CONSCIENCE

TWO SOLDIERS, TWO PACIFISTS, ONE FAMILY—
A TEST OF WILL AND FAITH IN WORLD WAR I

LOUISA THOMAS

PENGUIN BOOKS

PENGUIN BOOKS

Published by the Penguin Group

Penguin Group (USA) Inc., 375 Hudson Street, New York, New York 10014, U.S.A. •
Penguin Group (Canada), 90 Eglinton Avenue East, Suite 700, Toronto, Ontario,
Canada M4P 2Y3 (a division of Pearson Penguin Canada Inc.) • Penguin Books Ltd,
80 Strand, London WC2R 0RL, England • Penguin Ireland, 25 St. Stephen's Green,
Dublin 2, Ireland (a division of Penguin Books Ltd) • Penguin Books Australia Ltd, 250
Camberwell Road, Camberwell, Victoria 3124, Australia (a division of Pearson Australia
Group Pty Ltd) • Penguin Books India Pvt Ltd, 11 Community Centre, Panchsheel Park,
New Delhi—110 017, India • Penguin Group (NZ), 67 Apollo Drive, Rosedale, Auckland
0632, New Zealand (a division of Pearson New Zealand Ltd) • Penguin Books
(South Africa) (Pty) Ltd, 24 Sturdee Avenue, Rosebank, Johannesburg 2196, South Africa

Penguin Books Ltd, Registered Offices: 80 Strand, London WC2R 0RL, England

First published in the United States of America by The Penguin Press,
a member of Penguin Group (USA) Inc. 2011
Published in Penguin Books 2012

1   3   5   7   9   10   8   6   4   2

THE LIBRARY OF CONGRESS HAS CATALOGED
THE HARDCOVER EDITION AS FOLLOWS:
Thomas, Louisa.
Conscience : two soldiers, two pacifists, one family : a test of will and faith in
World War I / Louisa Thomas.
p.   cm.
Includes bibliographical references and index.
ISBN 978-1-59420-294-0 (hc.)
ISBN 978-0-14-312099-5 (pbk.)
1. World War, 1914–1918—Moral and ethical aspects.   2. World War,
1914–1918—Social aspects—United States.   3. World War, 1914–1918—
Conscientious objectors—United States.   4. Brothers—United States—
Biography.   5. Soldiers—United States—Biography.   6. Conscientious objectors—
United States—Biography.   7. Thomas family.   I. Title.
D524.T53 2011
940.3'162092273—dc22
2010047855

Printed in the United States of America
DESIGNED BY AMANDA DEWEY

For my sister
Mary

CONTENTS

PREFACE

Norman Thomas was expecting bad news. His country was at war, his brothers were in danger, and he was the subject of suspicion. Even so, the telegrams that arrived in the hot days of late August 1918 were worse than he feared. One said that his brother Evan, a conscientious objector, had been hospitalized at Fort Riley, a military training camp in Kansas, during a hunger strike against the draft. Then came word that another brother, Ralph, a captain in the Army Corps of Engineers, had been wounded by a German artillery shell on the western front in France.

With two sons who were pacifists and two sons who were soldiers, Norman's mother, Emma, had already felt anxious. Now she was beside herself. She had misgivings about Norman's pacifism and worried that his activism would get him in trouble. She believed that Evan's hunger strike amounted to suicide, and she had no idea what exactly had happened to Ralph or where he had been taken. Even her youngest son, Arthur, wasn't safe. He was at training camp in Texas flying flimsy practice planes.

Yet she was proud of them all. Her relationships with each of her sons were as complicated as theirs were with one another.

Norman and his mother could do nothing to help Ralph on the western front. They could, however, go to Evan in Kansas. They left New York City on August 28. As the train sped west, Norman dwelled on his brothers and the demands of citizens and the state. "The situation of Mother—Evan—Military—myself has no promise of simplicity and ease," he wrote to his wife, Violet.

Late in the summer of 1918, the Thomas brothers' conflicts were apparent—and irreconcilable. All of them believed they were fighting for freedom. Evan had become a conscientious objector to protest the government's conscription of life and conscience. Ralph had enlisted in the army immediately after the United States declared war, and Arthur had followed several months later, answering President Woodrow Wilson's call to fight for "the privilege of men everywhere to choose their way of life and of obedience." Norman, too, wanted to make it possible for all men and women to pursue their own ends, but he thought that violence undermined Wilson's aims. So did the repressive atmosphere at home, where saying the wrong thing could land a man in jail, and being radical, or being black, or being foreign could get a man lynched. Through his work as a Presbyterian minister in New York City tenements and as an officer of antiwar organizations, Norman had seen unconscionable degradation and despair, too much inequality and too many abuses of power. American society had to change, Norman thought, and he was starting to believe he had a part to play.

✛

Brothers have always disagreed; families have always fought. Some fights are bigger than others. When the Thomas brothers staked out their positions during that war, they had to reckon to an unusual degree with the questions of how to live, what to fight for, and why. They had to answer to one another, and they had to answer to themselves. That process of reevaluating, explaining, defending, and acting on his beliefs during World War I changed the course of Norman's life. And after the war was over, he dedicated himself to trying to help others change their own.

Norman Thomas is now largely forgotten, but for much of the

twentieth century it was commonplace to call him America's conscience. In a special remembrance that ran two days after his front-page obituary in 1968, the *New York Times* wrote, "He spoke to the feelings that most Americans have about themselves: that they are a fair people; that it is somehow wrong for poverty to exist amid plenty; that it is a perversion of justice to be jailed for political reasons; that Constitutional rights should be respected regardless of race or creed." He understood that these political, economic, and social problems were moral problems, and he confronted those problems publicly. He wanted others to do the same.

At the end of World War I, Norman became a Socialist. He would go on to run for president six times on the Socialist ticket, and he represented democratic socialism until the day he died. Though many of his goals for social reform, from civil rights legislation to unemployment insurance, are now law, he was not a good politician, and he always fared badly at the polls. His failure as a politician, though, matters less than the reasons he traveled down the path he did. He became a Socialist because he despaired at what he saw and held out hope for something better. He thought society had lost the balance between opportunity and equality, creativity and security, the individual and the community. He was convinced that the capitalist emphasis on self-interest and profit engendered injustice, irresponsibility, and class conflict, and that it was perverse that money was treated with greater reverence than the lives of workers. He was a pacifist before he was a Socialist, believing methods of force were antithetical to freedom. But his pacifism helped lead him to socialism, after he came to see war as the result and ultimate expression of capitalist exploitation.

As a politician he never managed (nor really tried) to put forth a coherent political philosophy, except to say what he was not: not a Marxist, not a communist, not a liberal, not a capitalist. At times, during party battles, he tried to adopt a more orthodox socialism. He was pessimistic about the state bureaucracy from the start, however, and he became less dogmatic after long and bruising fights with communists, of whom he was an early and determined opponent. With his hand in many causes, he spoke everywhere, in chapels and high school gyms, atop soapboxes and on the stage at Madison Square Garden. He cut a striking figure: tall and thin, with a high forehead and penetrating blue eyes. His voice resounded, and when he made a point he cut the air with the jab of a finger. He connected freedom to justice and justice to human beings.

But that came later. When World War I broke out, Norman was an unknown minister, more extraordinary for his promise as a pastor than for his politics. Soon after the United States entered the war, he lost his church. He also lost his faith in the aims and efforts of many liberals, including his old professor Woodrow Wilson. Yet it was also a time of discovery. Norman developed a new sense of purpose and a new understanding of what makes men free: freedom of conscience. Every person, he believed, has a conscience—a sense that he is more than a creature of instinct, an awareness of ultimate ethical ends—but not everyone is ordinarily free to heed it. A person is not free while fighting in war or living in extreme poverty. A person is not free if he is censored or unjustly jailed. During the war, Norman's own brother Evan was sentenced to life in prison for refusing an order to eat.

The politicians who led their countries into World War I described it as a war for freedom. But Norman became convinced that an ethical society could not emerge from the inferno of battle. Courage was important, but what was necessary was courage in daily life—the courage to judge right from wrong and oneself before others. He thought freedom required the conditions that would satisfy the basic needs of men and women so they might have the chance to cultivate their own way of life, and so they might also treat others and be treated by others with dignity and respect.

Norman's faith in freedom of conscience raised questions about citizenship and responsibility that could not easily be answered, if at all. His brothers answered those questions differently than he did. No brother was always right, nor always wise nor always fair. Still, each understood that he was not alone; he had brothers.

—┿—

Norman Thomas was young, only thirty-three years old, when World War I ended. Yet his journey had already been long. Its lessons, many of which would remain with him always, were evident in his application for membership in the Socialist Party. He has been both praised and disparaged for being an idealist or a utopian. He did have ideals, but he was less naïve about human nature or about schemes of salvation than those epithets suggest. In the letter that accompanied his application, he wrote that he believed in the necessity of establishing a more just economic order than capitalism provided, but noted that he was applying with reservations. "My accepting of the Socialist platform is on the basis of general principles rather than of details," he wrote. He was wary that the Socialists had not always guaranteed civil liberties. He harbored "a profound fear of the undue exaltation of the State and a profound faith that the new world we desire must depend upon freedom and fellowship rather than upon any sort of coercion whatsoever." Despite his qualms, he believed that socialism represented the best hope for a better world.

Norman's application to the Socialist Party was returned, "not because of the exceptions you wish to be recorded upon, but because you have not filled out the other side." Caught up in his statement of principles, Norman had forgotten to include his address and personal information.

The criticism that Norman was more concerned with listening to his conscience than attending to practical considerations has been leveled many times. But the accusation assumes that he considered himself a solitary arbiter of right and wrong, removed from the mess of daily life. In fact, his conscience was formed by practical experience and was responsive to it. He had a moral instinct, but his convictions and actions were also shaped by his family, friends, school, and work, by what he did and what he saw. His story is part of the shifting intellectual, social, and religious context of the early twentieth century. It is also part of his family's story. For the Thomas family, conscience was not an empty word. It made demands.

─┼─

This book ends just after the end of World War I. It has little to say about Norman as a politician, because Norman was not then a politician. It is instead about his turn toward politics and the experiences that shaped him and his enduring commitments. He is the central figure in this story, but it is also a story about his family, and especially about his brothers. It moves from the crowded rivers of Bangkok to the clipped lawns of Princeton

University, from the tenements of New York City to the West Wing of the White House. It traces the fault lines between liberal Christianity and fundamentalism, civic duty and civil liberties. During the early twentieth century, the American government began to play a role in the lives of its citizens it had never played before. New technologies, immigration, scientific advances, religious conflicts, and ideological battles were changing the world. There emerged a new language about the common cause of humanity and cooperation among states, women's suffrage, a new conception of civil liberties, and the groundwork of movements to come. The most vivid manifestation of that turmoil was a war that killed nine million soldiers and sailors by the time the guns were silenced, lives lost in the mud of Argonne, Verdun, Tannenberg, the Somme.

After World War I, Norman wrote a book called *The Conscientious Objector in America*. The first page read:

TO

THE BRAVE

WHO WENT FOR CONSCIENCE' SAKE

TO TRENCH OR TO PRISON

THIS BOOK IS DEDICATED

The dedication was to his brothers, with whom he had so often disagreed. That book was, therefore, a family story, and so is this. It happens to be my own family—Norman Thomas was my great-grandfather—but Norman took a more expansive view of brotherhood, and so will I. In the Thomas brothers' history, we all might find some of our own.

CONSCIENCE

One

FERVENT WRESTLING PRAYERS

Welling Thomas

Emma Thomas

Norman came into the world "the wrong side down," Emma Thomas reported to her mother in December 1884. He would grow to be over six feet two, but he was tiny at birth, only four pounds. "Now for the boy's looks," Emma wrote when her son was hardly three weeks old. "There is no use I know telling you he is not beautiful, but all the same he is not yet"—at least not compared with his older sister, Mary, who had been born with thick dark hair and a sweet, small mouth. Norman's nose was bigger and his head a little squashed. All the same, Emma added, "his mother and father are quite proud of him."

That mix of frank evaluation and tender pride was characteristic of Emma. She could be blunt in her appraisals, probably harsher than she meant to be, but she was also loving. She demanded much of her children, and she gave them her support in return. Her husband, Welling, the minister of the Presbyterian Church in Marion, Ohio, tended to defer to her. She was, as Norman later wrote, "the more outstanding personality, and Father was content to have it so." Welling was more restrained, traditional in his habits and reserve.

"What a setup for the modern psychologically minded biographer or novelist!" wrote Norman decades later, reflecting on his hometown and upbringing. "A study in revolt born of reaction from Presbyterian orthodoxy, and the Victorian brand of Puritanism in a *Middletown* setting! The only trouble is that that isn't what happened. I both loved and respected my parents."

They were tested during the first few weeks of Norman's life. Mary fell sick in January, crying when Welling touched her. Emma had to hold her in her lap while cradling Norman in her other arm. Mary's parents thought she was teething. They learned too late that she had diphtheria. She died two months after Norman was born. Understandably, Welling and Emma were protective of their son when he was young. He was a sickly child, gangling and frail, prone to croup. His mother kept him out of public school until he was in the fourth grade, sending him to a neighbor's for tutoring and keeping him home when the raspy, barking cough overcame him. She lulled him to sleep with hymns and told him stories from her childhood. She described a near mutiny aboard a ship and trips to the palace of the king of Siam. She told him what it was like to be shunned by other white girls in North Carolina because her parents taught blacks, and how she learned to make friends. He knew, from an early age, that she was not like most of the mothers he knew.

+

There is a photograph of Emma Thomas—then Emma Mattoon—as a child, but she is not in view. Her mother, Mary, sits near her father, Stephen, on the second-story veranda of their large house in Bangkok, shaded by the long overhang of the pyramid-shaped roof. Her sister, also Mary, stands primly in a full-skirted white dress and a small straw hat, carrying a little basket and looking out of place among the soaring, ragged palms and the tropical foliage so dense that the house looks nearly overtaken. An inscription on the photograph says that six-year-old Emma "is somewhere in the bushes."

She was a mischievous child, difficult to handle but much adored. Growing up in Bangkok, Siam, as the daughter of missionaries, Emma was stubbornly independent and often got into trouble. "I don't see why you have to watch me all the time," she would tell her older sister.

Emma's father, Stephen Mattoon, was born in 1816 in Champion, western New York, a land where some believed the Holy Spirit was abroad. The Second Great Awakening had begun, and religious fever burned through the frontier. The Fox sisters of Hydesville conducted table-knocking séances; Shakers shook; and Joseph Smith followed the angel Moroni to the Book of Mormon. The Congregationalist farmers of Stephen's own hometown cultivated a more temperate atmosphere, but religious enthusiasm seized Stephen all the same. At the age of sixteen, he stood up and publicly declared his faith, and the following year he announced that he felt called to become a minister. The college he attended in New York offered a liberal arts education and stressed nonsectarian inclusivity, but when he finally reached the Theological Seminary at Princeton, at the age of twenty-six, he entered a fortress of reaction.

"I am not afraid to say that a new idea never originated in this Seminary," said Charles Hodge, a leading nineteenth-century Princeton theologian. Suspicious of the unbridled emotional spirituality of the Second Great Awakening, the professors in Princeton taught their students to revere the Bible's authority over personal religious experience. Stephen absorbed this dogma, but the kind of religion that Princeton professors so distrusted had already made its mark on him. He did not doubt that those who refused the path of Protestantism would be consigned to a fiery hell. Nor did he doubt that man was hopelessly sinful and depraved, hopeless but for the grace of God. But he had an optimistic disposition and a more democratic inclination. He took something simple from the lessons of conservative Presbyterians: If Scripture was the single source of revealed truth, then spreading the Word meant teaching as many people as possible to read it.

In the summer of 1846, after his ordination, Stephen embarked for Siam as a missionary. He took with him his wife, a plain, thin teacher named Mary Lourie, whom he had met while preaching in upstate New York. His family in Michigan took one look at his emaciated bride and thought she was dying. She was tougher than she appeared, though, and intensely pious. In between bouts of seasickness aboard the ship to Siam, she read the work of Professor Hodge and memorized the Gospel of Matthew. "Cleanse me in my Dear Redeemer's blood," she began her diary. Her husband, meanwhile, peppered his letters with joyful thoughts of life after death.

In Bangkok, the handful of missionaries in the small compound of Presbyterians constantly fell sick, died, or left, to be replaced by others who would fall sick, die, or leave. Dysentery, typhoid, cholera, and tuberculosis swept the city in waves, killing the Mattoons' own young son in 1851. They recoiled, at first, from the people they lived among. "They are not destitute of natural abilities or ingenuity," Stephen wrote to his sister and brother-in-law soon after arriving. "But there is no motive sufficiently strong to call forth abilities especially in the right direction." A few months later, he worded his view more bluntly: "We are surrounded by an ignorant, superstitious and depraved people." The Mattoons disgust with the "idolatrous" worship and the mores of the Siamese would not change over the next twenty years, and neither would their ethnocentric view of their own civilization's superiority, their clothes and science and customs. Yet Siam became home, and the people became their neighbors. They half adopted and raised one girl, Esther, and they made friends. They liked, too, the man who became king.

In 1851 King Mongkut assumed the throne, after the Mattoons had been in Siam for nearly five years. Mongkut had a powerful intellect and ranging curiosity, and before becoming king he had been a Buddhist scholar. A missionary had taught him English, and he trusted and tolerated the Mattoons. He would visit their home on occasion; he liked, especially, to discuss science. In 1855, Mongkut asked Stephen to help translate treaty negotiations with the British, and Stephen served as an adviser for both Mongkut and an envoy from the United States a year later. Before he left Siam, the envoy appointed Stephen as the United States' first consul to Siam. It was clear, the envoy wrote, that the king and the people liked and accepted him—at least in nonreligious matters. Mongkut helped the missionaries secure land for their compound and a school for Siamese children, and he enlisted Mary Mattoon and two other female missionaries to teach his children and wives. But after he learned that the women mixed lessons with evangelism, he ended the classes. When the missionaries directly urged the king to convert to Christianity, he politely waved their words away. "We esteem you and your Christian character most highly, but your religion is best for you, ours for us," Mongkut would say to them.

Mongkut could afford to be philosophical. If the number of converts was the measure of their success, the Mattoons were failures. It took more than a decade for their small band of Presbyterians to make a single convert from among the Siamese. The Mattoons, who never doubted the singular truth of their faith, could not exactly accept Mongkut's words. With the arrogance of the benevolently disinterested, they had come to start a revolution. But the nature of their faith itself would curb them. Their Presbyterian conception of religion was demanding, and they did not think faith could be forced. With a limited awareness of their indirectly coercive power—the influence of their schools, their medicine, their books, the strangeness of their fervor—they believed that converts would become Christians freely, through their encounter with the Bible.

Those who did not would go to hell, they assumed. Even for those who did, life on earth was a punishment for men's sins, a burden to be endured until God released them. The Mattoons tried to focus on the next world, but the events of this one kept a hold on them. From afar they watched the Civil War in America with a horror that turned into hope. Their understanding of slavery was transformed, too. In the early months of the Civil War, they believed that slavery could be a state of mind and of the soul. "There are slaves in the north—there are slaves in the south—there are slaves in the east—there are slaves in the west—there are white freemen that are slaves—there are black slaves that are freemen—there are white masters that are slaves," Mary wrote in her diary on March 4, 1861, the day

Abraham Lincoln was inaugurated as president. A year later, that pious resignation had disappeared. By the time of the Emancipation Proclamation, the war had become a fight for freedom, for blacks and whites alike. Now Mary wrote, "If [the rebellion] is not put down, crushed out, will not our whole country become enslaved?"

The fate of the Union was still uncertain when Mary and her two children left Siam for good, on June 30, 1864, after eighteen years. Mary's health was too frail for her to remain in Siam. "I have just the old report to make to you," she wrote to her sister before leaving. "Asthma!! Asthma!!!" East of Sumatra, the *Eastward Ho* struck a rock and foundered. Mary clutched her crying daughters close, and "with sinking Peter we cried, 'Lord save we perish!'" Inhabitants of the island arrived to right the ship just as the crew attempted to mutiny. After a "terrible affray" of fists and a flashing knife, the ship floated free and the mutiny was quelled. Mary gave thanks to God. After five months at sea, the ship arrived in New York in December 1864. Before rejoining his family, Stephen remained in Bangkok to finish his translation of the New Testament. It would be, he believed, his legacy.

"It can scarcely be said to be either seed time or harvest time with us yet," Stephen wrote to his sister seven years after leaving the United States. "It is rather the time for clearing the land and breaking the soil preparatory to sowing this seed. But the seed time and harvest will surely come when we shall reap if we faint not. We need more faith, more zeal, more love, more patience, more perseverance, more fervent wrestling prayers. . . . Religion is after all a personal matter between our own souls and our God."

·⫙·

When Stephen returned to the United States, he accepted a position as pastor at a church in Ballston Spa, New York, not far from where Emma's mother had grown up. But in 1870, the family was uprooted once again. The Mattoons went south, past fields of tobacco and cotton, and through towns and by houses wrecked by the Civil War, to Charlotte, North Carolina. In 1869, the Freedmen's Bureau and Northern Presbytery asked Stephen to become the first president of a new college for blacks in Charlotte. (Mary taught there, too.) Biddle Memorial Institute, soon to become Biddle University (now Johnson C. Smith University), aimed to prepare its students—mostly former slaves—for lives of Christian service. The Mattoons' missionary purpose was different here than it had been in Siam; their students were already Christians. The religion of the Presbyterian Church, however, was vastly different from the antebellum religion of slaves, which had generally served cross-purposes: either as a tool for control by owners or, on other plantations, as an illicit protest and means of asserting human dignity and grace. The process of institutionalizing and refashioning that religion was complex, but the Mattoons saw their task as simple. The challenge was that before the war it had been illegal in North Carolina to teach a slave to read.

The education was rudimentary, especially during the early years, but the Mattoons were undaunted. Stephen expanded the curriculum; Mary had her students memorize the Sermon on the Mount. The Mattoons' white neighbors in Charlotte were wary at first. Not all were hostile—one townsman donated some land for the school—and some became friendly, but only two or three townspeople called on the Mattoons when they arrived, and the slights could sting. Emma was sensitive to the slurs hurled at her parents and sometimes at her, but she got used to them and the townspeople got used to the Mattoons and, eventually, the college. She would later tell her sons what it felt like to be shunned, to be called a carpetbagger and worse. At the same time, though, she emphasized that her friends came to look past her parents and her background. She did the same of her classmates.

The students at Biddle called Stephen "the Champion," after his home-town in New York. He did not champion his students as he might have. He focused on teaching and raising money for the school, and in town he kept his head down. He believed that his mission was to cultivate Christianity, not to fight for social justice. He deplored the terrorizing of blacks during Reconstruction only in private. In one letter he called giving the vote to freedmen "a doubtful boon," since violence, disenfranchisement, and sectional politics—"a curse to the nation"—were the terrible result. What he did he did quietly, buying land adjacent to campus and selling it to blacks at a bargain price when land was hard for blacks to buy, or inviting students into his home and library to sit by his fire and read. While some other all-black colleges emphasized vocational training and manual labor,

Stephen wanted black leaders to be preachers and teachers, and Christians
above all. Stephen and Mary could not see far past their mandate as missionaries. They might have done more. Still, at a time when blacks were
being attacked across the South, offering friendship was a place to start.
When Biddle students and graduates wrote letters to Stephen and Mary,
they addressed them as "Friend." When one of the first Biddle alums
reflected on his time there, his thoughts lingered on Mary. "She was ever
my best friend," he said. (To those who strayed, the Mattoons could be
frightening and severe. Years later, their grandson Norman met a Biddle
graduate who told him the scariest punishment at school was to have Mary
Mattoon pray over the offender.)

   "When I think of the influence for good [the students] may be from
this place," wrote Mary, "I do not desire a more honorable position than is
ours." By "for good," of course, she meant for Christianity. Yet she treated
the students with genuine care and affection, and they returned it. Before
she died, in 1885, she asked that the pallbearers of her coffin be students
from the school.

                                    ·+·

"We must not scrutinize too keenly the great deeds of great men," Emma
said, delivering the Commencement Essay at Elmira College in 1878, "for
we would be disenchanted, no doubt. All incidents, especially those coming down to us from the past, have a glamour of romance which would
probably be dispelled if we could know the practical circumstances under
which they actually occurred." Judge not, the twenty-year-old added, lest
you be judged. It was a lesson her parents had taught her, but it was also
something she had learned from the experience of being their daughter. She
had paid a price for being the child of people driven by a powerful sense
of duty. She had become accustomed to difficulty. Even college, in upstate
New York, had been a lonely place at times. Still, Emma had done well at
Elmira, studying Greek, trigonometry, chemistry, and literature, among
other subjects. She won the prize for highest scholarship.

   This was unusual training for a young woman in the nineteenth century, and it would not have boosted her marriage prospects. She was not
particularly attractive—unusually tall, with a long nose, thin, wavy brown

hair, and clear eyes that were just slightly too close set. With her college degree, she did not exactly fit the Victorian image of the gentle, subservient housewife. At college, though, she did also find a husband. She met Welling Thomas when he came to visit one of his sisters, a student at Elmira. The young man, just finishing up his studies at Princeton Theological Seminary, was mild-mannered and looked it, with large and solemn eyes and a slight build, only a little taller than Emma.

Welling was the son of Welsh immigrants. His father, insistently named Thomas Thomas, had left a farm in Carmarthenshire, Wales, with his family at twelve years old and sailed to New York in steerage. After a brief stay on Water Street, a blighted strip near the southern tip of Manhattan, the Thomases followed the Welsh migration to a community near Neath, Pennsylvania, where the green hills evoked Wales. Hardly had they arrived before Thomas's father died from sunstroke suffered while helping a neighbor build a house. Thomas was indentured to his older brother on the family farm after that, but he studied whenever he could. He was twenty-five by the time he made his way to college, at Lafayette. He traveled there by foot, walking more than a hundred miles in three days. To pay his way through school, he took time off to farm and to quarry stone for the college's construction.

Thomas wanted to be a minister. Religion was, in fact, one reason his Presbyterian family had come to the United States, in protest against having to support the established Church of England. After graduating from college at thirty-one years old—the oldest man in his class—he headed to Princeton Theological Seminary, where he was a classmate of Stephen Mattoon. When Stephen sailed to the other side of the world, Thomas returned home, where he married another Welsh immigrant, Mary Evans. Thomas Thomas was known for having memorized long stretches of the Bible and for his tirelessness. On Sundays he would travel from church to church, town to town—Orwell, Rushville, Rome—by horse or buggy, using Welsh in the mornings and English in the afternoons. He did not retire from preaching until he was eighty-two.

Welling was Mary and Thomas's only son. He was a good student, the best in his class at Lafayette, and decided to become a minister like his father. He went to Union Theological Seminary in New York and quickly

realized that he had made a mistake. His professors at Union had studied in Germany and brought back ideas that questioned the traditional
emphasis on the perfect accuracy of Scripture. These apostles of "Higher
Criticism" taught that the Bible would be best understood as a narrative
embedded in a specific period, written by a certain ancient people, over
a changing span of time. They did not suggest the Bible was false; Welling's teachers did not mean to question its ultimate authority—or indeed
many of the standard interpretations. Most of Union's professors considered themselves moderates, trying to grapple with modern realities and
seizing upon new insights as new paths to revelation. Far from imagining
some antagonism between modernity and Christianity, they believed their
study enriched religion and religion enriched modern times. Their critics
believed they were wrong and, worse, dangerous, that their rereading of
the Bible threatened to dim the faith.

Welling transferred to the stubbornly stolid confines of Princeton
Theological Seminary, where Darwinism was called atheism and where life
was not a matter of chance. There was an intelligent designer who had a
specific end—man—in mind. Welling was not hostile to modernity, but
he was wary of slippery slopes. It was human folly to chip away at the
foundations of faith. Chance shrugs off meaning and makes a mockery
of morality. Fathers died helping their neighbors; young children died of
dysentery; scoundrels succeeded and good men failed. If, despite all of this,
life was morally motivated, there had to be a purpose behind it, a Father
above it.

✛

Welling did not have a forceful personality, but he was apparently attracted
to one in a woman. Still, he did not rush Emma to the altar. The two began
a long-distance courtship, while Emma returned to her high school in
North Carolina as a teacher. They were married in 1881, when Emma was
twenty-four and Welling twenty-nine. After the Presbytery assigned Welling to a church in Ohio, they made their home in the Midwest. Mary was
born a year after their marriage and Norman two years after that. Their
second son, Ralph, was born in 1887, when Norman was two years old,
and Evan followed three years later. Arthur, Agnes, and Emma were born

at regular intervals over the next ten years. When the younger Emma was born in 1899, Arthur exclaimed, "What? Another one!"

One child died, six lived. The Thomas parents explained that inexplicable calculus to themselves the same way that their own parents had: The ways of God are unknowable, and tragedy is a fact of life. Yet they took a more optimistic view of humankind. They were creatures of their era, and their era was one of hope. One popular poem went:

> We are living, we are dwelling
> In a grand and awful time,
> In an age of ages telling—
> To be living, is sublime!

Welling was so fond of it that he had the verse printed on a bookmark for parishioners at Christmas. "To be living, is sublime" is hardly an orthodox Calvinist sentiment, but by the end of the nineteenth century the harshness of Calvinism had softened. Welling believed in hell, but as Norman later liked to point out, he wouldn't consign anyone to it. He believed in progress.

And yet the relentless optimism expressed in so many poems, speeches, sermons, and books of the time belied a pervasive unease. Things were changing, and however strong the prevailing ethos, Welling suspected that change was not always for the better. He had to work hard to remain sanguine in the face of doubt. In his letters and sermons he forcibly reconciled ideas and desires that pulled away from each other. He tried to turn scientific discoveries into religious metaphors, to show how they were in concert. He referenced the philosopher William James, willfully or ignorantly circumventing the substance of James's psychology and beliefs ("Says Professor William James, 'We believe ourselves immortal because we believe ourselves fit for immortality.'"). The agony of Christians like the Mattoons had given way to spontaneity and optimism, but grinding effort lay behind the transformation. To overcome the remnants of a moral system that assumed the worst about mankind, men of Welling's generation would spend their days convincing themselves that they were the shepherds of progress. At night, they wondered if it was true at all.

✛

Emma did not have to deliver sermons, but she did speak her mind. She had an unusually sophisticated social conscience and, for a woman of the era, unusual intellectual forthrightness. Her energy was boundless. In addition to raising children spanning fifteen years in age, she helped run her husband's church, sat on church and civic committees, and presented papers to women's clubs. She helped her children with algebra and Latin homework. As soon as her four sons left the house, with two younger daughters still at home in school, she ran for election to the school board on the Democratic ballot—the local Republicans were rumored to refuse to run women—and she won.

Education, like temperance (which Emma also championed), was one of those traditional "women's issues"—concerning, as it did, child rearing—about which more than a few women felt justified in taking a leadership role. Emma did not call herself a suffragist, but she was not afraid to speak up and speak loudly. She cited Mary Wollstonecraft's *A Vindication of the Rights of Woman*, knew of the American activists Margaret Fuller and Lucretia Mott, and admired Frances Wright, a Scottish woman who became one of the first female lecturers on politics in the United States. She was orthodox enough to believe the story of Adam and Eve, yet unconventional and droll enough to point out that Adam was blaming Eve for his own sin.

She had a sharp sense of humor, but she was also a warm and caring mother, and—having grown up the way she did—she wanted her children to see more of the country, if not the world, than most Marion children did. So, apparently, did Welling. There were trips to visit Grandfather Thomas in Pennsylvania; canoe and biking excursions in the countryside; a journey to Charlotte, North Carolina, through the hot cotton fields. When Norman was eight, Emma took him to the Chicago World's Fair, a landscape of wonder and ingenuity, art exhibitions, a Ferris wheel, and prize pigs. Welling took the six-year-old Ralph to the World's Fair later that summer and sent his son home alone, in the care of the railroad conductor, while Welling continued on to a Presbytery meeting. Self-reliance was expected in the Thomas household from the earliest age.

Freedom to roam and play, to camp and catch catfish in the creek, was encouraged, but so was a sense of responsibility. Emma and Welling expected the boys to earn what pocket money they wanted and to help around the house. They raked leaves for small change, delivered the newspaper, beat rugs, fed chickens, and canned fruit.

Sometimes Welling would take Norman into the yard under the tall oaks to play catch. Welling tried to teach his left-handed son to throw a ball with his right arm, and Norman felt clumsy and awkward. For the most part, Welling kept to himself, and to his study, kind and distant.

Two

PREACHER OF THE WORD

Ralph and Norman Thomas   Evan and Arthur Thomas

The Presbyterian Church had one of the tonier congregations in Marion. As its pastor, Welling ministered to some of the town's richest residents: the industrialists who oversaw Marion's threshing and steam-shovel manufacturing production, the businessmen and bankers. One of them was Amos Kling, whose daughter Florence had scandalized the town by running off with a local rogue when she was several months pregnant. After a quick divorce, Florence set her sights on the editor and publisher of the *Marion Daily Star*, a charismatic younger man named Warren Harding, the future president of the United States. Harding resisted Florence's advances, but Florence wore him down, and they married. For a time, Kling disowned his daughter.

Welling didn't like to condemn anyone personally, but the rumors about Florence were the kind of stories that made him uncomfortable. He was prudish and strict. He frowned on dancing and denounced gambling. He disapproved of cards, he forbade drinking, and his house was Sabbatarian—Sundays were reserved for church and reading. Fastidious and proper, he kept his mustache trim and his frock coat neat. His study was his domain. On the bookshelves of his study and the local library, within Norman's long-armed reach, were Gibbon, Scott, and Dickens, with a few trashy Victorian novels in between. Sundays in the Thomas household would have been dull beyond measure for Norman if not for the loophole in the rules that allowed for reading. The rest of the day was dominated by two church services. Welling's sermons were something to be suffered through: boring and vaguely erudite, delivered in a monotone. He may have been a Calvinist, but he spoke of hell with tepid words and abstract indirection. "There is immortality for the unsaved as well as for the saved," he warned his congregation in one sermon, "but not a blessed immortality."

✢

William Jennings Bryan was the one who showed young Norman the power of speech to stir a crowd. When Norman was eleven, Welling took him to watch Bryan speak from Marion's courthouse steps during his 1896 run for president. Thirty-six years old, Bryan had a barrel chest, a broad mouth, and a gaze that could fix the distance. He cut the figure more of an evangelist preacher than a politician, and indeed he had something of the evangelist in him, having declared his faith at a revival meeting. Bryan's religion animated his life and his politics. He promised salvation to all comers and turned his faith into a potent politics. Radicalized by the depression of the 1890s, he proposed policies to ease the plight of farmers and some laborers—a graduated income tax, workers' rights, a more flexible monetary system—but what captivated people was his populist appeal. He called upon an old vision of an egalitarian, agrarian America and promised to restore the mythic past. In the America he described, the machinery and swollen pockets of wealth in the Northeast would not abuse good men, nor treat them as cogs easily replaced and discarded. He showed them how to draw strength from their outrage.

Bryan took his message directly to the people. In a tactic unprecedented for a presidential candidate, the prince of populism delivered an average of five speeches a day during his run for the presidency in 1896. That July, at the Democratic National Convention, Bryan delivered his famous speech advocating a monetary policy that included a silver standard, hoping that it would relieve the crippling debts farmers faced and reverse deflation. "You shall not press down upon the brow of labor this crown of thorns," he said. "You shall not crucify mankind upon a cross of gold." Then he spread his arms, as if he were hanging from a cross. For five seconds, the crowd was silent. Then shrieks and cries rose from the throng as it rushed the stage, reported the *New York Times*, a "wild, raging irresistible mob." No mobs rampaged through Marion, but Byran's magnetic presence traveled across the space like the shimmer of heat on the hottest days, and Norman was transfixed. He never forgot the sight of him, or the power of that voice.

It was the politician's voice—so unlike his father's—that captured him, not the politics. At the time, he was more interested in the campaign pins produced by the McKinley camp, which he and Ralph collected, than in the issues of the race. The pins themselves, though, said something about McKinley's campaign. Instead of barnstorming the country, McKinley campaigned from his porch in nearby Canton and trusted his adviser Mark Hanna to strategize. Hanna raised $3.5 million from financiers and industrialists dismissive of Bryan's policies and terrified by the thought of that raging, irresistible mob.

Welling voted for McKinley, and McKinley won. But Bryan carried the county. His ability to channel the people's discontent resonated with an underlying turbulence shaking the nation, and his legacy would inflect the cultural currents for decades, for good and for bad. Populism can be ugly, infused with racism and xenophobia. In those days, many populists encouraged farmers to fear foreigners, who, they suggested, would take their work and "dilute" their culture and blood. They sometimes embraced economic policies potentially more ruinous than the ones they meant to fix. At the same time, populists kept alive egalitarian ideas that countered the inequalities and excesses of the Gilded Age. The people demanded to be heard, and their demand was backed by a combustible energy.

While Norman, ignorant of any turmoil beyond the confines of his small town, went to Sunday school and summer picnics, nearby towns and cities cracked under stress. Workers' movements were on the rise, developing a vocabulary to describe the dispossessed. In places like New York, immigrants and intellectuals used phrases like "class struggle" and "the proletariat"; in the Midwest, the labor movement was freighted with homespun values and reactionary zeal. Sometimes, those movements contradicted one another. Some people gravitated toward Bryan, some toward socialism, some toward violence. In Chicago in 1886, a bomb exploded at a rally for striking workers. Eight anarchists were tried for murder; four were hanged, and one committed suicide in jail. During the depression that began in 1893, employees of the Pullman's Palace Car Company went on strike outside Chicago after layoffs and wage cuts. Violent fights broke out along the railway lines between strikers and "scabs," and federal troops moved in to break the strike. Those, like Welling, who got their news from papers and magazines would have easily identified the villain: the head of the American Railway Union, Eugene Debs, a thin man with a hawk's stare. Growing up in Terre Haute, Indiana, Debs had absorbed the middle-class virtues of work, thrift, kindness, and the cultivation of manhood. He had become a leader and organizer among workers. The Pullman strike vaulted him into radical politics and national renown. Imprisoned for his role in the strike, he read Marx's *Das Kapital* and emerged a Socialist. But he was more in debt to the American Revolution than to Marx, and he believed he was restoring democracy to America.

As a boy, Norman did not care, and probably did not know, who Eugene Debs was. He and his friends played a game they called "Coxey's Army," but they had little idea that the name referred to Jacob Coxey and a march he led from nearby Massillon, Ohio, to the nation's capital, demanding food and work for the unemployed. When Norman's mother took him as a small boy to visit his grandfather, he had noticed that blacks worked in the fields while whites watched. But these glimpses into life outside Marion glanced off his consciousness, leaving only the smallest mark.

Norman was hardly aware of the depression of the 1890s. The class distinctions he could see were real but fine-grain: a train conductor's wife ranked above a brakeman's. His teachers and father tended to attribute real poverty to bad luck or alcohol. The newspapers he might have read did not convince him otherwise. The flood of immigrants into Ellis Island; the Supreme Court decision legitimizing "separate but equal" facilities for African Americans; William Randolph Hearst's sensationalist newspaper campaign against the Spanish in Cuba—if Norman heard of these things, they did not bother him; he was a kid, and his world, like his town, was small and pleasant. But he did like to look out the window at the tracks that ran by his house and watch the long trains heading out of Marion into the blank plains and empty horizon, their whistles sounding a resonant note suggestive of unknown places.

-+-

In early 1898, in Havana, Cuba, the USS *Maine* blew up, killing 266 men. President McKinley had sent the battleship to Havana after clashes between Cuban patriots and the Spanish government threatened perceived U.S. interests there. After the explosion, the sensationalist New York press fell over itself trying to drum up a cause for war (and a spike in circulation). In April, McKinley—somewhat reluctantly—declared war; in July, Teddy Roosevelt and his Rough Riders had charged up San Juan Hill; and in August, Spain gave up. Cuba had its independence (under United States jurisdiction), and Spain ceded Puerto Rico and Guam and sold the Philippines, which the United States had also invaded and effectively captured, to the victor. Secretary of State John Hay wrote to Roosevelt, "It has been a splendid little war . . . begun with the highest motives, carried on with magnificent intelligence and spirit, favored by that Fortune which loves the brave."

The invasion of Cuba was poorly organized, and the soldiers were ill equipped, but most Americans found the Spanish-American War entirely satisfying. As one *Atlantic* writer described it, the war was "the most wholesome exercise in constructive patriotism that this generation of Americans has had." Weak-kneed "mugwumps" were pacifists; the warriors were the heroes. To counter the widespread anxiety that Americans were losing their pioneer spirit, becoming too domesticated, men like Theodore

Roosevelt heralded "the strenuous life." Lodges and saloons, places where men could escape their wives, were popular across the country, including in Marion. Widespread belief in social Darwinism fueled men's anxiety: The fittest survive, and the test of fitness is war. A race that is not a fighting race, went the thinking, would atrophy like unused muscles. Theodore Roosevelt voiced this disquiet when he addressed the Naval War College in 1897. "No triumph of peace is quite so great as the supreme triumphs of war," he declared, and warned that the "race" had to guard against losing "the hard fighting virtues." Now that the frontier, which for centuries had allowed Americans to flex their muscles in the conquest of nature (not to mention indigenous peoples), was closed, Americans had to look for new places (and people) to conquer. Many argued that the time had arrived for the country to assert itself as a world power.

From his pulpit Welling cheered the United States Army against Spain, just as he had delivered a sermon championing Grover Cleveland's right to use force against Great Britain in a border dispute over Venezuela a few years before. Righteousness could be, must be, backed by force. While Welling never sounded like Teddy Roosevelt, it's possible that he shared some of that anxiety, so pervasive among his class and generation, over the diminution of the American spirit. After all, Welling's father had walked a hundred miles to go to college; his mother- and father-in-law had braved sailors' mutinies and cholera epidemics in the name of their faith. His sons argued about who was going to milk the cow.

✛

In the summer of 1901, right after Norman graduated from high school, the family moved east, to Lewisburg, Pennsylvania, where Welling had been offered a new pastorate. On the way they stopped in at Grandfather Thomas's home in Bradford County, as they did every two or three years, for a family reunion. All nineteen of the grandchildren attended this one, some from as far away as France. By then Thomas Thomas was eighty-nine years old, his cropped hair completely white and his cheeks deeply hollowed. He lived in a white frame house next to a small white church, up the hill from the creek and the county store and the flour mill. Behind the house, shielded from the woods and pastures by a stone wall, was Thomas's vast, well-tended vegetable garden. To Norman, the place was an idyll, and Thomas family reunions were the highlight of the year.

That reunion always remained for Norman the picture of paradise. When he described his forefathers later in life, Norman would summon this image: his grandfather holding a large-type Bible on his lap, there to prompt him even though he knew so many passages by heart, "so perfect a knowledge had he of God's word," wrote a local paper. Around him sat his grandchildren, aware of a sense of blessing. "Dimly at least we understood from him the sources of a light which gave meaning," Norman wrote in an unpublished autobiography, "yes, and glory, to the humdrum task, and all the vicissitudes of the year, a light which bathed, in beauty greater than the sun's, the fields, the shining river, the wooded hills, the cottage and the cherished garden in which this Preacher of the Word lived out his days."

Decades later, he looked back upon those summer evenings in the Pennsylvania countryside as a prelapsarian time. He had no reason, as the twentieth century dawned, to think that the light would change.

Three

THE WORLD'S HONORS

*The Thomas family, from left to right: Emma (Jr.), Agnes, Emma (Sr.),
Arthur, Welling, Ralph, Norman, and Evan*

N orman was sixteen, president of his high school senior class, and taller
than his father. He had ambitions. He wanted to go to Princeton.
As a boy, Norman had read and loved Jesse Lynch Williams's *Princeton Stories*, a sentimental account of undergraduate life. His father and
grandfathers had attended Princeton Theological Seminary and one of his
cousins had just graduated from the college. Attending Lewisburg's local
school, Bucknell, was a disappointment. Living at home with five siblings
underfoot and a cow to milk was probably considered an even worse fate.

But the Thomases did not have enough money to send Norman away, and so he had no choice. While the younger Thomases found plenty to love about Lewisburg, with the Susquehanna River down the street for canoeing and a diving board on the pier under the bridge, Norman breezed through his classes and wished he were elsewhere.

Then a "blessed miracle" occurred. Norman's uncle Frank Welles—Welling's brother-in-law, now an executive with Western Electric in Paris—offered Norman four hundred dollars toward tuition at Princeton. Princeton's campus was indeed a dreamscape for Norman. For a young man who grew up in a town where the cemetery was considered the scenic attraction, it was overwhelming—the spires and sandstone, the oaks and elms, the grand arch under which seniors sang in the moonlight.

Always congenial to pomp and circumstance, Princeton was then in its highest ceremonial mode. Only weeks after Norman arrived, Woodrow Wilson was inducted as Princeton's thirteenth president. The inaugural procession included J. P. Morgan, William Dean Howells, and Mark Twain. But it was Wilson who commanded attention that day. Dark-haired and long-jawed, with a pair of pince-nez perched in front of clear gray blue eyes, he struck a commanding figure. "We are not put into this world to sit still and know," he told those gathered. "We are put into it to act."

Norman took every class from Wilson that he could, studying constitutional government and absorbing a mostly Anglo worldview. Wilson had been the most popular professor at Princeton before becoming the school's president, and his lectures were still a great draw; at the end, students would stamp their feet in approval for the lean man standing on the stage.

Norman entered Princeton as a sophomore on the condition of passing extra exams at the end of his first semester in two subjects. He was woefully underprepared. At the end of a semester of frantic study, though, he not only passed the exams but also received top grades. He never let them drop. His academic success, at a time when few at Princeton prided themselves on their scholarship, was less impressive than it would be today, but his drive in such a culture was perhaps even more so. Wilson was only starting to implement the reforms intended to attract away from Harvard and Yale the very best students, not merely the best connected. He faced tremendous resistance. Students and alumni alike were proud of their reputation as "the most agreeable and aristocratic country club in America," in the words of the *New York Evening Post.* "Princeton is becoming nothing but a damned educational institution," one student was overheard saying. The *Daily Princetonian* ran a cartoon of a lonely Wilson sitting in a cobwebbed Nassau Hall, suggesting that Wilson's exacting standards would drive (or flunk) out all the students. In truth, Wilson was not sorry to see the bottom quarter held back and would probably have been happy to see more than a few students go.

Norman, called "Tommy" in college (as Wilson, too, had been called when he was a Princeton undergraduate), did not know Princeton's president very well, but Norman was one of the students Wilson liked. Wilson's biographer John Milton Cooper Jr. singled out Norman and one of Norman's best friends, Raymond Fosdick, as two students that Wilson considered models for the Princeton he imagined. Later in life, Norman claimed that he admired Wilson as a teacher but was ambivalent toward him personally. He liked to repeat a few anecdotes that illustrated Wilson's merciless manner: a sharp comment by Wilson criticizing Norman for wearing the wrong color trousers at a debate, or his superciliousness toward other faculty. But Norman's memories were shaded by his disillusionment with Wilson's entry into the First World War and all that followed. That Wilson was cruel to those who disagreed with him or offended his sense of propriety is well-known. He could be cold and strict. But when Norman was a student, he worshipped Wilson and he loved Princeton with few, if any, reservations.

Wilson took a special interest in debate, and that was where Norman really excelled. His deep voice was so lovely that one of his Bucknell professors had pushed him toward a career in opera; his Princeton classmates voted him as their best debater. Wilson's own prowess at public speaking surely encouraged Norman's interest. Princeton was the right place for a would-be public speaker, with a tradition that extended back to the revolutionary era. When Norman's three-person varsity debate team took on Harvard, the front page of the *Daily Princetonian* broke down the pre-debate analysis as if it were a football game, and the university band led a crowd of cheering students in a "P-rade" into the debating hall. When

Princeton won, coverage (and a large front-page picture of the three victors, with Norman looking very serious) dominated the school paper. Letters of congratulation arrived from Marion and Lewisburg. A Princeton dean wrote a glowing note. Even Norman's usually reticent father sent a telegram to his son when he heard the news.

·+·

A few months afterward, Norman graduated as valedictorian. Only twenty years old, he was selected to Phi Beta Kappa, voted "brightest man" and "most likely to succeed" by his classmates, and won the top prize for history, jurisprudence, and politics. His mother, as usual, mixed her warm words of pride with a harsh warning against hubris. "You better keep a collection of these notes," she wrote to him. "The world's honors are rather fleeting and sometimes it may do you good to look over the old times and see what a big toad you made in a big puddle. Yes, I suppose it is good for us to remember our failures," she added, and then proceeded to remind him of them. "Mrs. Hayes asked me the other day how many prizes you had taken. I said I didn't know all, but you had tried for a good many you didn't get, which the boys thought rather disloyal."

Being selected valedictorian was an honor. But as he confessed in his unpublished memoir, being elected to the Colonial Club, one of the "eating clubs" that had begun to crop up around Prospect Street in recent decades, "pleased me most." Though several of his friends were members of Colonial, he had not expected to be asked to join, nor had he particularly desired it. The clubs were for rich kids with connections. The most exclusive of the clubs, Ivy, would not accept its first public-school student for another forty-six years. Even Norman's place in Colonial was partly on sufferance; the officers offered him a part-time managerial position to help him pay the club fees. Edmund Wilson (Princeton '16) later complained that Colonial, "like a Hollywood set, had almost nothing behind it." Maybe so, but for Norman it offered a sense of acceptance that sustained him his whole life. It gave him the confidence to know that "if I espoused unpopular causes it wasn't some personal incapacity for ordinary social success which drove me to them," he later reflected. His classmates considered him bright but not a grind—not someone who walked in a furtive stoop as if he had his head in a phantom book or anticipated some heavy blow from behind. They gave him the confidence to think he could walk alongside anyone. As a young man, he did not seem to worry too much that the men who joined eating clubs in those days tended not to walk alongside anyone but their own. Woodrow Wilson himself was not immune to Princeton's social culture, even as he pushed to reprioritize academics and social life. When Wilson first hired "preceptors," the young teachers who lead small seminars, he reportedly dined with them first to evaluate their table manners.

Students cultivated their elitism and exclusionary instincts along with their traditions. Princeton could be the most unjust and hateful of atmospheres toward students who weren't of the "right" background. One Jewish student wrote to Wilson about the "gap of racial hatred which yawns black and gloomy indeed at your democratic and free university." Students who hadn't gone to the right prep schools or didn't have money to waste tended to have a hard time, too. Though hardly impoverished, Norman was poorer than most Princeton students, and he had to apply for a tuition deferral in addition to the help from Uncle Frank, work during the summers, and tutor rich students during the term. The class yearbook reported that the average expenditure for senior year was $941.61—which would have been nearly two-thirds of Welling Thomas's annual salary. This might have inspired disquiet or resentment, and it did in some, but not in Norman, at least not then. He was proud of his success—all the more so, probably, because of its improbability—and happy in his friendships. He considered himself, without reservation, a Princeton man.

--+--

Norman's friend Fosdick also spoke at commencement, as one of the orators. Fosdick took as his inspiration *How the Other Half Lives*, an account of life in the packed slums on the Lower East Side of New York City by the muckraking journalist Jacob Riis, which Fosdick had read earlier that spring. He was about fifteen years late in coming to Riis's work. The book had been a sensation since its publication in 1890. Riis's vivid, self-righteous indignation resonated with readers, and his ornate descriptions of the utter poverty appalled them. It was a book of his era—ethnic groups

were stereotyped and prejudices pandered to—but it also had the power
to effect real sympathy and surprise. What made his book revolutionary,
though, were the photographs. He captured young boys sleeping on the
ground next to a church, a tangle of limbs and tattered clothes. Children
looked out from the pages with the grim faces of adults; the reader looked
down long and narrow alleys without escape. The pictures affronted the
complacency of many Americans. When Riis went on tour, showing the
images to groups of upper- and middle-class New Yorkers, some ladies
fainted. In a culture predicated on duty, work like Riis's—and that of the
muckrakers that followed him, as well as the more sober work of early
social workers and reformers—presented a troubling problem for late-
Victorian Americans. Where did one's duty to be good begin and end?
They had been raised in the language of personal obligation, and such
squalor made them uncomfortable. More insidious sentiments were at
work, too: If they did not do something about that "foul core" of those
dirty tenements and the foreigners Riis described, some men and women
urged, wouldn't the rot spread through American society?

After reading Riis's book, Fosdick spent two weeks wandering around
the slums in New York, in neighborhoods that had not changed much
since the last decade of the nineteenth century, despite tenement reforms
(enacted in part because of Riis's work). Burning with a youthful indignation, he used Princeton's commencement as an occasion to launch his own
salvo against the wealthy. He aimed the polemic against the rich members
of the audience in front of him and against the mayor of New York, who
happened to be sitting on the platform behind him.

Norman also felt some compulsion to confront the problems of the
day—the "social question," as it was quaintly called—though with less
a sense of aggrieved urgency than Fosdick, despite his friend's efforts to
stoke his outrage. He thought about becoming a lawyer, a profession that
promised to combine his natural interests in debate and politics. He figured that he could probably become wealthy and successful, and possibly
influential. Near the end of the school year, a job at a high-profile lawyer's
office was "dangled before my eyes." Fosdick, too, was thinking about the
law, in hopes of exposing injustice and prodding change. But everyone,
including Norman himself, expected Norman to become a minister.

At the time, the church was part of the engine of social reform, no less than the law. The progressive spirit drew some of its fervor from a sublimated Protestant moralism. Duty and charity figured in, but shot through it was a desire for spiritual renewal, a desire to move out of sin into righteousness. The church, with its easy access to a moral vocabulary, was a natural vehicle for this kind of conversion and uplift. And as the church influenced progressive reform, so progressive reform altered the church. Its responsibilities expanded from focusing on personal salvation to exposing injustice, devising a rational and scientific solution to social problems, correcting imbalances, and educating rich and poor alike. In the twentieth century, it was widely believed that the Gilded Age, its polished veneer disguising the dull, tin center of selfish individualism, would turn into a golden era. The Victorian attention to personal morals and pieties would be transferred to constructing the commonweal. A new enthusiasm for science—social, mechanical, biological—sprang up, and the more liberal factions of the church embraced this, too, targeting their programs at practical measures like sanitation and health programs and playing a significant role in the growth of sociology. Social and spiritual concerns fused. What the historian Richard Hofstadter later called the Age of Reform had begun.

Norman sympathized with the evolving ideals of progressivism as a twenty-year-old, but he did not feel drawn to extremist politics or rebellion. In ways that neither he nor his parents realized yet, though, his Christianity was not quite theirs. Unlike his grandfathers, he felt "no mystical sense of call." His faith was more social, more ecumenical, than the gospel of personal salvation embraced by his parents and grandparents, and it was more concerned with practical problems than theological ones. He was not secular; he thought change would be most true and lasting if it was accompanied by a spiritual transformation as well. But from the start he was more inclined toward earth than heaven.

It's helpful to understand the religious character of Princeton in the early twentieth century, because by the time he had graduated, its influence upon Norman seems to have been as strong or stronger than that of his father's Sunday sermons. By 1905, the place of religion at Princeton was strong enough to be taken for granted and weak enough that it hardly intruded on those who wished it away. Wilson was the first president of the school not to be a clergyman, and he oversaw much of the jettisoning of parochial Christian (and Presbyterian) requirements. He stopped the informal practice of orthodoxy tests in hiring faculty, ended the compulsory four years of Bible classes, and reduced compulsory chapel to twice a week and Sundays. He had the university officially declared nondenominational. To his incensed conservative critics, he said that religion "cannot be handled like learning. It is a matter of individual conviction and its source is the heart."

Yet it would be a mistake to say that Princeton's religious character had really diminished, or that its president was unconcerned with the spirituality of his students. Wilson may not have been a clergyman, but he was the son of a Presbyterian minister, and his faith informed his entire worldview—as he believed it should. He hardly opened his mouth in a public forum without making reference to God. The student body did not worry over theological controversies and were very happy not to have to go to church so often, but save for the handful of ostracized Jews and a lone self-declared atheist in Norman's class, they invariably described their ideal character as "Christian." The Philadelphian, Princeton's branch of the Young Men's Christian Association, had a vibrant campus life, and Norman was an active member. Less than three weeks after his graduation, Norman went with the Princeton contingent, led by his good friend Dumont Clarke, the Philadelphian's president (and president of the Colonial Club), to the annual YMCA conference at Northfield, Massachusetts. Norman's brother Ralph, an incoming Princeton freshman, came, too. On the campus of the seminary founded by the evangelist Dwight Moody, Northfield operated like a summer camp for overgrown boys. Teams of college students competed for athletic prizes, and manliness was stressed as a great virtue. One oft-told story had Moody loudly interrupting a minister's rambling prayer to say, "While our brother is concluding his petitions to the Almighty let us sing 'Onward, Christian Soldiers.'" Enthusiasm blended with religion, and Norman could not help but be caught up in it. Though he had no kind of mystical epiphanies, he said the experience "probably brought me as close to an emotional religious experience as I ever came."

The offer from Spring Street Presbyterian Church came upon his return from Northfield. Tom Carter, a friend from Princeton who had graduated the year before, told him that H. Roswell Bates, the minister at Spring Street, was looking for another young assistant. At a conference at Yale, Norman had heard Bates speak on "the ministry and the working man" and about his church set among the tenements by the docks on the west side of Manhattan. Norman took the job.

Four

THE FATE OF THE UNIVERSE

*Norman Thomas and Ted Savage on camels during
their 1907 trip around the world*

At Spring Street Presbyterian, Reverend Bates had set up a veritable
internship for idealistic Harvard and Princeton graduates, cycling
them through in one- or two-year stints between college and seminary. When Norman arrived at Spring Street in the summer of 1905, Bates
was thirty-four years old, charismatic, neurasthenic, a bachelor and a bit
of a dandy, needy and prone to depression but extraordinarily committed to his parish. He infected his young subordinates with some of his
dedication. He was asking them to do difficult and sometimes unpleasant
work, for five hundred dollars a year and a room in a half-empty tenement

owned by the church. The young assistants did everything from singing in the choir to sitting by sickbeds, offering consolation when they knew what was needed was a doctor. At night, they walked along the Hudson and through the warren of gaslit streets, swapping stories, debating philosophy, and discussing politics.

There was plenty to talk about. In the fall of 1905, the colorful owner of the *New York Journal*, William Randolph Hearst, ran for mayor on a third-party ticket. Hearst spoke in a high squeak, but he talked like a king. No more oppression from the trusts, no more Tammany, no more graft: only Hearst and the people. The Tammany machine tried to portray him as insane, "an apostle of riot." On election day there was widespread intimidation at the polls against Hearst's supporters. Tammany was rumored to have thrown boxes bursting with ballots for Hearst into the East River. It was a game of special favors, disenfranchisement, and demonization. And it was exciting.

It was also alarming. Norman could easily see the consequences of corruption in municipal politics. Tenement regulations were not enforced. Sanitation standards were ignored. Around Greenwich Street by the elevated train track and on the worst blocks of Renwick, Norman visited tenements and overcrowded buildings, ministering to sick mothers and gaping at dirty children who played upon floors. The stink would rise up from trash piled in air shafts and yards; outdoor toilets had to serve whole buildings. Sitting on broken chairs as he listened to the parishioners' problems, Norman would watch cockroaches travel in intersecting lines upon the broken plaster of the walls. On one Sunday, a child came running, screaming, "Come quick; Papa's killing Mamma!" The child led him to a drunk longshoreman threatening his wife with an ax.

Unsurprisingly, the ubiquitous saloons were among the first things that Norman noticed. His father's temperance sermons and his parents' vocal disapproval of drink would have primed him to be aware of the deleterious effects of alcohol—the deadened gaze, the whiff of rotten grain on the breath. The degree of poverty, though, was something unimaginable. Eventually, he came to see liquor as an "escape" from, as well as a cause of, such misery. He developed a more nuanced view of drinking than his parents and teachers growing up in Ohio had imparted to him. The rampant alcoholism was not simply a sin, a failure of will and personal responsibility, but something that was part of a deeper problem, a communal despair that turned into "sodden apathy." It frustrated Norman to go to the poor areas on the east side of downtown New York, where the Jewish neighborhoods were marked by an "abounding vigor of life, that tremendous intellectual and social interest," he later wrote. The men's club he ran at Spring Street, by contrast, was "anemic." The people were bored and hopeless.

A young Socialist minister came to preach at Spring Street and tried to push Norman toward socialism. "What new anesthetic have you been putting on your soul to keep you from declaring your allegiance to the Cooperative Commonwealth . . . Comrade?" he wrote, offering Norman a job at his church in Boston. But the Socialist Party—founded in 1901 by an eclectic group of agrarian democratic populists, intellectuals on the Lower East Side, and some German Americans—did not have enough of a following to mobilize even the exploited and unhappy workers around Spring Street. Norman could not blame his neighbors. His economics courses at Princeton had convinced him that socialism would not work, and he was more interested in reforming capitalist society than abolishing it. He even considered writing a book attacking socialism.

Nevertheless, his old preconceptions were cracking. His Princeton friend Tom Carter's mother saw him and told Tom that Norman was "going all to pieces." But he did not experience a crisis at Spring Street. The city, with all its problems, energized him. Late into the night the young men at Spring Street—Norman and Tom Carter and, once Carter left, Harvard graduates Ted Savage, Charles Gilkey, and Ralph Harlow—pondered and debated what they saw in New York, learned in school, and believed. As Carter half kidded to Norman, they were solving "the fate of the universe . . . every night."

‡

It was a feeling that Norman did not want to leave behind. He was now committed to entering the ministry, but this presented its own problems. In fulfilling his parents' wishes, he was also breaking with them: Norman wanted to go to Union Theological Seminary in New York, the bastion of liberal Christianity, and his desire upset his parents. Emma was the one who pushed him hardest. "Papa would be willing to have you go to some other Presbyterian seminary that is not too far gone into the Higher Criticism idea," Emma wrote. Norman tore the letter in half.

At Union, the professors and theologians did not reject the immortality of the soul, but they were not much concerned with heaven or hell. They emphasized society over Scripture. It is hard to overstate what a radical change this was for an important current in mainstream Protestantism, and Welling sensed where it could lead. He was not bothered by the rejection of hell as a pit of flames. Yet to deny or diminish life after death, he believed, would suggest that God's omnipotence had bounds. It would suggest that the Bible was not revealed truth, but only a set of suggestions, to be picked through at will. On Easter Sunday, 1907, while Norman was mulling whether to go to Union or take the more conservative path to Auburn, Welling preached a sermon on what he called an alarming development: the trend of disputing the inerrancy of the Bible.

Welling warned the congregation there were people who called themselves Christians but denied the virgin birth, or the hard fact of the resurrection, or the existence of heaven and hell, Welling told his congregation. Agnosticism was gaining a foothold. He quoted a professor saying "that life beyond the grave is a fond illusion, at best a platonic speculation, that man at last lies down and dies like the dog," a death that "consequently cancels all moral distinctions and levels the greatest benefactor with the worst enemy of his kind." It was a "horrible belief," said Welling. He ended the sermon on an upbeat, if forced, note, by saying that he hoped and trusted that the reports of agnosticism and the rise of disbelief in the literal truth of the Bible were overstated. He must have known he was being optimistic. He knew he was describing his own son, who was writing letters home questioning the existence of hell.

✢

Norman dreaded having to choose what to do next. He was relieved when his uncle Frank Welles offered to pay for Norman to accompany Reverend Bates and two of his Spring Street Presbyterian coworkers and friends on a trip around the world. They traveled through the Philippines, Japan, Korea, China, Nepal, and India, visiting schools and missions and sometimes old Princeton friends. It was an eye-opening but not an always easy trip for Norman. Bates suffered from bouts of depression, sometimes severe, and the burden of caring for him fell to Norman. The other challenges were less pressing but left a lasting impression on the young assistant. Norman left for India with a fondness for Rudyard Kipling and an admiration for imperial Britain. What he found there, though, shook his confidence. When he met a student in Allahabad involved in the Indian nationalist movement, he found himself questioning the justice of British rule. The sight of a British civilian striking an Indian conductor over a dusty streetcar seat deepened his disquiet.

At the same time, when Sherwood Eddy, a YMCA missionary, took the group of American travelers to visit a village of outcasts, the Indian caste system horrified Norman. Eddy's own attitudes toward the Indians probably influenced him. Eddy, who would become one of the major figures in the international evangelical movement, strained to reconcile his respect for some local traditions with his revulsion for others, like female infanticide, and with his assumption of his own religion's superiority. His outlook could shed light on Norman's thinking as a twenty-three-year-old minister: "I took little interest in theological, ecclesiastical or organizational work. It was the life of the people that concerned me, as to whether it was impoverished or abundant, materially, spiritually, culturally and socially. I believed we had a way of life that would in time introduce a whole new civilization, with its religious, educational, economic and social values." Norman would later echo these words. He most likely did not take the sentiments directly from Eddy, but Norman would have been listening and paying attention to the ways and thoughts of his guide.

However uninterested Eddy—like Norman—was in theology, though, he believed that the "way of life" was Christianity. He was a missionary. Norman was not, but he was likewise enthusiastic about missionary work. A trip to Siam to visit Esther, whom his grandparents had raised, reinforced that conviction. Norman found her a "remarkable woman"—back straight, feet bare, graceful and caring. She was now a nurse very much in demand, Norman bragged to his mother, and her devotion to the Mattoons was still evident. She explained that she had worn Siamese mourning dress ever since she had learned that Mary Mattoon had died, Norman reported—"even in the palace where it is forbidden. They can't have her any other way." Esther even called Norman her own grandson.

Norman admired Esther for her indomitable character, but he was just as impressed at the strength of her faith. He considered her a "true Christian." He found nothing embarrassing about missionary work, and he did not jettison its specifically religious aspect. His mind coupled Christianity with what he saw as self-evident virtues: law and order, education, thrift. Reform of schools, prisons, government bureaucracies—all this anticipated the "better things" of Christianity. "Siam's progress is marvelous," he wrote to his mother, and he credited her parents and those with whom they worked.

> Missionary work in Siam is unique. No mission ever had greater indirect results—that is, social results. . . . And yet in Siam proper the *direct* results in the line of converts is pitifully small. I think not yet 700. Buddhism bends in tolerance but does not break. Its ideal is one of calm indifference; the agonizing love of Christ is inexplicable to many. . . . Christianity's demands of purity and love are too high. Yet I believe that the time is ripe for better things.

Perhaps it's natural that Norman would have written to his mother about her childhood home and her parents' work in this way. Perhaps he was only trying to make her proud. But more likely, he believed what he said. Stephen Mattoon had spoken of clearing ground and planting seeds: Now that half a century had passed, his grandson looked for ripeness.

This was a mainline view among American Protestants, but there were those who saw things differently. Among them was Violet Stewart, a young woman with an interest in tuberculosis care who had traveled to India to study hospitals and clinics. When a missionary told her of the sometimes violent punishments that converts faced from their disapproving families, Violet asked if it wasn't "selfish" of the missionaries to

"inflict such suffering" on the native community. Her question did not go
over well with the missionaries. "I'm right just the same," Violet wrote to
her mother. It was one thing to tend to the bodies of the sick, but as for
their souls, she said, "I think they'd be just as well left to God." She never
changed her mind but later she would help change Norman's.

⁘

After visiting Asia, Norman left the group to visit Europe, likely stopping
to stay with the Welleses in Paris or in their country home in Bourré. It
was a vacation. Though Norman surely told his aunt and uncle about his
travels, international politics were probably not the topic of much conversation. Still, he might have heard of an extraordinary conference that had
taken place the year before, in 1907, at The Hague—and traveling through
Europe, he might have sensed a growing mood of hostility among European powers.

The family of European monarchs formed a twisted tree. King Edward
of Great Britain was, among other interrelations, the uncle of both Wilhelm II, kaiser of Germany, and the German wife of Nicholas II, czar
of Russia. Nicholas and Wilhelm, cousins by other branches, called each
other "Nicky" and "Willy" and wrote to each other often. Major and
minor royalty married and moved, crisscrossing the continent and graft-
ing one country to another. But rivalries took precedence over blood and
friendship.

Empires cannot easily coexist, and in Europe at the turn of the twentieth century, the balance had grown precarious. In 1898, Czar Nicholas
called for an international conference on the subject of disarmament and
"universal peace." In his open letter, he warned that a balance of power
secured by armaments and armies "will lead inevitably to the very catastrophe which it is desired to avert." It was a surprising proposal, but less
altruistic than he hoped it would appear; the czar had just learned that
the Austrian army was stocking up on a type of rapid-fire gun that the
Russians were too poor to afford. But Nicholas was also motivated by
the six-volume work of Ivan Bloch, published in English as *Is War Now
Impossible?*, which portrayed full-scale modern warfare as absolutely
devastating to European economies—and predicted that civil revolutions

could follow. That got Nicholas's attention. His counterparts were unimpressed, though. His uncle Edward, king of England, called the conference proposal "the greatest rubbish and nonsense I ever heard of," and his cousin Wilhelm responded with dismay. "Imagine!" Willy wrote to Nicky. "A monarch dissolving his regiments sacred with a hundred years of history and handing them over to Anarchists and Democracy!" It was a horror too great to contemplate.

But all, including the United States, sent delegations to The Hague in 1899 and then again in 1907. The more serious reforms—arms limitations, enforcement mechanisms, measures that might have made a difference—were quickly off the table. But the conference did manage to establish an international arbitration court, where nations could mediate disputes without resorting to arms. The arbitration movement had attracted some of the brightest diplomatic minds. The delegates to the conference laid out rules for respecting neutrality, treating prisoners of war, adjudicating disputes, and, in theory, increasing the transparency of international affairs. War might not disappear immediately, but perhaps it could become more rational, more humane, less destabilizing, and less frequent. Few, however, were willing to limit national sovereignty to make that possible.

Even as leaders worked together at The Hague, at home they whipped up their populaces into frenzies of nationalism. They built up their armies and navies and worked to expand—or at least hold together—their empires. They nursed old grudges and encouraged their populations to do the same. The Hague was supposed to help clarify international relations but, as they preached the virtues of transparency and arbitration, diplomats formed a labyrinthine series of alliances and counteralliances that became as hard to trace as the royal family tree.

·✦·

In the spring of 1908, Norman returned to New York newly awake to its strangeness, mindful of what he had seen abroad, and unsure of where his future lay. He wandered through the city streets lost in thought. Princeton had offered him an attractive position as a teacher. One of the missions he had visited in Japan wanted him to return as a missionary. The Reverend Allen M. Dulles (father of Allen and John Foster Dulles, who was a year ahead of Ralph at Princeton) offered him a job as his assistant in Auburn, which he could do while attending seminary there, which would please his parents. Or he could stay in New York, attend Union Theological Seminary, and continue to do the kind of work he had done at Spring Street Presbyterian. William Sloane Coffin, a businessman and philanthropist involved with the church on Spring Street, urged him to accept an offer to be the assistant at Christ Church, on the edge of Hell's Kitchen. More than Norman's career was at stake in his decision. Different options promoted different conceptions of Christianity, and every step Norman took in one direction would make it harder to go back. It was a question not only of what to do, but also of what to believe and how to live.

He chose Union, Christ Church, and New York City. For all its problems, New York had enchanted him. He marveled at how it worked and how it didn't, at how prosperity and poverty were so enmeshed, and at how a panoply of peoples could more or less coexist. On one warm night in early June, Norman walked from Christ Church, at West Thirty-eighth Street and Ninth Avenue, to Union Theological Seminary, then located on the Upper East Side. As he came out of Hell's Kitchen, he wrote to his mother, "my mind was full of the problems of poverty and sin about us (it's not all bad)," when he came upon a man in the street, preaching to a crowd, and was struck by the force of that faith—so crazy and exuberant, alarmingly incoherent, intensely palpable. From there he went up to a socialist club and "had their position called vividly to mind." He walked through Times Square, with its blinking nickel shows, past a black woman singing, and wondered, "What story might lie behind?" He passed a man with long red hair hawking cheap jewelry and moved along the rows of theaters, the Tenderloin and Fifth Avenue, where elegant town houses were dimly visible behind two poor men asking for a place to stay for the night. Over them loomed the spires of St. Patrick's.

As he came upon Central Park, his mind spun. "I almost stopped to ask a man with a cheap little telescope . . . to let me look awhile at the quiet stars."

Disoriented by the kaleidoscopic city, he found his bearings a few days later at his third class reunion at Princeton. The familiar green expanses and the solid stone arches reassured him. He felt at home. At Princeton, he knew his way around. He was grateful for the feeling, and he knew whom to thank. Norman still adored Woodrow Wilson. After an unexpected dinner with Wilson at a friend's place in New York, during which Wilson entertained the table with limericks, Norman may have even felt an exaggerated sense of his own proximity to the school's president. After returning to New York from his weekend in Princeton that summer, he sent Wilson a gushing letter of gratitude. Norman wrote, "Every day I live I am more thankful that I am a Princeton man."

·+·

Then Norman began to turn away. Not from Princeton—not yet, at least, and perhaps not ever—but from its traditionalism. From that moment on, Princeton's privilege would start to rankle. His classes at Union Theological Seminary pulled him further from Princeton's conservative ethos—as his father had known they would. At Union, traditions were regarded ambivalently at best. Union's professors looked forward, not back. They considered themselves modern men using modern tools to excavate the truth of religious experience from the accretion of time. Francis Brown, the school's president, was eager to pursue a "scientific study of theology." The students nicknamed him Yahweh.

Whatever Union's critics said, the school's professors had no intention of abandoning the Bible as the prime source of wisdom. But to them, the Bible was a book written by inspired men, and not the total sum of truth. Theology was crucial, but so was the psychological experience of spirituality. Religion provided an ethical system—a way of life, not just a path to heavenly salvation. Union's professors thought that Christianity had a progressive social mission. They called it the Social Gospel.

Social Gospelers emphasized love, not retribution, and potential, not inherent depravity. Social Gospelers like Roswell Bates at Spring Street Presbyterian went into the tenements and slums and set up settlement houses, delivered sanitation lectures, and tried to marry the idea of urban renewal with spiritual renewal. In this, they were not unlike settlement-house workers, like Jane Addams, whose Hull House in Chicago had begun to change the way people understood the relationship between dignity and opportunity. For progressives, real reform was psychological as well as material. For Social Gospelers, it was also spiritual. They believed only Christianity could transform society in a true and enduring way. The sick and hungry need more than medicine and bread. Social Gospelers were convinced they could offer what secular leaders couldn't: the power of God's love and justice.

Norman had already been exposed to the Social Gospel during his days at Spring Street Presbyterian. He was committed to a vision that linked social and spiritual reform; that was why he had chosen Union in the first place. Union completed his conversion to a social conception of Christianity. His classes exposed him to thinkers like William James, who focused on the psychology of belief and religious impulses. James himself held aloof from the reforming fervor of the Social Gospel, but in his work he sought to shift the focus away from the truth of dogma toward the issue of what significance faith held for *this* world. The professors at Union taught Norman that, far from representing a distraction from the main business of nurturing souls, the cause of reform lay at the heart of the Christian method. Their theology centered on love and treated love as an ethics. What was the Sermon on the Mount, they asked, if not the most profound answer to the social question? Norman's professors, including William Adams Brown and Harry Emerson Fosdick, made a rhetorical and aesthetic appeal, as well as an intellectual and religious one. They inspired in Norman a sense of beauty and grave purpose. A minister, they suggested, might do more than guide his flock on Sundays. He could help make the world a better place.

A more conservative Christian, like Norman's father, might have found much to like in the language of the Social Gospelers' sermons, their words of love and solace and duty. But there was the small matter of squaring the practical reality of world with Scripture. Norman learned how to interpret doctrinal works in a way that preserved the spirit but dodged claims of literal truth. He attended lectures where economic justice was considered central to salvation. He learned about men like Washington Gladden and Richard Ely, who somewhat floridly called for employers to follow Christ and treat their employees like brothers, returning the fruits of the labor to the laborers. Gladden and Ely did not impress Norman very much. But the book of another Social Gospel writer did. *Christianity and the Social Crisis*, by a theologian named Walter Rauschenbusch, called for a Christianity of prophetic social justice. Here was a minister who had worked in conditions not unlike those around Spring Street Presbyterian, in a church in Hell's Kitchen, and diagnosed society's problems in a language that combined a familiar religious vocabulary with the confident language of social science. He argued that the essence of Christianity was antihierarchical, radically democratic, and essentially socialist. "Christian idealists must not make the mistake of trying to hold the working class down to the use of moral suasion only, or be repelled when they hear the brute note of selfishness and anger," he wrote. "The class struggle is bound to be transferred to the field of politics in our country in some form." Rauschenbusch believed he had written a revolutionary book that would shock the nation and make him a pariah. Instead, he was treated as a star. By the time Norman graduated, *Christianity and the Social Crisis* had gone through thirteen printings.

Few who read the book became Christian socialists. Its central message was lost on many readers who confused it with the polemic of an optimistic reformer or a utopian. Rauschenbusch was neither. He believed that progressive reform did not go far enough. He also did not consider his vision inevitable or even possible: "We shall never have a perfect social life, yet we must seek it with faith." He placed more importance on that quest than on a transcendent God. At times, his version of Christianity was hardly Christianity at all. "Ethical conduct," Rauschenbusch wrote, "is the supreme and sufficient religious act." If good behavior were enough, men might be able to grant their own grace.

This kind of language resonated with Norman while he was at Union, but it did not radicalize or completely convince him. In fact, he was more wary than many of his classmates and good friends, who were "disciples" of Rauschenbusch. A colleague of Norman's from Spring Street, Ted Savage, spent that summer studying the dockyard slums in East London before joining Norman at Union. He was, he wrote, "heartily in sympathy with the general principles of Socialism." Another of Norman's Spring Street friends, Charles Gilkey, went to Berlin that fall and declared himself "less and less of a Socialist," fearing that it would end in a "dead-level society"—a fear Norman himself would express years later. But Gilkey added that "the great truth and service of Socialism lies in the just protests against deep-rooted evils."

Norman had not yet traveled that far. That fall he voted for William Howard Taft for president, and in his part-time job at Christ Church, he followed the lead of his boss, James Farr, who was "conventionally and cautiously liberal." Farr was a Princeton graduate, and Norman appreciated him for his connections as much as anything else. Like most people, Norman never neglected the importance of social contacts. He made friends with bankers and magnates and dined in well-appointed rooms; when he wore himself out with work, he went to the Saranac Lake lodge of Cleveland H. Dodge (Princeton class of 1879) to rest up.

During the summers, he lived and worked at Christ Church, only a few blocks from Hell's Kitchen, one of the most violent neighborhoods in America. Gangsters strutted near the church in stolen cops' uniforms (no real cop was stupid enough to enter the area alone) and residents were accustomed to scattered pops of gunfire. When he moved between the tables of wealthy philanthropists and helping parishioners who never had enough food, Norman bifurcated his life. Inequality alarmed him, and he wanted to work to ameliorate it. But he wanted to eat pancakes at Saranac Lake, too.

Five

SYMPATHY FOR THE UNMARRIED

Violet Stewart

One of Norman's favorite dinner tables in New York was at the elegant home of Mrs. W. A. W. Stewart, on East Thirty-eighth Street, just off Fifth Avenue. Norman knew her daughters, Mary and Violet, from their volunteer work at Christ Church—Mary ran the Sunday School, while Violet helped the church's volunteer doctor—and he probably knew Mrs. Stewart through his friend Will Coffin, who was another favorite of hers. The Stewart sisters were a few years older than he and probably unlike any girls he had ever spent time with. Mary, a slightly deaf redhead, blew hot and cold, but Norman thought her a "wonder." Frances Violet—"Violet" to everyone—had a spirited personality that belied her small stature; she reached just the height of Norman's shoulder. Both sisters were outgoing, stylish, and a little provocative. Norman later said that he fell in love with their mother first. He was only half joking; he was enchanted by them all.

Their mother was a widow. Their father, William, had disappeared in 1888, when his cutter yacht, the *Cythera*, was lost at sea in a freak March blizzard. Frances Stewart had the veneer of a gracious, proper society woman, but underneath she was a live wire. She wrote her daughters lively, gossipy letters from her frequent travels (Europe, Southampton, West Tisbury, summer haunts ad infinitum), her cheerful voice flashing with irreverence and wit. Raised a Unitarian and married to a Presbyterian, she was the kind of woman who went Episcopalian when in England and Established Church of Scotland when in Edinburgh—unless she found herself fancying the Free Church that morning. She called her grown children by their childhood endearments: Violet was "Babs" or "Daddy's Bear"; Mary was "Polly Ann" or "Jane." Frances's favorite sister, Isa, was "Wawa."

Frances Stewart was born Frances Loring Gray, of Boston. Her family traced its lineage to the *Mayflower*; as befit her background, she was neither forgetful nor forthcoming about it. Her father, William Gray, was a merchant, financier, Harvard overseer, and city leader, one of the wealthiest men in Boston. But Frances's life did not exactly follow the path she most likely saw ahead for herself when she married William. He was a lawyer and avid competitive yachtsman. His father, John Aikman Stewart, was the chairman of the U.S. Trust Company and had been appointed assistant secretary of the Treasury by Abraham Lincoln.

The first shock came in 1886, when William Gray Jr., Frances's brother (and her husband's friend and sailing rival), was charged with embezzling half a million dollars from the textile company of which he was treasurer. Newspapers in New York and Boston splashed the revelations—along with rich details of Gray's extravagant lifestyle (the yachts, the extensive gardens, the "fancy fowl," the profligate sons)—across the front pages. "Developments that Startled Staid New-England" read one *New York Times* headline. It briefly appeared that Gray had gone on the lam, but on the third day of the scandal he drove from Boston to Milton, walked into the woods, and killed himself. The affair was deeply painful to the family, so much so that William Gray Sr. refused to execute his own son's will. A year and a half later, Frances's own husband was dead.

Her brother's travails and the independence thrust upon her may have made her more circumspect about wealth, more willing to let her daughters spend time outside the gilded confines of her world. And it may have made her more inclined to smile upon the very tall, very thin—only 155 pounds and well over six feet two when he graduated from college—young man with no money and not much of a plan to earn it. It helped that he had gone to Princeton.

Princeton was important to the Stewarts. The Stewart girls' father had gone there, as had their brothers; their cousin, John A. Stewart III, was a classmate of Norman's. (Even in a class with its share of Roman-numeraled names, Stewart represented, perhaps a little obviously, such an "old" family that a humorous essay in the class's yearbook called him "John A. Stewart XVII.") Violet and Mary's grandfather, John Aikman Stewart, had been a trustee of Princeton for forty years. Princeton alumni were welcome in the Stewarts' home. Violet and Mary's mother even kept a Princeton songbook open on the piano.

-+-

Norman had competition for the affections of the Stewart ladies (including from his own mentor, William Sloane Coffin, who was only a few years older than he). But the Stewart sisters had competition for his favor, too—not least from each other. Mary, who was dangerously approaching spinsterhood, was the early contender, and Violet deferred to her. Anyway, Violet had other things on her mind. She had badly wanted to be a nurse, but her family wouldn't allow it. After helping a doctor implement a tuberculosis home-treatment program around Christ Church, one day in 1909 the tiny, pale-eyed young woman came home and announced that she wanted to go to India to study tuberculosis and nursing. Violet was stubborn, and her mother consented. Her unofficial guardian, "Uncle Ed" (her father's former law partner, Edward Sheldon, who was now the president of the U.S. Trust Company), accompanied Violet and her companion, a

licensed nurse, aboard the luxurious *Lusitania* to London. From there, she
and her chaperone continued on alone.

Norman had provided letters of introduction to his own missionary
contacts in Asia, and he wrote to Violet frequently. She began to look forward to his letters as she moved from England to France, to Egypt, and
into Asia, growing tired of desultory flirtations with whatever eligible
bachelor happened to be around. She also grew tired of her sister's fick-
leness toward the younger suit back in New York. "I'd not be surprised
to hear next letter that you *hate* him and aren't speaking," she wrote half
playfully, half hotly to Mary from Amritsar, India. "Just to quote from
your last 3 letters—'A man *can't* be friends with two sisters so I mean'
etc! Next 'I think I want half of Norman after all'—3rd opinion 'I mean to
have all I want etc'—Well take him if you can get him, and the same holds
true of Anna and Sara. But it does seem to me that the Brick Church is all
getting foolish about him!"

From the start the good-natured ribbing was sharply edged, and as
time passed, Violet became more and more testy toward her sister when
the subject of Norman Thomas arose. She was starting to want Norman
for herself. She had grown to enjoy his letters—and liked the fact that he
had written to her five times in a row without hearing back. She could
describe the sights she was seeing to him with frankness, knowing that he
had seen similar things, and there was a seriousness to their exchanges that
her letters home usually lacked. (The possibility of courtship, remote or
not, would have made them especially formal.) To her mother and sister,
she wrote about bargaining at bazaars, seeing the Taj Mahal, and the men
with whom she idly flirted, and gave funny and cutting descriptions of
the missionaries whom she met. Her mother's replies were always spirited
and entertaining, but they often concerned shopping, art exhibitions, dinner parties, gossip—familiar subjects. Norman's letters, on the other hand,
were "full of news," and she found them enthralling. She replied to him
in kind. "I'd hate to be England just now with such a responsibility," she
wrote from Delhi. "I just feel that the people hate us . . . and the looks they
throw after us are not the same as the salaams with which they face us."

As their letters sailed back and forth across oceans and continents, their
relationship deepened. Violet's sister, though, still presented a complication.

In letters between Violet and her mother and Mary, the name "Mr. Thomas" cropped up more often, but always as gossip about Mary's fickle feelings for him. Violet insisted that she did not "mind" Mary's inconsistent chatter about Norman; it was all very amusing—until it was no longer very amusing. "Don't tell her that I told you she told me," Violet anxiously and rather torturously wrote to her mother from Lucknow, India, "but she says she's tired of Will Coffin and realizes he's rude and spoilt—Says Norman Thomas makes her feel 15 years younger—wish she'd not talk like that, makes me feel I've got too much of him, but I have certainly appreciated his letters."

By the time Violet arrived home in early 1910, Mary's infatuation with Norman was over (Mama doubtlessly getting more nervous with every passing year), and Violet's path was clear. "Mr. Thomas" became "Norman," and when he faced a stretch in the hospital with phlebitis, she invited him to recuperate at the Stewart home. He would be no trouble, she assured him. "You are quite sufficiently popular with Kate and Annie"—the maids—"to have them enjoy bringing you trays, to say nothing of me. And Minnie"— the cook—"will fix you whatever you like to eat." He wanted to accept the invitation, badly. But his sense of propriety propelled him forward—perhaps he was imagining what his proper parents would think. He could not be nursed by Violet at her home unengaged, and so he made a proposal of his own. From his hospital sickbed, he asked her to marry him, and she said yes. And so he went to convalesce at the Stewarts', where Minnie and Annie and Kate doted on him, and he lived, for a moment, like a wealthy man.

✢

While Norman was still in the hospital, the pastor of Brick Church on Fifth Avenue, around the corner from the Stewarts' house, died, and Norman's former Princeton English professor Henry Van Dyke became acting minister. A popular poet and essayist, Van Dyke was short, warmhearted, and vain; he wore his doctoral hood while preaching. Norman was a natural choice for his assistant. He had excelled in Van Dyke's classes at Princeton, was a close friend of the deceased pastor, and ranked at the top of his class at Union Theological Seminary. For Norman, it was a tremendous opportunity, the kind of job that could fast-track a career. For a seminary student on scholarship with an eye to marrying a society girl, the granddaughter of one of the grandees of the congregation, the prestige of the position (and the nice salary) mattered. When Norman, heart thumping, went to tell Violet's grandfather of their engagement—he lived a few blocks from his daughter-in-law and grandchildren and often saw them—he was not sure what the patriarch's response would be. But Stewart could see the potential in the nervous young man before him and was quick to give his blessing.

When Norman brought Violet home to meet his parents in Lewisburg that summer, the visit went less smoothly. They supported the engagement, but they did not totally hide their misgivings. It is easy to see from Violet's letters not only why Norman loved her so much but also why she made his parents wary. She spoke differently, dressed differently, and acted differently. Someone from Siam might have seemed more familiar than the sophisticate from Manhattan. In Lewisburg, when she and Norman walked down the street openly holding hands, the neighbors whispered. It's unlikely that she expressed her somewhat unorthodox religious views on that trip to the minister's manse, but she was prone to honesty, which others often took as irreverence. (Of course, she didn't mind that either. Her idea of "real preaching," she once said, was "some high priest haranguing the multitudes." "I have great respect for the Mohammadans even though I didn't quite believe them," she wrote from India. A hair from the beard of Islam's founder didn't excite her, but his old worn sandal "gave me quite a thrill".) She liked shocking people, and anyway, sometimes she could not help it. Who knows what Violet might have said to alarm Norman's parents? They were already worried enough about their son.

Violet and Norman were married on September 1, 1910. Henry Sloane Coffin, the minister at the Madison Avenue Presbyterian Church, married them. The petite bride wore a white chiffon and lace dress with a long satin train, and a garland in her hair. Norman's friend from Princeton Dumont Clarke served as best man, and his brothers Ralph and Evan were among the ushers. (Arthur, still in high school, was probably too young for the role.) A host of Stewarts and Grays attended, along with a little cluster of society names that were duly noted in the newspapers. Welling and

Emma Thomas were not there. It wasn't a snub—Welling had planned to help officiate until he had come down with typhoid—but their absence still would have been conspicuous. Norman's parents were uncomfortable with the match and the world that Violet came from. It's hard not to imagine that they would have felt out of place at the wedding, too.

Thus the presence of Norman's brothers mattered all the more. Evan stood out among the wedding party; he always stood out. He was six feet five, with dark brown hair parted sharply on the side, and arresting gray green eyes. His large, slightly pointed ears and narrow face made him look a little bit like an elongated elf. Evan was starting his sophomore year at Princeton, where he had thrown himself into work at the *Daily Princetonian*. Unlike his older brothers, Evan wasn't one to balance school and extracurricular activities. He did not do anything in halfway measures. Evan's extraordinary devotion to his activities had an edge of anxiety that Norman had a hard time entirely understanding. The two had not spent much time together until Evan arrived at Princeton and his brother would show up to visit his old New Jersey haunts; Evan had been only twelve when Norman left Lewisburg for college. But Evan was in awe of Norman, and Norman had grown closer to his intense younger brother. Violet, whom Evan had met in Princeton, helped. She was just as independent and spirited as he was.

Norman had been closer to Ralph growing up. They had worked side by side during the summers, even when Norman was in college, spending long hours together at a chair factory in Lewisburg or selling aluminum wares door-to-door. Ralph had followed the course that Norman set, excelling at Princeton, from which he had graduated the year before Norman's wedding. He made Phi Beta Kappa and finished fifth in his class. He earned a spot on the *Daily Princetonian*'s editorial board and, like Norman, won prizes in oratory and debating. But in other respects the brothers were quite different. Ralph had entered Princeton thinking he wanted to study classics, but the practical world of science captured him. By the time he graduated, he had decided to go into engineering or business. He loyally accepted the traditions in which he had been raised. He was much more like Welling than Norman was.

Ralph was kind and responsible, perhaps less sensitive to the relative incomes of the neighborhoods in Manhattan, but also more sensitive to

his personal debts and responsibilities. He, like Norman, owed money to
Princeton (each of the brothers had received a tuition remission, in addition to the generosity of Uncle Frank's check), but it weighed on him as it
seems not to have weighed on Norman, who was less conscientious about
repaying it. Like Welling, Ralph was suspicious of excessive wealth and
possessed a profound sense of personal duty. That summer, while tutoring
a young student in Connecticut, he described his employers to Norman:
"Considering their wealth and desire for social position, I think they are
very sensible," Ralph observed. "But what a handicap it is to a boy to be
brought up thus! I appreciate my home more and more all the time. Isn't
it a wonderful home, and oughtn't we to commit to something with such
a training?"

·+·

When the wedding was over and the guests had disappeared, Norman and
Violet left for their honeymoon. Instead of the European tour that had
launched the marriages of many of Violet's friends, she and Norman went
bicycling and canoeing near Princeton. When they returned, they moved
into a ground-floor and basement apartment at West Forty-second Street
and Ninth Avenue. It was only a few long avenue blocks from Mrs. Stewart's, but in another sense it was a world away. Violet knew what she was
getting into; she was not a stranger to the neighborhood. The *New York
Times*, the *Tribune*, and the *Observer* all called her "the angel of Hell's
Kitchen." The truth was both less and more dramatic than that description
implied. Christ Church wasn't in the dangerous part of Hell's Kitchen. At
the same time, though, she was not an "angel" dropping in to do her good
deeds and then returning to a more rarefied realm. She was not volunteer-
ing anymore. She was home.

Norman, no less than Ralph, wanted to commit himself to service—but
noblesse oblige was easier to entertain when it involved something short
of substantial sacrifice and when he had only himself to worry about. He
knew that even as it was, Violet's upbringing had prepared her for a more
comfortable life than the one he offered. He also knew that it was in his
power to provide a conventionally bourgeois life in the future, if without

grandeur. He was twenty-five years old and already the assistant at one of Manhattan's upscale Presbyterian churches. Everyone, including Violet's family, saw a bright future for him, and they saw it on Fifth Avenue—not on Ninth.

For the moment, Norman did not worry too much about the future. He was very much in love and ecstatically happy. "With sincere sympathy for the unmarried," he cheekily signed his letter to Princeton's class of 1905 alumni record a few months after his wedding. He later remembered that time between his marriage and the United States' entry into World War I as a period of "all this and Heaven too." But it was not as heavenly as he suggested.

✢

Brick Church rushed Norman to the pulpit. It had to, as Henry Van Dyke became less and less inclined to make the long commute from Princeton. Since Van Dyke's regular absences meant that Norman often had to preach, it was decided that he should become licensed and ordained before he had finished his course work at Union.

He was ready for the Presbytery's examination, or as ready as he would be. He knew his ecclesiastical history, his Church rules and governance, and his theology. But the ordination exam would not just test his comprehension of facts. The examiners were interested in the *nature* of facts, the literal factuality of the Bible. The examination was more than a test of Norman's fitness to be a minister. It was a contest between conservatives and liberals within the Presbyterian Church. The New York Presbytery that assembled to examine Norman behind closed doors in January 1911 was a divided body, and each side had something to prove.

Conflicts within the church were nothing new—as Norman's father and grandfathers had learned—but tensions were running especially high at that moment. As the conservatives in the Presbyterian Church saw it, liberals drained Christianity of its power to save the soul, leaving behind a pale and vague humanitarian ethics. Only the previous year, the General Assembly of the Presbyterian Church began publishing the five-volume *Fundamentals*, which reaffirmed the inerrancy of Scripture, the

virgin birth and divine nature of Jesus, the doctrine of substitutionary
atonement through faith and grace, the bodily resurrection of Christ, and
the authenticity of the miracles. So-called fundamentalists accused some
liberal Christians of heresy. After Norman's professor William Adams
Brown had delivered a lecture titled "The Old Theology and the New,"
in which he celebrated the blurring of the sharp distinction between the
religious and secular, he had been attacked on the floor of the General
Assembly as a "Hindu pantheist."

The ordination tested the church. Conservative members pushed the
young seminarian to account for his interpretation of the virgin birth
and to say whether or not he believed the resurrection was of literal flesh
and blood. Norman hedged, delivering practiced answers. The evidence,
he replied, was contradictory and incomplete, and his understanding of
theology suggested that it was possible for Christ to be resurrected without
being a breathing, bleeding body. His answers displeased his most insistent
questioners, and Norman had to deploy a little sophistry to satisfy the
majority. In the end, he passed. However skillful his performance, he knew
it was not his most principled hour, and he emerged feeling bruised.

At Brick Church, Norman was cheered for his plucky performance.
William Adams Brown delivered a sermon in support of his young pupil,
and Norman's friends in New York voiced their support. "We are all
delighted to know that you passed through your trying ordeal the other
day so successfully," wrote Cleveland Dodge, "and I am very thankful that
you stood up so nobly." But Norman's pain lingered, not least because his
own father was mortified.

"I was feeling pretty blue, one day, as I do frequently of late, thinking
of Norman's distressing tendency to liberalism and several other things
that have disturbed my peace of mind," Welling wrote to the more sympathetic Ralph. This was an understatement. To Welling's horror, reports
of Norman's fraught examination were printed in several newspapers. Ten
members of the New York Presbytery signed a protest against Norman's
ordination; that, too, was picked up by the press. The controversy was
"very painful," Welling admitted to Ralph. "The papers both secular and religious are giving wide circulation to rumors, some of which are surely false,
some, I fear, are true." Reminders of his son's wayward beliefs dogged him

when he stepped outside or even opened the mail. A flier advertising a clipping bureau included the signed protest against Norman's ordination in its solicitation material. "And the people here are astonished, as our friends everywhere will be," he told Ralph. "I can hardly go on the street before someone asks me about it."

Welling tried to convince himself that the news reports of Norman's test were distorted. Norman had hastily sent a postcard to Lewisburg clarifying that "he emphatically affirmed the resurrection of Christ, but was in doubt whether the [resurrected body] was a body of flesh and blood." Welling wrote to Ralph, "That is an unimportant matter and very different from denying the rising from the dead."

Welling was so upset and embarrassed by the controversy that he wrote to the New York Presbytery and asked them to put an end to the public discussion of his son's examination. "These sensational rumors are exceedingly painful to me, who am conservative in my views and anxious that my son be not made to appear more liberal than the facts warrant," he wrote. His words betrayed his wishful thinking, his desire to make distinctions between rumors and facts that he could seize upon to demonstrate, by the force of his insistence if nothing else, that he and his eldest son agreed on all but "unimportant matters"—never mind that those unimportant matters just happened to be the particular ideas that Welling had dedicated his life to defending.

Norman's unpublished autobiography and recollections downplayed his father's disappointment over his examination before the Presbytery. He often minimized conflict within his family, or else he tacitly acknowledged their disagreements but called them inconsequential. In his autobiography, he wrote that "in the winter of 1910–1911 my mild heresies were well enough received and my father, to my delight, willingly took an impressive part in my ordination."

Welling did travel to New York and deliver the charge to Norman on January 25. He may have done it "willingly" but not without misgivings and sadness. In fact, he asked the head of the New York Presbytery to meet with him on the morning of the ordination so that Welling could plead in person that his son did not deserve the "deplorable notoriety." It should have been the happiest of days for Welling. It was his birthday. His son was following him into service to God, and he would be there himself to anoint him. If only the circumstances had been different, he wrote to Ralph, nothing would have made him happier. "Even as it is," he added, "I hope Norman may be used of good to do much good, and that a riper experience will rectify his faith."

Six

A LAND OF BROTHERHOOD AND JUSTICE

East Harlem,
New York

Norman also wanted to do much good, but that meant something different to him than it did to his father. A sense that it required more than living a scrupulous life of private piety and charitable generosity nagged Norman. His conception of faith was more outward-looking, more immediately ambitious. He wanted his influence to extend beyond the radius of a comfortable parish, and he wanted to make changes now. His desire to serve more than the thin corridor between Park and Fifth Avenues was, in some respects, absolutely in line with the dominant thinking of the day. Even the richest members of Brick Church understood that they had some obligation to alleviate the extreme inequality between their privilege and the poverty rampant in other areas of the city. They wrote large checks and supported reform efforts, and some trekked a few blocks to volunteer at churches and charities in rougher parts of town. Brick Church considered its outreach efforts central to its mission and lent support to Christ Church, where Norman had worked while a student at Union Theological Seminary. But Brick's members, like most wealthy New Yorkers, extended their generosity only so far. For the most part, they did not question their privilege.

With youthful confidence, Norman tried to unsettle Brick Church's congregation. On Easter Sunday, 1911, he summoned himself to his most heroic heights and chastised the men and women arrayed before him. The church was too pleased with itself, he declared. It had caused so much suffering. Cynics who said that it "had literally cursed the world" spoke some truth, he said. Manipulations of Scripture had been used to justify slavery, and the church's emphasis on the afterlife, with the promise that all would be righted in heaven, had been used to excuse earthly injustice. Christians—like those who sat before him—had exploited the poor, forgetting that all men were their brothers in the eyes of God. Such men hardly deserved to call themselves Christians.

During the sermon's climax, Norman fixed his gaze on a particularly noxious pew holder and hurled his accusations in the man's direction. The same man later told John Stewart that he thought Norman had a bright future at Brick Church: "He preached a good sermon."

The accolades poured in, and Norman was devastated. He had wanted to provoke the wrath of the guilty and the perplexity of the complacent. Perhaps emboldened by his marriage and his early success—he was twenty-six and delivering the Easter Sunday sermon at a major New York church while still at seminary—he had fancied himself the champion of the impoverished, challenging the oppressors. He felt, now, a bit like a fool, and it is easy to see why. But it is also easy to see why that pew holder was so pleased with the sermon. Norman's message was, at base, a gentle admonition to do better and be better, and it ended with the reassuring line "So we rejoice." This was hardly the stuff of a Walter Rauschenbusch.

Perhaps if even Rauschenbusch had been standing in the pulpit, though, that pew holder would have nodded his head. The Social Gospel of the kind that Norman preached that Easter Sunday had been so thoroughly incorporated into the mainstream church that by now it hardly seemed revolutionary. The year before, the United Presbyterian Church created a statement that embraced the Social Gospel's central themes: "the proclamation of the gospel for the salvation of humankind; the shelter, nurture, and spiritual fellowship of the children of God; the maintenance of divine worship; the preservation of truth; the promotion of social righteousness; and the exhibition of the Kingdom of Heaven to the world." Shelter, nurture, social righteousness, bringing heaven to the world—it was no wonder that conservatives were incensed about the diminution of orthodox teachings and the de-emphasis on sin and depravity.

Two months later, upon his graduation from Union, Norman left Brick Church. The congregation wanted him to stay. "I am overwhelmingly distressed that you felt it your duty to give up your position just now," one of the church elders wrote to Norman. "Duty" is precisely the word Norman would have used. He was not driven out of Brick by disgust with it or any burning passion to right the world's wrongs. It was some smaller sense of obligation that he couldn't shake, the need to do good. Norman wanted to be more "useful" than he could be at a church like Brick, he later wrote, drily and evasively. Inadvertently or not, his words echoed those of his father.

For Norman, Christian duty assumed an inescapably secular cast. He had followed with interest the mostly Jewish needle workers' strikes on the Lower East Side over the past two years. He sided with the workers. He had been horrified by the fire at the Triangle Shirtwaist Factory just a mile downtown that killed nearly 150 workers, mostly young women, who were unable to escape when they found the door to one stairway locked and the other impassable. The single frail fire escape broke. More than sixty of the workers jumped, some of them ablaze. If the photographs of Jacob Riis had startled New Yorkers, the sight and later accounts of women in flames and falling to their deaths stunned them. Reformers seized the moment—and the fact that so many of the dead were women—to push through legislation protecting worker safety.

The Triangle Shirtwaist fire and other signs of injustice and unrest did not radicalize Norman or explain why he left Brick. It's impossible to know exactly why he resigned. It may have been as simple as wanting to let Van Dyke's replacement hire his own assistant. But Norman probably did desire to feel of *use*. So many did. The desire was reinforced by the sense, especially among the wealthy and young, that reform should require some kind of test and hardship—a slight revision of the late-Victorian emphasis on the strenuous life. It is also possible that Norman had a harder time moving between the grim streets around Christ Church and the elegance around Brick than the parishioners who volunteered at Christ Church's Sunday school did. He may have wanted to show that he meant what he said that Easter Sunday. He had seen the corrosive effects of poverty and those of wealth, yet here he was offering shelter, nurture, and spiritual fellowship to those who needed it least and who assumed their right to it most of all. Whatever Norman's reasons, when he graduated from Union that June, he had options, and he took the hardest one. He could have stayed at Brick or continued his studies. He graduated from Union first in his class and was offered Union's prestigious seminary fellowship, which would have funded two years of theological studies in Europe. Instead, he took a job running a parish set among tenements in East Harlem.

The Home Missions Committee, an organization that helped to run churches in immigrant areas around the country, had decided to consolidate several churches in East Harlem into a single parish, the American Parish, and needed someone to lead it. Norman's professor William Adams Brown, the chairman of the Home Missions Committee, wanted Norman. Looking at his young student, Brown wrote in his memoirs, he saw the combination of experience and "a penetrating and original mind, a keen sense of social justice and exceptional initiative and courage." For his part, Norman recognized that Brown could be a mentor, and he saw that the job offered exactly the kind of challenge that the Social Gospel demanded. It was the chance to change society along with the church. One transformation would reinforce the other.

Much of what his job would entail, he knew, was social work. Still, spreading Presbyterianism was the great cause. He was technically a missionary, as his Mattoon grandparents had been. His job, explicitly stated in the contract he signed each year, was to convert immigrants to Protestantism. When he was older he downplayed this aspect of it, but when he was young he took it for granted that social work and Church work should not be separated: A well-functioning society would naturally embrace Protestant Christianity.

Yet the decision could not have been easy, and not only because the work would be hard. Violet was pregnant and gave birth to a boy, Norman Jr.—called Tommy—that August. Already Norman was sensitive about the material sacrifices his wife had made for his sake, leaving behind genteel luxury for a relatively threadbare existence. But Violet had a sense of adventure and a streak of compassion. Growing up, she had wanted to be a nurse; she, too, wanted to be useful. In East Harlem, she would have to be. And so that fall she installed her silver tea service in a town house at 220 East 116th Street, across from the church with the large rose window tucked between tenements. Wherever Violet lived, she was the proper hostess—even if, as was sometimes the case, she and her guests could not speak the same language.

Norman's own church had several foreign-language services and Sunday schools, and there were four separate churches under his watch, two of them under construction. He faced an enormous challenge. Only twelve people came to Norman's first Sunday service at East Harlem Presbyterian. Most, he could guess, were there out of curiosity, wondering what on earth he was doing there.

✢

The American Parish covered what was called a "polyglot district": It was a place of many languages. Italians predominated, but there were Jews, Swedes, Hungarians, and immigrants from all over eastern Europe. Most of them had arrived during the mass migration to the United States at the turn of the twentieth century. According to the 1910 census, more than a third of the country's ninety-two million people were first or second generation. Many of the immigrants in East Harlem did have more hope and mobility than where they came from. Others found that life in America was just as bad as, or worse than, what they'd left behind.

Some blocks of East Harlem could have been transplanted villages from rural Italy. About a third of southern Italy's population had fled Europe in the first decade of the twentieth century alone, and millions had ended up in New York. Life in the New World was hard, but it wasn't "The Midday," *Il Mezzogiorno*, what they called the sunburned land. There, people suffered almost biblical afflictions: earthquakes, plagues of insects, cholera. Social hardships burdened them, too. Italians were saddled with high taxes, compulsory military service, and widespread illiteracy. They had little hope that things would change. The Italians came to Mott Street and the Bowery in lower Manhattan, and when those places became unbearably overrun, they started arriving in East Harlem—pushing out many of the Irish who were already there. Jews came fleeing pogroms, while Waldensians (Italian Protestants) and even some Catholics came to escape the stranglehold of the institutional Catholic Church. When they arrived, they looked for work; what work they found was tedious and often dangerous, with machinery and chemicals unregulated by any safety standards. Some sent money back to their relatives who had stayed behind. Others could not make enough even to support the family that they had brought. By 1910, around 15 percent of children between the ages of ten and fifteen worked for a living. One survey, conducted by the Department of Labor between 1917 and 1919, showed that working children's income accounted for 23 percent of their total family income on average.

East Harlem had one of the highest infant mortality rates in the city. Tenements were "substandard" and teeming. Typically, the houses were five or six stories connected by dimly lit stairs, usually with a shared toilet in the hall and sooty coal-fired stoves. The residents had little privacy, scant light, and no silence. Four large families might have access to a single latrine. Single blocks held thousands of people. With so little room inside, the streets became the playground, the meeting place, the store, the battleground. Children formed groups and then gangs; they used rocks for weapons unless they could get a hold of a length of pipe. The older ones kept brass knuckles in their pockets; some carried guns.

Immigrant and second-generation children fought not only with one another but also with their parents. Schools that made an effort to "Americanize" their students taught only in English and offered no history relating to the children's various ancestries (unless Christopher Columbus counted—but never as *Cristoforo Colombo*). Students heard slurs hurled at them and brought them home to fling against their own parents. "We soon got the idea that 'Italian' meant something inferior. . . . We were becoming Americans by learning how to be ashamed of our parents," recalled one man raised in East Harlem.

Among native-born Americans the argument was generally over whether assimilation was possible—or even desirable. A few public figures thought that the texture of other cultures and customs gave immigrants traction and dignity and their communities coherence, and a few believed that America was richer for its panoply of cultures, but they were a tiny minority. Most regarded the flood of immigrants with horror. Between 1901 and 1910, 70 percent of those who came to the United States were from southern and eastern Europe (mostly Catholics and Jews), and by 1910, immigrants accounted for some 40 percent of New York City's population. Many native-born Americans feared for civilization. They believed that races—and they used the word "race" not only for blacks and whites but also to describe Europeans, even to distinguish northern Italians ("Europeans") from southern ("Africans")—were inherently stratified. Scientists and pseudoscientists alike discussed cranial circumferences, fossil records, and the inheritability of characteristics. Those who did not view immigrants as a threat to civilization believed it was their duty, as much because of their "superior" status as in spite of it, to ameliorate the degradation. They tried to introduce education and sanitation measures, acceptable religion and good manners, into immigrant communities. They tried to instruct the "lesser" races not to be so emotional or superstitious. Even the most well-intentioned tended to view race hierarchically and, often, hysterically.

It is hard to tell what, precisely, Norman thought about race at this point. Most likely he had never really been exposed to racial conflicts growing up, except, significantly, in his mother's stories about her experiences in Siam and North Carolina. To his Princeton classmates, he occasionally indulged in a little bigotry (of his growing family, he wrote, "I have done reasonably well in seeing to it that the future population of America is not entirely of Italian or Jewish ancestry"). But such instances were relatively rare. For the most part, he did not employ racist—or, notably for a missionary, proselytizing—language. In one speech he delivered to the Women's Board of Home Missions at the beginning of 1912, he criticized the superior and dismissive language sometimes used to describe immigrants. "These people who are coming here are men and women," he said. "These people are not criminals of the world or the scum of the earth. . . . I doubt very much if we were poor laborers whether we would have the courage to come to a land which spoke a different language." They faced unfair social and working conditions, he said, and yet they persevered. "These people are the new pioneers."

·+·

On June 8, 1912, a sunny Saturday morning in Princeton, Norman slipped on his Princeton reunion jacket, a black and orange blazer, over a pair of white trousers and took his place in the gentle rowdiness of the alumni parade. That afternoon, the members of the class of 1905—nearly half had returned—gathered under and around a tent pitched in a grove of trees. As the light faded, the class supper ended and a few alums rose to deliver short talks.

Norman spoke about social work and life in an immigrant community. Already he had been designated as the group's social conscience, the one who reminded his classmates that the world was less fair than they generally cared to imagine. His audience, many of whom had just bought their seats on the Stock Exchange or were settling into law firms, listened receptively. Even among conservatives, even within the manicured confines of Princeton, there was an openness to the idea that the government had a role to play in correcting some of society's imbalances. Elsewhere on campus that summer evening, the recently elected reformist governor of New Jersey, Woodrow Wilson, dined with his own classmates, some of whom were bankrolling his campaign for president of the United States. His Princeton friends brought in $85,000. Norman's friend Cleveland Dodge alone was good for $51,000.

How far reform should go was a less settled question, and some were answering it in ways that would have disturbed the magnates and the bankers on Wall Street. The next afternoon, Commencement Sunday, Norman's younger brother Evan strode across campus toward Murray-Dodge Hall, a long gothic brownstone that looked like a disproportioned church. He was on his way to be inducted into a new club. This, for a Princeton student, was not at all unusual, but the club itself was. Its aim was to change the world. John Nevin Sayre, a twenty-eight-year-old minister, had founded the fellowship for Christian action with the earliest underground followers of Jesus in mind. He and Hugh Burr, the secretary of the Philadelphian, picked seven other Princeton men, mostly from the graduating class. Sayre called them the Crusaders.

Evan wondered why he had been chosen. On Tuesday he would graduate, but he felt unaccomplished. The others there that Sunday had won Phi Beta Kappa keys, honors, varsity letters; they tended to have distinguished themselves further by their faith and their commitment to Princeton's religious community. Evan did not consider himself particularly successful or spiritual. He did not plan on joining the ministry. He thought he wanted to become a lawyer. At Princeton most of his energy had been devoted to the *Daily Princetonian*, where he was on the editorial board, but he had not been particularly interested in his classes or the Philadelphian; he was not a member of one of the fancier eating clubs. Unlike Ralph and Norman, he was going to graduate without honors. He often compared himself to his older brothers, especially Norman, and he found himself wanting. He had a hard time understanding that people were inclined to like him and to look up to him, and not only because he was the tallest man in his class. He distrusted his own charisma, quick wit, and charm.

When everyone had arrived and settled, John Nevin Sayre began to read the service. Sayre had graduated from Princeton in 1907, attended seminary, and briefly tried missionary work in China before returning to Princeton that fall to become a preceptor and assist with the Philadelphian. His wife of a year had died only months before, a blow from which he had hardly recovered. His work with the Philadelphian had sustained him through his grief, and now he wanted to take it further. His brother, Francis, had founded a similar group at Williams College during the previous year. It seemed a noble thing—idealism considered practically.

Sayre had devoured Rauschenbusch's writings and other Social Gospel texts, and he took their message to heart: Jesus had a social, not merely a personal, mission, and the traditional Church had obscured his true character. He was a misfit, a pacifist, and a rebel. Sayre and Burr asked Henry Van Dyke—the professor and Norman's erstwhile boss at Brick Church—to write a service for the Crusaders. They then rewrote it to make it more radical, finding plenty of material in the Bible. "The Son of man must suffer many things," Sayre read aloud to the group from the Gospel of Mark, "and be rejected of the elders, and of the chief priests, and scribes, and be killed, and after three days rise again."

Together the men recited a Promise of Dedication—the Social Gospel distilled into a few lines. Led by Sayre, they prayed for God to gird Princeton against "the deceitfulness of riches, the narrowness of class, the selfishness of power," and they prayed for America, for a "new Emancipation Proclamation . . . so we may gain for the world a land of brotherhood and justice." Sayre spoke, and eight men responded, *Amen*.

Evan was the last to sign the Brotherhood of Consecration. He did so solemnly. He had attended thousands of church services and heard thousands of sermons. Calls for service to God and Christ—at home, at his father's church, at Princeton's chapel, even in class—came as regularly as the rising sun. Yet for a moment that Sunday afternoon, he felt he had heard something urgent and new. When he went outside into the bright blue afternoon, the feeling faded and the frenzy of commencement took over. But when a small book with the Crusaders' prayers arrived at his parents' house in Lewisburg a few months later, the humbling awareness returned with force.

"I have a confession to make, but I am mighty glad to say that it doesn't apply to the present time," Evan wrote to Sayre after rereading the Crusaders' service. "I don't think that I understood very well just what an honor was being offered, nor just what membership in the club meant. Had I really understood it, I am afraid that I couldn't have honorably joined at that time." He now understood that he had made a pledge that moved beyond bringing social services to crowded cities. He had committed himself to the kind of transformation that comes only when a man risks persecution and rejection.

"As you read the service that Sunday afternoon, I got my first inkling," Evan wrote. "For a minute it frightened me."

·+·

That Tuesday, Norman and Violet watched Evan receive his degree. Though Violet, three months pregnant with the couple's second child, was feeling a bit under the weather, it was an especially joyful occasion for the couple. Violet's grandfather, having finished his time as president pro tem of Princeton, was also honored with a long ovation as he received an honorary degree.

A few days later, as Stewart, who was approaching his ninetieth birthday, recovered from the festivities at his home in Montclair, he took the time to answer a note from Norman. "I am always glad to hear from you and Violet and to learn from others, as I am constantly doing," he wrote in his perfectly formed hand, "of the excellent ... work you are doing amongst the foreign population on the east side of New York." He was sincere. The American Parish was the kind of progressive reform effort of which a man like John Stewart would have approved. Reform was at a high point in 1912, and Stewart's friend Woodrow Wilson was riding its currents to the White House.

Seven

THE PROMISE OF AMERICAN LIFE

*Norman, Ralph, and Arthur, with two
of Norman's children, in 1913, in the
garden at Norman's summer home in
Ridgefield, Connecticut*

In the 1912 race for the presidency the man who received Norman's vote in 1908, William Taft, faced a challenge from within his own party—by the man who had once handpicked him, former president Theodore Roosevelt. The Democratic candidate, Wilson, was of course Norman's own former professor. Norman didn't think for a second about voting for the Socialist candidate, Eugene Debs, but Debs was a major figure in the race, too. In 1911, hundreds of Socialists had been voted into office in elections around the country, including fifty-six mayors and a congressman. Debs was more radical than the other candidates but not by too much. All the candidates shared a basic conviction that reform was necessary and possible and that the federal government had a responsibility to bridle big business and redress excessive inequality. The challenge was to use new technologies and institutions to combat new problems, while preserving democratic principles and traditional values. They wanted to wash away "the muddy tide of commercialism, of materialism, which has swept over our country, and which is leaving its stain," as one novelist at the time put it. But the campaign itself was a mudslinging affair.

In 1908, Roosevelt handed the Republican Party and the White House to Taft. So confidently had Roosevelt expected Taft to continue to carry out his own program that he had left the country in 1909 to go big-game shooting with his son in Africa. (The trip's purpose was also partly to dispel the appearance that he was pulling the strings of Taft's administration.) He was dismayed to come back and learn that Taft had not simply picked up where he had left off. Though he did more trust-busting than had the trustbuster Roosevelt, Taft's inclination was conservative. "A National Government cannot create good times," he said. "It cannot make the rain to fall, the sun to shine, or the crops to grow, but it can, by pursuing a meddlesome policy . . . prevent a prosperity and revival of business."

Roosevelt sometimes spoke with the confidence of a man sure he could make the rain fall and the sun shine. At the Republican convention in Chicago, where he was hoping to wrest the nomination from Taft, he described his followers as "fearless of the future; unheeding of our individual fates; with unflinching hearts and undimmed eyes; we stand at Armageddon, and we battle for the Lord." When Taft and the Republicans refused to defer to him, Roosevelt's supporters walked out, while both sides cried foul.

Undaunted, Roosevelt simply founded his own party, the Progressive Party, known as the Bull Moose Party for its larger-than-life leader. Its rallies had the character of religious revival meetings and often ended with hymns; "Onward, Christian Soldiers" and "The Battle Hymn of the Republic" were favorites. When he accepted the Progressive Party's nomination, Roosevelt delivered "A Confession of Faith." His program went

by the name "New Nationalism," a phrase taken from a book, highly flattering to Roosevelt, called *The Promise of American Life*, by a journalist
named Herbert Croly. The time had come, Croly said, for a new nationalism built around the cause of economic and legislative reform. "The trust
reposed in individual self-interest has been in some measure betrayed,"
Croly wrote, and the result was "a morally and socially undesirable distribution of wealth."

"The Bull Moose has stolen the Socialist Platform!" some Socialists
cried. (Taft's supporters were only too happy to agree.) Even so, the Socialists distanced themselves from the Progressive Party, arguing that the Progressives had watered down the Socialist platform so much that it would be
ineffectual. Whereas the Progressives called for the abolition of child labor,
the Socialists called for the abolition of labor for children *under the age of
sixteen.* Whereas Roosevelt called for an eight-hour workday for industries
on a twenty-four-hour cycle, the Socialists called for an eight-hour workday, full stop. Whereas Progressives were for women's suffrage, Socialists
were . . . for women's suffrage. The differences between the Socialists and
other progressives were real, though. The Socialists made bigger demands
for a minimum wage, a graduated income tax, health care, and safety regulations, and they had a long-term goal of converting banks, railroads, and
municipalities to public ownership. Debs was not a reformer but a radical,
and he wanted not just change but revolution. Ultimately, he conceived of
extending democracy through collective ownership—something Roosevelt,
who supported responsible private ownership, never dreamed of.

The Socialist leader Debs captured more hearts than votes. That he won
as many votes as he did was impressive, considering the fractious nature
of his own party. He had to deal with antipolitical Socialists and Industrial
Workers of the World (or "Wobblies") who advocated sabotage and were
willing to use violence. He faced trouble, too, in appealing to the broad
base of organized labor. Samuel Gompers, head of the American Federation of Labor, had no interest in dismantling capitalism; his goal was to
extract concessions from employers for his own members, who tended to
be more-skilled craftsmen. Debs struggled to hold together a coalition of
orthodox Marxists and farmers who had never heard of Marx.

But Debs had a genius for making moral appeals without moralizing.

He communicated an abiding belief in America's inherent possibilities, if only those who had been unfairly deprived of their labor and dignity would band together. His compassion was evident in his every encounter. He crisscrossed the country in his vest and bow tie, speaking to overflowing crowds. He would lean out over the audience and his voice would burst forth, clear and resonant, and people leaned toward him in return. No one expected Debs to win, Debs included. No one expected him to do as well as he did, either. Debs tallied 901,873 votes on election day, more than twice his 1908 count, nearly a quarter of Roosevelt's total, and well more than a quarter of Taft's. The Socialists' prospects looked bright. Nearly 120,000 people paid dues to the party that year, and it seemed like only the beginning. Few realized that 1912 would be, in fact, the peak of the Socialists' prospects.

The race came down to a choice between Roosevelt's New Nationalism and Wilson's New Democracy. The two men sometimes seemed like inverse images of each other—the northerner and the southerner, the hunter and the professor, or, as one historian has noted, the warrior and the priest. In other respects, they were not so different. Like Roosevelt, Wilson had great confidence in his power as a leader. He was not a populist like the other leading figure in the Democratic Party, William Jennings Bryan (though securing Bryan's support was essential), but he, too, was an excellent speaker capable of stirring audiences. As a scholar he had spent decades studying the structure and possibilities of practical government, and he was eager to put his ideas into practice. He believed that it was a leader's task to divine the will of the people, to understand how it was reflected in the spirit of the age, and to anticipate where it was going. Unwilling to cede the progressive label to his rival, Wilson refused to call Roosevelt's new party by name, referring to it instead as the "third party" or the "new party" or the "irregular . . . Republicans." His progressivism was different from that of Roosevelt. It was more laissez-faire, rooted more in a desire to protect and promote individual freedom through competition than in a desire to eradicate social injustice.

Wilson capitalized on the turmoil in the Republican Party and won handily. Norman admired the rest of the Bull Moose ticket, but for president, he naturally cast his vote for his old professor, Woodrow Wilson.

+

"Evan came home to vote, and voted for Teddy!" Welling wrote to Arthur, who was now a sophomore at Princeton. "I thought his admiration for Wilson would hold him." His mother, typically direct, gave what was probably the correct explanation for Evan's vote. "Well I guess Evan is sorry in a way that he didn't or couldn't vote for Wilson, who is still one of his great heroes," she wrote Arthur. But Evan's friends "think all righteousness centers in the 3rd party and its platform and Evan certainly wants to stand for righteousness." Righteousness may or may not have been on the line, but the rest of the Thomases were pleased with Wilson's win. They treated it a little like their own. Not only had Norman voted for Wilson, but Ralph had also helped form a student group supporting Wilson at the Massachusetts Institute of Technology, where he was now studying engineering, and he had taken the part of Wilson in a public debate. Even the Republican Welling declared himself "glad" at the result. "Some of the stand-patters are predicting dire consequences to the business of the country, but I think that is foolish," he added. "The Democrats can't afford to ruin the country."

Perhaps none of the Thomases felt the thrill of Wilson's election quite like Arthur, even though he was not yet of voting age. He was on the spot with Wilson, watching history transpire. On election day, Woodrow Wilson strolled around town and campus after voting at the firehouse. Students buzzed with the power of proximity. That night, when the results came in, the bell in Nassau Hall tolled over and over, as if the Princeton football team had beaten Yale. The home team had won.

Arthur needed the boost. He was struggling badly with his classes and felt himself unable to live up to his older brothers. He had finished his freshman year in the third group—not even the top half—and received bottom marks in two classes. He threw himself into trying out for the *Daily Princetonian* and had so far failed. Princeton could be a difficult place if you couldn't answer the question "Where'd you prep?" with an appropriate response or if you didn't prove yourself with some extraordinary skill. But Arthur could not explain this to his mother. Instead, he wrote vaguely despondent letters home, where they were received with sympathy ("I know just how he feels—I have a test tomorrow," said his youngest sister, Emma, who was starting high school, after one morose letter) and returned with instructions to get enough sleep. "Just remember that righteousness and health come first," his mother wrote.

"What is the particular cause for thinking there is no room for your sort?" Emma asked at one point.

Arthur may have felt like an outsider, but when Wilson won, Princeton was at the center of things, and so was Arthur. The school recessed for the inauguration and the students went en masse to Washington, where they formed the escort for the president-elect. Inauguration day, March 4, dawned warm and overcast. Wearing white gloves and sashes, the undergraduates walked Wilson's carriage to the White House. Their old leader came out onto the front porch to lead the students in a rendition of "Old Nassau," their hands waving in time to the music.

Wilson took the oath of office, drawing the crowd into the empty space in front of the stand before he began. In his inaugural address, he made a classic progressive plea to not forget the forgotten, to not ignore the hidden price of industrial advances—"the human cost, the cost of lives snuffed out, of energies overtaxed and broken, the fearful physical and spiritual cost to the men and women and children upon whom the dead weight and burden of it all has fallen pitilessly the years through. . . . The great Government we loved has too often been made use of for private and selfish purposes, and those who used it had forgotten the people." He ended as he had begun, by calling the crowd forward.

Arthur was among them. In his unhappier moments, he considered himself a "gloom," a misfit. But for a moment, at least, he was part of something great, a procession that streamed toward the White House. He was part of the flow of history, among those Wilson had summoned to his side.

⁜

From the start, Norman had trouble holding the people of his parish together, and it troubled him. He considered his first task to be encouraging cooperation, and he could not fathom why this was not a self-evident virtue. He wanted the residents of East Harlem to consider themselves one people who lived according to the "universal" (Protestant) values he was pushing them to embrace. On this front, he had trouble not only with the differing immigrant communities but also with the minority of American-born Protestants living nearby, who were not always pleased with his aims.

East Harlem was well delineated—Jews on this block, Italians on that. Tenement landlords learned to keep the Italians and Hungarians on separate floors. Norman wanted to scramble all of this, to create a harmonious neighborhood. That community, of course, whether he would have admitted it or not, was very much modeled on the bourgeois Protestant community further downtown. Because he saw that many of the Italian Catholics were "already hostile to the Roman Church," he supposed that the shrines and appeals they made to the saints and the Virgin Mary were merely trivial superstitions. He deplored what he considered their lax morals and their primitive customs. As he saw it, he wasn't even converting Catholics: He was offering religion to the irreligious and unity to the divided.

Or so he thought. "You have no right to disgrace us by carrying the bad element of other streets up here," complained "some residents in 116th St" to Norman. "We hope you will heed this warning else we will be obliged to use some methods Uncle Sam has taught us to use against undesirable cranks." It was hard for Norman to recognize the hierarchies in his new neighborhood and even harder for him to respect them. What he regarded as cooperation others saw as contagion, a threat to the success of their exhausting individual efforts. They had succeeded on their own, without the help—indeed, despite the hostility—of the dominant class, and they had no intention of letting an interloper like Norman pull them down.

The immigrants in East Harlem were no more happy than Norman was about the overcrowded tenements, with a foot of trash piled in the stinking air shafts, the sense of enclosure and claustrophobia, and the violence among gangs of boys. But they already had a way of life, and it was the way of neither Union Theological Seminary's Social Gospel nor a manse in Marion, Ohio. Some regarded the work of the missionaries in East Harlem as condescension, or even bribery, and in a way it was. Ministers funded by the congregation on Fifth Avenue and Park would give children American-style clothes and invite them to Sunday school, where they were taught English and sometimes sent home with food or toys. The hope was that they'd bring their parents to church. When parents did come, they, too, were taught English, supplied with new clothes, and encouraged to adopt virtues that sometimes ran counter to their own.

Norman did order coal for his parishioners, and he tried to win the allegiance of children through Sunday school and Boy Scout meetings before reaching out to their parents. At Christmastime he gave children presents that were donated by members of churches along Park Avenue. He paid parishioners' rent when they lost their jobs and faced eviction, and he negotiated with butchers and grocers demanding payment for bills that could not be met. He would have been baffled by the suggestion that there was anything wrong with any of this. He did not see it as bribery. He thought the problem was that he could not do more of it.

He was especially proud of the Neighborhood House that he established for the area, located in a large, rambling Victorian building by the East River. There was a playground for kids, and sports teams had a gym. Sewing clubs, language classes, social and educational groups met there. Violet's sister, Mary Stewart, came uptown to lead children in skits and plays. The Neighborhood House, though, did see its share of conflict. Sidney (Sid) Lovett, who had worked with Norman at Christ Church as a student-volunteer from Yale and was now a Union seminarian helping at East Harlem Presbyterian, once refereed a basketball game where a brawl began. He broke up the fight and made the boys stand in a circle, singing "Blessed Be the Tie That Binds." As soon as they went outside someone pulled a pipe and broke the bind. Lovett found one of the boys on the sidewalk, bleeding from a gash in his head.

The work was not easy. No doubt Norman did sometimes wish everyone could speak English and handle a fork and knife like a Princeton preceptor. Norman took Italian lessons from the Italian pastor at East Harlem, Reverend Giovanni Tron, and taught English to the new Hungarian pastor, Ladislas Harsanyi—a graduate of the University of Berlin who knew half a dozen European languages but hardly any English. The difficulty Norman had communicating with his colleagues and neighbors underscored the difficulty of what he was trying to do. The gulf between them could seem vast, even to a man who so badly wanted to cross it. So could the gulf between what was necessary and what was possible.

+

"Norman's letter sounded tired—and somewhat cynical in regard to the little interest the Church in N.Y. and at large took in his work," Emma wrote to Arthur that fall, 1913. It was not an unfair observation. Norman was exhausted; he had the kind of job, he later wrote, that never ended. But his frustration was with the attention given to his work, not with the possibilities of the work itself. He gave talks about social work among immigrant populations in New York. He joined the graduate board of Princeton's Philadelphian, heading its social work committee. He helped organize and teach a social work training course in conjunction with Columbia's Teachers College. He joined the local school board, like his mother, and threw himself into work as its secretary. And informally, he took it upon himself to be the prod and gadfly to his friends. In a class letter, he wrote:

> With all my love for Princeton I sometimes think, unjustly of
> course, that my education really began when I left there and
> that not the smallest part of it has been the life here in this dis
> trict. It is a sort of school which sets hard lessons and asks some
> difficult questions. . . . How shall we make [democracy] apply
> to our social, industrial and political problems? Are we prepar
> ing well . . . when so many of our workers cannot even under
> favorable conditions make the proper living wage? I wish more
> Princeton men were students in this school—but that is preach
> ing, which is against the rules in a class letter.

It was the right moment to hope to be forgiven for breaking that rule. Woodrow Wilson had begun his presidency with a flurry of reforms. Those who had backed Roosevelt as the candidate of government action were thrilled to imagine that Wilson was actually a New Nationalism man. In fact, Wilson had always had more admiration for Roosevelt's ambitions (if not for the man personally) than the partisans had given him credit for. Now Roosevelt's champions were swinging quickly to Wilson's side, and Wilson was repaying their support with progressive banking and labor legislation.

Hints of trouble at home and around the world belied the nation's confidence. Norman was disturbed to read about a mining strike the following spring in Ludlow, Colorado, that led to skirmishes between the mostly immigrant strikers and the Colorado National Guard. Twenty people, including eleven children, died, and the subsequent fighting was so fierce that Wilson called in federal troops. Norman's own neighborhood hardly seemed much improved since his arrival, despite the growing parish rolls. He could blame himself only so much. The problems went deeper. The popular language of "wage slavery," the exploitation of workers by capitalists, was starting to make sense.

By this time, Norman found himself more often on the workers' side. But he was not one of them. Never was that more apparent than in the summer months: The Thomases could escape the muggy heat and stench of the urban streets, and they did. Violet's sister, Mary, had just built a brick Georgian summer home in Ridgefield, Connecticut, called Stornoway. Violet and Norman bought a place nearby, and Violet took her children there for the entire summer. East Harlem was her home, but it was not her world. In mid-July, while Norman's children chased fireflies in the garden in Connecticut, the huge *festa* on East 115th Street at Our Lady of Mount Carmel washed East Harlem in colored lights. All night the sounds of celebrations and carousing, the smells of fried dough, sausage, and garlic, kept the neighborhood awake.

Norman headed out to Ridgefield whenever he could. In photographs from that summer, 1914, he is always the picture of happiness—his tie askew, his smile shining, his children always by his side.

They were in Ridgefield when war broke out in Europe.

Eight

LONG WARS WILL OCCUR

*Only months after the war began, large swaths of Europe were wrecked.
Here, Polish infantry move through Prussia in the fall of 1914.*

When a Serbian nationalist shot an unpopular aristocrat on the edge of Europe in late June 1914, few people paid much attention. Hardly anyone imagined that the death of Franz Ferdinand and his wife, Sophie, would be the spark that burned so much to ash. Tensions among European nations had been rising for years, but the peace had held for so long that most people had forgotten how fragile it was. Since 1881, when the czar of Russia had been assassinated, heads of state or royalty had been assassinated in France, Italy, Greece, and several other nations (including the United States) without engendering a worldwide war. It was not clear why this time would be different.

Kaiser Wilhelm II learned the news when a telegram was tossed aboard his yacht enclosed in a cigarette case. It was an inconvenient moment; the kaiser was hosting a squadron of British warships at his annual regatta in Kiel. The event was tricky enough to navigate without trouble in the Balkans; a naval arms race was fueling enmity between Great Britain and Germany. When the kaiser put his British naval uniform on to visit the battleship *King George V*—he was technically an admiral in the British Royal Navy—everyone noted how well everyone was getting along. Now Wilhelm had to head back to Berlin. Still, at dinner aboard the prince of Monaco's yacht that evening, dignitaries and diplomats all agreed that there was, in the words of the American ambassador, "no chance" of war. As the British fleet left Kiel two days later, the commanding admiral sent a message to the German fleet, "Friends in past, and friends for ever." A week and a half later, the American ambassador to Germany reported to Wilson's trusted foreign policy adviser Colonel Edward House that Berlin was "as quiet as a grave."

Apart from Austria and Serbia, only Russia, where the memory of a humiliating war with Japan a decade earlier exacerbated the debate over how to support Serbia, was seriously (if haphazardly) planning for war in the days immediately after the assassination. In Paris, the chatter was of a sensational murder trial; in London, the unusual heat and trouble with Ireland dominated the conversation. Though Wilson's adviser House, on a mission in London to loosen tensions among European powers, had earlier registered with alarm the militant atmosphere in Berlin, he barely noted in his diary the stress mounting throughout July.

In the United States, the newspapers reported news of the assassination and then returned to baseball. Whatever talk there was of war concerned trouble with Mexico on the southwest border. European affairs were not of much concern to most Americans, and with the success of the arbitration movements, the Hague Conferences, and the economic integration of nations, large-scale war seemed like a distant possibility anyway. Only five years earlier, the British journalist Norman Angell had published a book, *The Great Illusion*, arguing that the European economies had become so interconnected that one nation would gain no commercial advantage from seizing another's land or subjugating another. The book sold well over two million copies in twenty-five languages around the world. War on a catastrophic scale seemed next to impossible.

It was unthinkable to Norman. Later in life he would look back on those days in 1914 and marvel at his naïveté. Only later would he conclude that the conflict had the quality of an inevitability. Colonial conquest and subjugation and clashing empires had both reinforced and destabilized the alliance system, tangling commitments. No one really knew who was on which side or which agreements would be honored and which broken. Even within single states, various military and political factions usually held information and intentions from one another. War was not inevitable, but the safeguards that states had established to keep conflicts from careening out of control were weak. The careful balancing of powers, the tenuous arrangements of local minorities under distant rulers, and the stability of stratified—and repressive—societies had begun to break down.

The culture of militarism was strongest in Germany, itself a recent creation, the result of a conflict. The 1870 Franco-Prussian War unified the Prussian and German states, won Alsace-Lorraine from France, and marked the end of the Second French Empire. The infant state was immediately powerful. The legacy of Germany's creation was more than geographically formative, however; it was seen as culturally instructive. The Franco-Prussian War had linked the country's power to the strength of its armies. To fulfill its destiny as a great empire, bigger and better—and ever more victorious—forces were required. This conviction was not held by all Germans; there were antimilitarist forces within Germany. Still, it was dominant, and it had a logic that went beyond bluster. The kaiser saw himself as encircled by hostile powers, especially after the formation of unprecedented alliances between Great Britain, France, and Russia. Imperial rivalries and the competition for colonies in the second half of the nineteenth century had gradually made the nineteenth-century alliance system unavoidable, even for Great Britain, which was traditionally wary of continental power politics. Struggling to quell unrest on the margins of its massive and far-flung empire and fearful of Germany's military expansion, Britain countered with its own naval buildup. France kept the memory of its defeat during the Franco-Prussian War fresh; at the Place de la Concorde in Paris, the statue representing Strasbourg, the capital of Alsace, was draped in black for mourning. In Russia, Czar Nicholas II was dealing with domestic discontent and the country was slipping from his grasp. Still, no one wanted to discount Russia. Its peacetime army alone numbered 1.5 million, with another five million ready to be called up. Some Europeans took it for granted that within a few years Russia would become unbeatable. (The United States, by contrast, had a standing army of fewer than a hundred thousand.)

Germany's ally Austria-Hungary also had something to prove. Nationalist movements had frayed the net cast over so many minorities, and the empire had become fragile. Ferdinand's assassination required a response, but Austria-Hungary knew it would need the backing of its more powerful neighbor to make a meaningful riposte. Action against Serbia would likely draw Russia into war. The kaiser assured Austria-Hungary of Germany's support, but not all Germans, including some senior officials (and including at times the kaiser himself), were prepared to risk a war on two fronts just to assist Austria. Russia was unsure of what to do—and unsure of what Germany planned to do—and waffled accordingly.

As armies do, the German military had a contingency plan in the event of a European war. For years, Count Alfred von Schlieffen, chief of the German General Staff from 1891 to 1906, had tinkered with a scheme to split the army to attack France from above and below and then snap the claw shut. The geography of the continent meant that one "pincer" would have to march through Belgium, which was neutral, protected by clearly articulated international law and the explicit guarantee of Great Britain. Schlieffen's plan, which took inspiration from Hannibal, disregarded Belgium's neutrality, reasoning that the Belgians would not resist—and in any event the Germans would win before anyone could make an issue of the breach of Belgium's borders. Schlieffen gave Germany six weeks to defeat France.

Fighting France would likely mean fighting Russia, too. But the Russians, who had to cover vast spaces even to reach their border with Germany, would be at a disadvantage from the start. Schlieffen was confident that one-eighth of the German army could hold off the Russians until France was defeated. It would work, though, only if Russia was not permitted to get a head start in mobilizing. It would work only if the timing was exactly right.

That July 1914, crowds gathered outside the kaiser's palace. Inside its walls, the excitable kaiser grew sick with worry. He had wanted to draw the sword, but the prospect of actual battle frayed his nerves. Serbia, to everyone's shock, more or less capitulated to Austria's demands and asked only that the question of punishing those connected with the archduke's assassination be put to the International Tribunal at The Hague. (The safeguards established at The Hague might actually work!) Wilhelm reversed course once more, writing in the margin of the Serbian response that "every reason for war is removed." His advisers told him he was too late. Hardly an hour later, Austria declared war on Serbia. Russia, coming to the aid of its Slavic ally, mobilized partially, still hoping to avoid war with Germany. After a telegram from "Willy," the czar tried to countermand his order, but—like a refrain—an aide said it was too late. The army was too big and too slow to start up, shut down, and start up once more. The czar ordered Russia's full mobilization.

The German chief of staff, Helmuth von Moltke, frantically tried to push on, while the German chancellor, Theobald von Bethmann-Hollweg, tried to pull back. After the czar mobilized the Russian army, General Moltke telegraphed the Austrian chief of staff and told him to mobilize immediately. At the same moment, Bethmann-Hollweg telegraphed Austria's foreign minister, Leopold Berchtold, and urged the Austrians not to mobilize against Russia. "Who rules in Berlin," asked Berchtold, "Moltke or Bethmann?" Moltke won out. A nervous man, he had long feared that the moment to set Schlieffen's plan into motion would someday come, but even more, he feared that the moment would arrive and that he would miss it. If France and Russia were allowed to mobilize against Germany first, all was lost. For the plan to work, Germany had to be able to dictate the unfolding of movements. In July of 1914, Moltke saw a chance to seize control. Germany could not let Russia get the advantage.

During the last days of July, men at or near the top of every major European government voiced the confidence and hope, either privately or publicly, that a cataclysm might be averted. But in the end all capitulated. It was too late, the holdouts were told; it was too dangerous to wait; the war was not their choice. They had no choice.

✛

On July 28, 1914, with war only days away, the *New York Times* editorialized: "A general European war is unthinkable. . . . Europe can't afford such a war, and the world can't afford it, and happily the conviction is growing that such an appalling conflict is altogether beyond the realm of possibility." The Thomases had reason to hope the editorial was right. Welling's sister, Aunt Anna, and her husband, Uncle Frank, lived in Paris; one of their sons was in Vienna. Another of the Thomas brothers' cousins, Arthur Adams, was in Belgium.

The Thomases' sympathy was with France and England, and they were concerned for their family members abroad. But if they were particularly anxious in the days leading to war, then the evidence of that has been lost. More likely, they were paying little attention that July. Norman was probably not even aware of what he would later call "one of the supreme opportunities of history," the French Socialist and journalist Jean Jaurès's campaign to encourage support for a general strike in opposition to war. Socialism was a real force in Europe, with sizable memberships in several countries, including Germany, France, and England. Norman's retrospective admiration for Jaurès's effort was wistful; few took seriously the practicability of a general strike. But tragedy colors retrospection, and Jaurès's story is tragic. On the night of July 31, the date of Germany's ultimatum, Jaurès was dining at a café in the Rue Montmartre when a French nationalist held a pistol to the window and shot him dead. The workers did not revolt. Nationalism turned out to be stronger than socialism.

When mobilization was announced in Berlin, the air reverberated with song. In Paris, men and women poured into the boulevards shouting, "To Berlin! To Berlin! Alsace! To Berlin!" Londoners spent their bank holiday gathered outside Parliament, while inside the divided cabinet argued over whether to keep its traditional distance from the continent or honor the promises it made. German troops were moving toward the Belgian border.

A few Cassandras foresaw a nightmare. "I wonder if this is the end," the American ambassador to France said. "The end of civilization as we have known it." On Monday evening, August 3, the British foreign secretary, Edward Grey, stared out the long windows of his office at the throngs of Londoners who had gathered. Only a few days before, popular opinion had been weighted against entering the war. Now, it was almost unanimously for it. Earlier that day, Britain had delivered a final warning to Germany to respect Belgium's neutrality. As the dusk settled, Grey watched the lighting of the streetlamps and said aloud, "The lamps are going out all over Europe. We shall not see them lit again in our lifetime." Grey's foreboding is now famous, but at the time, the voice of doubt was quiet and private. Jubilation swept through the crowd outside.

German newspapers called the war "holy." In Austria, one diplomat—perhaps anxious to play up popular enthusiasm for war—described how the crowds went wild with joy. "Blow, bugles, blow!" the poet Rupert Brooke wrote a few months later,

> They brought us, for our dearth,
> Holiness, lacked so long, and Love, and Pain.
> Honour has come back, as a king, to earth,
> And paid his subjects with a royal wage;
> And Nobleness walks in our ways again;
> And we have come into our heritage.

Not everyone was so sentimental, and popular support for the war was not as universal as newspaper and diplomatic accounts sometimes made it out to be, especially outside of major cities. Yet few could deny that a force was sweeping through Europe. The war gave men a sense of purpose, a common spirit, a cause. To die for one's country became a reason to be alive. Brooke wasn't the only poet enraptured. Wrote Guillaume Apollinaire: "We arrived in Paris/At the moment when they were posting the mobilization order/we understood my comrade and me/That the little car had taken us to a new age/And that though we were both mature men/We had just been born."

Both sides longed for rebirth. Neither side imaged how much death they would see instead. Husbands told their wives they would be home by harvest, Christmas at the latest. Swaggering young soldiers flashed smiles at swooning girls. As the big guns rumbled east through Paris, women jumped onto their limbers to kiss the men aboard. The Scots donned their tartan, the French bright red pants. (Proposals to change the French uniforms to make them less visible to enemy gunners using smokeless gunpowder had been declined. *"Le pantalon rouge c'est la France!"* cried one former minister.)

Most of the European armies were dressed and equipped for a nineteenth-century war, the Belgians perhaps most of all. They pulled their machine guns in dog-drawn wagons. No one expected them to put up much resistance, least of all the German soldiers, who had been told that the way would clear before them. The kaiser believed reassurances that the Belgians would not be so stupid as to fight back. As his troops massed at the German border and prepared for the invasion, Wilhelm wrote to the Belgian king, Albert, to say that he had "the friendliest intentions." Albert responded by blowing up the bridges on his border.

The Belgians' aggressive fighting surprised and unnerved the Germans. For a moment, it seemed as though the invaders might slow, that Goliath might stumble, but then the Germans smashed the Belgians—civilians along with soldiers—with a cruelty previously reserved for colonized non-Europeans. Paranoid about snipers and mindful of their strict timetable, the Germans punished any hint—imagined or not—of civilian resistance. They called town mayors "ringleaders" and women and children "coconspirators," and they shot them en masse, bayoneting those who didn't die instantly. In small towns and villages, the piles of corpses formed ridges, and the Germans marched on. They moved into Brussels, 320,000 soldiers in lockstep, with cavalry carrying lances hung with pennants like medieval knights. The parade took three days and three nights.

Then the Germans curved into France, toward Uncle Frank and Aunt Anna Welles. Suddenly the war was not so far away.

⁜

Three weeks passed before letters from Anna and Frank arrived in Lewisburg. Frank had been arrested as a German spy, the Welleses reported, on his way from Paris to their country home in Bourré. Their son, Robert, had also been arrested repeatedly on his way from Austria to join his family. (Spy mania was pervasive. At one point the mayor of Brussels was chased through the street after someone yelled, "Espion! Espion!") Arthur Adams, to the Thomases' relief, had made it out of Belgium in time. "The European war is a most distressing thing," Welling wrote to Norman on August 25. "It is a comfort to know that God is over all, and that he can make the wrath of men to praise him."

The day that Welling wrote those words, the German army, startled by rumors of Belgian civilians shooting from the rooftops, set fire to the medieval university town of Louvain. Its library, among the world's most precious, was reduced to ashes. Over the course of several days, German soldiers destroyed more than a thousand buildings and killed civilians indiscriminately. Louvain became synonymous with German brutality. "GERMANS SACK LOUVAIN; WOMEN AND CHILDREN SHOT," read the front page of the *New York Tribune*. American newspapers were filled with accounts and descriptions of the smoldering ruins and swollen corpses. Reports of Louvain and the terror that German soldiers had left in their wake shocked Americans. They drove many who had felt impartial about Europe's war into sympathy with the Allies. In Britain—a country that had rounded up civilians into disease-ridden concentration camps in the Boer War—the Germans' rampage through Belgium helped turn the war from a Continental power struggle into a war for freedom. Never mind that one of Britain's allies, Russia, was ruled by a despot. Posters went up around Britain depicting the fight for democracy and righteousness against tyranny and evil, personified by the marauding Hun raping pretty Belgian maidens. So sensational were the reports coming out of Belgium in those early weeks that it was easy for the British to convince themselves that they were the guardians of liberty and virtue.

The British needed a sense of gallantry to galvanize them. Unlike Belgium and France, Great Britain had not been invaded; it could not rally to cries of self-defense. Meanwhile, the Germans were overrunning the Allies. They progressed so fast that their horses fell to their bloody knees and soldiers collapsed from exhaustion. By the first week of September, the German soldiers were nearing Paris. The kaiser knew that the Schlieffen plan required turning against Russia by the fortieth day. Remarkably, thirty-five days into the campaign, he was on track. In Paris, the French were laying charges on the graceful bridges over the Seine and preparing to blow up the Eiffel Tower so that the Germans could not use it for radio. Just as the end seemed close, though, Germany's overextended and splintering lines swung away and France and Britain counterattacked. The Germans retreated to the Aisne River and dug in—literally. And across a small buffer of space, a no-man's-land, the British and French entrenched themselves, too. By late November, parallel tracks of makeshift fortifications sliced through Europe, like row upon row of badly stitched sutures, from the North Sea to Switzerland.

·+·

The accounts from the battlefields, the reports of casualties, and the descriptions of destruction were shocking. At the first battle of the Marne in September 1914, France alone suffered 250,000 casualties. Millions of men on both sides had been mobilized to kill one another and given the means with deadly technologies. News of other theaters of war opening around the world—on the Mediterranean, in Africa and Asia—reached New York. Japan declared itself on the side of the Allies and seized a few German colonies. Britain's colonies began assembling regiments of troops. Europe's war was becoming a world war. The eyewitness accounts of brutalities and violence were painful to contemplate and impossible to ignore.

But from a great distance, it was possible to regard them with detachment. "War unlooses men's worst passions," Norman wrote, a little smugly, to his mother after she called his attention to a horrific report from the front. It was easy for the minister to draw the lesson and make a little sermon, to despair that civilization's arduously constructed dam against hate had broken so easily. Dispassionately—and with echoes of President Wilson, who was calling for neutrality in thought as well as deed and suggesting that the Allies were not without blame—he wrote that the endless cycles of blame and revenge indicated a deeper sickness, the "unbrotherly attitude" between nations. He turned his early critique of the war into a warning against arrogance and hubris. French *civilisation*, German *Kultur*, British rule of law . . . "As long as each thinks the world's progress rests exclusively with it," he wrote to his mother, "long wars will occur."

In the fall of 1914, Norman was not a pacifist. He would not say that no war was justified; he might not even say that *this* war was not justified. His friend Lovett told his mother that but for his young wife, he would have enlisted with the British. Lovett (who later became Norman's assistant) was around the Thomas home so often that he called Violet "Mom," and was usually a good barometer of Norman's own opinions. Writing to his mother, Norman went out of his way to be judicious. Germany "typifies . . . that deification of might which is the anti-Christ," Norman wrote to his mother, "but historically no nation in the old world or the new can throw many stones, for we've all sinned."

It was a reasonable response for a minister to make, and it was easy for Norman to be reasonable. He had nothing at stake. The ease with which he was able to turn his thoughts away from war is apparent in the turn of the lines of his letter. "We are well and happy—I doubt if anyone could be happier," he wrote.

Norman's family had just returned from Ridgefield, and his wife was pregnant with their fourth child. Perhaps it was easy for him to talk about love as the sublime solution to the world's problems, because love was such a persistent and stabilizing force in his own life. The woman he called "Beloved" made "this old earth paradise enough for me," he wrote to her in one letter. "It seems as if the passing days just increased my love for you," he wrote in another. The war was so far away.

Nine

WHICH WAY SHALL IT BE?

The Crusader Fellowship in 1915. Evan, tie askew,
stands in the back, third from the left.

E van was restless. Like his oldest brother, he felt obligated to serve and
searched for how best to do it; unlike Norman, he was furious. In the
fall of 1914, to his parents' dismay—and at Norman's urging—he had
entered Union Theological Seminary. Union was an obvious choice for Evan,
even more so than for Norman. He had already been introduced to the Social
Gospel through the Crusaders—several of whom had gone on to Union—
and he looked up to Norman enormously. But moving between studying at
Union and helping his brother with his parish in East Harlem did not have
the same effect on Evan that it had on Norman. It radicalized him.

Evan could not abide insincerity. A hatred of hypocrisy may be a hallmark of youth, but for Evan it became an obsession. He recoiled from the self-congratulatory atmosphere at Union, and the lessons in how to skirt heresy seemed to him exercises in dissembling. To Evan, the techniques of "reconciliation" that made church doctrine palatable in the modern world were a dodge. The ideal of the Social Gospel attracted him, but in practice it seemed more and more like a sham. Students at Union "take a couple of courses in Sociology and think that they have done their duty," he complained. In his view, wealthy churchgoers were even worse: They justified effectively ghettoizing workers and immigrants by writing checks to support churches for them. The church preached the Sermon on the Mount, but it was not about to relinquish its comfortable perch. Evan loathed what he saw as the church's hypocrisy.

If Norman's liberal tendencies made Welling worry, then Evan's views must have made Welling despair. At Christmas, Evan wondered aloud whether he should commit himself to overthrowing the social order. He would often write an incendiary letter to his parents and then apologize— sort of ("I have half regretted my letter of Sunday night ever since I wrote it")—before launching into another attack on the church, Union, and the complacency of everyone he met, including himself. It was "plain as day" to him "that the church was run by and for a privileged class," he wrote to his father, who, of course, ran a church. He confounded his professors at Union, as well. A theology professor took a liking to Evan, who was a top student, and spent hours with him discussing various theological questions, only to hear Evan say that he thought the subject "a damnable mistake or words to that effect." Yet Evan got away with being difficult. People liked him—his dry, self-deprecating sense of humor, and his obvious, even painful, desire to do the right thing. This side of him emerges in his letters to his young sisters, Emma and Agnes, letters that are funny, irreverent, and unfailingly tender. Those who met him, who heard him laugh and saw his ease with others, even in an argument, simply could not take his stridency seriously. His teachers and acquaintances tended either to dismiss it or give him credit for caring so much. He did care; that was clear. It was also clear that he was unhappy. He felt like a failure, trapped in a world he couldn't fix, with a personality that was too selfish, too lazy. "I wish that I was a greater help than I am," he wrote to Violet after she had written to thank him for his work in East Harlem. "Please don't make your opinion of me too high."

Unlike Norman, Evan could not reconcile the poverty he saw in East Harlem with the prosperity of the churches downtown. The church that emphasized charity over total commitment was not the religion he had glimpsed that commencement Sunday when Sayre had read the Consecration to the Crusaders. "Yes, [the church] preaches LOVE with all its might," he wrote. "But the sort of love that I want is not the sort that says, 'Here you poor, poor man, take this secondhand pair of shoes or this dollar and get yourself and children a good meal.' I want the sort of love that says, 'Here, I want to see you make the biggest and best man of yourself that is possible, I want to see you grow nearer to God every day you live, and to do this I know you must have room to develop.'"

Union wasn't teaching Evan what he wanted to learn. He wanted to learn how to follow in the footsteps of a revolutionary Christ, not to learn how to interpret the Bible in a way that would not offend people. The professors at Union only tried to smooth the rough edges of society, Evan complained. He was desperate to make his parents understand him. He was "not such an awful heathen," he begged them to see. He just wanted to recover what was best and true about religion as he understood it. It would take a heroic figure, a Luther, to inspire people to change their lives. Evan's words strained with the desire to be that man.

-+-

It was a different kind of leader, though, who had people buzzing. He was an evangelical preacher named Billy Sunday, and in the spring of 1915, he brought his barnstorming routine to Princeton, New Jersey. Arthur Thomas, then a senior at the college, could not help but be curious. William Ashley Sunday was a force to behold. He looked like a fop with his patent-leather shoes and diamond stickpin, but he acted like a gladiator fighting the devil every time he stepped onto a stage. Billy Sunday had been a National League outfielder in the 1880s. When he left baseball, he found God. He became a star, a performer, and, to many, a hero. Swinging his arms, punching the sky, arching his back, he delivered electrifying sermons denouncing drink, gambling, vice, and blasphemous "modern" ideas. "Take your evolution theory, take your gland grab bank, take your protoplasm chop suey," he roared, boxing his invisible opponents, gyrating and leaping, dancing and shouting across makeshift wooden stages in front of rapt thousands. All that so-called science, all that intellectual posturing, was a "rotting, vile, shriveled, stenchful corpse of unbelief!"

How the crowds loved him! Billy Sunday told them what to think and what to do, and they worshipped him for it. He *knew* he was right, as certain as the sun, and he promised people that if they shook his hand and signed a pledge card, kicked the booze and stopped their sinning, the truth would be theirs, too. At the end of his sermons, the aisles would jam and heave with people scrambling over each other to reach him. They seized his outstretched palm and his message as if they had been waiting for it—and in a way they had. Self-reliance, piety, and courage were familiar virtues. Sunday reminded them that *they* were responsible for their sins—not their parents, not their brothers; not the coddling government or arrogant know-it-alls. A man had to make it to heaven himself, and if he did not, he would go to hell. But Sunday took that old message and gave it a fresh style. He made hatred feel good, which made people feel powerful.

When Sunday arrived at Princeton that spring, he had already come a long way from the midwestern towns where he had gotten his start. Earlier that year, he had met with President Wilson and Secretary of State Bryan before preaching to a crowd of senators, congressmen, Supreme Court justices, and cabinet members packed into Convention Hall. He told them how disappointed Christ would be if he came to Washington. The same week he visited Princeton, he spoke at Carnegie Hall in front of a crowd so delirious that horrified observers wondered if it might riot. Andrew Carnegie himself had wanted to attend but couldn't (or wouldn't) push his way through the mob to reach the entrance to the building.

The professors at Princeton were not so happy to see Sunday there. He was uncouth, colorful, more of a boxer than their kind of minister. His outspoken anti-intellectual stance probably did not bother too many students, but it set some of the faculty members against him. The faculty vetoed a movement to invite Sunday to speak on campus, and so he was in town speaking off campus at the request of the Princeton Theological Seminary. Professor Andrew West defended the faculty's decision in the

Daily Princetonian, citing objectionable passages in some of Sunday's prior sermons but explaining that his real quarrel was with Sunday's manner. "In the name of decency and of the purity and sanctity of our Christian faith," West wrote, "Princeton University positively refuses to approve of Mr. Sunday's performances as suitable for the edification of our students."

Those words only roused the students' desire to see the preacher in action. They turned out en masse on that March Monday afternoon. When the pews filled, they spilled into the aisles. Arthur wasn't sure what to think of Sunday, but he was certain he wanted to see the show.

Still, when it came time for the event to start, the students grew suddenly wary. Sunday's advance man, Homer Rodeheaver, instructed the students to cheer. There was a moment of hesitation before a shout rose up. Rodeheaver told the students to sing their college song. More hesitation; it was anxious this time. They weren't about to give Billy Sunday their "most sacred hymn," Arthur reported to his father later that day. Whispers of "Not 'Old Nassau'!" rippled through the crowd. Finally the glee club led a rendition of "Princeton, Forward March," assuming Sunday wouldn't know the difference. Sunday appeared and did his usual jabs and jogs around the pulpit. It wasn't quite the rousing performance the students wanted, but Sunday wasn't stupid; he knew the audience was holding back, too. When Sunday asked for a show of those who intended to repent and reform, less than a tenth of the students raised their hands. Yet when he asked for the converts to come forward, some six hundred approached. Even those who were embarrassed by Billy Sunday wanted to be able to say that they'd shaken his hand.

After the service, Arthur hurried back to campus to write a report for the *Tribune*. His editor rejected his "straight and true" story, he told his father, for "a rankly unjust sensation" instead. The papers all reported what the people wanted to read. "If they didn't have all the students weeping and flocking down the trail, they went to the other extreme, which was almost more untrue, of having the whole student body take Billy as a joke," Arthur complained. He admitted that he was confused by the whole performance. Sunday "didn't move me in the least," but it had to be possible, he added hopefully, to extract the good part of Sunday's message and forget the rest.

This wasn't Norman's view. He found Billy Sunday dangerous, a man who encouraged the worst impulses of human nature by suggesting they were virtues. But Arthur wasn't the only one who combined skepticism with some admiration. Arthur may not have wanted to admit it, but it was invigorating to watch the former athlete swing his fists and promise that one *could* fight evil, that it wasn't merely an intractable abstraction. Thirsty crowds drank this up. Sunday had something of Teddy Roosevelt in him—the barrel chest, the apocalyptic vision—but in the place of the Pure Food and Drug Act, Sunday delivered screeds against *boooooooze*. In place of the Sherman Anti-Trust Act, Sunday promised salvation. He even had something of Eugene Debs in him, if the Socialist had worn a diamond stickpin. Sunday's message, like Debs's, appealed strongly to those who felt unjustly punished by societal changes, but who distrusted the power and place of the government to return to them the respect they felt was their due.

Yet his message also appealed to the congressmen and college students who flocked to hear him speak. Some part of them was attracted to his message: Defend the righteous. Pummel evil. Fight.

·+·

When Norman picked up the newspaper on Saturday, May 8, 1915, a cascade of black block type ran down the front page, row upon row of headlines spelling out disaster. The ocean liner RMS *Lusitania* had been torpedoed by a German U-boat the day before off the coast of Ireland, with heavy loss of life. For Violet, the news was even more shocking. She had loved her time aboard the *Lusitania* on her way to London the year before she had married Norman—the flowers that filled her room, the silence of the elevator as it rose and descended, the jigsaw puzzles on the deck, the concerts at night, the champagne. . . . But that was another life, and now the boat was sunk.

In all, 1,198 people died. To Americans, though, the horrifying figure was 128—the number of Americans who were killed. Ten years later, a journalist found that most people he interviewed remembered exactly where they were when they heard the news. The sinking is now sometimes misremembered as the event that triggered the United States' participation in the war. In fact, only the most extreme hawks, some of whom had been agitating for the United States to enter the war since the invasion of Belgium, considered it a casus belli. A poll of a thousand newspaper editors found that only six of them wanted to enter the war right away. All the same, editorials were calling the Germans "miscreants" and "savages drunk with blood."

Americans had been complacent about the European war until the *Lusitania* went down. They were neutral, they were innocent, they were supposed to be safe. And now it didn't seem to matter; Americans were dead. The sinking of a passenger ship offended the American sense of fair play. Submarine warfare was sneaky, ignoble, and against international law. The Germans would be held to "strict accountability," Wilson declared. He was not ready to go to war—but he knew it was a close thing. U-boats threatened American lives and the American economy, which depended on trade with the Allies and the merchant ships that carried goods, as Germany knew all too well. Wilson knew he had to be firm without being belligerent. He flailed as he tried to find the balance, but fortunately for him, Germany was not ready to draw the United States, with its money and men, into the war.

Germany apologized and the two countries backed down for the meantime. Still, the enmity that had formed between the two nations deepened, and Wilson's warnings took the country one more step toward war. However strenuously Wilson urged Americans to be neutral, the country had already tilted slightly but decidedly toward the Allies. The *Lusitania* gave it a hard push. Americans were indignant, eager to respond if not to fight. They faced a difficult question, one never fully answered: How can a country be at once powerful and pacific? How can a hawk be a dove?

"I wish with all my heart I saw a way to carry out the double wish of our people," Wilson said—the wish to prove the country's strength, the wish to keep the peace.

⁜

In pockets of the Northeast, there was no question as to which side the nation should be on. Wall Street had practically joined the Allies all by itself. J. P. Morgan acted as the Allies' purchasing agent and, four months after the

Lusitania sank, arranged a $500 million loan to the British and French, the largest foreign loan in Wall Street history. The most forceful advocate for an aggressive war policy was former president Theodore Roosevelt. In private he called Wilson a jackass; in public he declared that peace was worth it only when backed by righteousness and strength. The torpedoing of the *Lusitania* was "murder." Roosevelt wanted the government to implement conscription and to raise a standing army of two million men, and the old Rough Rider wanted to be the one to lead them into battle.

Roosevelt was a shrewd and incisive observer of international affairs, but when the Great War began he became a shark in bloody water. Haunted by deep insecurities and driven by high ideals, Roosevelt was consumed with the idea of war. The defining moment of his life had been leading the charge up San Juan Hill in Cuba during the Spanish-American War. War is "terrible and evil," he wrote in January 1915, "but it is also grand and noble." It made men heroes. He did not place all the blame with Germany or all the righteousness with the Allies (yet). It was war itself that he wanted, and he considered himself—not Wilson—to be the true idealist. Soldiers in Europe "poured out their blood like water in support of the ideals in which, with all their hearts and souls, they believe." Roosevelt was so fanatical about war that former President Taft said, "The truth is, he believes in war and wishes to be Napoleon and to die on the battle field. He has the spirit of the old berserkers."

Other men, less eager to storm into the deadly mire of Flanders, argued that there was another way to make the nation stronger. They called it "preparedness." The United States, they said, could deter the Germans, and at the same time summon some of that patriotic fighting spirit without actually having to go to the battlefields. Expanding the military forces would be "preparedness for peace." The United States' standing army of not even a hundred thousand hardly befitted a world power, they argued. In 1915, the support for preparedness shot up, and money soon followed. A formidable group of businessmen, with names like Vanderbilt and Guggenheim and Morgan, banded together to bankroll the National Security League. Senator Henry Cabot Lodge, Taft's old secretary of war Henry Stimson, Princeton president John Grier Hibben, and scores of other influential men waved the preparedness flag. An officer training camp in Plattsburgh,

New York, under the auspices of Roosevelt's friend Leonard Wood, the commander of the Rough Riders, attracted scores of college students and graduates, who practiced their horseback riding skills and experienced the salutary benefits of shooting things. "In the Plattsburg camp a man ceased to be thought of or to think of others as of Harvard or Yale or Princeton," a Harvard graduate wrote in 1915, amazed.

Thus far, Wilson had resisted the preparedness calls. He heard too much jingoism in the preparedness chorus, and he was convinced that keeping the country neutral would preserve his chance to broker a peace agreement for the ages. Wilson also knew that outside the Northeast, feelings about the war were more conflicted. Great swaths of the Midwest were inclined to stay out of the war, especially those areas with high concentrations of German Americans or Irish Americans loath to fight alongside the British. Newspapers carried stories about the carnage in Europe. Most Americans at that point saw little reason to send men so far away to die when the United States had little to gain. But Wilson did not consider himself an isolationist (a term that was hardly used then); he was an internationalist. He had a grand vision for a new leadership role for America. He wanted to be a peacemaker.

✢

Norman had trouble enough without worrying about war in Europe. He needed help in East Harlem. That spring he hired John (Jack) Darr to be his assistant. Norman may have seen something of himself in Darr—a Union Theological Seminary graduate from Ohio who had, like Norman, suffered an ordeal during his ordination, barely passing the Presbytery's examination after he offered figurative, not literal, interpretations of the Bible. Even with Darr by his side, Norman had his hands full. Only a few weeks after the Germans had sunk the *Lusitania*, Italy had entered the war on the side of the Allies. Even though it had been a member of the Triple Alliance with Germany and Austria-Hungary, Italy had not declared war, and the Allies promised the Italian government territory from the Austro-Hungarian Empire if it would join their side. This pitted the Hungarians and Italians living in East Harlem against each other, and they carried the conflict onto their streets. Hungarian and Italian children threw rocks through their "enemies'" windows and at one another. Tempers ran high, and Norman blamed the war.

Norman himself was caught between the Hungarian minister and the Italian pastor, who had begun to distrust each other. The whole parish felt the threat of violence. One night the Italian church's sexton was shot in the leg as he locked up the church. There was no evidence to point to a perpetrator—and it was not the first time a stray bullet had flown through the neighborhood—but the sexton began carrying an automatic pistol for protection. At a meeting at Norman's house, it slipped from his pocket and skittered on the floor. Everyone in attendance held his breath.

The Hungarian minister, Harsanyi, finally suggested that they might try organizing a "transnational" children's orchestra. The idea that a handful of kids playing the flute and trumpet could help was almost absurd—but Norman and Violet could not do much besides solicit the New York Presbytery and Mrs. Carnegie for funds to buy instruments. And, for a while at least, the tension was diffused.

·÷·

On Sunday, June 13, 1915, Princeton's graduating class filled Alexander Hall for baccalaureate. It was a day that, in his lowest moments, Arthur must have thought would never come. Princeton's president, John Grier Hibben, was the speaker. His sermon was titled "Martial Valor in Times of Peace." With the sinking of the *Lusitania* only weeks before, war was on everyone's mind. Hibben encouraged it. A slight man, he had a reputation as a calm conciliator, but on the subject of the Great War he was a passionate leader of the preparedness movement. He was not so much worried about the Allies as he was envious of them. Men at war had the opportunity to exercise those "muscular Christian" virtues of sacrifice, service, courage. A willingness to go to war ensured a nation's honor and integrity, he had argued the month before, for a peace "bought" with compromise is "a living hell."

Hibben had once been Woodrow Wilson's dear friend, but now Wilson couldn't stand him. After Hibben had opposed Wilson's plan to reorganize the social life and graduate school at Princeton, Wilson had broken with him forever. The year before, at the 1914 commencement, the president of the United States had used his remarks at his class dinner to say, "There are some pretty grim things I have learned in life. For one thing, I hope never again to be fool enough to make believe that a man is my friend who I know to be my enemy. . . . If he has proved himself unfaithful, he is unfaithful; and in performing public duties you should not associate yourself with him." Everyone knew he was talking about Hibben. It is even possible that Wilson's reluctance to expand the military was related, if only in small part, to Hibben's (and his other rivals') enthusiastic support for preparedness. Wilson was thin-skinned and bore grudges; his instinct was to use his power to punish those who crossed him. In calling for the country to arm for war, Hibben was crossing him again.

Hibben's baccalaureate speech did not question Wilson's foreign policy directly, but it was unquestionably provocative. Instead of talking about the dangers of war, Hibben told the graduating class, Americans should talk about the dangers of peace. During times of peace, there was little chance for heroism. In war, on the other hand, "the choice men of the nation [are] called to take their stand at the place of greatest danger, united by the common bond . . . fired by the spirit of courage and manly endeavor." The blameless knight, Sir Galahad, was his example for the Princeton man—a man of action, self-sacrifice, and romantic nobility. The young men who had gone to war, Hibben warned, held an advantage over American men. "It would be a pity, a very tragedy indeed," he told the assembled students that Sunday morning, "if the youth of Europe should attain this new view of life . . . and here in this land of peace far from the horror and disaster of war, our young men should fail of such a vision, and such a new birth of moral and spiritual power." Obsessed with the cultivation of valor, Hibben seemed not to notice or care that the youth of Europe was being wiped out.

This kind of sermon would have outraged Norman, but it is harder to imagine what Arthur thought as he sat in the audience and listened. Arthur, like all the Thomas brothers, was overcome with the Thomas sense of duty "to commit to something," as Ralph had put it. But he could not figure out what that something was. It's easy now to mock Hibben's use of the legend of Sir Galahad, but at the time it captivated many young men—especially those who groped for a way to forge their identity and prove their worth. Arthur had no idea what to do with his life. When he filled out his applications for his Princeton tuition remission, he listed "undecided" next to career choice—except when he once, tellingly, wrote "unsettled."

·**÷**·

All the Thomas brothers were at Princeton that weekend for Arthur's graduation and their own reunion festivities. While Norman conducted the memorial service in the chapel for those of his class who had died, Evan joined nineteen other Crusaders for the group's annual meeting in Murray-Dodge Hall. For three years the group had used words like "war" and "crusade" in a metaphorical sense: a crusade against poverty, a battle to establish God's kingdom on earth. No longer. The war that now loomed before them was fought with guns, and, a month after the *Lusitania*, it seemed possible that they would be asked to join it. Actual knights and holy wars had been far from Sayre's mind when he called the group the Crusaders. Now he had to contend with their example and decide whether or not to reject it. He knew maintaining that battles should be only metaphorical when a real war threatened might prove more controversial than suggesting that the virgin birth of Christ might not be literal.

Of all the men in Murray-Dodge Hall that day, John Nevin Sayre had the most at stake. He was the oldest, the group's founder, the leader. The seniors there had probably told him about Hibben's baccalaureate speech that morning. It was one thing for a Princeton graduate to condemn poverty and injustice; it was another to contradict Hibben. And it was something else entirely to urge others to resist the president of the United States if he asked the nation's men to go to war. For Sayre it would have been especially hard. Wilson's daughter had married Sayre's brother, Francis. Only the previous month, Sayre had stood with the president in the small chapel of St. John's Episcopal Church in Williamstown, Massachusetts, as the two men were named the godfathers of Francis and Jessie Sayre's son. Woodrow Wilson was more than Sayre's commander in chief; he was part of his family.

"A year ago, when we met together in this room for our Service of Consecration, no one of us could have believed possible the things which have occurred since then," Sayre began. He told them he would talk about war, though he could not tell them what to think. Each had to believe as his "conscience and judgment dictate." But he came quickly to his point. One after another, he refuted readings of the New Testament that showed that Jesus advocated violence. "From the very beginning of his ministry he saw clearly that answering force with force provoked more force," Sayre told the Crusaders. "To have set up the Kingdom of Peace with the sword of war was a fundamental inconsistency." The sword was the way of the world, and it was set against the way of the cross. "Which way shall it be?" Sayre asked.

-+-

Evan did not return to Union that fall. He transferred his seminary studies to New College in Edinburgh, Scotland, because he wanted to see for himself a country at war. He crossed the Atlantic with his Greek New Testament and Tolstoy's *My Religion* and *The Gospel in Brief.* When a customs official in Liverpool asked him if he was carrying seditious literature, he briefly considered saying yes—for Tolstoy and the Bible were, he thought, *truly* seditious.

Evan's train passed sandbagged trenches and through stone walls. Once he eached Edinburgh it was hard to see through the inky dark; the tops of the streetlamps were painted black; headlights were off, window shades drawn. But by daylight the city enchanted him. He liked to walk and look out over the Castle Mound onto the magisterial sights of Princes Street and the hills and the woods beyond, seen through the shroud of fog and soot. He moved into the New College Settlement, one of the early settlement houses. He felt most comfortable where he felt most indignant, in places with pubs on the corners and drunks in the gutters.

In theory, Evan opposed war, but his heart leaped at the sight of soldiers leaving for France. One Saturday night soon after he arrived, he watched a company, elegant in tartan, march down the street, led by bagpipers playing their eerie, wailing skirl. To see them "makes your blood run faster sometimes," he wrote in a letter to his younger sister Agnes. It had been a terrible fall for the Scottish. At Loos, two Scottish divisions had been smashed; the Fifteenth Division had lost more than three thousand men in a single day. The gas had hung like a mist, and when the wind turned

against them, it blew back into their own trenches. They pushed on anyway, into the stretch of hell where they had hardly a chance of surviving.
"The enemy could be seen falling literally in hundreds, but they continued
their march in good order and without interruption," recorded a German.
The Scots in particular were famous for their fortitude.

Even the Scots, with their tradition of sacrifice and fighting men,
could not make a heroic myth of Loos, so painful and astounding were
the losses. By the time the war had ended, more than a quarter of Scots
who enlisted had died. Still, young men continued signing up in droves.
Between August 1914 and December 1915, 320,589 had volunteered,
emboldened by the tradition of "Highland heroism" and the image of the
fighting Scots. Seminary students were no different. Of a class of a hundred or so at the New College, hardly more than twenty were left by the
Christmas break; the rest had enlisted or entered another form of wartime
service. Six students enlisted in one week alone after his arrival, Evan told
his mother. He suspected that the class would dwindle even more after the
Christmas break, when the students returned to their homes and saw their
families and friends—or felt their absence. Unlike France, Germany, and
Russia, Britain did not yet have compulsory service, but the pressure to
go to war was tremendous, as was the guilt of those who stayed behind.
Evan was appalled that the New College's faculty seemed so eager to urge
their students into the trenches. But a few of the remaining students were
fierce pacifists, and they introduced Evan into their circles. They took him
to meetings of the pacifist Fellowship of Reconciliation and the Union
of Democratic Control, and brought him to talks by pacifists and politicians like Bertrand Russell and Charles Trevelyan. Back in his room, Evan
read the Gospel of Matthew over and over and rehearsed Paul's Letters
and Acts. "I am ready to take the out and out non-resistant basis so far
as war is concerned," Evan wrote to Norman in early November. "Nonresistance" was the term many pacifists used to describe an active—not
passive—resistance to war. What "active" nonresistance meant was hard to
define, though, and the pacifists' best attempts were eloquent but airy. The
minister John Haynes Holmes called it *the lifting of resistance to evil from
the physical to the moral plane.*" In the fall and winter of 1915, this meant

that nonresisters attended a lot of meetings. Without compulsory service, there wasn't much else to do.

Day and night, in letter after letter, Evan tried to work out what non-resistance entailed. "Love is the ideal and love alone," he wrote to Norman, repeating the word "love" like a mantra. He wrestled with the allure of martyrdom and looked for role models in figures like Henry David Thoreau. He conducted thought experiments in which whole populations became pacifist and concluded that if the people of France, Great Britain, Russia, and Belgium had refused to fight the invading Germans, the force of their love would have overcome Germany in the long run. This was, Evan assured his brother, "the practical point of view."

It was certainly not the practical point of view. Evan's ideas were often confused and contradictory. He mixed grand and inchoate ideas for a new utopian social order with discussions of the Gospels and pacifism. But one conviction began to stand out: the idea that war is inimical to the freedom of conscience. For a soldier forced to obey orders—including orders to kill—"nothing is his own," Evan wrote to Norman, "least of all his conscience." To his mother, he began to flesh out the idea—defensively, at first, sensitive to charges of egotism. "There is no such thing as an external authority," Evan wrote, underlining his words. This was both a radical idea for the time and an old one, and he knew it. "I will continue to fight for what I believe to be right," he wrote to his mother, "but I will have respect for the other side if they believe they are right, and I will know that no matter how I fight the right will win anyway."

That November, he sent Sayre a postcard that simply said, "Have thought much about your Crusaders' talk of last June. You were right in what you said of war, I am sure."

Ten

COURAGE OF THE HIGHEST TYPE

*On May 13, 1916, well over a hundred thousand people
marched up Fifth Avenue to call for a bigger military.*

Norman encouraged Evan, but he was also a little concerned about his brother, and he wasn't convinced that Evan's explorations were leading him in the right direction. Norman worried that Evan was prone to moral egotism and sentimentality. Evan's statements about love and nonresistance were abstract, vague, and separatist, especially when compared to the quotidian material and social problems that Norman faced at the time. The United States was in a recession, and the war had made it worse. The stock market was closed from July 31 to November 28, 1914. With Europe in a continent-wide war, the export market shriveled, and cotton prices fell by half, sending ripples through the economy that quickly reached East 116th Street. After unemployment spiked, Norman partnered with Union's Settlement House on East 104th Street and secured funding from the mayor's office to set up a workshop where 450 people earned fifty cents a day making baskets and flowers. Norman and Violet had to turn away hundreds more people looking for work.

That experience, along with daily life in East Harlem, showed him how economic and industrial dynamics shaped his neighborhood and the country. He was already convinced that a pastor must help his parish meet basic needs, but he was starting to feel that he was no match for the forces that often governed behavior. What could Norman say? It was little comfort—for him, let alone his parishioners—to say that God works in mysterious ways when he saw employers exploit labor all too clearly. When bankers strengthened their ties to the Allies in 1915 and the economy began to recover, Norman still despaired. First, the war had caused hard times. Now, as the economy recovered, the industrialists and bankers were profiting—far more than the workers—and, in doing so, strengthening their own economic ties to the Allies, giving them a vested interest in the success of one side over the other.

He had a hard time seeing that there wasn't much of an alternative. The U.S. government, which had depended upon tariffs (not taxes) for revenue, faced the prospect of a deficit of sixty to a hundred million dollars unless it could find a way to regenerate trade. When war had first broken out, Secretary of State Bryan had made a point of saying that private loans with the belligerents offended the "spirit of neutrality." But by the following spring, the administration had announced a change in policy, and J. P. Morgan and other American bankers were setting up attractive credit arrangements with the Allies. Much of the discussion surrounding the economy was secretive, which gave rise to rumors, falsehoods, and oversimplifications, though some of the reports were true. Norman was inclined to believe the worst. It reinforced his sense that there was something wrong with a system in which bankers made money from war and workers struggled.

More than the upper class's relationship to the belligerents bothered Norman. He was frustrated with the established avenues of relief and reform, including the efforts of some of his well-meaning associates. When streetcar workers went on strike in New York, he sided with the strikers. "Some of my friends who are very philanthropic and genuinely sorry for the suffering of the poor can always be trusted to be on the side of the capitalists in any specific quarrel," he wrote to one colleague. The self-proclaimed defenders of labor were not much help either. At a wire factory he witnessed management playing different nationalities off one another, exacerbating the misunderstandings produced by language barriers. Norman tried to become involved in unifying workers for their common interest. Following a spontaneous strike, Norman organized a meeting at the Neighborhood House and brought in an American Federation of Labor (AFL) organizer. The organizer appeared so bored that "a good phonograph record would have been better," Norman recalled. The workers were bewildered. After the crowd had left, Norman later wrote, the organizer turned to him and said, "Well, that's done. The I.W.W. and the priests have it right; you have to crack a whip over these Hunkies. My wife says she can tell what kind of wops I've been talking to by the smell of my clothes when I come home."

Reform organizations weren't much better. Programs like the Charity Organization Society (COS) and the Association for Improving the Condition of the Poor (AICP)—"alphabet societies," he called them—"have failed miserably in many of their efforts and are wholly inadequate," Norman declared to the New York Presbytery that fall. "Minister Attacks Organized Charity," read a headline in the *New York Times*. Norman, embarrassed, responded that in fact he believed that charities were absolutely "necessary" but that "experience proves that the Church can help her own far better than the societies; therefore, she ought to arouse herself to the task." His hope was still with the church, however frustrated he was with its inconsistent attention to social reform. This was partly by default and partly due to his persistent belief that the church should do what government organizations couldn't: reach into the hearts of people and connect a message of brotherhood with practical measures. Norman still believed that countering the warping predatory instincts of the powerful and the mean want of the weak required an understanding of the moral and spiritual connections among people. A floating ethical system wouldn't hold, and appeals to self-interest would fail as soon as the wind shifted. Reform that would last, he believed, was rooted in unity and common purpose. It was rooted in God.

·+·

Welling was struck with apoplexy (likely either a heart attack or a stroke) before his regular Sunday service on November 14, 1915, and died two days later, at the age of sixty-three. He had left his sermon for that Sunday on his desk.

Stunned, the Thomas brothers (except for Evan, still in Edinburgh) returned to Lewisburg, where they spent a difficult week. That Sunday, they faced the pulpit where their father had preached so often and watched as one of their father's friends, a professor at Bucknell, read Welling's final sermon, "Realizing God's Presence." It may have surprised them. Its subject was the war, and it was a reevaluation. Welling had championed the Spanish-American War, advocated the necessity of force, and stressed the obligation of loyalty during wartime. Now, at just the moment when the calls for preparing the nation for war grew loudest, Welling called for them to stop. He rejected the truism that war brings out the best in men. This war, Welling wrote, "is a war in which hate is extolled as a virtue and inculcated as a duty"—words that he could almost have lifted from one of Evan's letters.

But Welling did not use Evan's strident tone. His words were chastened and sad. "We have had to revise many of our most cherished opinions," he wrote. Progress had produced more efficient weapons of destruction, not a more just society. Deterrence had failed. Speaking directly to the advocates of preparedness, Welling pointed out that the belligerents had maintained vast forces as guarantees of peace, only to see deterrence turn into destruction. His generation's faith in progress had been misplaced: "All these assumptions are now shown to have been vain."

In the end, though, Welling rejected cynicism. The righteous did not win every battle, and not all battles were righteous, but righteousness persisted.

It was the minister's task to help people realize that God's presence was always among the faithful. There were church leaders, he cautioned, "who need to have their own eyes opened to spiritual things." Almost as if he were speaking to Norman directly, he wrote, "They emphasize the humanity of Christ and minimize or ignore His divinity. In their attempt to make Christianity more comprehensible they rob it of its divine authority and power."

God was incomprehensible in his all-powerfulness. War had to be part of his plan, too, though men could not understand it. Welling was not a pacifist; he would not go that far. "I do not know how he will do it, but I firmly believe that God will overrule this dreadful war in Europe for the working out of his gracious plan," Welling wrote. "In doing so he may use the means and instruments that seem to us least likely to be used. He may use this war to break down imperialism and give a larger and truer liberty to mankind." This was the kind of language that Wilson would use when he took the country into war.

Yet Welling also anticipated the language Norman and Evan would use when they objected to Wilson's course. "What Christians need is the faith to believe where they cannot see, and to trust in the unseen," he counseled. "It does not require much faith or courage to be a Christian when the multitude is with you; but to stand alone, or to be one of a few in opposition to the multitude, requires courage of the highest type."

÷

A man whose gaze is trained on the mass of humanity can sometimes suffer from farsightedness, unable to see clearly the needs of those closest to him. Norman had spent a week with his mother, brothers, and sisters, discussing what would happen to them and beginning to organize his father's things. He was also supposed to handle Welling's will and take care of his mother's finances, a task all the more pressing because there wasn't much of an estate to speak of. His mother and two young sisters were facing straitened circumstances, and soon they would be out of their house (the manse in which they lived went with Welling's position). Arthur was not in a position to support them; he'd yet to find work. Evan was in Scotland, and Ralph had just moved to Baltimore to begin a new job. Norman was the oldest and the responsibility fell to him. He was distracted, though; he had a wife and four children, and he was already overwhelmed. After he returned to his work in East Harlem, he seems to have put his mother and siblings out of mind.

Norman's lack of attention to his family bothered Ralph. He looked into their mother's finances and saw she was in bad shape. He researched her investments and made suggestions. "Please answer at once," he had to plead with Norman, "as Mother is losing money and prices are rising." Before long, Norman deferred to Ralph, and Ralph ended up doing more than handling their mother's money. Since their mother and sisters had nowhere to live, the family agreed they would move to Baltimore and live with Ralph.

Ralph was twenty-eight years old, living in a boardinghouse at the time; he was accustomed to a life without furniture. Buying a home and living with three women—including his mother, who was not exactly the retiring type—would have been an extraordinary change. "He looks thin and sober," his mother wrote to Norman a few months later. With a note of guilt and perhaps reproach, she added, "I do hope your family burdens are lighter."

This was how Ralph understood duty—differently from Norman, and certainly differently from Evan, whose apologies for being unable to send money from Scotland were so emphatic that both Ralph and Emma offered to send some to *him*. He thought about his personal debt before his social one. He was not unmindful of urban poverty or injustice, but he wanted to provide for and protect those closest to him first.

·+·

When Norman wrote to Evan about their father's death, Evan responded with guilt as well as grief. He had harangued and provoked his father for two years, with letters that were "so absolutely needless," Evan admitted to his oldest brother. He had never understood his father, he confessed, and he searched to find some kind of lesson to draw from Welling's life. What he finally concluded said more about Evan than his father: Welling "lived what he preached." Evan could not unpack what "lived what he preached" meant; he was wound too tightly. He turned the phrase into a cliché, rephrasing the platitude that a man's character is what matters.

Evan could not see even his own father except through the prism of his obsession with sincerity. Of course, abstracting his father's life and death had advantages. It was a way of sealing the guilt and pain of their difficult relationship, of cauterizing the wound without having to probe it.

Mourning Welling would have been difficult for Evan in any circumstances, but alone in Scotland he was clearly in no position to come to terms with his fraught relationship with his father. He was consumed by thinking about the war, the corruptions of society, the primacy of the individual. Still, the weeks after he learned of Welling's death were hard and solitary. Just before Christmas, he traveled alone to the Highlands. He spent days walking through the deer forests in the fresh snow and nights staring at the ghostly moonlight on the blanketed glen. Over the New Year, he and his friend from Princeton John Mott sprayed golf balls across the empty hills.

Ralph and Norman thought it might be time for Evan to come home. It was clear that he had found no more answers in Edinburgh than he had in New York, that he was still desperately hammering at the same unyielding questions. John McDowell, the minister at Ralph's new church in Baltimore, Brown Memorial, was willing to give Evan a job there. McDowell already knew Norman; they were both on the graduate board of Princeton's Philadelphian Society. Norman, Emma, and Ralph all wrote to Evan, urging him to accept the attractive offer. The salary was high, the prestige of the position would help secure his future as a minister in the United States, and he would be close to Ralph, his sisters, and his mother.

But Evan said no. His reason must have surprised his family: He had already been offered a job as the assistant to John Kelman, the minister at St. George's in Edinburgh—a church, as Evan himself noted, that would have stood comfortably on Fifth Avenue in New York. (In fact, Kelman would later become minister of Fifth Avenue Presbyterian.) Kelman and Evan argued terrifically about the war. When Evan had first met the minister he had dismissed him as a warmonger and a snob, but he had come to like him, and Kelman liked him in turn. Kelman was gregarious, friendly, honest, and colorful, never losing the expansive curiosity that had led him to write a book on the religiosity of Robert Louis Stevenson. Before long the Kelmans were treating Evan like "one of the family," and part of the Kelman clan even asked Evan to come live with them. Evan defended his choice to his mother as an opportunity to see up close the kind of church he instinctively opposed, and then he appealed to his father's memory. Writing to her on Welling's birthday, he said, "I believe he would want me most of all to be true to my own conscience, and that is what I want to be."

True to my own conscience—this would become for Evan a mantra, a trump card. It was indefinable and unassailable, all he needed to say to end a conversation. Even Evan could sense that this rhetorical move was too facile. As the early days of the new year passed by, Evan became more and more tangled in his attempt to determine what conscience was for him, and what it told him to do. Anxiety and frustration radiated from his letters, as he raised the stakes in his attempt to find some grand purpose. The grandest purpose was the establishment of peace and justice. He was genuinely bothered by the extreme inequality he saw, between the drunks in the gutter around the settlement house on Castle Mound and the pew holders at St. George's, and by the hot air of sermons exhorting men who had already lost friends and brothers to march to their deaths in the name of Christ and country. The repetitious, manic quality of his letters, though, was the result of more than his concern for others. He had an urgent need to act, to do something heroic. In several letters, he told Norman that he was convinced that history could turn on the idealism of a few great men who shone light on the truth simply by the radiance of their own example, by being true to their consciences. Blinded by his intensity, Evan argued even with those who were inclined to agree with him. After one tirade against the church and war in a letter to the Crusaders, he had to apologize to Sayre for writing as if he were preaching to a group of prowar Tories.

Norman thought Evan was "groping in the dark." The two brothers were so close in so many ways, certainly closer to each other than to Ralph or Arthur. They shared an impulse to make social problems their own, a sensitivity to injustice, and a commitment to do something about it. Because of their closeness, as much as in spite of it, they argued sharply and sometimes woundingly in 1915 and 1916. For all their mutual sympathy, they differed in important ways. Evan had a romantic streak, an individualist impulse that owed more to Americans like Thoreau than to social progressives. Moral indignation came much more easily to Evan than to Norman, who tended to see problems as more structural.

Inevitably, complicated sibling dynamics were at work, as well. The younger brother who had always been in awe of the older was driven to prove himself by staking out a more extreme position. When Norman pointed out the inconsistencies in Evan's logic, Evan replied with more heat than reason. "I question it," Evan once simply dismissed one of Norman's arguments. Norman found Evan's obsession with lone examplars and his fixation on "love" to be simplistic and a bit silly. But the arguments sprung from sources deeper than these disagreements. Part of the problem, perhaps, was due to Evan's difficult year in New York, where Norman had encouraged him to come. However profusely Evan expressed his admiration for Norman's work in East Harlem, Norman must have felt stung when Evan went to Scotland. Evan had begun down the path that Norman had followed and then noisily rejected it. It must have been painful, too, for Norman to watch Evan flail under the immense pressure that he had placed upon himself.

Evan did try to catch his breath and calm himself. He thought that his new job at St. George's might give him a "new start," he wrote to Sayre, and free him from the "rancor and criticism" that ate at his heart. He made lots of friends—many of them pacifists, but not all. He was close to Kelman and to Kelman's predecessor, Alexander Whyte, who—whatever Evan liked to say about the fanciness of St. George's—was self-educated and born out of wedlock, and who had begun as an apprentice shoemaker before becoming the minister of St. George's and Principal of New College. The new lightness of Evan's tone, though, soon faded. Great Britain had just implemented the draft. The posters declaring the new Military Service Act deployed tremendous euphemisms, describing a conscript as a man who "will be deemed to have enlisted." Evan began writing agitated letters home about the noble stance of conscientious objectors. Just the term, with its resonance of lonely protest and conscience, excited him. It suggested a repudiation not only of conscription but of conformity, which Evan detested. When he preached in a small village in Fife, he looked at the stone-faced crowd and had to resist the urge to hurl his Bible into the pews, to see if *anything* would rouse a reaction. Visiting a friend's family in the Highlands, he envied them their freedom. "Such people can be themselves, say what they think and enjoy it," he wrote to his mother. "No king can have that joy." His thoughts turned bitterly toward his own situation. "Likewise the pastor of St. George's can't have that joy, for he too must be true to his position."

For his first sermon at St. George's, Evan delivered a message that he thought was radical and even seditious, "the work not of a week, but of years of far from easy and not always happy striving and thinking," he wrote to Emma. The thrust of it described what he had been saying for some time: The man who was true to himself would want to live in a more socialistic society and would condemn war. It was, actually, a pretty tame sermon. Only at the end did Evan reveal his radicalism to the well-heeled congregation. The man who had found real love within himself would inevitably become a target, Evan said. "In the words of Jesus: 'Blessed are ye when men shall revile you, and persecute you, and say all manner of evil against you falsely for my sake. Rejoice and be exceedingly glad.' . . . He, who has faith, may be persecuted, reviled, and killed; but, if so, with Jesus, he can say, 'my life is given as a ransom for many,' and with Him, he can say, 'I have overcome the world.' " With that, Evan closed his sermon and waited to be reviled.

What came instead was praise—"chiefly for the way my voice 'rang out,' " Evan wrote to his mother. "It disgusts me. . . . No one can know what that sermon meant to me." Evan's speech—like the young Norman's Easter Sunday sermon at Brick Church—was not the fiery cri de coeur he had imagined. Any half-regular churchgoer would have heard most of it before. Words like "faith alone saves," no matter how passionately uttered, were not the stuff of radical revolution. Nor were the lines "That means LETTING GOD DO THE JUDGING OF OURSELVES AND OTHERS. He alone is good." Who among the audience of regular attendees would not smile and nod indulgently at their young preacher's passion when he said, "The earth may shake and the mountains be moved, but such a faith will know no fear"? His heart was in the right place.

So much desperate effort had gone "up in a puff of light praise." Evan was devastated. People thought he was cynical—but he thought these churchgoers, with their rented pews and their breweries and their wars, were the cynical ones. They were the ones who could hear anything on a Sunday morning and mildly approve of it. The whole thing, he told his mother, was "a bitter disappointment."

"You might send sermon to N," he added, "who will probably say it is sentimental."

⁜

Norman had always loved to speak, and he would do it wherever he could—not just from the pulpit. The church had given him one platform, and he used it to seize others. He began to deliver speeches from stages and soapboxes, in dingy halls and in the open air. He spoke about the church, immigrants, and social work, and more and more he spoke against the war. He already had the orator's skill, honed during countless debates at Princeton and in hundreds of sermons. He had a sly sense of humor and an elastic, expressive face, a supple voice that he could throw against the back walls of large rooms without apparent effort. He was inspiring but also sharp. When hecklers stood in the balcony, he would push back. "Sit down," he'd say, "you're as foolish as you look." His words had a magnetic quality, even to people who did not speak enough English to understand them. One evening at a Harlem school, Sid Lovett watched him debate and dismantle the arguments of a downtown lawyer on the subject of preparedness. Lovett told Norman's biographer W. A. Swanberg that "the audience was so enthusiastic that they surged around Norman to shake his hand or just to touch him."

Norman was not much of a missionary for the church, but on the subject of war he was evangelical. This was risky. Mainline Presbyterianism, with its Social Gospel inflection, was pliant enough to absorb his criticism of the economic status quo, and even of the church itself. When he spoke about politics and preparedness, though, he moved out of the mainstream (at least in the Northeast). President Wilson had changed his mind that November, proposing a limited expansion of the military and then embarking on a speaking tour to persuade the public to support his bill. Wilson's bill did not go nearly as far as many preparedness advocates wanted. Still, Norman was alarmed by the ferocity of the nationalism summoned to support it. This nationalism masqueraded as patriotism, but it was militant and xenophobic, and Norman was convinced that it was among the reasons he was having so much trouble encouraging the residents of East Harlem to get along.

He was also convinced that the same kind of mass hysteria, a lust for power and national glory, had led to the war in Europe in the first place. A book by Henry N. Brailsford, *The War of Steel and Gold*, which argued that the deeper causes of the conflict lay in the imperial system in Europe, made a deep impression on him. Brailsford suggested that economic competition, a scramble for resources, the substitution of military prestige for selfless service, arms races, and secretive diplomacy had set the stage for a cataclysm. *The War of Steel and Gold* had a prophetic quality; it had been published just before Archduke Ferdinand was shot. In Brailsford's book and other pacifist and antiwar literature, Norman found an indictment of the whole system of conquest underpinned by military power. It was a simplistic view, but for Norman its simplicity was clearly a part of its power. Brailsford's argument seemed to confirm his idea that capitalism meant the "practical denial of brotherhood" in favor of greed and distrust. A war of annihilation was the most horrific evidence for the argument that exploitation leads to violence. The more Norman read about the economic and psychological causes of the war, the more he was sure that he had found a worldview that could help explain not only what happened in Europe in the summer of 1914, but also what was happening in the United States at that moment. It even helped explain the power of Billy Sunday.

✢

Billy Sunday was on Norman's mind. He embodied the militant nationalism that Norman so feared and loathed and the conservatism that Norman found closed-minded and distinctly unchristian. For Norman, Billy Sunday's name was shorthand for the country's biggest problems. But this presented its own problem in the spring of 1916, when Ralph expressed his qualified admiration for the preacher.

Sunday had recently preached in Baltimore, and Ralph had been impressed. Sunday's style may have been gauche—and Ralph did not deny it—but at least it brought people into the church. This was a common defense of Sunday: When Sunday came to town, the saloonkeepers shut up shop, church membership spiked, and men swore a little less. He also reminded people of the absolute authority of the Bible. If he was a little heavy-handed, where was the real harm? In condemning those who took license to sin, he pulled people into line.

That was precisely the problem, Norman replied to Ralph. There were things to admire about the preacher, he acknowledged, and he sometimes had positive effects on personal morality. More often, though, he pulled people into the rut of unthinking conformity, and he encouraged hate and intolerance. Norman could never accept Sunday's God, "a 'moral' but vindictive God who apparently takes pleasure in condemning men to an eternal hell unless they happen to accept a rigid and somewhat unethical scheme of salvation." ("It's a good thing for some fellows that I am not God for about 15 minutes," Sunday liked to say. "I wonder that God lets some people live.") Sunday appealed to that part of human nature that wants to be told what to do, Norman charged. He excused men and women from thinking for themselves. He offered a morality based on fear instead of forgiveness and love. He encouraged a mindless belligerency instead of real patriotism. He confused force with strength.

Ralph and Norman were really arguing about preparedness. Ralph was for it, Norman against it, and Billy Sunday was the proxy subject. Ralph was no Billy Sunday. He believed that it had to be possible to defend his country's values, to the death if need be, without descending into jingoism. In several letters to Norman, he defended the preparedness movement's patriotism against accusations of selfish profit motives.

"Are you sure that you have understood our position?" Norman asked hotly before confirming, inadvertently or not, that that was just what anti-militarists thought. Historical study suggested, Norman wrote, that the buildup of armies in preparation for war in the name of defense "always results in taxes for the masses and benefit for munitions makers, and big financial interests which want to exploit weaker nations." He added, sharp and condescending, "This is not theory. Have you studied the question or read anything but newspaper articles?"

What had begun as a civil exchange turned into a fight, and the gloves came off. Billy Sunday drew a crowd, Norman was perfectly willing to admit, but crowds rarely flocked to the best and most thoughtful leaders. "By thinking men I do not mean your lawyers and brokers," he wrote to Ralph, who happened to count lawyers and brokers among his close friends. "My experience is that most of them do very little thinking outside of their own groove. I mean that small company of men of every class who really care about the scientific, social and intellectual problems of our time. They are a minority but in the long run they move the world."

It was an argument neither brother would win. "I do not suppose that any further discussion about Billy Sunday will get us anywhere," Norman wrote—and then went on to attack Sunday for four more pages.

-+-

Norman was touchy and frustrated for long stretches of 1916. Another public controversy over the ordination of three Union Theological Seminary students who refused to admit the literalism of biblical miracles had him fuming. "It's the old story," he wrote to Ralph. "I'll spare you my comments except to point out the worse than futile waste of time in this day of great spiritual and ethical problems." A bad hernia, exacerbated by stress and overwork, kept him in pain. He was "not at all well," wrote Lovett to his mother, adding that Norman needed a "long respite from work." Of course, he would not get it.

He worried about his wife's health and the vulnerability of his children. Violet, who had problems with her heart—perhaps from rheumatic fever as a child—was often ill. At times it could seem that death was all around him. His neighborhood had one of the highest infant mortality rates in the city. A polio epidemic swept the city and countryside. When children near the summer camp he had established for urban children in Oak Ridge, New Jersey, came down with it, he was forced to sequester some campers and turn others away. Most painfully, Lovett's young wife, Rebekah, died in childbirth at the end of the summer. The Thomases had adored her, and she had been an important part of their small community, coming for dinner or to play the organ at Norman's church. Lovett, despairing, turned to Violet and Norman, and they gave him a room in their home and cared for him as best they could. They also grieved for his wife, so much that they named their next-born daughter, Rebekah, in her memory.

The persistent threat of war darkened everything. The newspapers reported worse news by the day. German sabotage plots and sensational rumors of conspiracies (some real) stimulated anti-German sentiment. Another U-boat attack that year brought Wilson perilously close to severing diplomatic relations with Germany, while British infractions of maritime law infuriated him, too. On top of everything, Wilson faced hostility from Mexico. Throughout the spring and summer of 1916, that trouble threatened to flare into full-scale war.

Wilson had stumbled with foreign affairs in Latin America since the start of his presidency. He had sent troops into Haiti, Nicaragua, and the Dominican Republic, hoping to use the United States' traditional sphere of influence and military might to encourage democratic governments and found himself instead embroiled in messy occupations. Mexico, with its long U.S. border, was the most persistent threat. After a coup in 1913, Wilson privately condemned the "government of butchers." He saw the establishment of a constitutional democracy in Mexico, he told Congress, as a chance to expand "the field of self-government," but he checked himself, too. "We can afford to exercise the self-restraint of a really great nation which realizes its own strength and scorns to misuse it." Mexico's so-called constitutionalists were hardly more pliant to American interests than the prior regime, though, and before long Wilson undertook a botched military landing at Veracruz. One observer noted that the affair left Wilson looking "almost parchmenty." The disaster at Veracruz may have chastened him somewhat, but he still waffled about what to do. With revolutionaries making border raids in the southwest, some Americans were agitating to cross into Mexico to pursue the fight—which, eventually, Wilson did, with troops under the command of John Pershing. The shadow of Germany's presence in Mexico made any move even riskier. Germany, eager for the United States to become embroiled in a guerrilla conflict on its southwest border that would distract its attention and resources from the Allies, was actively and openly prodding the Mexicans.

"I should like to be in Washington now to hear the President," Norman wrote to Ralph. "Things are serious, Germany terribly in the wrong, but as yet I can't feel that war is the way to mend the matter. . . . Poor

Woodrow, with Mexico, Germany, Congress, the country and TR on his hands!" Norman watched Wilson anxiously that spring. "I still feel as I did on this preparedness propaganda and expect to speak a couple of times on it," he added. "It's an unpopular position."

·ᛏ·

The preparedness movement was concentrated in cities on the East Coast; it was far less popular across the country. But in the spring of 1916, for a New Yorker like Norman it would have been impossible to ignore. Preparedness advocates had managed to make their cause synonymous with patriotism, and "preparedness parades" became spectacles of flag-waving. Norman would not have been able to overlook the Stars and Stripes bathing the city on the morning of Saturday, May 13. Flags lined Broadway and fringed Fifth Avenue. Between the St. Regis and the Gotham Hotel hung the largest American flag in the country. The Ritz-Carlton trained a searchlight on its own giant Stars and Stripes. From lampposts and storefronts, from long poles and small sticks clutched in thousands of hands, American flags rippled as the breeze brought them to life.

More than 120,000 people processed up the island, marching twenty abreast, accompanied by some two hundred bands and fifty corps of fife and drum, reported the *New York Times*. The participants included a whole range of professions, from carpet traders to haberdashers, and fifteen thousand bankers and brokers. All through the day, until the spring sun had set, the marchers made their way up the route to the edge of Central Park. At Twenty-fifth Street, they passed a reviewing grandstand where Rear Admiral Nathaniel Usher and General Leonard Wood watched approvingly. Roosevelt himself—or perhaps even Wilson—might have been there but neither was invited. The marshal wanted patriotism, not partisanship, to be the theme of the day. Lest the crowd forget the importance of its allegiance, over Fifth Avenue hung an electric sign blinking the words "ABSOLUTE AND UNQUALIFIED LOYALTY TO OUR COUNTRY."

The parade was like a beautiful machine. The *New York Times* admiringly noted "its celerity of movement, the unfailing perfection of alignment." The people were swept into the forward motion of the march, united by their common momentum and the prospect of where it might take them. There was a darker side to that unity, and to the flags, the matching clothes, the signs, and the songs, though. Any note of difference or dissent could threaten to throw the "perfection of alignment" out of whack. Patriotism wasn't enough. A different word was used: "Americanism."

To drum up support for preparedness, it helped to rally people against something or someone. President Wilson knew this as well as anyone. He, no less than the hyperpatriots who organized the Preparedness Parade, was obsessed with unity. The enemy wasn't Germany (yet), but that did not mean there was no enemy. "There is disloyalty active in the United States," Wilson said on Flag Day, "and it must be absolutely crushed."

Eleven

MUDDLE HEADED

*Ridgefield, Connecticut, was a refuge for
Norman—here with his son Billy
perched on his shoulders.*

In the spring of 1916, Germany decided to "bleed France white." If the
Germans could beat the French at Verdun—a place of symbolic significance to the French, a stronghold since the days of Gaul—it might be
able to break not only the Allies' armies but also their spirit. In the hilly
terrain along the Meuse River in late February, Germany set one million
men upon two hundred thousand French defenders. By the end of the day
the Germans had gained only the front lines. The two sides traded attack
and counterattack every few weeks. The French knew the wound at Verdun
would be bad but gambled that it would not be fatal and that they, too, could

wreak incredible damage. It was one of the worst battles of attrition in history. By its end—nearly a year later, making it the longest battle of the war—each side had inflicted around half a million casualties, to no advantage.

The British launched their attempt to win the war on July 1 along the Somme River. The commander of the British Expeditionary Force, a Scot named Douglas Haig, planned to blast the Germans on the front lines and then send wave upon wave of men to overwhelm the enemy positions. Serene and spiritual, Haig carried himself "as if guided by some inner voice, speaking of a higher purpose and a personal destiny," writes the military historian John Keegan. For days, British artillery hammered the German trenches. More than fifteen hundred guns fired a million and a half shells. When they stopped, there was silence, and above the smoke the sky was blue and clear. At 7:30 A.M., a series of British mines buried under the German lines exploded, and the "big push" began. Afterward, British soldiers would call it "the great fuckup." The Germans on the front lines were sheltered by their solidly constructed trenches, and when the barrage ended they climbed to the top of their dugouts and opened fire. They had plenty of targets. Many British soldiers were caught in the snarl of barbed wire the initial explosives had failed to destroy. Some of them were killed by friendly fire. By the end of the first day alone, twenty thousand British soldiers were dead and another forty thousand wounded. It could have been worse. Some Germans became so sickened by the sight of the carnage that they stopped firing and allowed those who could to turn back and make it through the bloody mud to safety. In the end, the Germans weren't spared either, and suffered heavy losses. By the time the Allied offensive at the Somme officially ended in November, over a million men had died or been wounded, and the Allies had gained seven miles of ground.

The more who died, the more who had to die. This was true for both the Allies and the Central Powers. Each side would accept only a resounding victory, to justify their enormous sacrifice. The psychological effects of the Somme were particularly damaging to the British. Nothing, it seemed, could justify such losses, so many dead and wounded. Still, they kept fighting. The *Punch* cartoons that had so merrily urged the people to join up "For King and Country" now bore the bleak slogan "Carry On!" For many citizens and soldiers, the Somme broke the cracked dam. The country's ebullient enthusiasm for the war—and the self-assurance and easy confidence built by centuries of empire and self-mythology—drained away; now there was only grim perseverance.

·+·

Evan was "sick" of the war, he told his mother, but he could not let the subject go, and he could not avoid it anyway. As the shells fell along the Somme and Verdun, Evan went to France, passing through Paris on his way to visit his aunt Anna and uncle Frank Welles. When he returned, war was still the subject of nearly every letter. Something had changed, though. He concerned himself less with the religious basis for pacifism and more with the pacifists themselves, especially conscientious objectors. Objectors were loathed in Britain, but they were not ignored. The Anglo intellectual and social tradition had long privileged individual liberty and resistance to the state—before the war, the term "conscientious objector" had described those who refused compulsory vaccinations—and unlike the continental European nations, Great Britain did not have a tradition of compulsory service. In part *because* of that, it depended upon loyalty and "voluntary" service. Even before conscription was implemented, social pressure could be almost as severe as the law, if not more so. The Military Service Act did allow exemptions or provide for alternate service for conscientious objectors, not only religious objectors but anyone judged sincere by a tribunal. But the policy was more generous in theory than in practice. Few men were granted unconditional exemptions, and most nonreligious objectors were declared insincere. Some who were declared sincere refused noncombatant service. Nearly six thousand men landed in jail, where conditions could be brutal—plank beds and hard labor, severe hunger, beatings, and an enforced rule of silence, which some found the worst punishment of all. Objectors were shunned even by some men who thought the war was folly. While so many Tommies were dying, "Conchies" became synonymous with cowards.

To Evan, they were heroes. A conscientious objector admitted no authority but his conscience. Like a soldier, he faced a force that would break him if it could. He had to neither submit to the compromises that politics required nor compromise his nonviolent ethics with the violent overthrow of government that revolution required. And he proved himself by his imprisonment.

No small part of Evan wanted to be punished as a martyr. He wrote that he was convinced that your conscience required you to "take the consequences if the majority believe it right to persecute you. If your ideal is true your suffering persecution will make it shine all brighter in the darkness; if it is false it will die with you." He surely had the Gospel of Matthew in mind: "Blessed are ye when men shall revile you, and persecute you, and say all manner of evil against you falsely for my sake." Trying to live up to Jesus's example, Evan was bound not only to fail but also to feel miserable. Contradictions tore him apart. His letters burned with self-righteousness against the self-righteous; he charged the complacent with inaction, while he wasn't doing much himself. He hated hypocrites, but he thought he was one. He adored his boss, Reverend Kelman—almost in spite of himself—but hated what he thought St. George's represented. He was against the war, but he admired soldiers. He idolized his oldest brother but criticized him often.

He especially criticized Norman's new involvement in politics. Evan was a pacifist, but he did not support the antipreparedness movement in the United States. Evan was such an individualist that he made a sharp distinction between the obligations of the individual and the state. The individual's duty was to live life according to his highest ethical ideals and hope that the people would see the truth of his actions. The state had to make compromises for the safety and security of people that the individual did not. The state would change when enough people understood that true freedom comes from within themselves—but that moment had not yet come. Norman, in Evan's view, was confusing what a person should do with what a democratic government must do. The state had to consider the security of its citizens and the will of the popular majority. As far as he could tell—at least from reading the papers and letters from America—that will was for preparedness, and preparedness, considering Germany's actions, was wise.

Emma, who constantly passed her sons' letters between them, sent along a letter to Norman that Evan had written in which he questioned Norman's "political moves." "As an individual I will preach pacifism for all I am worth and get every one else to come with me I can . . . but politically you must consider the majority," he had written. "Nothing could be worse than to have a nation unprepared for war one way or the other. Far better prepare than to go unprepared with the great bulk of the people not knowing their own minds." The antimilitarists, he wrote, were "muddle headed."

Evan had contempt for the tepid compromises made by many liberals. On a train to Manchester, Evan listened to a couple of British soldiers ribbing each other when another man, reading the *Nation* in the carriage's corner, interrupted. He asked the soldiers what they thought about the argument, which he had just read, that the Allies should negotiate immediately because they probably could not win the war. A soldier laughed, glancing around, and then quieted his voice. "Well, by God! We can try." That was the kind of spirit Evan admired. The *Nation* reader, not the soldier, was the one who disgusted him.

"What in the world do these good liberals want?" he exploded in a letter to his mother. "What would they have—a war waged with one hand and the other used for twiddling one's thumb?" In Evan's mind, there were two ways to fight Germany: to crush by force (and risk becoming like Germany) or to resist by nonresistance. There could be no timidity. If the people of the United States were not capable of or willing to embrace pacifism altogether, then it was Wilson's duty to commit himself to war—just as Evan believed that it was his duty to fight for peace. Evan worshipped Wilson. "My admiration for Pres. Wilson steadily increases," Evan wrote. "Personally I have tremendous faith in American idealism."

Wilson had once been Norman's hero, too. No longer. Norman's discouragement with his old professor had been building for a long time. His experience in East Harlem had given him a very different theory of government than the one he learned in Wilson's classes. He had been heartened by the way Wilson talked about expanding democracy, but he was disappointed by his actions. What Norman really considered a betrayal, though, was Wilson's preparedness bill. It was yet another sign of inconsistency and political pandering. The president's turnabouts, Norman wrote to Evan, "to a certain extent justify the widespread distrust of him as an astute opportunist rather than a tremendously sincere statesman." He hastened to add, "I shall certainly vote for Mr. Wilson and hope that he will be reelected." Still, he was disappointed that Wilson had not been nearly the reformer that Norman had hoped he would be, and he was not convinced that Wilson was committed to keeping the country out of war.

Norman was not the only progressive surprised by Wilson's preparedness endorsement. The country's leading antimilitarists hastily formed the American Union Against Militarism (AUAM) and launched their own campaign. Leaders of the Women's Peace Party, including Jane Addams, the founder of Hull House, Lillian Wald, who had founded a settlement house on the Lower East Side of New York, and Crystal Eastman, a beautiful, vivacious feminist lawyer, joined, and Eastman became its head. Her younger brother, Max Eastman, the aesthete and editor of the socialist paper *The Masses*, also became a member. The Reform rabbi Stephen Wise, the Unitarian minister John Haynes Holmes, Paul Kellogg, the editor of the social work journal *The Survey*, and other influential progressives all joined. They opposed Wilson's bill to expand the military, increased military training in schools, provisions for the draft in certain states' legislation, and intervention in Mexico as well as Europe, and they worked both through backdoor channels and through grassroots efforts. When Wilson took his tour of the country, so did members of the AUAM, matching packed halls with packed halls. They took with them their mascot, a papier-mâché dinosaur named Jingo that wore a sign on its collar reading "ALL ARMOR PLATE—NO BRAINS."

Norman looked up to the leading members of the AUAM and knew some of them personally, though slightly, through social work channels in New York City. He was only thirty-one years old, a minister who preached often to empty pews, with no reputation outside the Presbyterian Church. As the antimilitarist cause became more urgent, though, he started associating himself more with them than with his church. He was turning to politics. It seemed to be, as he had said of the choice between Brick Church and East Harlem Presbyterian, where he could be of more "use." Writing to Evan in the fall of 1916, he launched into his defense of "our" position: sympathy with the Allies but condemnation of the "shameful measures" of all belligerents; opposition to increased jingoism; a protest against the sham of self-defense ("every nation in the world has said that it was only preparing to defend itself and no nation believes the others"); a defense of the conviction that the money would be better used for relief instead of battleships. "Our campaign has been by no means fruitless," Norman wrote to his younger brother, and then took a little credit. "You know there is a clause in the big naval bill authorizing the President at the close of the war to appoint commissioners to try to arrange for some plan of world peace."

"We are by no means 'muddle headed,'" Norman stiffly insisted.

᛭

Wilson's plan for world peace had begun to crystallize in his mind, and members of the AUAM were indeed among the first to hear of it. The AUAM had come to the White House to discuss its worry, as Lillian Wald told Wilson, that a big military would "neutralize and annul the moral power" of the United States when it came time to negotiate peace. "I am just as much opposed to militarism as any man living," the president reassured the delegates, and then explained that if the United States were to be part of a worldwide defense of righteousness, a "family of nations," it would have to supply some of the "bite" to keep other nations from pursuing actions that might lead to war. This was true for the United States, too, he allowed. There would need to be "some check" upon its power "by some international arrangement which we hope for." All this was sketchy and vague, but it was significant nevertheless. The AUAM meeting appears to have been the first time that Wilson broached his idea for an "international arrangement" backed by some kind of peacekeeping force with an outside group. The AUAM members were completely mollified and charmed by Wilson. Max Eastman, a self-proclaimed radical, marveled at how Wilson "always referred to the Union Against Militarism as though he were a member of it." Eastman approvingly added, "I believe that he sincerely hates his preparedness policies."

A few weeks later Wilson announced his plan for a "world league for peace of righteousness" to the public, during a speech to the League to Enforce Peace (LEP) in which he called for "a common order, a common justice, and a common peace"—a league of nations. This was not entirely his idea. Roosevelt, in fact, had proposed a "world league for peace of righteousness" years before, and the LEP existed to promote the establishment of mechanisms that would guide arbitration and diplomatic mediation. But where the LEP wanted to define the obligations of league membership, Wilson wanted to leave things more open-ended. He was convinced that the right rules would present themselves in good time. "I did not come here . . . to discuss a program," he said. "I came only to avow a creed. . . . I feel that the world is even now upon the eve of a great consummation." The principle of obligation mattered most of all, not the details. This kind of augury perplexed and enraged some of Wilson's critics. But however vague, the vision seemed sufficient to vindicate the hopes that liberals wove around him. Max Eastman called it "the most important step that any President . . . has taken toward civilizing the world since Lincoln." The *Independent* effused that the speech ranked with the Declaration of Independence.

But world peace by American fiat, some of Wilson's opponents noted, sounded a little rich, considering that both the Allies and Germany were currently ignoring the United States. Wilson's attempt to begin negotiations was rebuffed by both sides. The Allies refused unless the United States promised to enter the war if Germany failed to capitulate to their major demands; Germany would not think of giving up the huge territories it had gained in the first month of fighting. Neither side was inclined to defer to an American who lectured them about universal values.

·┼·

Europeans knew they might not have to worry about Wilson for much longer. If the election of 1912 had been distinguished by a sophisticated political discourse, the election of 1916 was marked by innuendo, contradiction, and confusion. The Republicans were running Charles Evans Hughes, recently resigned from the Supreme Court. The long-jawed, reserved Hughes was mocked as a "bearded iceberg," though Teddy Roosevelt liked to call him "whiskered Wilson." The former president had tentatively sought the Republican nomination for himself, hedging that it would be possible to elect him only if the country were in a "heroic mood" and then concluding that it was not. Wilson was pandering to citizens' fears that German Americans and Irish Americans could not be trusted, while at the same time criticizing the Republicans' bellicosity. Declaring that the theme of the Democratic National Convention would be "Americanism," he told the organizers to best the Republicans with patriotic displays and then became astonished when the crowd began chanting, "We didn't go to war! We didn't go to war!" "He Kept Us Out of War" became the incumbent's slogan. Wilson embraced the message publicly, but half-heartedly, trying to ride the support from noninterventionists while pushing his internationalist league of nations and at the same time touting his preparedness program and his patriotism. Privately, he admitted that the slogan was a problem. "Any little German lieutenant can put us into war at any time by some calculated outrage," Wilson said to the secretary of the navy.

But debates over war and peace did not dominate the election. Despite the preparedness parades and flag-waving, the Great War touched most Americans' lives very little. Outside the Northeast, war seemed especially distant. Meanwhile, liberals (and they were now "liberals" instead of "progressives," distancing themselves from the "berserker" Roosevelt) focused on the reform legislation Wilson had signed during his first term. At the *New Republic*, Walter Lippmann praised Wilson for "remaking his philosophy" and building a strong, effective party. Most members of the AUAM put aside their misgivings over his preparedness policies and convinced themselves, like Eastman, that he really "hated" preparedness, or focused instead on his league of nations proposal. Even Socialists were urging followers to vote for the Democrat. "I am a Socialist," Mother Jones said. "But I admire Wilson. . . . And when a man or woman does something for humanity I say go to him . . . and say, 'I'm for you.' "

Wilson needed the radicals' support. The race could hardly have been tighter, as Hughes dominated the Northeast. On election night, the *New York Times* actually declared Hughes the winner before the western polls had closed. In Princeton that evening with his family, Wilson stayed up, morose. Not only his presidency was at stake, he understood. He knew the country was closer to war than it had been hours before. Finally, glumly, he drank some milk and went to bed. Once the western votes were counted, though, his hope revived. It came down to California, where Wilson won by 3,806 votes, a plurality of less than four-tenths of a percent. "He Kept Us Out of War" had won, by the slimmest of margins.

Evan told his mother that he was "more delighted than I can say" with Wilson's election. His admiration for the president could not have been higher. "America has an opportunity never equaled before in history of bringing about a more secure and better world," he wrote later. "I never cease thanking God for Woodrow Wilson."

For Norman, though, the presidential race made a "very depressing commentary on politics." Wilson's first campaign had described a stirring vision of democracy, and he had, by many measures, been successful at pushing reform legislation through Congress, especially during his first two years. Yet progress looked more and more doubtful. What had happened on Wilson's watch? An expansion of the military, increased animosity toward immigrants, worsening race relations, and an economy ever more controlled by big business. Worst of all, there remained the persistent possibility of war.

·+·

Norman was cynical about Wilson's peace efforts, but the efforts were sincere. The president's advisers were amazed—and chagrined—at how desperately he was working to stay out of the war. During one conversation with his aide Colonel House at the beginning of 1917, when House lamented the poor state of war preparations, Wilson stated flatly, "There will be no war." After his reelection, he started drafting a peace note to send to the belligerents, laying blame on both sides and on war itself, a "vast, gruesome contest of systematized destruction." If either "German militarism" or "British navalism" was allowed to crush the other, he suggested, then peace would not last. War, Wilson wrote, was not the way to attain their common objectives of defense, security, and equality. He sounded not unlike Norman Thomas.

Colonel House was apoplectic when he read Wilson's draft. It would make the Allies "frantic with rage," he wrote to Wilson. Secretary of State Robert Lansing responded more plaintively. If the Central Powers responded positively to Wilson and the Allies rejected the note, Lansing worried, "would it not be a calamity for the nation, and for all mankind?" Germany had already sent its own bombastic, belligerent, and vague invitation to begin talking about peace terms. The hawks in the administration worried that Wilson's note might come off as an inadvertent endorsement of the kaiser's move. The letter that Wilson finally sent was more subdued than the draft, and it expressed some embarrassment about following the kaiser's peace "offer." Still, Wilson called "attention to the fact that the objects" of the belligerents "are virtually the same."

Secretary Lansing immediately undercut the president's message. Apparently behind Wilson's back, he went to the Allies to assure them that the United States was on their side and suggested to France that they demand Alsace-Lorraine, the democratization of Germany, and indemnity— in short, a punitive victory. To an American reporter, Lansing said, "We are drawing nearer to the verge of war ourselves."

Wilson was furious at Lansing, but he did not force him to resign. Why Wilson tolerated repeated acts of insubordination—this was not the only one—has puzzled historians. There are plausible explanations for why Wilson did not fire Lansing for such flagrant subversion: the sensitive international situation or Wilson's tolerance of disputes among his aides. Another reason might have to do with Wilson's particular disregard for his subordinates. The president hated to be crossed, but he sometimes acted as if those working for him did not reflect upon him or much matter. When his own ambassador to Germany, James Gerard, came to Washington to press the president to make a peace proposal, Wilson kept him waiting for ten days. When he finally met with Gerard, he hammered his desk and told him to tell the kaiser that it was wrong to attack merchant ships without warning. Wilson considered Gerard an "ass." Gerard had not exactly proven his worth, but Wilson could not seem to understand that he might be there for a reason (or, if he had such a low opinion of his ambassador, that he could replace him).

It was, in fact, an opening. Wilhelm had rebuffed Wilson before, but Chancellor Theobald von Bethmann-Hollweg had the slightest hope that the kaiser would listen now. Bethmann-Hollweg was desperate to end the war as quickly as possible. He knew that the Germans would soon resume unrestricted submarine warfare, and he knew that it would likely draw the United States into the conflict. He knew that Germany would probably lose. Both he and the foreign minister of Germany urged Gerard to go Washington and to plead with the president in person.

Wilson could not have known what was on Bethmann-Hollweg's mind, of course, and perhaps it is not fair to judge him for his failure to speculate. But it is fair to wonder why he did not try. Part of the answer, surely, was that Wilson looked inward for answers. While Lansing and House pushed him toward declaring war, while Roosevelt bellowed for arms, while foreign leaders pulled him, Wilson saw himself as the lonely champion of neutrality. And so, lonely is what he was.

Twelve

WHAT THEN SHALL AMERICA DO?

*To many Americans, the Zimmermann
telegram brought a distant war home.*

Norman joined the Fellowship of Reconciliation, a Christian pacifist organization, on December 2, 1916. It might have seemed a small gesture, considering Norman's opposition to preparedness (and the length of the list of organizations to which he belonged), but it was significant. "I have at last taken the step," Norman wrote to a friend. Before then, he had been unwilling to renounce all war. Now, he wrote to a friend, he could not ignore the conviction that one "cannot conquer war by war; cast out Satan by Satan."

This was neither an original thought nor an original expression. Many people had used some variation of this phrasing in the years leading up to the war. It described the classic religious grounds for pacifism. Norman's own brother had said something like this scores of times in the past two years, and even Wilson's peace note—or at least his draft—echoed some of the same sentiment. Indeed, the very derivative quality of the statement suggests something important: It was not far outside the mainstream. Before the Great War began, few would have blinked at the word "pacifist." The secretary of war himself, Newton Baker, had embraced the label only a few years before. That Norman had been reluctant to join the Fellowship of Reconciliation when it was first formed reveals more about his instinctive caution than the radicalism of the organization. Norman, more than many people (including some who had helped found the Fellowship only to resign as soon as the preparedness movement went into swing), recognized there was a difference between being antiwar and being a pacifist—someone opposed to all wars, not just this one. He also recognized that he was taking a risk and that he would be criticized. Pacifists were derided as tender-hearted dreamers and worse. They were accused of being disloyal and disrespecting the sacrifices of soldiers. To a friend, Norman hastened to explain that he had "all appreciation of the noble motives which have led many men to war and support it in all generations." But his revulsion for war—after the Somme and Verdun, after the endless bloodletting and the poison gas, the easy enmeshing of gears between American business and the Allied war effort, and the feverish promilitary rallies—had grown overwhelming.

Norman had several reasons for opposing this particular war—a mash of political, social, and practical considerations—but when he became a pacifist, he justified his general rejection of war in religious terms, saying that war ran counter to Christ's injunction to turn the other cheek. At other times, he said he did not believe in the utilitarian calculus that war could be used as a means for better ends. Still other times, he described his fear of the militarized state. Sometimes, though, he simply sounded vague and frustrated. In those moments, he did what Evan did: He appealed to conscience, as if it were unimpeachable, "I cannot fail to record the faith that is in me."

✦

"Peace now or at any time before the final and complete elimination of this menace is unthinkable," the new British foreign secretary, David Lloyd George, had declared in the fall of 1916. Only a "knockout" would be acceptable. The hard-liners were in; the conciliators, including Edward Grey, who had wondered aloud whether it was time to begin negotiations through "not-unsympathetic mediation," were out. Too much was at stake. After its opening storm across the west and east of Europe, Germany still sprawled across once-Allied lands. The Allies' economies were in shambles. A generation of young men, among them the best educated and most ambitious, had been wiped out. In Russia the economy had collapsed altogether and starving people had turned to barter. Soldiers threatened mutiny. The czar knew that if Russia were to accept peace now, his own people might revolt. France still had food, but it had been attacked and was aggrieved. It had to justify its sacrifice. So many had died.

On the map, things looked better for the Central Powers. They claimed territory from the middle of France to the blurred edge of Russia, from Baghdad to Jerusalem. But their troubles were no less severe than the Allies'. By the end of 1916, a million Germans had died at the front, and at home people were starving. Female mortality increased by more than 10 percent in 1916, mostly due to diseases of malnutrition. The dwindling food stores and freezing winter—"turnip winter," Germans called it—made things worse. Protests filled the streets of Berlin, and Socialists in the Reichstag were starting to shout. "The people don't want war," one yelled. "What they want is peace and bread and work." But the protest was overwhelmed by a flood of ridicule. There were no revolts in Germany, no question of who was in charge. The military autocracy was firmly in control. Even the liberals hardly challenged the desire for victory. The liberal Progressive People's Party was circulating a draft of a treaty proposing to partition Russia and claim the majority of Belgium and "the French coast from Dunkirk to Boulogne." The privation hurt, but the people were still willing to suffer. *"Durchhalten"*—see it through—Germans said to one another.

But Germany's military leaders knew that neither the armies nor the civilians would see it through for much longer. They also knew that the people expected a reward for their sacrifice. When an embattled Austrian diplomat pleaded for peace, the joint head of Germany's war effort, General Erich Ludendorff, replied, "I do not intend to end being pelted by stones." And so the military prepared to push for victory with all its strength. In mid-December, the German commanders decided to resume unrestricted submarine warfare. They waited a few weeks before informing the kaiser.

·+·

President Wilson, oblivious to what was happening across the Atlantic, declared that what the world needed was "peace without victory." Giving the Senate only an hour's notice on January 22, 1917, he delivered a speech proclaiming that old power politics and the "net of intrigue and selfish rivalry" would continue until the cycle of conquest and humiliation stopped. Wilson invoked long-standing American themes and called them universal: equality, consent of the governed, freedom of the seas. Peace based on such principles was the "world's yearning desire," he said, and the way to secure it was with a community of common interest, a league of nations. With characteristically grand and solemn purpose, eloquence, and self-importance, he appealed to the people of the world, not to their leaders. Wilson claimed to speak "for the silent mass of mankind everywhere," those who saw "death and ruin" and had no way to speak out.

The speech thrilled antiwar activists. It was "destined to an immortality as glorious as that of the Gettysburg Address," declared one group. Norman was also pleased, though less hyperbolically. Perhaps, he hopefully suggested, Wilson's moderate tone would quiet the "campaign of hysteria," the ultranationalism sweeping across the country. There might still be hope. But he had less admiration for the president than some of his more publicly visible pacifist allies. He admired Wilson's words, but he still believed that Wilson was pursuing his aims the wrong way. The country was preparing for war even as the president forswore it, and the nationalism that preparedness encouraged did not bode well for a peace without victory.

Norman said so, as often and as loudly as he could. Having taken "the step" to pacifism, he found himself on a bigger stage—among a dwindling cast. He found that the role suited him. His early efforts, though, were more earliest than effective. He circulated a petition that suggested that the machinery of war undermined all those American ideals that Wilson himself championed. While some were calling conscription inevitable, desirable, or even necessary to raise an army, Norman argued that it represented the antithesis of liberty and suggested that the movement to implement the draft represented an attack on freedom of conscience. "However impractical our ideals may seem at this time to the majority of our fellow countrymen, can America afford to deny her own highest ideals and attempt to coerce our consciences?"

In Norman's view, "freedom of conscience" was not reducible to some notion of minority rights found in the First Amendment, though he did have a more robust view of the Bill of Rights than many people at the time. Nor was it the self-declaration of a Martin Luther, though it drew some of its force from a Protestant tradition of connecting conscience directly to God. It was not the romantic self-reliance of an Emerson or a Thoreau, either, though it contained a strain of American romanticism. It was not quite like Evan's use of the phrase; it was not an endorsement of the absolute autonomy of the individual. Norman believed that freedom of conscience was the only way to ensure what he called—what liberal Christians called—the "reverence for personality," the latent potential of every person. He believed that humans were moral beings, made unique and special by their autonomous capacity for moral choices. Freedom of conscience ensured that people had the room to act on those moral choices. It did not give people blanket legitimacy for their actions. It obliged people to respect the moral choices of others (so that they could also have room to act on their moral choices). Having the freedom to act, though, required freedom from oppressive want, hunger, and pain. It also required freedom from an oppressive government.

As 1917 began, Norman looked around him and saw a state that threatened to tell people what to believe, think, and do. To preserve the right to dissent, he dissented. In the *New York Evening Post* that January, he published a protest to the Congressional Committee on Military Affairs against conscription. He began working more and more closely with the governing body of the Fellowship of Reconciliation. Around the same time he became the chairman of the New York No-Conscription League, which protested local laws granting the state the power to draft men and opposed military training in New York public schools.

Norman conducted his antiwar work with enthusiasm but not with particular skill. His boss and mentor William Adams Brown took a look at the No-Conscription League's mission, gently praised its purpose, and then pointed out, "When you come to the positive side of your programme . . . you have got nothing definite to offer." It was true. In the group's literature Norman mostly promised to offer to "work with existing agencies"—doing what, it wasn't entirely clear. A draft of the group's mailing to solicit members communicated more confusion than initiative. "If you are interested will you become a member?" it asked. "Can you suggest practical ways in which you might serve? Have you any plans to offer the organization?" The letter plaintively ended: "We must act!"

There was a will, but there was no plan. There was also no cash, and efforts to raise it were fumbled. "I would avoid the expression 'shy of money,'" Norman chastised the group's secretary, who was soliciting funds from the rich. The league sputtered along for a few more weeks, until the beginning of February, when Norman raised the issue of disbanding the group. Frustration underlined his words—frustration with the group, with himself ("I might do better service in the ranks or as an under-officer than as captain," he confessed to the secretary), and with the international situation. The United States had just broken relations with Germany.

·┼·

On January 9, 1917, the German leadership had gathered at a castle in Poland to make the decision that had already been made. "I guarantee that the U-boat will lead to victory," the head of the navy reassured the kaiser, who was now at the mercy of his own military. Bethmann-Hollweg, hollow eyed, a cigarette always in his hand, spoke against the plan. He rambled; he knew he had already lost. Finally he rubbed his head and said, "Of course, if success beckons, we must follow." Afterward an old baron found the chancellor sitting in the empty room. "Finis Germaniae," Bethmann-Hollweg said. The baron told him to resign, but Bethmann-Hollweg would not. Duty reigned.

On Wednesday, January 31, Wilson learned that Germany would

unleash its U-boats the next day. That Thursday morning, Colonel House found the president listless and depressed, pacing and organizing his books. He knew his aides wanted him to break diplomatic relations with Germany, but still he resisted. He told House that it would be a "crime" if an American entry made it "impossible to save Europe." The next day Wilson met with his cabinet. "What shall I propose?" he asked them. "What shall I say?"

Americans remained divided. "For defense of American rights on land and sea, let millions be called," said a Nebraska congressman. "For an allied European war of aggression, no men, no money." Others suggested that this was a businessman's war, a plutocratic conspiracy. Henry Cabot Lodge led those who questioned Wilson's vision of the international order. He asked how the map of the world could be redrawn according to self-determination without cleaving populations and destabilizing others, wondered what role force would play in guaranteeing collective security, and suggested that an international league might interfere with Congress's power to declare war. Would not membership in such a vaguely defined organization demand that the United States sacrifice sovereignty without limit? Lodge had supported a league based on a legal framework, a league with clear rules, expectations, and enforcement mechanisms; a mandate that went deep but not far. He understood that "everything here depends on details." To Wilson, details did not matter so much. The league was, he said, "in my view a matter of moral persuasion more than a problem of juridical organization."

The moral persuasion campaign at home had already begun. Wilson's supporters at the *New Republic* were calling Germany's aggression against the Allies "a war against the civilization of which we are a part." Large segments of the population still opposed sending soldiers to Europe, but the prowar drumbeat drowned out antiwar voices. The church was particularly belligerent, "the handmaid of nationalism," complained Norman. But hawks were hard to counter. They argued that the war was a fight for both freedom and security, and those who disagreed, they suggested, were weak and unpatriotic.

+

It was called a war for democracy, but the majority of Americans probably did not support entering the war. To Norman, that was a bitter irony, and if he could prove it, possibly a powerful one. Referenda had been a popular progressive measure, and several antimilitarists suggested that the government hold a referendum on the war. Norman wanted to help shape it; he had a plan. As a little-known minister in a poor neighborhood who had just passed his thirty-second birthday, however, he did not have much influence. So he turned to those who did. He wrote to the Executive Committee of the American Union Against Militarism and urged it to take the lead in conducting the referendum. It might "unite friends of democracy" whether they were pacifists or not, he wrote, and would be a "service to humanity."

The members of the Executive Committee were impressed by the young clergyman's letter, and they invited him to attend an emergency meeting to discuss his proposal. Around lunchtime on Saturday, February 10, Norman traveled the hundred blocks downtown and walked into a room that held nine of the leading antiwar liberals in the nation, among them *Nation* and *New York Evening Post* owner Oswald Garrison Villard, grandson of William Lloyd Garrison; the progressive *Survey* editor Paul Kellogg; and Emily Balch, a professor at Wellesley (and future winner of the Nobel Peace Prize). The lawyer Crystal Eastman was present, as was her brother, the bon vivant journalist Max Eastman. With his languid eyes and finely shaped mouth, he was as gorgeous as his sister, and as charming. Lillian Wald, the settlement worker, presided. Norman impressed them with his presentation, and at the following meeting they voted to invite him to join the Executive Committee. It was a significant moment in Norman's life. The AUAM was probably the most important antimilitarist group in the country. If any organization had a chance of throwing a wrench into the war machine, this one did. It also brought him into close contact with some of the leading reformers in the country—and gave him his first real exposure to politics and the workings of the state.

His referendum proposal sputtered out, but Norman immediately assumed an active role on the committee. Just after joining, he traveled to Washington to watch the Senate debates concerning a "spy bill." Created from several bills proposed by the Department of Justice, it would, among other measures, make it a crime punishable by life in prison to spread information causing "disaffection" or to "interfere" with the military. The law would not only punish treason but would also give the government the power to infringe upon speech and suppress dissent. The bill did not make it through the House before Congress's session ended, but its passage in the Senate disturbed and disheartened Norman and the AUAM members. A meeting with Wilson on February 28 was even more depressing. Pressure for war mounted with each passing hour. The day before, the papers had reported that a British liner had been sunk without warning off the Irish coast, and an American mother and child had died in a lifeboat. Where once Wilson had spoken like an ally, now he distanced himself, resigned, aloof, and stern. To a group of Emergency Peace Federation members that followed the AUAM delegates, he said that he had no choice. His hope, noted Jane Addams, was that entering the war would give him leverage in the eventual peace negotiations, instead of being forced to "call through a crack in the door." He needed a seat at the table.

·╬·

Wilson had good reason for being stony that day. He was about to authorize the release of a German telegram, secretly intercepted and decoded by the British, from the German foreign minister, Arthur Zimmermann. In it, Zimmermann encouraged Mexico to invade the United States as part of a military alliance with Germany and Japan and offered Texas, New Mexico, and Arizona to Mexico as spoils. Wilson knew what the effect of the telegram would be. The war had come home.

From Germany's perspective, the Zimmermann telegram was a disaster. Mexico had rebuffed the overture anyway, inclined to consider the withdrawal of the American commander in Mexico, John Pershing, and the American troops (completed by February 5) a satisfactory victory. But the British government's decision to give the telegram to the Americans worked brilliantly toward the Brits' purpose. The war, once "Europe's war," was now plausibly an issue of the United States' national defense. The matter of the U-boats and maritime violations had not incensed the public as it had Wilson; submarines were far away and below the surface, out of sight. Now the threat became vivid, especially in the West and Midwest, where the peace sentiment had been strongest. "The Prussian Invasion Plot," newspapers called it. Pro-Germans and erstwhile pacifists hastily proclaimed their undivided loyalty to the United States of America. Those who were already hawks could hardly contain their fury. If Wilson refused to go to war, Theodore Roosevelt wrote to Henry Cabot Lodge, "I shall skin him alive."

Norman was shaking his fist at an incoming tide. Tempers flared and old friends turned against him. At a Princeton class of 1905 dinner, the debate got so ugly that a classmate wrote to apologize to Norman afterward. "The fact that that meeting got rather out of hand has been on my conscience ever since," he said. After reading an account in the *Princeton Alumni Weekly* of a meeting at the Princeton Club in which General Wood described "a good Presbyterian" as "the last to let go of a friend's hand and of an enemy's throat," Norman whipped off a letter to President Hibben. It was bad enough, Norman said, that Hibben had barred the pacifist (and retired Stanford president) David Starr Jordan from speaking on Princeton's campus, but Wood's words were downright dangerous. "I live and work in a district where I have seen passions in labor disputes and similar matters run high," Norman wrote, "and I know the danger that threatens us from intolerance of opinion and of speech." Hibben replied by dismissing Wood's remarks as "half jesting" and then implied that Wood had been the one unfairly attacked at the debate. As for Jordan— and, implicitly, Norman—Hibben wrote, "I do not wish to have Princeton in any way directly or indirectly associated with the propaganda that seems to me at this particular time wholly unpatriotic and directly aimed at our country's honor and sense of national obligation."

David Starr Jordan could find few safe platforms as the country drew closer to war. On Sunday evening, April 1, he was speaking on behalf of the Emergency Peace Federation in Baltimore when a crew of nearly a thousand—led by professors at Johns Hopkins University—streamed in and started down the aisles to storm the stage. A quick-thinking person in the antiwar audience began to sing "The Star-Spangled Banner," and the rest of the audience joined in, bringing the mob to a halt; respect must be paid to the flag, even when a lynching was at hand. Jordan had time to sneak out the back to safety. Throughout the night the mob roamed through Baltimore chanting, "We'll hang Dave Jordan to a sour apple tree!"

The antiwar allies began to crack along numerous fault lines. The nature of the enemy had become clarified: Germany was hostile to the United States, eager to destabilize the country and threaten American citizens. Rabbi Stephen Wise, who had been one of the most outspoken antimilitarists, resigned from the AUAM, emotionally telling the Executive Committee that he thought that the threat from Germany was greater than the threat of militarizing the United States. Others became prowar because they believed their early support would give them the power to moderate the means by which it was waged, and that it would be easier to work from within the system than in opposition. Liberals like Wilson saw entering the war as an opportunity to participate in the peace, to shape a new liberal international order. Some liberals went further: They not only believed terrible means might justify exalted ends, but they were also convinced they could manipulate the externalities of waging war for the good of society, at home and abroad. The necessity of mobilizing the economy for war could create an opportunity to instill a more just distribution of goods and services, a smoother and more efficient bureaucracy, a more vibrant public life, and a new consideration of the social contract. If liberals established their position of power early, they could diminish the chance that businessmen would stand to gain the lion's share of profits from the reorganized economy. The pragmatist philosopher John Dewey used his perch at the *New Republic* to become one of the most eloquent exponents of hope—tentative but definite hope—for the possibilities of war. He wanted to turn the nation into a laboratory and thought that wartime could create those experimental conditions. Dewey hoped liberals could grasp the "instrumentality" of war and direct it for the good of mankind. Dewey was no Roosevelt; he was not jingoistic. Yet he was driven, he said, by "a vague but genuine vision of a world somehow made permanently different by our participation in a task which taken by itself is intensely disliked."

Norman read the *New Republic* regularly and admired Dewey, but this was just the logic that Norman found bankrupt. The Great War was not a "task" that was "intensely disliked"; it was slaughter, and Norman thought it was wrong. He did not respond to Dewey's article directly, but when others suggested that the war would have a positive social outcome, he tended to reply that was more likely to increase distrust and intolerance than produce order and democracy. If war was a tool, then it was a bludgeon, and one could not control what it smashed. Norman's own efforts to articulate a response to "the present crisis," though, did not produce his finest work. Drafting an article, he circled around the ideas that war cannot be ended by war; the irony of fighting for "freedom" alongside a Russian autocrat and for self-determination alongside the British Empire; and the dangers of militant nationalism. They never really cohered into an argument, and the article quickly devolved into a string of rhetorical questions. He ended them with a sentimental flourish. "What then shall America do? Acquiesce in wrong? A thousand times no; but let her protest be to the conscience of the nations."

"Deeper still," he added, lurked another question: "Where is God?" For that, for now, he had a minister's answer: "God promises us knowledge of this teaching as we do *His Will*, and answers to our prayers as we try to do the good we know."

Consolation was hard to come by, though. When, in March, Brown remarked that preparations for war had "the effect of a great revival on the life and spirit of young men at New Haven," Norman responded that that reactionary forces would follow, just as brutalities against blacks had followed the noble work of the Civil War. The spirit of internationalism would give way to a hateful nationalism and ethnic conflicts. His experience in East Harlem had made him sensitive to the persistence of strife and its manipulation by the upper classes. Wilson had already shown himself willing to use xenophobia as a way of uniting native-born Americans against the most convenient target, immigrants. His record on race was shameful, even for his own time.

Norman predicted the worst. "Race passions and prejudice will be terribly played upon by our papers," Norman wrote to a friend. "Conscription seems almost inevitable. Certain money interests will use the war for their own ends. This is no way to serve ideal ends."

-+-

While everyone waited for Wilson to act, convulsions wracked the world. In the United States, a general strike by railroad unions aiming to enforce the new and largely ignored law establishing the eight-hour workday was barely averted. Fighting in Congress became so aggressive that during a battle over a bill to arm neutral ships, the antiwar Wisconsin senator Robert La Follette placed a loaded gun in his desk; his alarmed son had to calm him down. In France, soldiers threatened to mutiny. Russia suffered the worst chaos—chaos that would change the course of history. The starving masses filled the streets of Petrograd, searching not for revolution but for food. There was none, and the crowd turned violent. The huge military and police presence did nothing at first. And then it joined the rebellion. The Russian Revolution had begun.

Through the dark glass of their hope, many progressives—liberals and socialists alike—watched what was happening in Russia with great optimism, Norman included. They were witnessing the overthrow of a despotic regime. Czarist Russia covered nearly one-sixth of the world's surface and had a population of 120 million, five-sixths of whom were peasants. Its literacy rate at the end of the nineteenth century was less than 20 percent. Nicholas's grandfather had instituted a series of reforms meant to liberalize Russia, including abolishing serfdom and opening up the press, but when he was assassinated in 1881 Nicholas's father had ended the reforms, cracked down on dissent, and banned local councils and local languages. Non-Orthodox religious believers faced discrimination. Jews were massacred. Nicholas could be sweet and intelligent; he was a loving husband and father. But he was needy and isolated, and his father was the only role model for a ruler that he had.

Nicholas and his German wife, Alix, cultivated a homey domesticity—dogs, children, plain food—but the food was served on silver platters, the imperial household boasted a staff of 16,500 (including four, dressed in white turbans and Turkish slippers, whose only job was to open the doors to Nicholas's study). The czar closeted himself so totally that he hardly knew he was closeting himself; he had little idea what was really happening in his country until it was far too late. The people were starving to death. When the president of the Duma, Mikhail Rodzianko, cabled Nicholas in March 1917—after civilians had begun to revolt—to tell him that the garrison was joining the uprising, Nicholas simply suspended the Duma. "Fat Rodzianko has sent me some nonsense which I shall not even bother to answer," he told his senior commander. He would not have had a chance to answer if he had tried. Eight months later, Lenin ordered Nicholas and his family shot.

But that was to come. When Nicholas abdicated on March 15, liberals across the world cheered. Wilson himself described the Russian Revolution as a demonstration of that "yearning desire" for freedom and self-governance. Some of the enthusiasm sprang from relief: The presence of a repressive despot among the Allied "freedom fighters" had been a source of some embarrassment for American interventionists, liberal and conservative alike. For liberals, the revolution was vindication of their hopes for a new liberal international order. It had become "as certain as anything human can be," wrote Walter Lippmann, "that the war which started as a clash of empires in the Balkans will dissolve into democratic revolution the world over." It would be the first real test of whether Marxist socialism would work. Norman was among those who were elated at the autocratic czar's overthrow.

Germany's chancellor, Bethmann-Hollweg, was wondering how to exploit the chaos. Deciding that the most promising strategy would be to boost the extreme radicals challenging the moderates for power, he arranged for a train to carry a group of political exiles in Switzerland— including the professional revolutionary V. I. Lenin—back to their home country. The train was sealed shut until it reached Russia.

-+-

And still Wilson remained cloistered. He almost never left the White House except to play golf. By mid-March, the country was more or less waiting for him to ask for a declaration of war, though it was still by no means united. A national referendum might still have rejected joining the war. But Wilson was trying to understand the implicit will of the people in his own way, as he always had. While passions ran so high, he kept his head down. He knew worse was to come. On March 19, Wilson granted a rare interview to his friend Frank Cobb, a reporter for the *New York World*. "Once lead this people into war," Cobb recorded Wilson saying, "and they'll forget there ever was such a thing as tolerance. To fight you must be brutal and ruthless, and the spirit of ruthless brutality will enter into the very fibre of our national life, infecting congress, the courts, the policeman on the beat, the man in the street." He did not say, "and the president," but perhaps he should have. A thread of ruthlessness had already wound its way into his own fiber, and the weave would only tighten. He had not been above stirring up paranoia about "hyphenated Americans" or anti-German sentiment. Wilson's words to Cobb sound, on the surface, noble and prescient, and that is how admiring historians of Wilson have tended to describe them. Critics of Wilson usually focus on disputing the conversation's veracity. Few notice the chilling passivity of Wilson's words. He was the leader—yet he was wholly absent from this scene, describing it as if from the distance of an observer, not the man who would make it happen. At least according to Cobb's notes, he did not say once, "*I* lead the people into war." He did not say, "*I* must be brutal."

The cabinet met the next day. They discussed the Zimmermann telegram, unrestricted submarine warfare, and the weakened state of the Allies. They also briefly talked about the larger grounds for fighting the war. Lansing recorded in his diary his suggestion that Wilson should stress "the duty of this and every other democratic nation to suppress an autocratic government like the German because of its atrocious character," and so appeal to "every liberty-loving man the world over." Wilson, Lansing wrote, responded simply: "Perhaps."

When Wilson asked the cabinet members whether he should request a declaration of war, they agreed unanimously. The postmaster general said that the public had made up its mind. Wilson answered, "I do not care for popular demand. I want to do what is right, whether popular or not." When a member asked him whether he had decided to ask for the declaration, he said he would "sleep on it." The following day, he summoned Congress for a special session on April 2, 1917.

Exalted ends had to justify terrible means. Wilson had a particular grievance: violations of neutral rights and maritime law. But he could not ask millions of young men to sail thousands of miles to a killing field because some submarines were sinking British ships. To find the myth that would justify the sacrifice, Wilson looked to his liberal internationalism. He brilliantly connected America's founding myth to the present demands, and to a vision of a future in which American ideals knitted together the world. It was an act of rededication that established new normative possibilities, that harkened to the hope of universal human rights. But it was also mythmaking. When he stood before Congress on April 2, he promised something he could not deliver.

Thirteen

LET EVERY MAN BE FAITHFUL

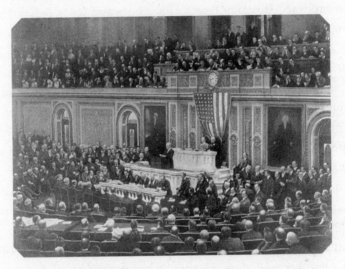

*"It is a fearful thing to lead this great peaceful people into war,
into the most terrible and disastrous of all wars," President
Woodrow Wilson told Congress on April 2, 1917.*

They withstood the rain and wind to cheer him. When Wilson traveled along Pennsylvania Avenue from the White House to the Capitol on Monday, April 2, Americans lined the route and waved their sodden flags. Once Congress was ready—it had been a long and contentious day on the floor—Wilson entered the House to applause. Gravely, he asked that Congress "formally accept the status of belligerent which has thus been thrust upon it" and then sounded his great themes: a peace based on the principles that were native to America but that he believed were found within the heart of every man and woman across the world. The close of his speech included its most remembered lines. They not only reflected but also impacted the nation's sense of itself, as one historian put it, "in all its arrogance and innocence," and of the promise that the Declaration of Independence had so boldly made.

> It is a fearful thing to lead this great peaceful people into war, into the most terrible and disastrous of all wars, civilization itself seeming to be in the balance. But the right is more precious than peace, and we shall fight for the things which we have always carried nearest our hearts, for democracy, for the right of those who submit to authority to have a voice in their own governments, for the rights and liberties of small nations, for a universal dominion of right by such a concert of free peoples as shall bring peace and safety to all nations and make the world itself at last free. To such a task we can dedicate our lives and our fortunes, everything that we are and everything that we have, with the pride of those who know that the day has come when America is privileged to spend her blood and her might for the principles that gave her birth and happiness and the peace which she has treasured. God helping her, she can do no other.

The last line comes from Martin Luther. "To go against conscience is neither right nor safe," Luther had said. "Here I stand. I can do no other."

✛

"I have just finished reading President Wilson's speech, and a very wonderful thing it is," Evan wrote his mother the next day, April 3, from a train moving through the green hills and small towns of northern Wales and England. Evan "personally" was no less a pacifist, he emphasized, but neither was he any less an admirer of Wilson. "As president of the USA I suppose he had no other choice really than that which he took," Evan conceded rather cheerfully. Germany's government was "wretched" and the American people apparently wanted to fight. Wilson had done his duty as the representative and champion of the people's will. He had done what he had to do. Now it was up to Evan to do the same, but he still needed to figure out just what that was.

For a moment it seemed as if a weight was lifted—but then, just as quickly, Evan felt the burden as never before. With a frenetic urgency extreme even for Evan, he searched within himself for what to do, think, and believe. He had a central animating idea, but since that idea was precisely that man is obligated to search within himself for what to do, think, and believe—which he was already doing—he had little way of grounding his obligation in practical action. Fixated on the idea of following his conscience, he neglected the content of it. His ultimate desire was to be able to stand up and say, *Here I stand and can do no other.* But he overlooked Martin Luther's other famous words about conscience: "If conscience is separated from the Word of God, it is like a ball which is kicked about the earth." Luther believed it would be dangerous to disconnect conscience from the Bible. Evan had long ago rejected the idea that Scripture contained the infallible word of God. He believed that man's inner voice reflected God's voice, however distorted by human understanding. There was *no external authority*, he wrote again and again, underscoring his words. Not even the Bible. Now with renewed pressure on himself to follow his logic to its end, he went even further. He had taken the idea that the truth of Christianity was found not in theology but in the life of Jesus as far as it could go. Now, he abandoned the idea of Christ's divinity. Jesus was not the Son of God but only a man; and a man is on his own. "There may be some truth in the trinity," he wrote to his mother, "but I can't fathom it."

Evan had said vaguely irreligious things to his parents in the past ("I still think theology is the work of the devil," he had written in 1916), and the idea that there is no external authority—that man can discover the truth within himself—can be seen as an extension of the Protestant conscience. But he knew he was breaking a connection. He was the son and grandson of ministers, and he had spent more than three years studying to be a minister himself. Repudiating the pulpit would change his identity, and it would raise the stakes of his actions. If he could no longer justify his intransigent insistence on his conscience as a religious belief, then the burden upon him to stick to his stances was even greater. In the past, he had suggested that even his most heretical statements actually reflected the true Christianity, cleansed of the corruptions of the institutional church. Now he was saying there was no such thing as the true Christianity. Always mindful of hypocrisy, he decided that if he could not accept the fundamental idea of Christianity, then he could not call himself a Christian.

He knew that leaving the church would hurt his mother. Telling her may have been the hardest part of his decision. It took him more than a week to write the letter, composing draft after draft and discarding each one. He pleaded with Emma to understand that he was not trying to reject his parents' and grandparents' central commitments. "Your lives for me will always be an inspiration and a help," he wrote. "They will always quicken my aspirations, serve to hold me more faithfully to the ideals I long for, help to keep me from discouragement, and strengthen my faith in that which is beautiful, and true and loving."

That January, he left Edinburgh and his job at St. George's Church to become a full-time YMCA worker in prisoner-of-war camps around Britain. He made his refusal to proselytize known to the YMCA before he accepted the job. In many respects, his religion remained what it had been: a theology of conscience. For years, he had insisted that truth did not reside in Scripture (though some truths did) or rest in the judgment of experts (though they had insights to teach) or emerge from the organization of society (though social circumstances mattered). Truth was not wholly the provenance of Christianity and the United States. It lay within every person, and it was accessed by his or her conscience. The primacy of the individual was the fixed principle around which he had spun for a long time. The fundamental challenge—what to do, how to act, how to follow one's conscience—remained. The entrance of the United States into the war made the challenge more urgent. After reading Wilson's war message, Evan had spent a week questioning his pacifism. When he triumphantly declared himself a pacifist once more, he had traveled far to come full circle. He had, after all, sailed across the Atlantic to Scotland in the fall of 1915 carrying a book by the apostle of nonresistance, Tolstoy.

Still, Evan lurched through the spring. In early June, he said that he "felt like a man who had been on a three months' debauch." He quit his job with the YMCA, uncomfortable that it involved "using the name of Christ," but a month later, he was still working for the YMCA in the POW camps around Great Britain and Ireland. He confessed to his mother that he so badly wanted "something positive to do" that he sometimes thought of enlisting as a soldier, before the certainty that war was wrong would wash over him again. Those moments suggest there was something painful about the demands of conscience, something that drove him to seek an escape from his lonely road of grueling inaction. To be at the front, to fight alongside others, he wrote, would be a "relief."

"To my mind there are only two ways of humbling Germany," he wrote to his mother that spring. "Beat her soundly at her own game. That she will understand, because it is her way. Or there is the other way." That, of course, was to abjure force altogether and embrace nonresistance. He was not deaf to the argument that going to war was the lesser of two evils, but he believed there was a way for an individual to resist evil without doing evil. "The abandonment of the use of force altogether," wrote Evan, marked "the way of the only true freedom, and therefore the way of love." It was his old theme, barely reworked. Still, there was a softness to him now. His words had lost the swollen and bruised quality of being beaten against the wall. He wrote with a degree of care, even tenderness, that lightened his lines.

> There is only one way by which I can prove that mine is the true way, and that is by my life and example. That is the only way any of us can prove the value of our different points of view and ideals. To compel a man by physical force, against his will, is not to establish the truth one way or the other, unless it be true that force is the greatest power and greatest truth in the universe. . . . Let every man be faithful to his own vision, granting the same privilege to his neighbor, and for the first time the truth will be given an opportunity to come to its own in the heart of mankind. But, if each individual waits for his neighbor to be tolerant before he begins, the Kingdom of God will never be seen on this earth.

He thought about returning to the United States to see if his life and example might make a difference there. He wanted to test the value of his point of view and protest conscription. "If I could be of more use in America I would like to return," he wrote to Norman. "Or if there is really likely to be conscription, I would like to return."

+

Norman thought there was really likely to be conscription, but he was not ready to tell his brother to come home. He was still trying to decide what to do himself. The declaration of war put Norman and his antimilitarist colleagues in a bind. They had to ask themselves whether it was more important to be true to one's principles and accept a role defined by protest, or whether it was better to compromise one's convictions with the hope of gaining influence. This question is one of the central problems of politics, but Norman felt it powerfully and perhaps for the first time.

To some, the choice was obvious. Now that the war was a settled fact, liberals—especially progressive pragmatists, who focused not on niceties like natural rights but on how to organize society with a view to the common good—were determined to make the most of it. They were practical, they argued, where the antimilitarists were impractical; they could get things done. Some of the antimilitarists were pragmatists themselves, and the indictments of their erstwhile allies made them uncomfortable. The mood was tense on Tuesday, April 3, the day after Wilson's speech, when the Executive Committee of the AUAM met to discuss the next phase of its existence. The members knew well that any overt criticism of the government might endanger their access to the upper echelons of Washington. It might also make them appear disloyal to their nation in a time of war. To emphasize its patriotism, the group "ceased all opposition" to the United States' entry into the war.

If the American Union Against Militarism was not to going oppose military intervention by the United States, its members had to rethink what "Against Militarism" meant. A few saw an answer. If militarism was objectionable because it used coercion to demand absolute submission, then it was important to preserve the right to live free from coercion. It would be especially important during a war ostensibly waged against the tyranny of "Prussianism." Because a fully mobilized society tended toward absolutism and conformity, then there was a role for those who reminded the government of their obligation to preserve freedom. This position had practical policy implications. Conscription was naturally coercive. So were limitations on free speech. There was a role for people who worked to defend citizens' rights to freedom of conscience. "Unless a people retains its liberty to discuss freely according to conscience," Norman wrote, "it loses its soul."

Americans had said this kind of thing since the nation's founding, but they usually thought about freedom of speech as an ideal or platitude. In the early twentieth century, there was no legal tradition establishing the First Amendment as a protected right and no organizations seeking to establish such a tradition, save for one tiny group called the Free Speech League founded a few years before. Nearly everyone accepted the idea that free speech could be limited when the national interest demanded it. "Rights" themselves were suspect. During the early twentieth century, many liberals associated individual rights with Victorian selfishness, too often used to justify an individual's own interests against the common good. Natural rights tended to be framed in economic terms, like the right to contract. Progressive liberals tried to not be careless with talk of rights—the discourse of democracy relied upon the open exchange of ideas—but their emphasis was on the common good. Rights were human constructs, and like any human construct, they were contextual, not inherent. As John Dewey reasoned, if the government could ration sugar and gasoline, then it should be able to limit some speech. Other citizens had a more basic sense that maximum freedom was fine during peacetime, but extraordinary circumstances called for extraordinary measures. Only hours after Wilson's war message, the Justice Department again called for a spy bill. The only measure in the bill that engendered serious opposition was censorship of the press (something Wilson wanted but newspapers campaigned vigorously, and successfully, against).

The AUAM loudly advocated the right to free speech. This made sense, since some members were journalists, and since the group's role as a watchdog depended on its ability to air grievances against the government. The Bill of Rights seemed clear enough. The antimilitarists were less united, though, on what to do about conscientious objectors. Defending "freedom of conscience" was like defending the right to life, liberty, and the pursuit of happiness—good in theory, but intangible and practically impossible to secure directly. Trying would only distract them and damage their ability to prevent more pressing wartime abuses, some members argued. How could the AUAM oppose conscription without opposing the government's efforts to raise and train an army? How could they oppose the government without becoming a "party of opposition"? For the moment, the group tabled the issue, but a few of the younger members, especially one named Roger Nash Baldwin, would not let it go.

Baldwin, a Harvard graduate Norman's age, was more forceful and more inclined to lead than Norman was. Baldwin had been living in St. Louis before moving to New York to work for the AUAM. In St. Louis, he had founded the sociology department at Washington University, served on the St. Louis Juvenile Court and in the National Probation Association, worked in a settlement house, and gained a reputation as a leading social worker. He moved easily between high-society balls and meetings attended by the anarchist Emma Goldman. Strong-willed and quick-tempered, Baldwin did not mix easily with everyone, but he and Norman became instant friends and natural allies. Baldwin came to his conception of freedom of conscience from a secular humanitarian, not a religious, perspective, but their similar backgrounds and shared cause cemented their friendship. They shared, too, the conviction that real freedom requires freedom of conscience, and though they were both younger and less established than their colleagues, they were both stubborn. Their colleagues sometimes found their implacability irritating and obstructionist. "I believe that mutual understanding with the government is very important," wrote one Fellowship of Reconciliation member to Norman. She recommended that the group abandon the word "conscription" in favor of the government's euphemisms, as a show of good faith.

Suggestions like this could make Norman testy, but he, too, struggled over what tone to take. Immediately before the United States had entered the war, he made it clear that he would resign from any organization that embarked on a high-publicity anticonscription campaign. "The only kind of organization that I will support is one that exists quietly and not for definite propaganda purpose," he warned, "save as each of us as individuals may be able at our own discretion to further our cause." But existing quietly sometimes seemed like not existing at all.

·+·

The war divided friends and colleagues across the country. The Socialist
Party split. When the war had broken out in Europe, the American Socialists
had remained united in their opposition to it, calling it an imperialists' war
and clear evidence of the impending death of capitalism. Once the United
States was in the war, however, American Socialists faced the same problem
as their European counterparts: During peace, socialism was an international movement, but when one's country was at war, nationalism was more
powerful than Marx. At an emergency convention, the majority of Socialists produced a proclamation more or less following the party's earlier line,
arguing that the war was the result of the forces of capitalism, pledging con-
tinuous and active opposition, and calling for "mass action to shorten this
war and to establish a lasting peace." The intellectuals voted against it and
then left the party altogether. John Spargo's defection made the front page
of the *New York Times*. The moderate Socialist W. J. Ghent signed his letter
of resignation to Morris Hillquit, who led the antiwar faction:

> You are my enemy and I am,
>
> Yours,
>
> W. J. Ghent.

The dissenters from the proclamation wrote their own statement in
support of the United States' entry. "Having failed to prevent the war by
our agitation, we can only recognize it as a fact and try to force upon the
government . . . a constructive program," the "Dissenting Fifty" wrote.
"We must seize the opportunity presented by war conditions to advance
our program of democratic collectivism." "A constructive program"; "the
opportunity presented by war"—the words almost sounded like they
came from the *New Republic*.

The debate in Congress that preceded the declaration of war was just as
angry. Some antiwar progressives bitterly noted that the same conservatives
who embraced the war as a fight for democracy fought legislation to expand
democratic opportunities at home. Others pointed to close financial ties
between northeastern bankers and the Allies. When Senator George Norris
suggested that the nation was "going into war upon the command of gold,"
other senators cried, "Treason! Treason!" For four days the men (and a lone

woman, Jeannette Rankin, the first ever to sit in Congress) wrangled and fought. Rankin's experience is instructive. She opposed war—she had joined the Women's Peace Party in 1915—but she was under pressure from suffragists to support it in order to increase favor for a constitutional amendment to give women the vote. During the roll call vote in the House, Rankin—reluctantly, hesitantly—stood up for herself. "I want to stand by my country, but I cannot vote for war." No speeches were allowed during roll call, and congressmen yelled, "Vote! Vote!" She voted no.

Only six senators and fifty representatives voted against the war. Onlookers, judging the tenor of the debate, murmured that if the vote had been secret, the outcome might have been different. Still, most of the votes were cast with excitement. A sense of making history spurred the yeas. Illinois representative Frederick Britten said that he felt "something in the air, gentlemen, destiny, or some superhuman movement, something stronger than you and I can realize or resist . . . forcing us to vote for this declaration of war when away down deep in our hearts we are just as opposed to it as are our people back home."

War was declared on April 6, 1917. Throughout his life, Norman stressed that his embrace of socialism and his movement away from the church were not the results of an epiphany. There was no day on which he felt he could say *After today, my life will be different.* But to this observer, reading his letters and diaries a century later, it is clear that April 6 was a day, perhaps *the* day, that changed his life.

Decades later, Norman would very occasionally open a marble notebook and reflect on the course his life had taken, and April 6 is a date that comes up more often than others. He cared most of all that it was Violet's birthday, and he would dwell on how much she liked to make a fuss of it. But he would also record that it was the anniversary of the day the United States declared war, and he would sometimes note that April 6, 1917, was Good Friday. On the page, they sat in a line: the birth of his wife, the death of Jesus, the start of war.

✛

Two days after the declaration of war, Billy Sunday started his New York campaign. It was Easter, and the sixty-five-year-old minister was still in fighting form. He preached in Washington Heights, at Broadway and West 168th Street, in a wooden tabernacle that had been specially constructed to "fit his voice," reported the *Times*. "In these days all are patriots or traitors, to your country and the cause of Jesus Christ," Sunday said that Easter, before leaping atop the pulpit and frantically shaking an American flag as tens of thousands of onlookers went wild.

Norman had dreaded Billy Sunday's arrival in New York, struggling to explain to the members of the Presbytery why he would not support Sunday's visit. He pointed to Sunday's "arrogance, narrowness, lack of perfect sincerity, trust in force rather than love." It was even harder to deal with some of his colleagues, though. Norman expected the worst from Sunday, but he was disappointed to find his peers trumpeting arrogant nationalism. A few days before Wilson's war message, one minister impugned a potential pacifist as a "coward and a sneak. . . . I believe there are times when to be a pacifist is to be perilously near being a traitor. You cannot mediate with murderers." Another minister said he would not forgive the Germans until every one was shot. The Federal Council of Churches was rallying to the war cause, and some of Norman's mentors, including William Adams Brown, were taking visible roles.

As Norman drifted away from the church, he thought it was drifting away from him. That April he handed more control of the American Parish over to his assistant, Sid Lovett, and became the co-executive secretary of the Fellowship of Reconciliation, the Christian pacifist organization. He was away from East Harlem more often anyway, delivering speeches and traveling to Washington, where he pressured Congress to reject conscription and the spy bill. Everywhere he went, he was appalled at how easily men parroted received arguments without thinking about their meaning. When he saw a slew of slogans pasted to the wall of a D.C. restaurant, he ruefully thought it a "parable of the state of our minds," as he told a group of Quakers. "My country right or wrong." "Let us have peace." "There is a higher law than the Constitution." The clichés were contradictory, but it hardly mattered. They had become meaningless.

Sometimes the debates over conscription were so absurd they seemed humorous. During the debate over the war declaration, the Speaker of the House, a Missourian named Champ Clark, had memorably quipped, "In the estimation of Missourians there is precious little difference between a conscript and a convict." Some congressmen who had voted for the war seemed to have forgotten or ignored the business of sending soldiers to Europe altogether. When an aide to the secretary of war testified before the Senate Finance Committee regarding the War Department's request for three billion dollars, he explained that the budget would cover "clothing, cots, camps, food, pay . . . and we may have to have an army in France." "Good Lord!" responded the committee chair. "You're not going to send soldiers over there, are you?" No one bothered to correct him. Testifying before Congress, Secretary of the Treasury William Gibbs McAdoo argued that if the United States gave large loans to the Allies, the dollars would be "substitutes for American soldiers." Some took him more literally than others. The draft was not a given. As late as April 18, the House Military Affairs Committee reported out a bill without military conscription by a 13–8 vote.

Americans remained suspicious of conscription for many reasons. The *New Republic* weighed in to argue that conscription would unfairly burden not only conscientious objectors but also the "nervously defective," men who would find battle too terrible to bear. Even those who wanted to fight worried that the draft diminished the glory of self-sacrifice. Was it really a noble sacrifice if you were among men who were not there by choice? There was little historical precedent for the draft. During the Civil War, the legal practice of buying substitutes had meant that only a small fraction of soldiers—less than 8 percent of the Union Army—were drafted, and even so the draft had caused huge riots in Northern cities. The supporters of the Civil War–era bill had tried to frame their scheme as a tax, not a draft, by pointing to the substitute provision. There was also historical, if not legal, precedent that conscription was unconstitutional. During the War of 1812, Daniel Webster had led the opposition to proposed draft bills, calling them illegitimate. "Where is it written in the Constitution . . . that you may take children from their parents, and parents from their children[?]" Webster asked. None of those bills had passed.

The nineteenth-century argument was about how to interpret the Second Amendment, which regulates militias. The anticonscription forces focused on the First. How the government treated conscientious objectors would be a test of its toleration for dissent. Freedom of conscience, after all, was among the oldest ideals in America. The government had long worked to protect it, even during wartime. During the Revolutionary War, George Washington had written to a Quaker leader to reassure him that Quakers would not be forced to fight. "I assure you very explicitly, that in my opinion the conscientious scruples of all men should be treated with great delicacy and tenderness: and it is my wish and desire, that the laws may always be extensively accommodated to them, as a due regard for the protection and essential interests of the nation may justify and permit." But Washington directed his words toward an established religious organization—the Quakers—and not toward individuals or secular groups. The question of "the protection and essential interests of the nation," furthermore, left a door wide open. It was a monumental task to expand the nation's small army into the force of millions that the government estimated was required. The situation in Europe was growing more dire each day, as an endless parade of Allied dignitaries and military leaders into Washington reminded Wilson and his advisers.

Wilson had a tremendous number of problems to deal with, and quickly. He was not about to be slowed by a few antimilitarists. He needed the draft, if only to keep Teddy Roosevelt from galloping onto the battlefield with a herd of Ivy Leaguers behind him. Wilson knew the war did not have the support of the whole country. Outside of Princeton, where so many students had wanted to enlist that administrators had promised to jettison academics for military training if war was declared, Wilson would have a hard time depending upon voluntary enlistments. There were other arguments for the draft. Some argued that it would forge a common American identity from disparate backgrounds, creating a brotherhood of the trenches. "Universal training will jumble the boys of America all together, shoulder to shoulder, smashing all the petty class distinctions that now divide, and prompting a brand of real democracy," argued one Wilson adviser. (Of course, there was a limit to how much "jumbling" would be permitted; there were still segregated units.) The *New York Times* put the sentiment more insidiously, editorializing that the draft "gives a long and sorely needed means of disciplining a certain insolent foreign element in this nation."

Wilson knew the draft would have to be conducted intelligently, though. He understood that one of the war's greatest battles would be for American minds. The country had not been united behind the decision to go to war, so Wilson tried to unite it after the fact. By philosophy and temperament, Wilson could not brook anything less than a display of unity. Almost immediately after he asked for a declaration of war, he began exploring options for dealing with dissent. He turned to a muckraking journalist named George Creel, who immediately told him not to use the word "censorship," and avoided the word "propaganda" himself. On April 13, Wilson established a "Committee on Public Information" under Creel. The committee comprised only the most visible part of the movement to combine the exigencies of war mobilization with the spirit of voluntarism. To conscript men and material, the government understood that it needed to conscript the mind and spirit first. Every wartime government becomes a machine oiled by euphemism, and the Wilson administration knew how to grease the wheels better than most. Immediately, it substituted the phrase "selective service" for "conscription." Selective—drawing from the elite, the special. Service—a voluntary sacrifice, an American ideal.

·+·

When Norman, Lillian Wald, and Jane Addams met with Secretary of War Newton Baker in Washington on Wednesday, April 11, to discuss the army bills being debated in Congress, Baker greeted them kindly. Addams was one of his heroes, and he knew and admired Wald as well. Before joining Wilson's cabinet, Baker had been a reformist mayor of Cleveland; in those days, he had called himself a pacifist. Now, of course, things were different, but peace activists considered him a potential ally inside the administration, or as close to an ally as they were likely to get.

Wald, Norman, and Addams were there to argue against limiting the exception from the draft to pacifist religious sects, such as the Quakers. Such a restriction, they pointed out, would run counter to their most basic conception of conscience: It is particular to a person, not beholden to a group, and in a secular society its integrity comes from its ethical commitments, not its religious sanctity. Different conscientious objectors would respond differently to various orders. Some would be willing to accept noncombatant service, working with the military but not in a position where they might be forced to kill. Others would accept alternative service, outside of the military but on farms or other areas of need. The "absolutists"—those who would accept no conscription whatsoever—would be a problem that the War Department would have to confront, but Wald, Norman, and Addams urged Baker to begin by preparing for those who would work in some capacity. They also encouraged him to study how conscientious objectors were treated in Great Britain. Mostly, they were trying to call his attention to the problem. Few others would. The meeting went well, they told each other when it was over. Baker seemed "genuinely interested," the group reported to the AUAM, and he had requested a memorandum to refer to the Senate and House committees. It appeared they might have accomplished something.

At the very least, it was a good sign. The attitude of the War Department and Congress toward them appeared to be open and generous. Members of the AUAM, led by the tireless Baldwin and the group's lobbyist in Washington, Charles Hallinan, were granted meetings and hearings. Norman appeared before the Sub-Committee of the Military Affairs Committee of the Senate on Saturday, April 21, and was pleased with how things went. By then, though, some of his optimism had already disappeared. Norman and Baldwin drew up an amendment for alternative service, and they were crushed when both the House and Senate quickly forgot it. When Norman sent the copy of the amendment to Baker, he received a response from an adjutant general instead. The inferior official replied courteously but with distance, saying that "it is contrary to its long established practice to make any comment concerning legislation pending." Norman was not Jane Addams—and it was almost too late, anyway. The bills were headed for a vote. In a last desperate attempt, Norman called Sayre, who was now the treasurer of the Fellowship of Reconciliation, and asked for help. Congress needed only a word from the president, he said. Sayre agreed to pass along a letter through his brother, Francis, Wilson's son-in-law, on behalf of the Fellowship. By the time the message reached Wilson, though, the bill had already passed both the Senate and House. "I can assure you that the point you raise . . . has by no means been overlooked," Wilson wrote to Sayre. "It has seemed impossible to make the exceptions apply to individuals because it would open the door to so much that was unconscientious," Wilson wrote. "I think you can see how that would be."

The more determined members of the AUAM refused to see how that would be. They employed Wilson's own words in their pleas. Writing to the House Committee on Military Affairs while the army bill was still in conference, Norman and Baldwin imploringly wondered how the country could "wage war 'for the privilege of men everywhere to choose their way of life and obedience' while we compel the conscientious objector to war . . . Conscience is individual or it is nothing." It did not make a difference. The version of the bill that passed did exempt objectors, but only members of a list of well-recognized religious sects.

The Wilson administration turned the draft into another opportunity to celebrate patriotic unity—"a festival," as Baker suggested to Wilson. The War Department printed up posters featuring a gaunt old man with a floppy bow tie and a poorly fitting suit, a hawk's gaze and a shaggy white brow beneath his large top hat. Scowling, he pointed straight out of the picture. This "Uncle Sam" had first appeared on the cover of the July 16, 1916, issue of *Leslie's*, under the headline "What Are You Doing for Preparedness?" Now the image said: "I want YOU." Wilson threaded the theme into his own speech. On Thursday, May 18, 1917, Wilson signed the Selective Service Act into law. "It is in no sense a conscription of the unwilling," Wilson declared. "It is, rather, selection from a nation which has volunteered in mass."

✢

By then, Ralph was already at officer training camp, a member of the Army Corps of Engineers. Since he supported his mother and young sisters, he could have claimed exemption from the draft and avoided fighting altogether, but he had little doubt of what he had to do. He was not yet thirty when Congress declared war; he was healthy, and as an engineer he had a valuable set of skills to offer the army. His country needed him. On May 14, he and the other officer candidates of New York's Fifteenth Company assembled at Plattsburgh, New York. Ralph was amused by the ragtag aspect of the other men in his company; most were older, bigger, and more experienced than the green Ivy Leaguers who had flocked to

Plattsburgh. Outside his company, though, Ralph ran into friends from all parts of his past.

Spring had come late and the trees were just beginning to bud. The days and nights were wet and cold. Violet knitted Ralph a gray sweater. He hardly ever took it off, even to sleep. Ralph was sure of his decision to enlist, but he did not dwell on it. Routine—drills, formations, marches, boiled meat and prunes—took over. When preachers sermonized on "the glory of self-sacrifice," Ralph shook his head, but he went to church services anyway. Only practicing the bayonet seems to have unnerved him: "I do not believe I would stomach it."

Fourteen

A CAGED AND CAUTIOUS LIBERALISM

"It is in no sense a conscription of the unwilling,"
Wilson declared in the proclamation of the
Selective Service Act. "It is, rather, selection
from a nation which has volunteered in mass."

Even before Norman had begun devoting time to antiwar work, he
had felt his work in East Harlem was "never done." With all the
added meetings and trips during the spring and summer of 1917,
one wonders how his pastoral work could have been done at all. Lovett
was a more than capable assistant, but the American Parish surely suffered
from Norman's neglect. He might not have seen it that way, however. His

antiwar work was related to his work in East Harlem. After all, his neighbors were the ones who would be drafted and sent to die in a war that Norman believed was waged for exploitative reasons in the first place, in a war that was not their desire. If war was in part an imperial conflict, as Norman thought it was, then it was only the most extreme manifestation of a system of brute coercion, the desire of one people to dominate another for their material and psychological gain. He could see its echo in the poverty produced by industrial capitalism. Whether from force or need, he met too many people who were crushed.

They were not even free to say as much. In the middle of April, Norman arrived at an anticonscription rally in Harlem at which he was supposed to speak only to find two thousand men and women gathered in front of the building. The door was locked, and police captain James Brady, backed by a large force, stood in front of it. This kind of treatment only exacerbated workers' rage, Norman thought. Class conflict divided the wealthy and poor, and what they shared was hate. He heard as much violence in the anger of the upper classes' indictments of pacifists and Germans as he heard in the workers' rage against the upper classes. It confounded Norman that rich men were willing to die (or send their sons to die) but refused to pay more taxes to support the war. The conscription of lives was good and necessary; the conscription of money, apparently not. Men who feared violence from the lower classes, furthermore, celebrated violence between nations. Was it only power and profit, Norman cynically wondered, that justified one conflict and not the other?

Some of Norman's friends repeated the old saw that war had a salutary effect on citizens, summoning them to sacrifice and noble virtue. But not that Norman could see. After some of his parishioners called his attention to worsening crime and lower standards of decency, he sat down at his typewriter and hammered out a letter to Captain Brady. There was increased shooting in the streets, "not only of fire-crackers but of revolvers," Norman reported to the police captain. Men were playing more craps games and for higher stakes. Small shops sold cigarettes to young boys, and—God forbid—"certain of the moving picture houses are getting very careless about admitting children unaccompanied by parents or guardians." "I recognize that you have difficulties in war-time because you may be short of men," Norman wrote, his tone more sniping than conciliatory. Everyone had difficulties. In a speech delivered that spring he mentioned that at a school in his neighborhood, 13 percent of boys had been arrested at least once by the time they finished sixth grade. This was "not because of unusual inherent depravity, but because economic conditions and the home environment denied them a fair chance."

When he complained to Henry Sloane Coffin that an article he had submitted to an ecclesiastical magazine criticizing the church's acquiescence to the "industrial autocracy" had been watered down, Coffin replied that he thought the "punch" was still there. "On the whole you may congratulate yourself in having supplied the most socially striking article that will have appeared in any distinctively Presbyterian publication," Coffin wrote. But Norman wasn't satisfied. "There is a very considerable body of literature of a caged and cautious liberalism which tries to say true things in a way that will not arouse anybody's antagonism," he wrote after receiving the edits to the article. "I shall be inclined to think that we will have failed unless some of our readers disapprove pretty strongly of what we have said." Then he added, as if unable to help himself, "Please do not think . . . that I want deliberately to stir up antagonism." It had become hard to offend without really offending, and the strain was showing. His attempt to soften his criticisms with understanding and deference was never a pose; it came reflexively. Still, it wasn't easy to push with one hand and pull back with the other.

-+-

Imagine what a "worthy citizen" would have looked like ten years ago, Norman told an audience of Quakers at a meeting house in Philadelphia in May 1917, and you would probably picture a married, sober pillar of the community, a man not stingy with charity, not overly concerned with politics, and somewhat dismayed at the loss of the nation's values—in short, someone "often lovable" in his personal life but "a bit smug" and narrow-minded with regard to larger social forces. He might have been describing his father, or the man Norman might have become. "The point is," he said, "that practically all of us, men and women, who honestly thought we were lovers of Christ, of our country, and of mankind, were really fairly content with a social order which contained in it the seeds of this world catastrophe and innumerable fruits of evil and injustice. We were blind to the terrible contrasts of the principles of self-seeking which inspired business and national life and the self-forgetting love incarnated in the Christ to whom we professed allegiance." The challenge for "Christian patriots" was not only to recover that "self-forgetting love" but also to examine the social order to see how those seedlings of evil might be rooted out. It was not enough to be simply "lovable." Transformation had to extend to social relations. He wanted to take transformation seriously. In 1917, that meant grappling with socialism. But no sooner had he suggested it than he dismissed it. Socialism presented its own problems and potential injustice. Under socialism, he asked, how could people "protect individual initiative and freedom from the deadly weight, if not the actual tyranny, of an unsympathetic and unimaginative bureaucracy?"

A better solution would be a "strong voluntary co-operative of individuals which compete with one another, not for the amassing of private wealth, but in service." He had no idea how this would work, he admitted. It was a vague ideal, a dream, really. But who were Christians to mock dreamers? "Men still laugh at Jesus the dreamer, or wistfully sigh for ideals beyond their grasp," he said; "yet the dreamer has the only hope for the world."

It was an explicitly Christian dream. Not everyone would have agreed that it was really Christian, though. As he spoke to the Quakers, Norman did not buttress his arguments with the Bible. He used the writings of Bertrand Russell, a man who was avowedly *not* a Christian. Norman didn't care what Russell called himself. He thought his work had a kind of spirituality that went deeper than simple humanitarianism. Later, he would write, "I bless the day I first read Bertrand Russell's *Free Man's Worship*. For while it did not give me the emotionally satisfactory equivalent for the liberal Christian faith that I was losing it gave me solid ground for believing that life was abundantly worth living." What Norman later said he wanted from the church was simple: "forgiveness of sin, comfort in sorrow, assurance that life has eternal meaning, that in very fact the Lord is my shepherd, Jesus the lover of my soul." What he wanted in 1917, though, was justice on earth.

When Norman became the head of the Fellowship of Reconciliation, he worked on drafting a description of the group and its purpose. (Now we would call it a mission statement.) The Fellowship was not a "mere anti-war society," he claimed. It sought to substitute "Christian principles of freedom, cooperation and good-will, in place of the old political, social, and economic theories of class superiority, ruthless competition, and self-seeking." Then, more grandly, he wrote—as if to reinforce the preceding claim that the principles were "Christian"—"We are the missionaries of an internationalism based on the universal brotherhood of the children of God." Certainly, there is a long tradition within Christianity of Christians who claim that the true Christianity lies outside the organized church. (Evan was one of them, for a while.) Norman was a different case, however. As he worked to "Christianize" the world, he was secularizing himself.

The prowar stance of the church hastened the transformation. A tenured professor at Union who had advocated neutrality was fired in absentia. Ministers like Harry Emerson Fosdick, whom Norman had once admired, were rabid in their support of the war, calling it a crusade and summoning righteous rage from congregations. The governing bodies of churches sometimes discriminated against pacifist preachers, and in some cases, their congregations forced them out. What really underlay Norman's changing beliefs, though, was a more haunting problem than the clergy's bad behavior. Amid the carnage, where was God? If he was with the soldiers at Ypres and Loos, why was there so much death and destruction? How could he be love when he was also power? If he was all-powerful, had he no responsibility for the men he had made?

·+·

On Friday morning, June 1, Norman went downtown to *Nation* editor Oswald Garrison Villard's office on Vesey Street for a special meeting of the Executive Committee. Registration Day was four days away. Once men began filling out their draft cards at polling places around the city— another way of connecting the draft to civic responsibility—conscientious objection would no longer be an abstraction lost among other abstractions.

Conscientious objectors would be opposing the law, denying their obligation to bear the greatest burden of citizenship because of their individual
scruples. This made the liberals of the AUAM uneasy. The mood at the
meeting was tense. Henry Mussey, a professor of economics at Columbia
University, said that he, Wald, Addams, Kellogg, and two other members
of the committee had discussed the group's work on behalf of conscientious objectors and were against it. They did not want to appear to obstruct
the draft.

Mussey, Wald, Addams, and Kellogg had reason to be concerned, even
beyond any ambivalence toward the legitimacy of conscientious objection. Mussey's boss, Columbia University president Nicholas Murray
Butler, was openly hostile to pacifists; within a month he would prohibit
disloyal speech on campus. Kellogg cared most about encouraging international cooperation for peace, and he thought the group's activities for
conscientious objectors would damage its credibility and hurt its chance
to take part in shaping whatever peace organizations emerged in the war's
aftermath. Wald and Addams worried that the more radical stance might
interfere with their settlement house work. Already it had affected their
reputations. After Addams delivered a speech in April arguing that free
speech should be protected during wartime, the Women's Club of Chicago
informed her that she and her groups could no longer meet at their club-
house. When, during another speech, she suggested that pacifists could also
be patriots, the chief justice of the Illinois Supreme Court—a former friend
and reformer ally—stood up to disagree publicly. Admirers turned against
her. "Jane Addams is losing her grip," wrote one women's club newspaper. "She is becoming a bore." Soon, the New York Times was calling the
AUAM "the little group of malcontents." The group's members had to
assess what was possible and responsible, and some of them suspected that
the mainstream view was right: Wartime conditions had altered what kind
of criticism was legitimate.

Immediately after Wilson's war message, the group had written, "We
are not, by habit or temperament, troublemakers." And yet that is how
they were seen. The problem cut to the AUAM's greatest dilemma: How
far could it go without losing its most important asset, its access to Baker,

the president, and legislators? How far could it push its agenda before it became irresponsible, or even dangerous? And what made conscientious objectors so special that they merited respect for violating the law?

The moderate liberals of the AUAM feared that some of the younger and more radical members (such as Baldwin, Eastman, the Socialist economist Scott Nearing, and, to a lesser extent, Norman) had more revolutionary aims than simply ensuring dissenters were treated humanely. Just before the special meeting at Villard's, pacifist groups from across the country had converged at Madison Square Garden for the First American Conference of Democracy and Terms of Peace. Many of them were Socialists or had socialist leanings. The People's Council, which had organized the First American Conference, was meant to bring together the disparate and besieged peace groups in order to coordinate and strengthen the effort. But the radical cast of the organization, which took its inspiration from "New Russia," unnerved the moderates of the AUAM. They had been as heartened by the overthrow of the czar as other liberals, but reports of anarchy spreading across Russia disturbed them. So when the Russian Revolution and the Russians' progressive peace plan were invoked and cheered repeatedly at the conference, the moderate antimilitarists blanched. Already the AUAM had publicly distanced itself from the conference, but a few members were on the People's Council board, and some worried that the group would be tainted even by that association.

At that meeting on June 1, Mussey proposed that the AUAM set up an independent group that would work for the rights of conscientious objectors. It would have the support, but not the sanction, of the AUAM, and Baldwin should lead it. An argument ensued, and at times it could seem to Norman as if Baldwin and he were against everyone else. For Norman, this was uncomfortable. They were the youngest (Baldwin was thirty-three and Norman thirty-two) and the least experienced. They had both attended the First American Conference and were considered a little too radical by some. Baldwin was more confident in his ability to work through the governmental establishment than Norman, who had a more grassroots instinct. At the same time, Norman was far more deferential to the senior members of the group than Baldwin was. "I feel very sorry that we were constrained to take the position which is so different from that of many of the wisest and most prominent of the Executive Committee," Norman wrote to Oswald Garrison Villard. To Wald he was even more direct, praising her "splendid courage." But Norman agreed with Baldwin that the conscientious objector question was the most important issue of the day, the question that most urgently threw the whole idea of war into doubt.

Villard stepped into the dispute to support Norman and Baldwin. The support of Villard, who often stayed quiet during meetings (at least if meeting minutes are an indication), meant something. The editor commanded respect. His credentials were impeccable, not only because of his work but also because of his background. The forty-five-year-old publisher was the grandson of the abolitionist William Lloyd Garrison and the son of a founder of the Women's Peace Party; in addition to being an active pacifist, he was also a cofounder of the National Association for the Advancement of Colored People. Baldwin and Norman may not have had enough gravitas to carry their point on their own, but Villard's support deadlocked the committee for the day.

Later that Friday afternoon, Norman and Villard arrived at a YMCA on Twenty-third Street for a meeting of the Fellowship of Reconciliation's directing committee. On the way, they passed under countless flags and streams of bunting; Registration Day was to begin the next morning, early. Norman had asked Villard to come to the meeting. The following day, those members of the Fellowship who were between the ages of twenty-one and thirty would have to present themselves and register. Those who weren't exempt would have to choose whether to request conscientious objector status or to become soldiers. Norman did not have to worry for himself; he was over the age limit. (Even if he hadn't been, he would have been offered an exemption because he had a dependent family and was a clergyman.) Outside, last-minute preparations were under way to create a festive atmosphere for the draft. Inside, Villard's presence made a difference. Just by showing up, the grandson of William Lloyd Garrison connected the group to the long tradition of the fight for social justice, the fight for freedom. For what was war, they asked, if not the violent attempt of one people to dominate another?

Evan's group, the Crusaders—founded by Sayre, who was now a leader in the Fellowship of Reconciliation as well—had called for a new Emancipation Proclamation. The Fellowship considered itself a kind of continuation of the abolitionist movement. For years, pacifists and reformers had made analogies between the abolition of slavery and the abolition of war and unfair labor practices; they used the term "wage slavery." Once, the abolition of slavery had been derided as a dream, just as the abolition of war and predatory labor practices were now derided. The religiosity of abolitionists had helped them keep the dream alive. It had rooted their activism in the first principles of their faith. So it was for the members of the Fellowship. They hoped to spread those "principles of freedom, cooperation and good-will" from Christianity into the secular world, until it became impossible to distinguish one from the other.

But it had taken a war—the very thing the pacifists fought against—for the abolitionists to win their battle. How could the pacifists possibly win theirs? And what, exactly, were they fighting for?

·╬·

The American Union Against Militarism had perhaps an even harder time defining its aims than did the Fellowship of Reconciliation or the Crusaders. As a secular organization adopting techniques and justifications from what had previously been the province of religious groups, the AUAM was trying to do something essentially new. It was doing it, furthermore, without the advantages of a common set of beliefs or justifications. Its membership was not even strictly pacifist (Fellowship members, on the other hand, had to sign a statement of pacifist principles grounded in Christianity). Compromises became all the more crucial and all the more difficult.

After Registration Day the Executive Committee voted to create a bureau, under the auspices of the AUAM but with some autonomy, to serve as a clearinghouse for objectors and those concerned with abuses of civil liberties. It could then claim to be working in the tradition established by the Bill of Rights. "We have no intention or desire to interfere with the government's plans for prosecuting the war," the group said in a draft of a statement to the press. "But it is the tendency, even of the most 'democratic' of governments embarked upon the most 'idealistic of wars,' to sacrifice everything for complete military efficiency." Not all the members were pacified. One committee member immediately resigned from the group, and others were wavering. Kellogg was still worried, and so was Wald. The efforts of the group to protect civil liberties, Kellogg privately wrote to Wald, could "so throw the organization out of balance" that the government would turn against the group and render it useless.

Already the AUAM had a problem. The United Press had written a story saying the group's offices were under surveillance by the Justice Department. Charles Hallinan, the group's lobbyist in the capital, reported to the committee that government agents had visited the AUAM's offices in Washington. Baldwin added that he, too, had spoken with agents, at the Justice Department's offices in New York. Neither man was concerned; both felt they had reassured the agents that the AUAM was functioning entirely within the bounds of the law and were in turn reassured that their activities would not be disturbed. Hallinan suggested suing one of the papers that ran the UP's surveillance story, but the group settled for a retraction. The AUAM's leaders could not conceive that the story might possibly be accurate. They were too confident of their good standing with the government, their good reputations. But the story was true.

The new Civil Liberties Bureau's job was about to become more difficult. That month, June 1917, Wilson signed the Espionage Act into law. The act gave the government power to fine up to ten thousand dollars or imprison for up to twenty years anyone interfering with wartime measures, and it gave the postmaster general the power to exclude from the mails anything that advocated breaking the law. This was considered the more "moderate" version of possible bills, since it did not censor the press specifically, and since it had dropped that contentious word "disaffection." But for all intents and purposes, the bill covered that, too. If a publication could not be mailed, it would not be widely read. The law, furthermore, required officials to judge the intent of speech, not just the letter. It would take a scrupulous and restrained man not to abuse such power, and Postmaster Albert Burleson, a Texas Democratic Party fixture, was not such a man. The Justice Department also took a broad view of its new mandate. Already, it had given some support to a civilian organization called the American Protective League. By June, one hundred thousand self-appointed vigilantes in six hundred cities watched their neighbors and townspeople and reported any sign of antiwar activity or dissent.

The members of the AUAM had fought the spy bill and despaired at its passage, but they hardly thought it would be used against them. They did not see themselves as enemies of the government but as friends. They did not trust Postmaster General Burleson, but they still had great faith in the president and his closest advisers, especially Secretary of War Baker. For all the Burlesons in the government, the antimilitarists could point to intelligent, capable men who were surely on the right side (their side), men who seemed a "guarantee of good faith," as Crystal Eastman put it. Wilson himself encouraged the activists to consider him an ally. He responded to their pleas to end the repression of civil liberties with a display of overt sympathy, at least at first. After receiving one petition, he replied that it, "of course, chimed in with my own feelings and sentiments." They believed him.

"We don't want to make a move without consulting you," Roger Baldwin wrote to the War Department at the beginning of June. The new Civil Liberties Bureau vetted pamphlets directly with the War Department before distributing them. It urged men of draft age who wanted to refuse to fight to register and declare their desire to be conscientious objectors, rather than dodge the draft altogether. ("Obedience to the law, to the utmost limits of conscience, is the basis of good citizenship," read its pamphlet on the draft.) It considered itself well within the bounds of the law. Baldwin went out of his way to place himself and his group "entirely at the service of the War Department in rendering any assistance that you think lies in our power to give."

What seemed like good-faith common sense turned out to be naïveté. Wilson considered unified support for the war to be essential. Tolerance of dissent was a virtue he could recognize, but it was not one he considered desirable or, in wartime, practical. Trying to drum up support for the unpopular war, he lumped together saboteurs and conscientious critics of wartime measures. He was no Teddy Roosevelt, who declared his contempt for the "white-handed or sissy type of pacifist" that represented "decadence" and "the rotting out of the virile virtues among people who typify the unlovely senile side of civilization." But in some respects, Wilson's words contributed as much to the climate of fear and hate as those of his colorful rival. Privately, the president offered reassurances to people like Lillian Wald. But publicly, he suggested that pacifists and antiwar activists were disloyal. Malevolence tinged the warnings that ran through his speeches. On Flag Day, in the summer of 1917, Wilson said that the forces of "sinister intrigue" had "learned discretion. They keep within the law. It is opinion they utter now, not sedition." He concluded, "Woe be to the man or group of men that seeks to stand in our way."

Later that year, he described his attitude toward the pacifists more honestly, but no less bluntly. "What I am opposed to is not the feeling of the pacifists but their stupidity," he said. "My heart is with them, but my mind has a contempt for them. I want peace, but I know how to get it, and they do not."

⊹

Max Eastman's magazine, *The Masses*, was among the first to fall. On July 3, Eastman submitted the next issue to the New York postmaster for inspection, as required by the Espionage Act. The postmaster called it "unmailable" due to its "general tenor." Norman did not particularly admire *The Masses*; it offended his somewhat prudish personal morality. When Eastman had asked for use of the mailing list of the Fellowship of Reconciliation for it, Norman had refused. Too many articles seemed written in order "to shock people," he responded. But he did not imagine that the federal government would suppress the paper. None of the civil liberties activists could believe it. The Civil Liberties Bureau held a press conference on July 13. "The worst thing I can say for this situation," Eastman told the crowd, stunned, "is that it actually surprises me." After Federal District Judge Learned Hand found that the postmaster had been too vague, Burleson charged *The Masses* with obstructing the draft. The subsequent trial hung two juries, but when Burleson rejected the magazine again in September, it collapsed. That summer, the Justice Department also seized copies of pamphlets published by the Civil Liberties Bureau, including one by Norman called "War's Heretics." In it, he argued for the value of free expression as essential to democracy, saying that the power of the state should never "grow to a control over men's convictions."

In October 1917, the postmaster general wrote a letter to the AUAM, published in the press, explaining his interpretation of the Espionage Act. He wanted to reassure the public, he said, that he was no tyrannical censor, but no one could have missed the implied threat: "No publisher who is at heart truly loyal to his country in this war should have any apprehension of embarrassment or inconvenience," Burleson wrote. Only the "treasonable press" that gave "aid and comfort to the enemy"—by arousing feelings against the government or its Allies or fomenting dissatisfaction among workers—need worry. Of course, radical publications existed to arouse the dissatisfaction of the workers, and talk of a negotiated peace could be construed as offering comfort to the enemy.

It was in this climate that Norman decided to start a Christian pacifist magazine. It would support conscientious objectors, oppose the Espionage Act, fight for industrial democracy, and commit any other number of offenses that Burleson would no doubt condemn. Over the summer and fall, the magazine began to take shape. It would be tied to the Fellowship of Reconciliation but not part of it. Modeled along the lines of a British pacifist publication, the *Venturer*, it would include articles about the church, war, labor, and society; it would explore conflict and encourage fellowship. It was tentatively titled the *New World*.

In Ridgefield that summer, Norman's children played games in the garden—the kaiser was the villain—while Violet, her sister, and her mother sat on the porch and knitted socks for soldiers. In New York, Norman was consumed with work. It was an exhausting summer, hot and muggy. But on the weekends, when he could get away, he relaxed in a boat on the lake, and Mondays invariably revived him. That was the day when the directing committee of the Civil Liberties Bureau met at the Civic Club on West Twelfth Street. There, perched on benches around a wooden table in a paved backyard, with a single ailanthus tree to give them shade, they lunched and talked and planned. They saw themselves as champions for those who had few defenders. When Villard had met with Judge Advocate General Enoch Crowder, the federal official in charge of conscription, Crowder had confessed that although objectors would be shipped to training camps after the draft, he had not drawn up plans for what would happen to them. There would be tribunals to set their punishment at some point, but no details had been worked out. They would be in limbo, without any clear idea of their fates. Months later, it was still that way.

At the end of the summer, Norman's work on behalf of conscientious objectors became all the more urgent and personal. Evan had decided to come home in order to register as a conscientious objector.

+

In the first week of September, Evan sailed out of Liverpool, bound for New York. It was a relief to be *doing* something. That summer in London, where the YMCA operations were based, Evan and his small group of American friends had discussed the strange numbness that sometimes overtook them, a fatalism as heavy as the English fog. When a squadron of German planes had released their bombs over London in the broad daylight of July 4, Evan's friend Kirby Page, another American YMCA worker, and hundreds of civilians had rushed outside to watch the aerial dogfight, unafraid and weirdly excited. At night, Evan lay in bed and listened to the rat-a-tat of guns and the rumbling of bombs, feeling so dejected that he hardly cared if he survived. Only the long discussions about nonresistance and pacifism awoke him from his stupor. He paced as he argued, always restless.

One evening in August, Evan and his friend Harold Gray, a Harvard student who had taken time off from school to volunteer for the YMCA, sat in a dormitory room in London discussing a recently published pamphlet called "I Appeal unto Caesar." The pacifist philosopher Bertrand Russell had ghostwritten it under the name of Mrs. Henry Hobhouse, a well-connected woman whose son Stephen, an Oxford student, had become a Quaker and was imprisoned as an absolutist conscientious objector. Its pages included the testimony of Clifford Allen, an imprisoned socialist whose objection was based on humanitarian and ethical, instead of religious, grounds. Allen, not much older than Evan, had repudiated the politics and religion of his father, an Anglican merchant active in the

Conservative Party, and become involved in the nascent Labour Party. He had already served two sentences, one of 112 days and another of six months of hard labor, for refusing noncombatant service, and he now faced prison again.

Gray flipped open the pamphlet to one of Allen's court-martial defenses. "You can shut me up in a prison over and over again," Gray read aloud to Evan, "but you cannot imprison my free spirit. The duty of every citizen is to serve his fellow-men. In all humility I believe I am being faithful to this obligation of citizenship by pursuing my present policy." Gray paused and then read the paragraph to Evan again. He did not need to; both of the young men already knew the speech so well that they had memorized parts of it. But Gray drew out the drama. *You cannot imprison my free spirit. The duty of every citizen is to serve his fellow-men.* He was acting the part.

Gray looked up from the page and told Evan that he would return to the United States to become a conscientious objector. For Evan, too, his task was clear. He left England as soon as he could, months before Gray.

Hardly had his ship pulled out of port when he ran into his friend Kirby Page and Page's boss, Sherwood Eddy, who was now the YMCA's secretary. Page and Evan's reunion—and the sense that they were sailing into the storm, even as they pulled away from war-torn Europe—made them euphoric. Without delay, they picked up the "hot old arguments" about war, challenging any comers aboard ship. Halfway through the journey, they sensed that Eddy's prowar resolve was cracking—a possibility that left them giddy. Evan had thought the YMCA was a lost cause, a tool of the military. But if he and Page could convince a man of Eddy's stature and influence to rethink the war, who knew what else they could do. Eddy's hesitation did not last, but it emboldened the young pacifists.

It thrilled them to know they were in real danger. They had heard and seen the bombs in London, but it was something else to know that beneath the ocean's steely surface lurked German U-boats. On the second day after leaving Liverpool, a cry cut through the air: "Submarine!" "Torpedo astern!" came the reply. The boat swung around and the missile sped by. The boat's guns shot at the torpedo's wake, and the sound of their report reverberated across the waves.

As the ship neared the eastern seaboard of the United States, it entered safe waters. But the young pacifists knew that they were steaming into trouble—less dangerous, but in some ways more difficult. Their families would not all or always understand. "What could pacifism do now?" Harold Gray's father wrote when he learned that Harold planned to become a conscientious objector. "Pacifists in America now are looked upon as shy mentally—'nobody home'—because they can't see or be made to see the true situation and what a calamity it would be to stop the war before the goal is reached." He was as straightforward as he could be. "Pacifism in this great crisis is disloyalty to the country."

Fifteen

A DEMOCRATIC RIGHT

American soldiers drill at training camp.

Evan's ship pulled into New York on Sunday, September 16, 1917.
Emma had come from Baltimore to meet him. It had been two years
since she had last seen her son, and so much had happened in that
time. Her husband was dead and her children were divided. She was working hard to keep them close. While they had lived apart, she had made sure
they knew of one another's thoughts and whereabouts. When she received
a letter she would list all their initials in the left-hand corner and circulate
it among the brothers, instructing each to mark himself off when he was
finished reading so that no one would be overlooked. She had sent them
articles and magazines, some that supported their own views but some
that did not. They might not agree with one another, they might not even

understand one another, but she wanted them to listen to one another. This was a considerable demand, and never more so than at that moment. All of her sons had come to New York for the reunion. With Ralph about to go to war, Evan about to test the draft, Norman pursuing his antiwar work, and Arthur—who knew what Arthur was going to do?—they must have known, even if they did not acknowledge it, that those days could be the last time they were all together.

Ralph, now a first lieutenant in the 302nd Army Corps of Engineers, Seventy-seventh Division, at Camp Upton, had taken the train into the city from Yaphank, Long Island. It was a short trip, but he was grimy and tired when he arrived. For weeks he had dreamed of a proper shower, tired, he told his mother, of washing at a faulty spigot while the training camp was still under construction. The past few days had been particularly heady and exhausting, as the first draftees arrived in camp—chauffeurs and plumbers, mechanics and accountants, an awning maker and an embalmer. Some of the men came wearing their best suits. Many did not know English. All had left their homes and families at the order of the government. They were doing precisely what Evan was protesting. So, of course, was Ralph, however hard the brothers tried to make justifying distinctions.

As complicated as the reunion must have been for Ralph and Evan, it may have been most unsettling for Arthur. He had one brother who was an officer in the United States Army. He had another who was planning on taking a decisive and difficult stand, risking prison. He had a third who was making a name for himself in prominent circles, meeting with the secretary of war and members of Congress. Arthur still searched for what to do.

He was supposed to be in China, at the Princeton Center at Peking, or Princeton-in-Peking, the Philadelphian Society's missionary outpost. The program had been founded in 1906 with the aim, as one fund-raising pamphlet put it, of countering evils that were "blasting character and enslaving men in sin. . . . PRINCETON MUST OCCUPY PEKING." In practice, Princeton-in-Peking did less character blasting than it did sociology. It had begun as a late-Victorian evangelical-imperial project and had become a classic Social Gospel venture, putting perhaps greater emphasis on vigorous exercise than the typical urban church. The organization was run by Norman's Princeton classmate and friend John Burgess, who also had a master's degree from the New York School of Social Work. Burgess had little respect for some of the more religious Princeton students he had met during his recruitment efforts; he considered them "too pious" and called them "gospel sharks." In Peking, he organized conferences with lectures like "The Relation of the Study of Sociology to Social Reform" and "The Problems of a Chinese City—What Students Can Do to Solve These Problems." At the end, he encouraged attendees to convert.

Arthur, who had been working for the YMCA in New Jersey, had initially turned down the offer to join the group, but then Robert E. Speer, a renowned figure in the Presbyterian Church, and Ralph's minister in Baltimore, John McDowell, had applied some flattering pressure. They were "very anxious indeed" that Arthur should accept. "The opportunity offered in this position is one of truly national influence." (This appeal was not such a stretch: One of Wilson's first acts as president-elect had been to offer the position of ambassador to China to John Mott, the YMCA leader. When Mott declined, Wilson wrote to his friend Dodge that he had never been "so disappointed.") In late March, just before war was declared, Arthur had accepted the Philadelphian's offer. It was unusual timing—perhaps a sign that he was ready for an adventure, or perhaps a decision made to avoid having to fight. Whatever the reason, he had spent the next few months preparing to leave. On Tuesday, July 19, his visa came through at the State Department, and he was scheduled to leave right after that.

Instead, he was in Baltimore in August, and September found him at the American Parish's summer camp and farm in Oak Ridge, New Jersey, pulling potatoes from the ground. Arthur now planned on becoming a soldier. It is unclear why he changed his mind. Any letters reflecting on Arthur's decision have not survived. He was not drafted; the visa to China was valid; he could have avoided the war. Even after he decided not to go to Peking, he spent months trying to decide which branch of the military to join (Norman advised the Air Service, because it still had "some sportsmanship in it"). He was probably like most people, not quite sure what to do or what to think but convinced that to not respond to Wilson's call would be unpatriotic. Ever since his time at Princeton, Arthur had had trouble seeing his way through the murky future. He lacked the confidence of his older brothers.

The flags and the posters, the songs and parades must have made it harder. The propaganda campaign of President Wilson's brainchild, the Committee on Public Information, for "the *minds* of men, for the 'conquest of their convictions,'" succeeded spectacularly. The CPI sent out 75,000 "Four Minute Men" who spoke as fast as possible to plug the war in four minutes. It published seventy-five million copies of more than thirty pamphlets promoting the war. It turned an unpopular war into a two-year-long Fourth of July parade. George Creel, the head of the CPI, was to keep the drive for war at a fever pitch, turning the nation into "one white-hot mass." Those who did not support the war—whether support was supposed to be "voluntary" or not—were held uncomfortably close to the heat.

After the brothers' reunion in New York ended, Arthur went down to Baltimore with his mother. Ralph returned to training camp. Evan moved in with Norman and Violet and worked as an assistant at East Harlem Presbyterian Church while he waited to be drafted.

⁘

Emma had visited Norman and his family in Ridgefield and New York earlier that summer, and she and Norman had discussed his work and the war. She was sympathetic to his causes and to his desire to act on his beliefs. (That year, she and her sister, Mary, made their own gesture, donating the land in Charlotte that they had inherited from their parents to Biddle University, in honor of the black college's fiftieth anniversary. The land was valued at thirty thousand dollars (more than five hundred thousand dollars, adjusted for inflation)—no small sum for a woman with financial worries.)

She was nervous, and Norman tried to reassure her. He was no extremist, he said; he followed his convictions as far as he felt he must but no further. Yet he moved further from the mainstream all the time.

When he had to take sides, he took sides with the radicals. The unresolved conflict over the AUAM's position on conscientious objectors flared again at the end of August and divided the group. Wald continued to worry that supporting conscientious objectors would damage the group's (increasingly notional) friendly relationships with the government, while

Kellogg, whose main concern had always been establishing a new international federation of democratic states after the war, still found defending objectors a distraction. It was impossible, he wrote to Crystal Eastman, to combine "an aggressive policy against prosecution of the war with an aggressive policy for settling it through negotiation and organizing the world for democracy." Whether idealism could survive the challenge of practical trade-offs was an unanswered question.

Norman continued to try to mediate between the radical and moderate factions in the AUAM, even as he found himself more consistently siding with the radicals. Like them, he was heartened by Russia's announced peace aims—"no forcible annexations, no punitive indemnities, [and] free development for all nationalities"—but he tried to encourage those who embraced the new Russia to reiterate their commitment to democracy. To Wald, he mixed anger with conciliation and tangled his feet. He began one letter innocently enough, emphasizing that he personally understood why the government had organized the army as it did but at the same time stressing the necessity of an "honest and open discussion" of peace proposals. He told Wald that radical groups like the People's Council played an important role in the cause. Unlike the AUAM, they reached beyond the "the great, rather stupid middleclass who are well-intentioned but easily frightened by words." Norman was usually caustic when addressing Wald, and it seems to have made him nervous. No sooner had he lashed out than he pulled back. "In times like these," he explained, "it is the more extreme opponents of the war who are likely to be the most active and the most emphatic, and there is the real danger . . . that we ourselves more or less unconsciously will tend very decidedly toward the radical wing." When he said "we," he meant "I." Wald was in no such danger. Finally, in full retreat, he wrote, "I am obliged to confess that I see with increasing clearness the difficulties which you and Paul Kellogg pointed out."

Norman tried to do more to placate some of the upset members. At an AUAM Executive Committee meeting, he proposed "for the good of both organizations no Executive Officer of [the AUAM] should accept a position on the Executive Committee of the People's Council." But this motion wasn't enough; Crystal Eastman's efforts weren't enough;

Baldwin's arguments weren't enough—and perhaps did even more damage. The divisions within the group had grown too deep. Wald and Kellogg resigned and others followed. Norman "is reasonable and has judgment," Wald wrote, "but Crystal, Mr. Hallinan, and Roger Baldwin much as I like them personally, are more than I can manage single handed."

The break was a long time coming. The radicals would have their own organization. At the end of September, the group voted to separate the Civil Liberties Bureau officially from the AUAM, and the National Civil Liberties Bureau (NCLB) became an independent body. Roger Baldwin was at its head, and Norman became vice chairman. The NCLB had a broad mandate. It provided legal services to combat the abridgement of free speech and protect civil liberties and served as a clearinghouse for advice and information for conscientious objectors. The idea was to give substance to civil liberties. Free speech, the new group announced, should not be an "empty legal right" but rather "the living essence of democracy." It's hard to see this as a truly novel or radical position now, but at the time it was. The attenuated AUAM continued to meet, but it had more or less ceased to function.

The AUAM was unable to withstand the strains of working in the repressive atmosphere of wartime and collisions of clashing personalities. On a deeper level, though, what killed the organization was its inability to resolve the question of whether it should focus on what was immediately attainable or on what was principled. Norman's mentor, William Adams Brown, spoke for many pragmatic liberals (if more kindly than most) when he said that he had "great respect" for pacifists but objected to their attempt to "apply an absolute ideal to a progressive society." It was a serious accusation, and it hurt. People like Wald and Kellogg feared being seen as utopian or impractical, or, worst of all, fanatics. They wanted to be effective.

Others—Norman, Evan, Baldwin, and Sayre among them—were more comfortable with the idea of one absolute: the absolute ideal of freedom of conscience. It did not mean license; none of them supposed that one person should be able to harm another under the blanket justification of conscience. All of them understood that freedom of conscience was not the same thing as freedom *from* conscience, that actions had consequences, and that when consequences affected others, they could be judged.

Convictions could be dangerous things if they led to intolerance. Freedom of conscience required that one respect the right of others to be free. But problems persisted: If conscience was contentless, wasn't righteousness a question of preference? What made the right *right*?

·+·

"You may justly be called anarchists," wrote one of Norman's Princeton friends, a former usher at his wedding. "There must be a limit to freedom of conscience." After all, he added, "the man who murdered McKinley thought he had a direct call from his God." Women working at East Harlem's Neighborhood House gave Norman's former assistant Jack Darr, now in charge of the place, an ultimatum: no pacifist workers, or they would quit. One of the women wrung her hands and, thinking of Norman's children, kept repeating, "Just think—five little pacifists." ("Ask Tommy if he is that," Norman wryly wrote to Violet.)

One of Norman's old colleagues at Spring Street wrote to Norman that he had heard "wild rumors" that Norman was being shipped to a camp as a conscientious objector and, while voicing his "sympathy," added that he didn't agree with him. "We're in the war and I thank God we are." Another Spring Street friend, Ralph Harlow, resigned from the Fellowship of Reconciliation in anguish. He had witnessed the Turkish massacres of Armenians and lost friends in the genocide. Some things were worth fighting against and fighting for. And if he was wrong—then "I would rather go with my country to hell than save myself," he wrote to Norman.

These tests of his friendships saddened Norman; he knew some of them would not survive. He knew, too, that he was making a gamble on his "ethical optimism." But if faith was not stronger than war, then what was it worth? "Your position may be the only practical one," he admitted to Harlow, "but what have you to say for a religion which leaves its followers with a choice between evils? Does it sound like the faith that will overcome the world?"

·+·

For the most part, though, Norman kept his focus trained on the societal, not religious, implications of war. The war was accelerating and accentuating his opinion that one did not need to look far to find real victims. He saw injustices that he had overlooked, and the heat of his frustration welded them together. It was not enough to talk about poverty. What about the mistreatment of black Americans? Before the war, he had hardly paid attention, but race riots that devastated St. Louis prompted him to add the oppression of African Americans to his indictment of an unjust and hypocritical social order. "Do you think Americans in general with their shameful record for race riots are purely disinterested redressers of the crimes to Belgium and Armenia? . . . Do you find now that we are in a war there is a real passion for conquering imperialistic tendencies and the exploitation of the weak anywhere else except within the territory of the German power?" he angrily asked one correspondent.

The war, racial injustice, economic injustice—Norman saw them as all of a piece. He watched his parishioners enlist in the military and could not blame them. Walter Bruno—whom Lovett had once found outside the Neighborhood House with his head bashed by a pipe—told Norman that he was joining the army because life at home was "intolerable," Norman reported to Emma. Work, for those who could get it, was "monotonous." Becoming a soldier would give him food, clothes, and perhaps some sense of belonging. Upton, or wherever Walter would be sent, had to be better than East Harlem. (Whether the trenches would be was another question.)

Those who weren't pushed into war by the draft or economic conditions were coerced by threat, and it wasn't happening only in places like East Harlem. Columbia University president Butler declared, "What had been wrongheadedness was now sedition. What had been folly was now treason," and fired two professors for their peace movement activities. The *New York Times* praised Columbia for having "done its duty." Norman took up the cause of three ministers associated with the Fellowship of Reconciliation who had tried to hold a meeting in Los Angeles. They were denied use of a municipal hall, locked out of an alternative site, and then arrested on charges of unlawful assembly when they moved to a third. At their trial, opponents called the organization a Socialist conspiracy. The *Los Angeles Times* reported that conference attendees included "negroes and Mexicans, bootblacks and disciples of Yogi." The *Times* also printed a letter from Billy Sunday, who was preaching in Los Angeles, suggesting that the Christian pacifists be lynched. In lieu of lynching, the court sent the conference organizers to prison. In East St. Louis, rumors of whites and blacks mingling at a labor meeting brought three thousand white men into downtown, where they began to beat African Americans indiscriminately. By the time the violence was over, around a hundred were dead.

Reports of brutalities against conscientious objectors in training camps streamed into the offices of the NCLB, reports so severe that Secretary Baker had already heard about them from his own men. Antiwar ministers lost their jobs; some almost lost their lives. Herbert Bigelow, a minister who preached against the war, was kidnapped and beaten nearly to the point of death. The mayor of Cincinnati whooped that Bigelow had gotten "what's coming to him."

Radicalism of any kind was cast in different shades of red. That summer, soldiers attacked a Socialist parade in Boston and beat the marchers, and vigilantes forced some of them to kiss the American flag. In September 1917, the so-called Green Corn Rebellion, a protest against the draft in Oklahoma, ended with the arrest of more than four hundred impoverished sharecroppers and tenant farmers. Members of the Industrial Workers of the World, which loudly opposed the war, were special targets. Around that time the Justice Department raided Industrial Workers of the World offices around the country and indicted more than a hundred IWW leaders on charges of obstructing the United States' participation in the war. (The NCLB faced some of its worst trouble after publishing a pamphlet protesting the IWW's treatment.) Business leaders—and American Federation of Labor leader Samuel Gompers—saw an opportunity to crush Socialism and the radical labor movements once and for all. In Bisbee, Arizona, the sheriff and a band of vigilantes broke an IWW strike by forcing thousands of unarmed strikers into cattle cars and then shipping them into the middle of the southwestern desert without sufficient food or water. The U.S. Army had to rescue them. In other parts of the country, IWW members were shot outright. In Butte, Montana, a labor organizer was dragged by the back of an automobile until his kneecaps were torn off. Then he was taken to a railway trestle and hanged.

Not all the manifestations of the anti-German and antipacifist hysteria were violent. Some were silly. Sauerkraut was verboten, replaced by "liberty cabbage." Boards of education around the country altered school curricula to diminish the American Revolution (when Great Britain was the enemy) and elevate figures like the French Joan of Arc. The California State Board of Education ordered that German folk songs be snipped—by hand—out of music books. People with German heritage formally changed their names to make them sound less German, as did the king of England in the summer of 1917, jettisoning "Saxe-Coburg-Gotha" and adopting the stolidly English "Windsor."

It was not easy for Wilson to engineer the right kind of patriotism while condemning the wrong. For the most part he stayed silent. Efforts to drop German-language instruction were "childish," he allowed, and lynching was reprehensible. But most vigilantes were never punished, and Wilson made few attempts to police his subordinates. He himself had said that to wage war, one must be ruthless and brutal. If his propaganda wizard George Creel was going to keep the patriotic fervor "white-hot," then someone, inevitably, was going to get burned.

Sixteen

COURAGE OF CONVICTIONS

*Arthur had always been a little slow
and cautious, his mother noted,
but he wanted his chance to fly.*

Norman could no longer keep to a couple blocks in a corner of New York and try to make things a little better here and there. The problem wasn't the excesses of capitalism; the problem was capitalism. He rejected the system altogether. His faith in the power of the church to combat inequality had nearly disappeared. He did not believe liberals had the solutions and expertise they claimed; he did not trust conservatives, convinced that they were beholden to big business. He was radicalized.

The crisis wasn't just the war, though the war was what awakened him. It was a question of how men could live together without killing one another. It was a political question, and it demanded a political response.

In the fall of 1917, Norman decided to support a Jewish immigrant named Morris Hillquit for mayor of New York. Hillquit, born Hillkowitz, was a Socialist. He had emigrated to New York's Lower East Side at the age of seventeen from a German-speaking Jewish colony in Riga, Latvia. The slender, dark-haired man had worked his way from a shirt cuff factory to a successful law practice. As the historian Richard Fox has observed, if Debs was the Socialist Party's "prophetic spirit" and heart, then Hillquit was its tactician and mind. He served on the executive committee of the Second International between 1905 and World War I and knew the doctrine well. Orthodox in ideology—a disciple of the "later" Engels—he was reformist in style. This was not really a contradiction, although it seemed like one to his more radical foes in the IWW, who accused him of selling out, and also to his foes at the *New York Times*, who noted the pitter-patter of ladies' gloved hands that greeted his speech to a bourgeois civic club. In Hillquit's view, revolution was not the result of a cataclysm but actually represented the final stage of a process of rational evolution. Socialism was not only the inevitable result of class struggle; it would also result from a more ethical, rational, and equitable society. In a widely printed exchange with Monsignor John A. Ryan, a Catholic thinker, Hillquit had described the promise of socialism in just those terms, saying that morality grew out of a "sense of duty of man toward man." He proposed that humans are most profoundly human when they want to act with justice toward others. Norman had read the debate and thought Hillquit the clear winner.

But it was the Socialist's antiwar stance that got Norman's attention. For his antiwar position, Hillquit's adversaries called him a "Hillquitter." One lawyer (listed affiliation: the Princeton Club) telegraphed Wilson urging him to have Hillquit arrested for "high treason" and then "shot at sunrise." The *New York Times* printed the telegram. Henry Van Dyke, Norman's own professor and erstwhile mentor—the man who had hired Norman as his assistant at Brick Church—said, "I'd hang everyone, whether or not he be a candidate for mayor, who lifts his voice against America entering the war."

On October 2, 1917, Norman wrote a letter of support to Hillquit. He explained to Hillquit that his decision to back him was based on the candidate's municipal program and his peace advocacy. Norman might have stopped there; some of Hillquit's supporters did. But Norman went further, bluntly stating that the war had convinced him that capitalism—a system that "exalts competition instead of cooperation"—was not a system that guaranteed freedom. Injustice was its natural result, and war its most extreme manifestation. He emphasized to Hillquit that he had no plans to join the Socialist Party. He found its propaganda crude and offensive, its structure overly disciplined, and feared that it diminished individual initiative and personality. But those were concerns to address another time.

A number of influential non-Socialists were supporting Hillquit, among them Amos Pinchot, a reformer who had once been part of Roosevelt's inner circle; Harry Hopkins, who would become Franklin Roosevelt's close adviser; and Roger Baldwin. Still, there weren't very many patrician clergymen at the proletariat rallies. Hillquit had no problem with Norman's Christian background. He had actually proposed an amendment to the party's constitution making religion a matter of personal choice, counter to orthodox doctrine. Indeed, Hillquit surely saw in Norman a handsome, articulate minister who could bring the Socialist message to new audiences and make it palatable. (A few years later, Hillquit, serving as attorney for five Socialists whom the state assembly refused to seat, literally produced Norman in court as evidence "to prove that Socialism was not hostile to religion and did not seek to disrupt the family ties.")

Norman's mother was upset and told him so. People were calling Hillquit's views "treasonable," she reminded him. She wondered how Norman's own positions could have changed so much since they had discussed his politics less than two months before. Things *had* changed, he replied. The repression of pacifists and radicals—not only by vigilantes but also by the government—had intensified in the early fall. Besides, he added, he supported Hillquit's municipal program. The task of addressing poverty had become too large for Norman to countenance. "If you lived here from day to day and saw the futility of many of our measures of amelioration," he assured his mother, "I am sure you would agree with my stand."

Hillquit lost, but the Socialist had actually had a fighting chance. His rallies reverberated with the noise and energy of people who felt that they might be given a political stake. This was not the sound of people pursuing a lost cause. When Hillquit took the stage in front of twelve thousand at Madison Square Garden, the people cried, "Peace! Peace!"

Norman's pacifism had already alienated many of his friends, but he acknowledged to Villard that supporting Hillquit would be the "last straw to break the back of their toleration." He was right, and it hurt. New friendships, reinforced by their common cause, sustained him, though. It was a heady time. He loved to feel the rush that came when he stepped onto a stage. He had always been drawn to public speaking, whether from the pulpit, the rostrum, or the soapbox. A political campaign gave speeches and debates a new urgency and purpose. He spoke inside and out, at meetings and atop a car at the corner of Ninety-sixth and Broadway. He spoke at Madison Square Garden. On October 31, a week before the New York City mayoral election, Amos Pinchot organized a rally of nonpartisan supporters for Hillquit. An assistant United States attorney and a group of official stenographers were in the audience, and Justice Department officials were waiting in the wings to scrutinize every word. Norman stood on the stage in front of twelve thousand people and hurled his booming voice into the huge void above their heads. The audience heard him and responded. The cheers were intoxicating. Norman never forgot that feeling.

·+·

Some of Violet's friends began crossing the street to avoid speaking with her. Her family was upset, and Norman's wasn't happy. His boss at the American Parish, William Adams Brown, called him down to his office late that fall and begged him not to support Hillquit. Norman's pacifism had made things hard enough, Brown said, "but to be also a Socialist!" They were having trouble raising money for the parish. Norman knew it was true, and he knew what Brown was hinting at. Brown never fired him, but when Norman offered his resignation, Brown accepted it with relief—before asking Norman to stay a few extra months while he looked for a replacement. (Two decades later, Brown told Norman that he had always regretted watching Norman go: "Oh, Norman, Norman, why did you ever leave?")

The break had come. Norman resigned from the Harlem school board—he would be moving downtown, anyway, to be closer to his office at the Fellowship of Reconciliation on East Twenty-eighth Street. Columbia's Teachers College, where he had been planning a course with Lillian Wald, was relieved when he excused himself with the acknowledgment that he might "embarrass" the college. (When Norman proposed that the school hire Emily Greene Balch, a well-respected professor and eventual winner of the Nobel Peace Prize, the school rejected her for her "objectionable" pacifism.)

Norman resigned from the Philadelphian Society, writing, "It would be idle to deny that I am—to my sorrow—out of sympathy with much of Princeton's social and intellectual outlook." He was not being polite or exaggerating his sorrow. It would be hard to overstate how much he had loved Princeton and how painful that estrangement would have been. So closely did he and his brothers and his wife's family identify themselves with Princeton that it must have felt like turning away from kin.

By the end of 1917, Ralph was excelling at Camp Upton, practicing his marksmanship and looking forward to joining the fight. Arthur was about to head to training camp to become a pilot. Evan, living with Norman and Violet and working in East Harlem as he waited to be called up, was very close to his brother, but even they did not have a totally smooth relationship. As much as Norman admired his brother's commitment, Evan's tendency toward extremism alarmed him. He wondered, sometimes, whether Evan's intense introspection and individualism made him forget other people. He worried that Evan talked about love and then forgot that real love needs an object outside of oneself. There was a militancy about Evan sometimes that was hard to ignore. He might have made an excellent soldier.

⁍

All the while, the war ground on. For both sides, it was going terribly. For the Allies, it went worse and worse. The Allies were confident (and the Germans were afraid) that bringing enough American soldiers onto the battlefield could break the stalemate, but whether Uncle Sam could reach the trenches before the Allies caved was an open question. The large regiments of U.S. troops were still preparing to leave the United States. In France, morale had sunk so low that, on the front, soldiers refused to attack. The underprepared Italians inched forward, gaining a few feet here and there but suffering heavy casualties. Some of the deaths were inflicted by the Italians' own generals, who ordered deserters shot in shocking numbers. One officer went to the front trenches and shot his own men if they hesitated. The Italian commander even resurrected the old Roman practice of decimation—shooting every tenth man, randomly, in regiments that had performed poorly.

The turmoil in Russia threatened to upend everything. A Russian offensive launched in the summer of 1917 collapsed almost as soon as it began. Some soldiers simply refused to fight. Those who made it as far as the trenches quickly deserted, looting and raping as they went. By the end of the year, the number of Russians taken prisoner exceeded casualties in the old Russian army by a stunning measure of three to one. The army had effectively dissolved itself. Germany's counterattack rolled through the lost land and kept driving, covering huge stretches of ground. It had help from its opponent. The Russian leadership was in upheaval. Lenin and his Bolshevik Red Guard seized power from the head of the provisional government, a moderate socialist named Alexander Kerensky, as soon as the Germans moved within striking distance of Petrograd, at the end of October. Lenin almost immediately formed the Council of People's Commissars, declared the countryside the people's property, and initiated a three-month armistice. The remaining beleaguered soldiers wandered off, heading home to claim their promised land, and the Bolsheviks waited for the world uprising. To their astonishment, it did not happen.

Lenin's cohort Leon Trotsky, appointed commissar for Foreign Affairs, had assumed that his role would be to declare "a few proclamations and then shut up shop." With Petrograd in chaos and the army collapsed, the Russians had little choice but to negotiate a treaty with the Germans. They did it at Brest-Litovsk, a ruined Polish town. It was an awkward scene for all; at one banquet, befuddled Austrian aristocrats tried to make conversation with a Russian peasant by asking him about planting onions. The conference stretched on as both sides played for time. The Germans hoped the non-Russian ethnicities on Soviet land would rebel, while the Russians hoped the workers of the world would rebel. Finally, Trotsky walked out, and the Germans broke off the armistice, fed up. The Americans still had not arrived.

-+-

What could peace look like? Wilson persisted with his vision. On January 8, 1918, the president addressed Congress just after noon. The events at Brest-Litovsk, he said, had compelled him to lay out the United States' peace aims. Americans were fighting, he said, so that the world would "be made safe for every peace-loving nation which, like our own, wishes to live its own life, determine its own institutions, be assured of justice and fair dealing by the other peoples of the world as against force and selfish aggression." To that end, he proposed "fourteen points" for the establishment of a new order. There would be no more secret diplomacy, an "absolutely impartial adjustment of all colonial claims," security for small nations, freedom of the seas, and welcome and assistance to the new, freely determined Russia, for "the treatment accorded Russia by her sister nations . . . will be the acid test of their good will." The crowning proposal was the last: "A general association of nations must be formed under specific covenants for the purpose of affording mutual guarantees of political independence and territorial integrity to great and small states alike." The international league was what liberals like Paul Kellogg had so badly wanted. But would it be enough, would it be in time, and what would it look like?

Norman was pleased with Wilson's speech. Indeed, events seemed to be improving, and so did Norman's prospects. While Evan handled much of the load in East Harlem until Norman could leave that spring, Norman focused on launching his new publication. In January 1918, the *New World* published its first issue. Prominent liberals chipped in: Oswald Garrison Villard wrote a story on blacks and the war; John Haynes Holmes weighed in on conscription. Other articles addressed economics, toleration, and the demands of Christianity. Almost immediately Norman and his colleagues decided to change the paper's name to the *World Tomorrow*. The new world had not yet arrived, but it was surely coming.

"Frankly my own feeling with regard to the war is undergoing something of a change," he wrote to Wald on March 1.

On religious grounds I am still obliged to think that war is a
hideously unsatisfactory method of righteousness but the Russian situation and the progressive abandonment of imperialistic
aims by the Allies under pressure from the President and British Labor remove the reproach of hypocrisy from us. Meanwhile the German people seem to be more completely under
the dominance of their cynical Junker class than I had thought.
Things change so fast that one is at a loss what to think.

Things did change fast, yanking Norman between despondency and
optimism. One week he was raising bail for Scott Nearing, arrested for his
pamphlet "The Great Madness," and the next he was applauding Wilson
and the War Department, unreservedly grateful to the administration for
clarifying its policy on conscientious objectors.

The president's March 20, 1918, order prepared the way for a board
of inquiry to travel from camp to camp to examine conscientious objectors. Those found sincere would be offered noncombatant service, Friends
Unit Service, or farm or factory furlough work. Absolutists and those
found insincere would be brought before a court-martial for sentencing.
Objectors would soon know their fates. The new policy on objectors truly
was a relief, if only because the War Department finally *had* a policy. Since
the start of the war, the NCLB and the Fellowship of Reconciliation had
pushed the administration to recognize conscientious objectors who had
ethical or humanitarian, not only religious, objections; to clarify and stan-
dardize the treatment of objectors; and to offer noncombatant or furlough
service for those who did want to serve their country in a time of war but
could not conscientiously participate in the military. Lawyers working with
the NCLB had hoped the courts would declare the draft unconstitutional,
but their challenge had failed that January 1918. By a unanimous vote, the
Supreme Court had upheld conscription, saying that the power of the state
depended upon its right to compel military service. To believe otherwise,
Chief Justice Edward White wrote, "challenges the existence of all power."
Power that depends upon consent "is in no substantial sense a power."

It was no small task to call up, train, outfit, and dispatch a military
nearly from scratch. The presence of a small number of recalcitrant draftees

who did not themselves agree on why they refused to fight was understandably low on the list of the War Department's concerns. Quietly and haphazardly, but in good faith, the War Department issued orders ending the arbitrary segregation of objectors and the practice of forcing Mennonites to wear a uniform. Baker ruled that noncombatants should not be forced to bear sidearms and ordered that objectors "be treated with kindly consideration," having learned that the best way to induce an objector to become a soldier was to treat him well. Still, officers and guards interpreted that vague order variously, and abuses continued at some camps. Some objectors were verbally harassed, sent to the guardhouse, and a few were beaten to death.

Now, though, the NCLB thought that what Norman called the War Department's "policy of drift" might finally be over. "We who are struggling against great odds and misunderstanding to help keep alive in wartime our traditional individual and minority liberties," the NCLB wrote to Wilson, "express to you grateful appreciation of your handling of the issue in such a way to remove it from bitter public controversy."

Norman had special reason to be relieved. The following month, Evan was drafted, and he presented himself to the local board as a conscientious objector. He was to be sent to Camp Upton. He just missed overlapping with his brother Ralph.

✤

While the soldiers waited, they sang. Camp Upton was rarely quiet in March 1918, as the men prepared to go to war. When they summoned friends and family to say good-bye, the reunions were raucous. The soldiers held parades and lit bonfires, and they banged their spoons and forks against kitchen tins in impromptu percussion performances. Some said farewell more than once, as rumored departure dates came and passed. Finally, on the morning of Wednesday, March 27, 1918, the men of the 302nd Army Corps of Engineers awoke to band music as the first contingent of the Seventy-seventh Division marched out of camp and to the train cars that would take them to New York City, where a ship awaited to ferry them to France. The 302nd Engineers would leave the next night. The jangled merrymaking that had burned through camp all month erupted into earnest celebration. When Captain Ralph Thomas sat down to write his last letter before shipping out, he could hear the happy tumult out-side. "There is a general feeling of relief and almost a gala atmosphere," Ralph wrote to Norman. "The men are singing and shouting in the bustle of moving. They are a good bunch."

Ralph was proud of them. The 302nd Engineers boasted the best marksmanship in the Seventy-seventh Division, the best football team, and the best basketball squad. Not coincidentally, the 302nd Engineers also had the best morale. When the assistant secretary of war reviewed the division in mid-February, the 302nd Engineers went first. And when the ten thousand soldiers from Camp Upton paraded down Fifth Avenue a week later, through a heavy snowstorm on George Washington's birthday, the 302nd Engineers led the way.

Ralph had done well at training camp. His commander, Colonel Sherrill, had recommended his promotion to captain in the beginning of January, in light of his "exceptional work" and his leadership of enlisted men. Training had been difficult at times—pulling stumps, building roads, and construct-ing trenches in ground that froze three feet deep in January, not to men-tion controlling those enlisted men. But the soldiers' exhaustion dissolved into excitement as the departure date drew close. They were not all there by choice, but for a moment they were united in the faith that they were serving their country and its cause. When they chose an emblem to stamp on their packs, the New York–based division chose the Statue of Liberty.

On that night of March 27, Ralph would board a train that would take him to Astoria. From there it was on to the Hudson, where the *Carmania* was waiting to carry him, forty-five other officers, and some 1,500 enlisted men. The Great Adventure was about to begin.

But before he departed, he had something important to say to his older brother. He and his brothers disagreed about the war, sometimes vehe-mently, but now was not the time for rancor. "I am sorry we don't agree in this, the biggest affair of our lives," he scrawled across the small sheets of paper, "but you know I respect your courage of convictions and idealisms."

+

Evan arrived at Camp Upton in May, the month after Ralph had left, and found nothing to do. His papers from the local board had not arrived, and even if they had, the process of examining the objectors and sorting them into categories had not yet begun. The first thing that struck him was how impressed he was with the army. "The interest of the officers in the men, the really worthwhile and efficient welfare work, the clean and abundant forms of entertainment, the fostering of sport and the real idealism in the addresses of the officers and the other speakers I have heard have all made a very great impression on me," he wrote to his mother. Wandering through the camp—he had few other options for passing the time—he was jealous of the camaraderie among the men and longed to join them. "Frankly the tug is very great to let go and become a part of it all," he confessed. "It seems so much the human thing to do and my position seems so aloof and so unhuman."

But he became inured. After three weeks in the casual barracks, where he could barely abide the number of "constitutional slackers," Evan was moved into the objectors' barracks. Despite some condescension about the intellectual caliber of most of the men, he liked the motley group of objectors. There were some "socialists of a not very intelligent type, two Seven Day [sic] Adventists with the most curious interpretations of the Bible, four typical colored brethren of a very courageous and devout sort—I like them—and one fellow who claims to be a great admirer of Nietzsche." Attitudes toward religion polarized the group, as some were "violently hostile" and others always clutched their Bibles, but they limited their fighting to petty stuff. And so his days were filled with chatter and walking around the simple grounds, over roads built by Ralph and through fields abundant with wild strawberries. He was assigned some work—planting garden beds, cleaning latrines—but nothing he could object to. He read and wrote letters. He endured the thick clouds of mosquitoes, and he spoke with the soldiers. "Was talking with Major Weeks from 2.30 to 7 pm this afternoon with one or two interruptions and found him a splendid man," he reported to Violet. "I almost wish they weren't so fine." Mostly, he waited.

His mother and Norman were waiting, too, not only to see what the government would do about Evan but also to see what Evan would be willing to accept. His mother badly wanted him to take some kind of non-combatant service. Norman had his doubts that Evan would accept such an offer—and doubted, too, that the board would offer it to him. Gingerly, he tried to prepare his mother for the worst, while hoping Evan might come around.

Evan, characteristically, was digging in. He threatened to become an absolutist objector and to accept no work at all. He had a point to make and wanted to make it. The government had no sympathy at all for absolutist objectors. To the religious objector, it would be accommodating; to those who objected on humanitarian grounds, it would go to lengths to resist forcing him to kill another man. But absolutists were another story. Major Walter Kellogg, who later joined the board of inquiry for conscientious objectors, allowed that "many of this class are unquestionably sincere. What, however, is their sincerity worth? They have been a burden in a time of world crisis. They have contributed nothing save discontent and disaffection. They come out from the war resolved to spread the gospel of their iniquity."

Emma knew that her two pacifist sons were courting trouble. The only thing that she could do was plead and hope. She could also remind her sons that there was another side to their positions. She sent Ralph's letters to Evan and Norman and Evan's letters to Ralph. "I should like to see some of Arthur's," Norman reminded her.

···+···

Arthur had been in the Air Service for about six months, assigned to the Army School of Military Aeronautics at Cornell, in Ithaca, New York. If Ralph's experience in training camp was exceptionally good and Evan's experience was simply exceptional, Arthur's was probably more typical: Pride and pleasure alternated with infuriation.

At ground school in Ithaca, he bridled against a superior officer, a Lieutenant Wolfe, who had "open scorn" for men who had not seen actual fighting and whom Arthur found slightly sadistic. One morning Wolfe put Arthur's squadron through an hour of bayonet fighting using rifles instead of bayonets and laughed when the rifle's sharp sights cut the men. He allowed Arthur only three hours of sleep between guard duty tours. Arthur fumed—at himself, at Wolfe, at the army. "I can't imagine why it is that I am still a corporal," he complained to his mother. Wolfe seemed to have some kind of vendetta against the men. "Since the day when I used to chase Evan and others with anything that I could throw, I have not been so mad as I was yesterday," he wrote Emma at 1:00 A.M., on one of his short breaks. "If I were not a slave I would have told Wolfe my opinions of him and left him or knocked him on the head but, as it was, I did neither 'because I'm in the army now.' What a multitude of things that phrase covers!"

But when his ground school course was over and he was granted leave, he arrived in Baltimore smiling and "very much pleased with his course," his mother reported to his brothers. He looked sharp in a new uniform, and he showed off the green and black cord signifying the flying corps on his hat. The neighbors clucked with pleasure at the sight of him; his mother cheerfully embarrassed him by fussing over his appearance. "His carefully wound spiral puttees brought out his calves so well that Mrs. Bond assured me she had no idea before that he was so well formed!"

That weekend Arthur had only good things to say, which Emma proudly repeated to her other sons: "he thinks aviation the best service of the army"; "he made some very good friends"; and so on. One can easily picture the beaming mother and her youngest son, handsome in his new uniform. Soon he would head off to flight school. The boy who had always been a little "slow and cautious" would have his chance to fly.

Seventeen

INTO THE FRACAS

*In the tent colony at Fort Riley, Evan (back row, left)
found his home in the Extreme Left tent.*

That spring, Norman and his family made the move out of East Harlem. In a few short months Norman had lost close friends and his job. He was arguing with his mother and had severed ties with groups that had once meant something to him. His wife's grandfather, John Stewart, was furious. There was talk of writing Violet out of his will. Violet shared her husband's views but bore the stress in an already weakened state. She had given birth to another child, Rebekah, on March 17. The Thomases now had five children, all under the age of seven. Violet was a "brick," Norman marveled, but he could tell she was suffering. Her weak heart worsened, and she never totally recovered.

For a few months, they stayed with Violet's mother off Fifth Avenue when they weren't in Ridgefield. The patriarch of the Stewart family may have disapproved of Norman's actions, but Frances Stewart's house was always, Norman liked to say, a port in any storm. The move downtown to a neighborhood of unassuming gentility just south of Gramercy Park made some things easier. Their new home, a spacious brownstone with long windows and a sweeping staircase, was near good schools—something they had worried about in East Harlem—and not far from Violet's mother and sister. And where their old block had been a cacophonous scene, now they lived in comfortable quiet. On East 116th Street, Norman and Violet had come to expect the knock on the door from a neighbor or parishioner needing help. They stopped what they were doing to fetch a doctor for the sick or take a neighbor to the hospital; they visited long coal lines in winter, bringing coffee. Norman could never entirely separate his work from his home life, and so their new place had a parlor large enough to host the entire membership of the Fellowship of Reconciliation—or whatever other group needed a place to land—for weekly tea or a talk. But when Norman made the short walk to his office at the Fellowship, he put some distance between his family and the persistent problems he worked to combat. He had asked much of his family, but he was sensitive—now more than ever—of asking too much. He was always aware that Violet's money was hers and not his.

·‡·

As spring turned to summer, the flowering of hope that Norman had felt about the war and Wilson's conduct died. After Russia and Germany finally signed the Treaty of Brest-Litovsk, in which Russia ceded 750,000 square kilometers—an area three times the size of Germany that contained a quarter of Russia's population and a third of its farmland—Wilson condemned Germany with a zeal that unnerved even his admirers. In a speech at a Liberty Loan drive in Baltimore, he railed against Germany's repudiation of "the principle of free self-determination of nations. . . . There is, therefore, but one response possible from us: Force, Force to the utmost, Force without stint or limit, the righteous and triumphant Force which shall make Right the law of the world and cast every selfish dominion down in the dust." The public did not have a chance to hear him backpedal a few days later, when he told a group of reporters that he had "no desire to march triumphantly into Berlin" and that "there isn't any one kind of government which we have the right to impose upon any nation. So that I am not fighting for democracy except for the peoples that want democracy." These remarks were off the record.

The talk of self-determination and democracy abroad galled Norman when he considered the escalating abuses of citizens' rights at home. Wilson pushed Congress to pass the Sedition Act, which made it unlawful to "utter, print, write, or publish any disloyal, profane, scurrilous, or abusive language about the form of government of the United States, or the Constitution . . . or the military or naval forces . . . or the flag of the United States, or the uniform of the Army or Navy." (In a private letter, the attorney general suggested to Wilson that the censorship provision might be unconstitutional. No matter; his department was happy to use it.)

Norman grew accustomed to spotting Justice Department agents in his audiences when he spoke. Whatever illusions he had entertained about being in the government's good graces disappeared. Roger Baldwin was more optimistic, at least for a while. Whether willfully or naively, he could not see that his civil liberties organization was regarded not with tolerant disapproval but with active distrust. It was not long before the Justice Department's Bureau of Investigation started keeping tabs on the NCLB. At the end of 1917, an intelligence officer sent a memo entitled "Suspects" to the chief of the Intelligence Section of the War College, asking the college to conduct an investigation into Baldwin and the NCLB. Shortly afterward, the chief sent a memorandum to intelligence offers around the country calling the NCLB intentionally disruptive—which, in the suspicious atmosphere engendered by the Espionage Act, was close to alleging criminality—and claimed that the AUAM and NCLB "have been pernicious from the beginning." By March, an agent was writing that "this man Baldwin should be checked in some way and . . . his organization should be broken up."

The top War Department officials knew of the investigations. They also knew Baldwin, Norman, and the other main members of the group personally, and they hardly considered them treasonous. Still, the NCLB's meddling—for that is how the War Department saw it—was getting out of hand, and the War Department let Baldwin know. The assistant to the secretary of war, Frederick Keppel, who had been the dean of Columbia University before moving to Washington for wartime work, had been on friendly terms with Baldwin. He was even, to a point, sympathetic. But however cordial he might have been to Baldwin in the past, he was getting annoyed. He reported to Baldwin that military intelligence agents regarded the NCLB closely and with suspicion, and that their relationship was creating an "embarrassing situation." The military, Keppel explained, was convinced that the NCLB was in "direct conflict with the Government." The War Department and the civil liberties group would therefore have to suspend their communications. Surprised (and probably a little hurt), Baldwin replied to Keppel that the NCLB was "entirely willing to adjust ourselves in the matter of dealing with the conscientious objectors" to "whatever policy seems wise in your judgment." In fact, he went on, he thought the NCLB and the War Department had actually been working *in concert*; the NCLB was alleviating "an administrative problem" for the department by serving as a clearinghouse for objectors and providing legal advice. So sure was Baldwin of everyone's good faith and intentions that he sent the War Department not only the NCLB's literature but also its mailing list.

"I am of the opinion that this organization serves no good purpose and that their activities should be stopped," wrote an attorney representing military intelligence. For the War Department, all this really *was* embarrassing. Baldwin persisted, writing letter after letter after letter on behalf of the objectors. Baldwin's typewriter, quipped Keppel, "ought to appeal to the Labor Department for relief." Keppel tried to break contact with the NCLB at the beginning of summer in 1918, but Baldwin kept writing. He was either determined or oblivious, maybe both. Keppel's exasperation with Baldwin and the NCLB was obvious.

Keppel finally lost his temper when Laurence Todd, the NCLB's Washington representative, went to see him in early August. "We are not doing business with you fellows," he scolded Todd in front of a group of people, "and you know it."

·✦·

Norman was not getting much more traction with Evan than the NCLB was with the War Department. After the NCLB tried to work with the

Board of Inquiry to offer farm furloughs to objectors, Evan fired off a
furious letter to his brother. "I would many times rather be sent to prison
on a clear cut issue than on this feather bed of unprincipled liberalism,"
he wrote. "More and more I hate liberalism from the bottom of my soul."
At the end of June, Norman mailed an application form for the Friends'
Reconstruction Work program to Evan. Evan had actually applied for
Friends' work himself, but he immediately rescinded it. "I can't help but
feeling that to take Friends' Reconstruction work now is really admitting defeat," he explained to Norman. "I feel that I have failed badly to
get a single thing across here in camp. I hate to quit this way." He could
hardly abide the stridency of some of the objectors, like the Socialists who
objected to his sweeping out the latrine because other soldiers used it, or
the YMCA workers who came up to him and questioned his "sincerity."
He hated to feel as if he was neither in prison nor out of it. He was more
aware than ever of his own powerlessness. In mid-July, he was, at least,
given a change of scene. He and thirty-odd objectors were herded into
an old railway car and taken to Fort Leavenworth, in Kansas, where they
continued to wait.

On Friday, July 19, Evan finally appeared before the Board of Inquiry.
The three members of the board—Harlan Stone, the dean of Columbia
Law School (and later a Supreme Court justice); Julian Mack, a Court of
Appeals judge; and Major Richard Stoddard, from the Judge Advocate
General's office—spent the summer crisscrossing the country, visiting
camps and interviewing thousands of objectors to determine their "sincerity" and then recommending them for one kind of noncombatant or
alternative service or another. They tried to determine the grounds of the
objection and the kind of religious faith that might motivate it, to learn
something about the person. *How often do you pray? For whom and for
what? Do you pray for the kaiser?*

Evan said what he always said: that he was fighting for his ideals just
like any soldier, but that he believed the best way of combating the "Prussian idea of the State," in which the state dominates the individual, is to
oppose the principle of conscription. He delivered his refrain: Every man
must be true to himself. Judge Mack called Evan's stand "philosophical
anarchy." Still, the board found him sincere and offered him farm furlough

service on a civilian farm of their choice. This was generous, and Evan knew it. But even this would be a military order. He would still be *conscripted.* "I want to establish the principle that governments do *not* have the right to conscript a man's working life," Evan wrote to Norman. He said he would not take the farm furlough. He knew that meant the government might send him to prison. "If so I certainly bear no malice nor do I feel that I am being persecuted," he wrote to his mother. "I am merely ready to take the consequences of my fight for a new freedom the same as men in the trenches."

Evan wanted Emma to do more than support him. He wanted her to *understand.* When it became clear that she didn't, he vented his frustration. "I left Upton happy because I thought . . . that you were coming to see that I consider that I am in an active positive fight for a new freedom just as much as Ralph and Arthur," he complained four days after his Board of Inquiry test. Couldn't she see that only their methods differed? If he had accepted farm furlough, he would have been making only his protest against his personal participation the war, instead of a positive stand for the argument that freedom begins in the hearts and minds of men and so cannot be won by force. He wanted to protest conscription, to protest the government's right to compel the consciences of it citizens. He wanted to be heroic, and he wanted his mother to see him that way.

"I am not sure that I know a correct definition for conscience but what I call conscience certainly is not merely a check, always inhibiting and suppressing, giving warnings you must *not* do this and you must *not* do that," he told his mother. "With me it tells me equally strongly what I must do."

She did, though, understand more than he suspected. When his mother passed the letter along to her other sons, she asked for its immediate return. "It's sort of a comfort," she explained.

Around twenty-four million men registered for the draft in America during the First World War. (An estimated three million dodged registration. A total of 64,693 claimed conscientious objector status. Of those, 20,873 were called up in the draft. By the end of the war, fewer than five hundred objectors were in prison or training camp—fewer than five hundred out of twenty-four million registered men. Nearly all objectors who were drafted accepted some kind of military or alternative service. Those who refused represented such an insignificant number that it was easy for most to dismiss them. Prowar conservatives saw them as troublemakers, radicals, and recalcitrants. Pragmatists tended to view them as anachronistic, men who misguidedly stressed the importance of individual liberty at the cost of the social good. (It is both ironic and revealing that many were Socialists, or at least inclined toward socialism.) Most people simply did not understand them. "The great mass of our citizens subordinated their individual consciences and their opinions to the good of the common cause," wrote Board of Inquiry member Harlan F. Stone. At the same time, "there was a residue whose peculiar beliefs . . . refused to yield to the opinions of others or to force." Stone's tone reveals a significant ambivalence. Conscientious objectors represented "a residue" with "peculiar beliefs"—and yet there is a note of respect here, the refusal to subordinate oneself and submit to the "opinions of others or to force." That ambivalence is part of the American ethos, in which community is forever balanced against the individual, the state against the rights of men. Conscientious objectors demanded to be released from the heaviest burden placed upon citizens, the willingness to kill and die for one's country. The health of a democracy requires minimal coercion. But the health of a state sometimes requires that men do things they object to. Conscientious objectors brought that tension to the fore. That is why they could not be ignored.

·+·

At the end of July, shortly after appearing before the board, Evan was transferred from Leavenworth to Fort Riley, about a hundred miles west. Changing locations did not solve his dilemma of how to resist conscription, nor the government's dilemma of how to treat absolutists. The day after arriving in Fort Riley, Evan called a meeting of objectors to apportion the chores in order to preempt military orders. Evan explained the options; a vote was called. Only about twenty-five of the hundred or so men even bothered to hold up their hands either way. Fed up, Evan resigned his "chairmanship." The real trouble began, though, when those who refused to work, about fifty men, were led to an isolated field, given stakes and unconstructed tents, and left to argue among themselves.

+

"The absolutists were no one's favorite American citizens," one historian has written, not unfairly. Even Norman found them exasperating, and his own brother was one of them. "It is not always easy to deal with this class of men," Norman allowed in an article that appeared in the *Nation*, "and few officers have the patience and tact to carry out the liberal spirit of the War Department's orders." The objectors disagreed about how much to cooperate with the army and with one another. The soldiers tested the objectors' limits to see where they would bend and break. If conscientious objectors would not cooperate with the army, they were told, they could not cooperate with one another, and they were issued raw rations—oatmeal, flour, potatoes, and beets—which they had to pick up individually and cook alone. There were no proper cooking facilities. Nor was there a latrine.

The days were hot and dry—108 degrees in the shade, Evan told Norman. Boredom was a problem. The men had nothing to do; they refused to do anything. Mostly, they talked. One objector later wrote in an unpublished memoir that it wasn't uncommon to come upon the long frame of Evan Thomas stretched out across a cot at the center of a "red-hot argument" among the "intellectuals" about the limits of conscription.

"I'll help keep my prison clean when it's put up, but I won't help build it," said an objector during one debate. "Aw, I hate these fine distinctions," replied Evan. "I want something *big* for an issue. As a matter merely of good-fellowship, I might even help build the gallows they were going to hang me on, if the hanging was going to make the issue clear!"

On Sunday, July 28, Evan and two of his closest friends walked the four miles along the macadam road to Junction City to post some letters beyond the censor's reach. One of the men was Harold Gray, Evan's friend from the YMCA in England, with whom he had happily reunited at Fort Leavenworth a few days before. The other was a man named Howard Moore, who, having left his family's farm in upstate New York as a fourteen-year-old with $11.72 in his pocket, had worked at the New York Telephone Company before registering as an objector. Moore was nearly a foot shorter than Evan, silent and dark. He projected a quiet bravery that was immediately apparent to those who met him. Evan was somewhat in awe of him. The men reached town hungry, hot, and tired. Their situation was untenable, they agreed. They decided to go on a hunger strike. But it lasted only three days—not even enough time to worry Evan's mother. The government relented and let the objectors draw their rations in bulk and prepare them together. But this felt like a weak victory, and with only a few men willing to do the cooking, it was bound to break down.

·+·

Even before Ralph's ship, the *Carmania*, arrived at Liverpool on Friday, April 12, 1918, Ralph could feel the nearness of war. Off the coast of Ireland, a torpedo shot by the boat's bow and knocked the propeller off an escorting British destroyer. As the destroyer limped into port, the Americans cabled their thanks and sympathy. "Carry on," came the reply. The engineers were shaken but charmed. *Carry on! How British!*

It was more unnerving to see the British themselves. They had carried on too long. The day before the *Carmania* pulled into port, the British Expeditionary Force's General Haig had called upon desperation to motivate his men: "With our backs to the wall and believing in the justice of our cause, each one of us must fight to the end." The Germans were doubling up on British divisions and inundating them with gas. Blood flooded Flanders again, as the Germans tried to ram through the deadlock as fast as possible. Four years of grinding mutual destruction had made a mockery of time. Now, suddenly, time was the biggest factor of all. Neither side knew exactly what impact the Americans would have, but both knew the Americans would have an impact. "Look! Look!" came the hopeful Allied cries when they spotted the lines of hale doughboys. "Here are the Americans!"

"It is best you know the truth," Ralph confidently wrote to his mother from France. "Since we landed we've been told with a frankness almost astonishing that it is absolutely up to the U.S. if the war is to be won." They could not reach the front soon enough. "Inferno continues," wrote one soldier. The other Allied commanders had a less exalted view of their so-called saviors, and with reason. They were poorly trained and unprepared. The 302nd Engineers arrived in France without the equipment they had packed and prepared, and there was a mix-up among the various

Allied commanders—the hazard of Wilson's insistence on keeping the American army separate from the other Allied forces—over which nation would supply new equipment. Ralph's cockiness was tempered by how obviously untrained the engineers were for the reality of trench warfare. "I think half our time at Upton was wasted," Ralph wrote to Emma. As they trained behind British lines, they were exhausted and a little unnerved. Yet it quickly became almost *normal*. "I remember as a boy how war seemed to be of another realm—how surprised I was to find that during the Civil War people built houses and churches, and went to the theater and dances," Ralph wrote. "And now it all comes in a day's work. . . . But I reckon it will be different when we get into the fighting!"

He badly wanted to fight. As the regiment settled into the Baccarat sector, a shattered area once known for its crystal, the men heard of Americans engaging in action and were jealous. Baccarat was considered quiet. A thick curtain of barbed wire separated the two sides. But at night the sky would come to life, and Ralph could hear antiaircraft guns thunder and shells whine, shrapnel burst and machine guns chatter as German planes buzzed overhead, looking to bomb. This was war, but on the ground the engineers were still observers, an audience for the "great show" of pyrotechnics overhead. (After one particularly "spectacular" bombardment from German planes, Ralph wrote, "It was really a wonderful show and made the night work very realistic.") Ralph was busy, "on the go day and night" when the company commanders headed to the active front for a week and left Ralph in charge of his battalion. The engineers were responsible for setting up communications, preparing roads, and laying bridges, and when the fighting was hot they knew they would be under fire and in vulnerable spots. They had rifles and were supposed to use them. They watched their British counterparts scramble through danger with envy.

War was an adventure for American soldiers during those first few months. The Seventy-seventh "Melting Pot" Division brought together all kinds of men. Some learned how to speak English by singing: "Oh the army, the army, the democratic army, / All the Jews and Wops, the Dutch and Irish cops / They're all in the army now." One night in June, under a bright full moon, as the Seventy-seventh moved into Baccarat, it passed the other New York Division, the Seventy-sixth. Good-natured taunts flew back and forth, curses and cheers. "Boys and girls together, me and Mamie O'Rourke, / We tripped the light fantastic on the sidewalks of New York," sang the two divisions as they walked along the roads of Lorraine. The experience of being the first Americans to enter a French town that had been caught in crossfire, Ralph wrote, was "like the circus coming to town."

"I think all of us want to get into the fracas," he wrote. "Personally I hope this division will have the chance to participate in a smashing drive." At the beginning of August, the engineers boarded the small train cars marked "Hommes 40, Cheveaux 8"—forty men or eight horses—and left the safety of Baccarat. They marched through the American sector along the Marne, "an experience of a lifetime" for Ralph. Their anticipation, and their revulsion, grew as they passed German equipment abandoned on the ground and blackened corpses stinking of rot. They traveled at night, moving down to the Vesle River. The summertime air was mild. As the soldiers marched, the band played.

When they reached their position, near Bazoches, they dug in. It was a hot spot, under fire. Ralph took refuge at night in a little wine cellar, grabbing for his gas mask when the gas seeped in and pooled, as it did every night. The Germans held on the north bank of the river. When the engineers moved to repair a trench, camouflage a road, or lay a footbridge, only the night sky hid them. Nothing obscured the battalion's headquarters, in the village Chéry-Chartreuve, from the full view of the Germans or the reach of their guns and artillery. Headquarters was an active target range. Ralph was there on Tuesday, August 20, when a high explosives shell thudded to the ground close by. It shattered into thousands of steel shards, like so many jagged knives. Ralph was hit.

-+-

At Fort Riley, in Kansas, the hunger strike had begun again, and this time the strikers meant to follow through with it. They told each other they did not have a choice. The cooperation within the tent colony had fallen apart. The objectors disagreed about everything, including why they were there. "I am not an American citizen, I am a *Citizen of Heaven!*" one Christian objector liked to say. Meanwhile, in the "Argument Tent," a group of New

York Jewish Socialists, arguments would range from how to cut onions for gefilte fish to how to classify kisses. The objectors disagreed about what they were willing to do for the army, for themselves, and for each other. Finally, inevitably, those who were willing to cook refused to do all the work while others made a show of their righteous stand. Evan had hated the situation anyway, feeling like a loafer and a slacker. The practice of drawing lines, of arguing about what it meant to pick up a rake or put a pot of water to boil, grew absurd to him. The objectors' situation was "ridiculous," he had written to Norman weeks earlier. "The question on both sides was where to draw the line, and I can assure you that no men ever spent more time splitting hairs than we. It had to stop." But it had not. A month had passed since he had been determined "sincere," yet here he was, in the same place. He was addressed as "private" and remained a soldier, though he was treated more like an army dog, alternately kicked and indulged. He hated letting others cook for him, even though it was his own doing. The only other solution, as he and his friends saw it, was to neither cook nor let others do it. Howard Moore was the first to declare it a strike against "the principle of conscription," but by August 21 Evan, Gray, and a University of Chicago graduate named Erling Lunde were calling it a strike against conscription, too. (A group of others refused to eat until their food was prepared for them, and it soon was.)

Evan could be prone to bravado. When Norman and Baldwin had tried to propose another furlough scheme for absolutists, Evan wrote Norman a swaggering letter telling him to back off. "Never will I work to keep myself a slave," he wrote, with Gray and Moore looking over his shoulder. "Quit bargaining with the government about us. There is nothing that the government can do with us except free us, or take care of us, or let us die. Is that plain? . . . Moore and Gray join with me in the above statement of our stand. We all send our best to you and Roger Baldwin." They egged one another on. "P.S.," Evan added afterward, "You must pardon the above heroics—couldn't refrain—besides, I thought it might be very impressive to Moore and Gray. . . . Give me liberty or give me death! Great stuff—always a big temptation." A big temptation indeed. Evan longed to be in real danger, to test the limits of his physical abilities, to be pushed to the point of death for his cause, to prove the strength of his determination as soldiers did.

But he was not just grandstanding. However clumsily, he grasped something that Norman and the liberals of the AUAM, who worked so hard to keep their voices down and to appeal to the proper authorities without making a fuss, did not. Nonviolent protest was not only a moral position but also a drama, and protesters had to play it out. In the days before the Freedom Riders and Martin Luther King Jr., before Gandhi was famous in the United States, he had few examples to draw on—the women hunger strikers for suffrage in England, perhaps, and Thoreau's civil disobedience. William Lloyd Garrison burning the Constitution. Jesus, of course. If Evan had had a public trial, it might have been different. If he had been able to make a grand statement of his principles, as conscientious objectors did in England, he might have not tried so hard to enact his struggle. "The policy of the War Department was resulting in making real slackers of us. . . . We recognized that the government certainly had a right to punish men who refused to obey the selective draft," he wrote in an article that appeared in *The Survey* after the war. "We felt that it was *honorable* to ask a man to take his choice between being shot and being a soldier, or between going to prison and being a soldier. But it was neither honorable nor just for the Government to attempt to force men by a long process of wearing down to recognize the military."

Norman could not understand. In his view, the hunger strike was neither necessary according to principle nor tactically smart. "You know how much I want to get your point of view," he pleaded. "In the case of the farm furlough it's easy; in the matter of work in preparing meals it is a little harder; in regard to the hunger strike it is very much harder." He tried appealing for help to Judge Mack, who responded only to say that his concern lay not with the men but with their "utter folly," which he found "completely anarchistic" and said "cannot be tolerated in a civilized society." Norman was so desperate that he asked Sayre whether it would be worth going to the president. He was afraid that Evan might not give in, and he was afraid that the military might let his brother die. "I am fully aware that there would be no great clamor of protest," he wrote.

This was not a hysterical concern. Already a very thin six feet five, after more than a week without food Evan was weak and staggering. The doctor monitoring the men found his pulse irregular and decided to send him to the post hospital. Norman and Emma left for Kansas almost immediately. Emma was determined to persuade Evan to stop the strike. Just before she and Norman left, the telegram with the news that Ralph had been seriously wounded arrived.

·+·

After twenty-four hours aboard the train, Norman and Emma had reached only St. Louis. At least good news was waiting there: Ralph had been hit in his lung, side, arm, and thigh, but he had made it to a hospital in Saint-Nazaire; he would recover. There was also a telegram from Villard with the news that the War Department had agreed to release a group of men from solitary confinement. "We are leaving here more cheerful because of Villard's telegram," Norman wrote to Violet before the train pulled out of the station in Kansas City, after reporting that "Mother will be less anxious" after the news of Ralph. This is a curious way of putting it. Doubtless, Emma was also happy about Villard's telegram, and doubtless, Norman was also happy to learn that Ralph's wounds were less severe than feared. But that's not exactly how the letter reads. It is, of course, important not to overanalyze a hastily written letter. But it is true, in this moment and others, that far-reaching compassion can blur one's sight closer to home. Norman had his brothers on his mind, but he was not thinking only of them. He felt a broader responsibility.

Reaching Fort Riley on Friday, August 30, Norman and Emma went directly to Ward 6, where Evan was held. They found him better than they had expected—and fed, in a manner. The night before, nurses had given him a mixture of milk through a tube shoved down his throat. He "can still walk, talks rationally and clearly, and is absolutely unshakeable," Norman reported to Baldwin. "I still by no means agree that Evan hit upon the right method. But there is something (to his fond brother at least) quite magnificent about his spirit, his calm, his interest in affairs, and the friendship he has won from men who on principle abhor what he is doing." After months in the sun and more than a week without food, Evan was gaunt and sunburned but in good spirits, and he cheerfully told them about the events of the previous day. When Evan had arrived at the hospital, the tough and salty medical officer, Captain Henry, had yelled curses at him and bound him in a straitjacket. At 11:00 P.M., Henry had commanded orderlies to scrub Evan with the stiffest kitchen brushes they could find. Evan told his family that he had told the men "to make some scratches 'to please the captain,' but that they didn't do much," Norman reported to Baldwin. An hour later, with Evan apologizing for the inconvenience he was causing, Henry had ordered him forcibly fed. Evan had decided that as long as he didn't have to swallow, he would allow it. Several orderlies and nurses had put a towel around his long neck, tilted back his head, and then shoved a long red rubber tube down his throat as he gagged. Through the tube they had poured milk and later a mixture of milk and eggs. Evan could not have found this experience pleasant—the friction from yanking the tube out when the feeding was over burned the throat—but it was not so bad. Evan had drawn yet another line: swallow no, sustenance yes.

Norman and especially Emma, who, because of her more orthodox religious beliefs, had the burden of worrying about Evan's soul as well as his health, were relieved. He was not going to die, and the suggestion of suicide was weaker. They both still thought his stand foolish, but for the moment they were happy that he was all right. "He's the same dear boy," Emma wrote to her daughters, "if only he would not go wild over things." Evan was trying. He even held his tongue when the chaplain stopped by to make a plea, telling him that the military officers and the president were simply in the use of the Lord in the same way Moses and Calvin had once been. "I just nodded my head," Evan told his oldest brother. He really did like many of the doctors and orderlies and some of the soldiers. And they liked him, as people usually did. Norman watched his brother interact with the military staff and felt a kind of reverence come over him. However misguided his brother was, Norman thought, he could not help but admire him. Perhaps, too, Norman felt some twinge of guilt. Two of his brothers were in the hospital; the third risked his life every time he strapped into an airplane. Norman spent so much of his time in meetings.

Emma felt no such ambivalence and immediately tried to talk Evan out of the strike. Evan was cheerful but unyielding. She cajoled him and reasoned with him, but still he would not eat. Norman, meanwhile, made

arrangements to visit the objectors' tent camp in the morning and to investigate rumors of abuses in the guardhouse, and at the end of the day he and
his mother made their way to the parade ground, where they were picked
up by the small trolley car that took them on down a tree-lined route to
Bartell House in downtown Junction City.

When Norman and Emma arrived back at the hospital the next morning, they found that Evan had been joined in the ward by Gray, Moore,
and Lunde, now all being forcibly fed. Evan's three friends greeted Norman like some kind of minor idol. Gray, especially, was eager to see him.
Craving guidance and affirmation—and finding only discouragement from
his own family—he longed to discuss his situation with Norman and was
disappointed to have "only a short talk." Norman told Gray, as no doubt
he told the others, that he did not think their course best but "made absolutely no attempt to change my attitude toward the strike," Gray wrote
home, "and urged me to be guided only by what I inwardly felt to be
right." The young men welcomed Emma as if she were their surrogate
mother, and she mothered them in return. She was there for one reason,
though: to get her son to eat.

That afternoon Norman received a telegram from Roger Baldwin:
"FEDERAL AGENTS HAVE TAKEN CHARGE OF BUREAU AND
ARE GATHERING EVIDENCE FOR PROSECUTION."

Eighteen

TREASON'S TWILIGHT ZONE

*For his seditious speech in Canton, Ohio, Eugene Debs
was sentenced to ten years in prison.*

At the end of August, the New York military intelligence office told its headquarters in Washington that it was prepared to move "against Baldwin and the Conscientious Objector group." A fourteen-page report on Baldwin accused the NCLB of "carrying on a very insidious and dangerous campaign . . . all the more harmful because of the subtlety with which it is conducted." The NCLB's propaganda offended "every high impulse and altruistic motive animating our President and Cabinet in this epochal cataclysm, and helps to indoctrinate our youth with a spirit of disloyalty and treason."

On August 31, while Norman was in Kansas with Evan, armed federal agents filed into the building off Union Square where the NCLB had its office, passing a scrawl of graffiti on the wall: "Treason's Twilight Zone." The agents brought with them a group of civilians from the American Protective League, led by a lawyer named Archibald Stevenson, a vigilante who called himself a patriot. Baldwin was apoplectic, telling the men to "lock him up, shoot him, hang him, or anything else," the agents reported, but when he calmed down, he let them take his files. Walter Nelles, the lead lawyer working with the group, warned Baldwin that the NCLB's entire Executive Committee might be indicted.

At just that moment, Norman received more distressing news: The *World Tomorrow* had been held up again by the post office censors. Norman had gotten into trouble with the Espionage and Sedition Acts before—once a censor had noted that one article was "written by some ass of a pacifist person" and said that the magazine "preaches disruption on every page"—but in light of the problems with the NCLB, the trouble could be more serious this time. It did not help that one article in question was by Norman, in which he criticized the United States for sending troops into Russia to intervene in the Russian Revolution. Norman had titled it "The Acid Test of Our Democracy," a cutting reference to President Wilson's line that the international treatment of Russia's new government would be the "acid test" of a nation's commitment to democratic self-determination. Military intelligence officials were now writing reports suggesting that the *World Tomorrow* and, "particularly the editor thereof," should be kept under "continued observation."

Norman and Sayre took the train together to Washington to see if anything could be done. While Sayre tried to reach the president, Norman went to see Postmaster General Burleson. "If I had my way, I'd not only kill your magazine but send you to prison for life," Burleson told him.

An official at the attorney general's office was more reassuring when Norman came in to discuss the situation of the NCLB. "I can't see what protection civil liberties will have in America if the Civil Liberties Bureau itself is to be prosecuted," Norman told him. The official said it wasn't "his business" to say so, but that Norman shouldn't worry. "You've got John Haynes Holmes"—the eloquent pacifist minister—"and Roger Baldwin and yourself," he said. "There would be too many good speeches. We're not taking that chance."

Sayre went to the White House. Wilson greeted him warmly; he wanted to hear about his grandchildren. Talk moved to the future of capitalism, the military intervention in Russia, and Norman Thomas. The president was at his most sympathetic on all fronts, from a socialized economy ("nothing that everybody needs should be controlled by a private interest," Sayre recorded Wilson saying) to the war ("terrible") to the Espionage Act ("very dangerous") to Russia ("President wants real freedom for the Russian people," Sayre noted afterward. "We've just got to trust him and some things can't be made public now, without spilling all the beans"). Wilson told Sayre that he could not engage with the world against the "white background of a Utopian ideal" but had to take those steps that could be taken. He had to be practical. Sayre handed him a copy of the latest issue of the *World Tomorrow* and told him about the censor's leaden hand.

Wilson picked up the magazine and glanced at it. "We now need sentiments that will quicken all to united action and that will not tend to put on the brakes," Wilson told Sayre. "The *World Tomorrow* should print its title in bigger headlines and editors should dwell on the Tomorrow." The problem with Norman, Wilson said, was that given his views, "he can hardly help throwing a wet blanket on the war." Norman should focus on the future, he added, and not criticize the present. "If Norman Thomas could live with me for a single day through its problems," Wilson said, "he would realize the necessity for this advice."

An hour and a half had passed; it was nearing the time for Sayre to leave. Wilson flipped the magazine over in his hands and considered it. He was in sympathy with the *World Tomorrow*'s aims, he insisted. But he told Sayre to give Norman a message: There is such a thing as "the indecent exposure of his private opinions in public."

After Sayre left, Wilson sat down at his desk and wrote to Burleson about the *World Tomorrow*. "I know the principal writer for this paper, Norman Thomas," he wrote. "He was once a pupil of mine at Princeton." Wilson told Burleson that he was confident that his talk with Sayre would influence "the policy and, to some extent, the point of view of men like Thomas; but I write this only to suggest that you treat these men with all possible consideration, for I know they are absolutely sincere and I would not like to see this publication held up unless there is a very clear case indeed."

·+·

Wilson intervened with his subordinates on such matters only a handful of times, and he did so on behalf of individuals even more rarely. His general policy was not to have a policy. Thousands were arrested and imprisoned, and Wilson stayed silent. Three days after the Justice Department ransacked the NCLB offices, the American Protective League led a "slacker raid" on New York City. Volunteer agents had already approached men at movie theatres and railroad stations in Chicago, Coney Island, and Trenton, asking them to produce their draft classification cards. The raid in New York City came just before the third registration day for the Selective Service. Between September 3 and September 5, an estimated twenty to twenty-five thousand men, including members of the Justice Department, police, soldiers, sailors, and card-carrying league members, questioned between three hundred thousand and five hundred thousand men who appeared of draft age. The agents blocked the doors of trains and approached diners in restaurants, "arresting" anyone who could not produce an adequate card. They moved through traffic, interrogating men at stoplights. Finally they were told to stop hauling drivers away because abandoned cars were clogging traffic. They interrupted trading on Wall Street. At the Equitable Building, they questioned thousands of employees and caught twenty-two without cards (all of whom would later be released). In the end, 60,187 men were detained. Of those, 199 were found to be dodging the draft and were later put into service. Even fewer were deserters. The raids divided opinion in the papers and Congress. Wilson said nothing.

A week after Sayre visited Wilson, Eugene Debs went on trial for a speech he had delivered that summer in Canton, Ohio. Wearing a vest and jacket in the rippling heat, so weak from illness he could hardly stand, Debs knew that radicals were being watched, but he spoke anyway. The government's prosecution of dissenters exposed the hypocrisy of their fight for freedom, he declared. But direct censorship was not the only gag on the people. They were fighting a war they had not asked for. He gripped the railing of the platform and leaned out over it. "If war is right, let it be declared by the people—you, who have your lives to lose." A newspaperman heard the speech that day and called a friend, the federal prosecutor for northern Ohio. The prosecutor appealed to Washington; the special assistant in Washington said that Debs's speech fell under protection of the law, if barely, and recommended against prosecution. The prosecutor in Ohio indicted Debs anyway. During his trial that September, the Socialist produced a copy of Wilson's 1912 campaign book, *New Freedom*, and read aloud passages in defense of his views. It was a smart gimmick, but not as moving as his own pleas. He was, he said, on trial for aligning himself with those who suffered, "their hopes blasted, because in this high noon of our twentieth century civilization, money is still so much more important than human life." At his sentencing, he delivered words that would long be remembered: "While there is a lower class, I am in it; while there is a criminal element, I am of it; while there is a soul in prison, I am not free." The judge gave him ten years.

·+·

At Fort Riley, Emma pressed her son to eat, but he was stubborn. The army had no better luck. On Sunday afternoon, September 1, Colonel M. O. Bigelow came over to Evan's bed and asked Emma to wait outside. Bigelow asked Evan if he belonged to a church. Evan replied that he did not, that he had a religion of his own. Bigelow asked him if he thought he was crazy. He asked him if he was wealthy and where his mother was from. Bigelow ordered him to eat when the orderlies brought in food, and Evan replied that he refused to obey any military order. Bigelow wrote the order down, and Evan refused again. He knew his refusal would mean a court-martial. He had disobeyed a military order from a senior officer—and whatever Evan thought, as the military saw it, Evan was part of the military.

When Emma was allowed back into the room, she was devastated—"all broken up," wrote Gray to his parents—that her son would go to jail for a stand that would be seen as suicide. Her tone in a letter to Norman, however, was flat. "You better collect the testimonials of Evan's past life and character and send them on to me," she wrote. Only the smallest suggestion of vulnerability betrayed her anxiety: "My pen is broken," she wrote to Norman, "and I have a poor pencil."

That night Evan stayed up late talking to Gray, who had listened to Emma say that starving oneself was suicide and worried that it might be true. Gray did not want to do something unethical, nor did he want to go to prison for the pathetic reason of refusing an order to eat. Evan told his friend he had to follow his conscience. The next morning, Gray and Lunde "wiggled [their] jaws" and had breakfast. It was hard for Evan to watch them eat and to see their ebullience, and it was hard for him to hear all the talk of suicide. It was hard for Emma to watch him bear it.

The next morning Emma arrived to see Evan, Gray, Lunde, and Moore excitedly surrounding an older man. It was Lunde's father, and it turned out that he had just been released from the guardhouse. The cause of arrest was unclear. One rumor was that officers had found letters among the younger Lunde's papers from his father supporting his son's opposition to conscription. Another rumor had it that the Chicagoan social activist had been arrested while looking for the hospital on suspicion of being a German spy. One objector, who knew that the senior Lunde wrote letters to his son saying things like "Never let the event master the will to do right!" joked that he was probably arrested for being too loud.

The elder Lunde wore his indignation a little vainly. Still, his arbitrary arrest shook Emma. As the day went on, she became more sensitive to the military's capriciousness. Later that afternoon she heard that her access to her son might be restricted, a thought she could hardly bear. She thought it unfair, she told Norman, that Evan was "getting all the blame." Captain Henry told Evan that he would be the scapegoat for all the hunger strikers, and that if the military machine decided to crush him, then it would. Evan's own stubborn tone began to creep into Emma's letters. "He insists [the strike] was his only way out of a position which was intolerable," she wrote to Norman, who was well aware of what Evan insisted. She was advancing the line against her own resistance.

One night, Emma sat on a park bench by her hotel and noticed that the ground was littered with sparrows killed in a thunderstorm the night before. She described the dead birds in a letter to her daughters, who must have worried at their mother's morbid turn. Newly alert to censors and spies, she said she worried about implicating her sons with some careless observation, even in a letter to her teenaged daughters. "Always nowadays it is best not to write much." As she sat and wrote, Emma thought not only about her son but also about the other absolutists. She was touched by Moore's situation most of all. Moore's mother had written to say that her son's stand was "killing" his parents, literally. "I almost cried over it, so sorry for the mother and yet sorry for him," she wrote to her daughters. "Like Evan he hates awfully to hurt his mother and also like Evan he thinks he would feel his life ruined if he gave up his position on war now." She added, "All the tragedies of this war are not at the front."

The next day, Evan was in a desultory mood, and Emma did not blame him. Only he and Moore were still on the hunger strike. When Norman had heard that Gray had begun to eat, he had sent him an enthusiastic telegram, congratulating him for doing as he saw right. Gray, having tucked in a nice breakfast, passed the telegram around. "That's fine," Evan offered when he saw it. Emma hotly told Norman he shouldn't have congratulated Gray so. "I'm not sure that I feel Harold needs so much praise. He strikes me as one who can feel quite sure he deserves praise—but there I may be doing him a great injustice." When she calmed down, she allowed she was being unfair. "I feared for Evan's feelings," she explained. When she looked at her son, growing thinner and more alone, she dug her heels in.

While eating lunch the next day, Emma devised a plan: She would carry a letter from Moore and Evan to President Wilson herself. She returned to find her gaunt son pacing, his long strides eating the length of the room. Emma had just launched into her plan when Evan cut her off. "I've been having a talk with three majors," he said, "and I'm almost ready to give in." An army psychologist had just come by and convinced him that continuing his strike would not help his cause, he wrote to Norman and Violet. To Emma, though, he was more revealing. "Oh," he said, "he told me I was an individualist and an egoist and just hold out from pride and will." That criticism hit its mark.

Evan walked back and forth, back and forth across the hospital room floor, agonizing over whether to abandon his position and call for dinner. If he gave in, wasn't he a failure? And if he didn't, wasn't he a vain, stubborn fool? Finally, his mother could not take watching her tortured son anymore. She stood up and paced alongside him.

And then she did something incredible: She tried to convince him not to end the strike. "Funny creatures that we are," she wrote afterward, "when I found him weakening I actually almost hated to have him give it up." She drew herself up and reminded him that nothing had changed, that the tent colony conditions were as bad as ever. He had not yet succeeded. He could not weaken. He had to be strong.

Evan replied that he was exhausted. He had been fed twenty meals through a rubber tube shoved down his throat, and nothing had changed. She told him to go back to the major and insist that camp conditions *must* change if he was going to give up the strike, and, wearily, he agreed.

Whatever ambivalence Emma had entertained vanished. She stood by her son because her son had taken a stand. She had not agreed with it—but he had tried to act on the best convictions he had. That was something a daughter of Mary and Stephen Mattoon could understand. He had taken a risk for his beliefs, and in his thin body and the anguish on his face as he paced she could see that he suffered. She hated to see him in pain—hated to see the conditions of the tent colony, hated to see him so defeated and despondent. She was angry now. When Harold Gray showed her a note he had written to Secretary Baker apologizing profusely for undertaking the strike, she bridled. The note was pitiful, she told Gray, who was so taken aback that he did not send the letter. (Emma's fierceness "tickled me greatly," Evan wrote gleefully to Norman and Violet. "Didn't know she was such a good sport.")

While Emma rallied, Evan gave in. He came back into the room and said, "I promised [the major] to eat while in the hospital but starve or desert if sent out to old conditions." The room began to buzz. The objectors who had come to the hospital to eat a prepared dinner gathered around Evan's bed. Captain Henry came over and shouted loudly, "Here, bring Thomas some supper!"

She could hardly understand herself, Emma later wrote, and yet she was filled with a sense of despair, some inexplicable mix of frustration and anger at her son, at the military, at what was happening. Emma turned away from her son. She walked over to Moore's bed; he was now the only striker left, and she did not want him to be alone. Captain Henry spotted them and came over. "Here, you," he addressed Moore, "you're the only one left now; just get up and eat your supper." Emma saw Moore stiffen.

"No," he said. "Poor Moore is such a fine fellow, proud and sensitive," Emma wrote to Norman later that night. "He said sadly, without much bitterness, 'Of course, Evan and Gray with their education and advantages will get off in some way, but I'm a poor nobody easily crushed,' and I'm afraid he's partly right." Emma told Moore that she was on his side. She would not let him be forgotten. She'd sooner have Evan go on another strike than see Moore suffer because he lacked the fancy connections that her sons had. Knowing that he was back on his family farm would bring her greater pleasure, she wrote to Norman, "than anything else I know of, except to have all my boys safe at home." Moore had proved himself to Emma, and he had found in her a defender.

The experience of watching Evan and Moore awoke a latent fighting spirit, and it only grew stronger. Cornering the army psychologist, Major Herman Adler, she pleaded with him to understand why Moore should be allowed to return home, why the young men had acted as they did, and why it must have been making a difference.

"Your son tried a method and failed," Adler responded. Evan had "won nothing." She mentioned the poor conditions in the tent colony and he waved her words away. "The soldiers put up with worse conditions," he said. This was true, and she knew it. Another of her own sons had spent nights in gas-filled dugouts. Still, there was something he just did not seem to understand: The treatment of the objectors was dehumanizing and dismissive, and the strikers' protest preserved some dignity. Adler "listens and agrees," she wrote to Norman, "but some way soon you lose all enthusiasm for your ideals and are left with a perfectly hopeless feeling of: what's the use of trying anything different? Certainly he was sorry for individuals, but one could not stop to consider them when multitudes must be considered."

Emma—who had come to Kansas in a state of despair, desperate for her son to give up the strike—looked at Adler with resolve and barely contained fury. "I wanted to ask him why he was here if my son had gained nothing," she wrote to Norman. She was not exactly hopeful—"yet I *know* the whole thing has stirred up Washington." Her son's fight had become her own. Emma repeatedly wrote to officials, including Secretary Baker and President Wilson, on her son's—and Moore's—behalf. Sayre passed along her message to Wilson. In his cover letter, Sayre called Evan "Christ-like." It was a claim that Evan would have hated to see, but it was also a description of what he desperately tried to be.

·+·

Soon after Evan was strong enough to return to the tent camp, he had to leave it. On September 16, he found guards waiting for him at his tent. It was the start of the "Colonel's Drive," during which officers gave orders to objectors and put them in the guardhouse when they resisted. Evan was the first one taken. In his case, the colonel in command of the post did not even go through the show of delivering an order and arresting him when it was disobeyed. The guards took him straight to solitary confinement, where he waited for his court-martial for refusing to eat. His cell was about six feet by five—too short for him to stretch out in. He had nothing to read, no paper for writing. After a few days he was brought some soap and a towel and some toxin to combat the bugs that scuttled across the floor and walls. Later he was given a Bible, two sheets of paper, and a pen. Major Walter Kellogg, a member of the Board of Inquiry, visited him in prison after he had been there a week and asked if he would change his mind about refusing alternative service. Evan said no. Kellogg said he was sorry for him. He wished Evan were older, because then Evan might have more "horse sense."

Part of Evan—a large part—was relieved to be in prison. It was better to be behind bars than imprisoned by the inertia he had felt all summer. He had hated the feeling of being ignored. Prison was a kind of platform, a place of protest. "My place is in prison as long as the American people believe in conscription or believe that the State has the right to do with individual lives what it chooses regardless of the individual's personality and conscience," he wrote to his mother. Uncertainty was worse than solitary. "I admit the 1st week cost me something but I needed just that," he said. More clarity about his fate came a few days later.

Evan was called before a court-martial at Camp Funston on the afternoon of October 3. Eight majors, five captains, and two second lieutenants were on hand to judge his case. He faced two charges. The first was "that Private Evan W. Thomas, Medical Corps, having received a lawful command from Colonel M.O. Bigelow, his superior officer, to eat such food as was provided him by attending surgeons, at the times prescribed by them, in order that he might regain his strength and be restored to duty as a soldier, did, at the Base Hospital, Fort Riley, Kansas, on or about the 1st day of September, 1918, willfully disobey the same." The second was more straightforward: he was charged with trying to weaken himself past the point where he could be an effective soldier.

Evan served as his own counsel. "I believe that America went into the war sincerely to end Prussianism and Prussian militarism," he told the assembled. "Nevertheless my experience in Great Britain made me believe that while perhaps it is true that in this stage of the world, at the present time, the war may be necessary, yet there must be kept alive the ideal of individual liberty, an ideal for which I believe America stands as no other nation in the world." When he arrived at camp, he said, "I was told repeatedly that I was in the army. I was told that I must accept the status of a soldier, in fact to do non-combatant work." This was why he had taken an absolutist stand. When conditions became unendurable, he felt he had to protest them, "not in the spirit of defiance, but merely in the spirit of trying to be true to myself and true to the ideals which I had."

The prosecution took its turn. "This is clearly a case of willful disobedience of orders by a superior officer in the United States Army," the prosecutor began, then immediately turned the argument against the legitimacy of conscientious objection, just as Evan had turned his argument into its defense. "The very foundation of every civilized government from the first beginning of history down to the present time has been based absolutely upon force of arms," argued the prosecutor. There were no such thing as conscientious objectors. There were only cowards. "Gentlemen, if we don't punish these cowards who appear in this land like the sore spots on our bodies, to the fullest limit of the law, this government cannot survive. . . . Gentlemen, I ask you to give this accused the fullest limit of the punishment to which he is entitled"—which was death—"because he refuses to go out with the soldiers of this land and fight in the trenches for the principles of our government."

Evan responded flatly. "I do not consider it a disgrace for any man to wear a uniform. Whether I am a coward or not is not for me to decide. It is my conviction if the principles of liberty need to be kept alive now, this is my way of believing that I best can keep it alive."

An hour after the court convened, Evan was found guilty on all charges. Twenty minutes later, his sentence was handed down: "Evan W. Thomas to be dishonorably discharged, forfeit pay, and to be confined at hard labor, at such place as the reviewing authority may direct, for the term of his natural life."

Norman was shocked when he heard the sentence. It seemed a farce: life imprisonment for refusing an order to eat. Evan had spent years trying to figure out how to fight for the principle of freedom of conscience, the right of a man to be his own master. Instead, he would be locked up for life because he refused to swallow at a colonel's order. If anything demonstrated the absurdity of Wilson's claim the country went to war for the privilege of men to find their own way of life and obedience, Norman thought it was this.

Evan—as ever—saw things differently. "I take my hat off to Wilson as a very great man," he wrote only ten days after his court-martial, when he learned that Germans had opened peace negotiations. "Very likely I will live in prison some time because of my refusal to accept conscription," he allowed, "but I can at least admire the greatness of the man."

﹢

On Wednesday, October 9, Roger Baldwin let the local draft board know that he would refuse to appear before it. The eligibility age had risen, and Baldwin was eager to join the ranks of conscientious objectors. (Norman's large family made him exempt, as did his status as a clergyman, though he refused to claim an exemption on the latter grounds.) He told the district attorney that he hoped for a quick trial and that he planned to plead guilty and refuse bail. A government agent came to his apartment and led him to the draft office in the basement of the American Natural History Museum, where the chairman instructed him to not be so "contumacious." He was taken to jail for a night to think it over. The next morning, a group of rowdy agents (including some he knew from their raid on the NCLB office) took him in a limousine to a "bang-up breakfast" and then to the

Bureau of Investigation office, where several attorneys begged him to register, he later recalled. That night he was indicted and taken to the Tombs, where he was treated as a kind of "pet prisoner." The agent in charge of his case rebuked one deputy for putting him in handcuffs and then asked, aware of the irony or not, if Baldwin could organize the seized NCLB files; the agents who had taken them had done the task so haphazardly that they were now in disarray.

·+·

For three weeks agents ferried Baldwin from his cell to "work" organizing the NCLB files and then sometimes to dinner or the theater (and one night a burlesque show). One afternoon, a Bureau of Investigation agent accompanied Baldwin to lunch at Norman's house. To the Thomases' horror and their young sons' delight, the agent entertained the children by showing them his weapons. As Baldwin and his armed chaperone left, the agent told his incredulous hostess to call if she should ever need anything. Afterward, Violet turned to her husband and said that she felt like she'd been offered assistance by an undertaker.

Baldwin was in terrific spirits, but Norman had trouble seeing things with a light heart. The situation was ridiculous, but it was hardly funny. His good friend was in jail, his brother was locked up for life, and another brother was recovering from wounds in a war that Norman believed should never have been fought. Even Arthur had to deal with useless tragedy. At just that moment, his closest friend in flying school died when his training plane crashed—and it looked probable that the training was for nothing, since the war was winding down. For Norman, a decade of frustrations in poor neighborhoods in New York City had built to a climax. It was time for him to demonstrate his convictions. "These are the days," he wrote, "when radicals ought to stand up and be counted."

On October 18, Leonard Wood, the commander at Camp Funston, where Evan was being held in the guardhouse, reviewed the transcript of Evan's court-martial and reduced his sentence from life to twenty-five years—out of mercy, Norman sarcastically noted in a letter to Ralph. On that same day, Norman applied for membership in the Socialist Party.

·╬·

It was not a rash decision. No single event drove him to it. A full year had passed since Norman had supported the Socialist Morris Hillquit's campaign for mayor. Thirteen years had passed since he had first moved into the New York tenements. He did not join simply because he was appalled by what he saw there or on Fifth Avenue (though he was sometimes appalled by both). His understanding of the social and economic dynamics in the city had not suddenly changed. Nor did he become a Socialist because it was the only major antiwar party, though his pacifism had led him in that direction. The war was nearly over, and Norman admitted he was not totally enamored of the Socialists' proclamation for peace anyway. He became a Socialist in October 1918 because he saw a country in crisis, and he felt the crisis within himself. He wanted to help workers who were powerless to change their situations, but the truth was that he was powerless, too. Joining the Socialist Party was a way of taking a stand. Unlike Evan's stand, Norman's was not lonely. The promise of politics, and of Socialism in particular, was that people act together.

Norman's move was less dramatic and dangerous than Evan's (or Ralph's or Arthur's). Unless the government or a zealous vigilante decided to crush him (which was, granted, a real possibility), he would not die or be imprisoned. Partly he was reluctant to risk hurting his wife and children or being taken away from them. But the way he expressed his convictions was also different because his convictions were different. Norman and Evan shared many beliefs about what the state should and should not look like; they had a common concern for civil liberties and freedom of conscience and a disgust for the inequality produced by the capitalist state. But Evan elevated the individual to the supreme position. He was almost anarchic in his principles and temperament, inclined to look inward and act accordingly. Norman's conception of conscience was more complex and almost paradoxical. Since he believed the deepest desire of every individual is to love and be loved, then being true to oneself means focusing on others. He tried to focus his brother's flailing attention. "I think you hold the only worthy faith, but that sort of individualism can only be realized in the fellowship with other individuals and in mutual service," he wrote to Evan soon after the hunger strike.

Evan acted from a position of privilege in becoming a leader of conscientious objectors. He was well educated and childless. When he was sick, he had doctors. When he was hungry, he was fed. He was free because he could be; he had already been given every advantage. Norman admired and even envied him for his courage. He saw him as an ally—more than an ally, as a hero. His understanding of freedom, though, meant more than freedom from conscription. It meant freedom from hunger, from exploitation, and from war. It meant that the sick would have doctors, the unemployed would have work, and the workers would have leisure. All of this, he knew, would take more than brave speech or heroic individual action. It would take laws and money—policy and politics.

Trying to negotiate the conflict between autonomy and responsibility, Norman and Evan ultimately came down on different sides. Evan had disparaged Norman's politics, finding him too optimistic about the kinds of compromises people and politicians would and should make. Norman, on the other hand, worried that his brother cultivated an "aloofness from life." In his obsession with being true to himself, Evan risked forgetting others, Norman gently told him after the hunger strike. No one lives entirely alone, in the citadel of his own being. "If we are to love our neighbors as ourselves," Norman wrote to his brother, "we must seek with might and main to bring about conditions under which the inner kingdom is not constantly mocked by outward circumstances, and in which its attainment is not rendered all but impossible for great masses of people." These were lofty, grandiloquent words, perhaps more suited to a minister's Sunday sermon than a letter from one brother to another. But Norman really believed them. And they explain, as simply as anything Norman ever said, why he became a Socialist.

Socialism was, for him, more of an ethical than an economic system, a way to reconcile the inner kingdom with outward circumstances. It was a way to start thinking about society in terms of people, "living, breathing men and women." He agreed with his brother that acting in the name of " 'society,' 'democracy,' 'the proletariat,' 'Christianity' " had led to unimaginable harm throughout history. But that did not mean that people should not search for some kind of transcendence. Norman wrote to Evan, "I am still enough of an optimist about the universe to believe that truth, righteousness, reason, not as abstractions but as the expression of the deepest desires of living men and women will ultimately triumph if we serve them with methods consistent with them and abandon the false and perilous maxim that the end justifies the means."

Norman believed in democratic socialism. He wanted workers to have a claim to the things they made and to things that every human needs. He wanted to end the cycle of violence and conflict that he saw endemic to capitalism. Later, he would focus on economic policies and theories concerning the means of production, use value, full employment, and other tenants of the socialist economy—embracing some, rejecting others, changing his mind—but what motivated him first and finally was a simple ethic, one related to his religious background but independent of it. It was the injunction to love your neighbor as yourself writ large. The socialism he embraced was hazy in its particulars at first, predicated too much on the possibility of eradicating war, extreme inequality, abuse, and indignity. It put too much faith in the idea that, given the chance, people will put others before themselves. He had read some literature by socialists and was familiar with its basic doctrines, but neither Marx nor Engels was on his mind when he joined the Socialist Party. When he applied to the party, he wrote that he thought "establishing a cooperative commonwealth and the abolition of our present unjust economic institutions and class distinctions" was not just necessary but possible. Still, at that point, he was almost entirely unconcerned with the grit of economic planning. This was his way of taking a stand.

He joined warily. "Perhaps to certain members of the Party my Socialism would not be of the most orthodox variety," Norman wrote in the letter that he submitted with his application. This was something of an understatement. His letter included a long list of protests against the party. He worried about the bureaucratic state and the conflict of individuality and collectivism. He did not believe the party was concerned enough with civil liberties. "I have a profound fear of the undue exaltation of the State and a profound faith that the new world we desire must depend upon freedom and fellowship rather than upon any sort of coercion whatsoever," he wrote. So ambivalent was he that he noted that if he were a farmer, he probably would have joined the Nonpartisan League, not the Socialist Party. Only three weeks before, in September, he had suggested to one correspondent that the Socialist Party was not sensitive to the dangers of the powerful state and tended toward force. "No theory of the state, whether socialistic or capitalistic, is valid, which makes it master not servant to men," he wrote.

He had not come up with any new answers since he wrote those words. Still, he was a Socialist. Liberals had failed, like the progressives before them. Roosevelt was jingoistic. Wilson's presidency had produced a country that seemed to Norman worse off and less free. Progressive efforts were superficial and ineffective. Class conflict was endemic. There was a structural element to injustice that the reform efforts of the liberals could not address. A philanthropist, a president, a man of conscience—a conscientious objector—could not do it alone. It would take society, and Norman had come to believe it would take Socialists.

The idea of self-fulfillment through fellowship, obviously, was not original to Norman. And yet Norman felt it with a rare urgency, and he had a talent for communicating that idea to others. He never argued that the greatest good should be secured for the greatest number, or that concerns for the commonweal trumped the rights of individuals, as many progressives held; that was "the false and perilous maxim that the end justifies the means." From the start, people called him naïve, and maybe he was. His conception of socialism depended on the idea that, despite so much evidence to the contrary, people would want to care for one another, not overpower one another, if they lived in the right culture and economic system, free from the warping effects of desperation and distrust. But what, he asked himself, was more naïve: perpetuating a system that allowed for a cataclysmic war, that allowed for lynching and repression, and that left so many in poverty and pain, or trying to change it? Were men condemned to kill each other, or could they be their brothers' keepers?

Nineteen

MEAN WHAT YOU SAY

*Ralph missed his chance to participate
in a smashing drive after being wounded
by a German artillery shell.*

Baldwin's court date was set for October 30. He drafted his statement sitting in his cell and showed it to only Norman. On the Wednesday morning of the trial, Baldwin's friends and colleagues filled the courtroom. So did reporters from the major New York newspapers. Baldwin didn't disappoint his audience. Speaking simply, he told the court that he opposed the conscription of life by the government in times or war or peace. He said that he knew that few shared his views, but that they were part of the country's strong tradition. Conscription, he told the judge, was "a flat contradiction of all our cherished ideals of individual freedom, democratic liberty and Christian teaching." By the end of his speech, even the judge was moved. But the judge had to consider the law, he told Baldwin, and the law was clear. He sentenced Baldwin to a year in prison.

After the sentence was delivered, Norman rose from his seat and walked forward to congratulate his friend on his performance. Baldwin had managed to turn a depressing occasion—the imprisonment of the leader of the nation's nascent civil liberties movement—into a reason for heart. No one knew how Baldwin's trial would affect his cause. Only a few days afterward, the Associated Press reported that officials were warning against making contributions to "so-called 'civil liberties,' 'liberty defense,' 'popular council,' 'legal advice,' or anti-war organizations," and they held up Baldwin's imprisonment as a warning. All the same, Norman knew, even then, that Baldwin's defense of freedom of conscience would make a difference, that his speech would be read and remembered for a long time. After the trial, he wrote to Baldwin's mother that watching his friend conduct himself with such dignity was "one of the rare experiences of a lifetime."

✢

News of Evan's hunger strike and Norman's decision to join the Socialist Party took time to reach Ralph. He did not hear anything, in fact, from the United States for months, while his mail was rerouted from the front to his hospital on the coast of western France. The days ticked by, slow and dull. There was still, of course, death all around him. Ralph did not write home about the maimed men at the hospital or describe the moaning that echoed down the halls. When he did complain it was because he was bored, with nothing to read but pulp novels, nothing to do but submit to dressing changes, nowhere to go but to the window, where he looked longingly at the fine weather outside. His wounds were slow to heal. He suffered from "proud flesh"—infection from the dirt and germs that had entered along with the shrapnel—and it would not hold a suture. Still, he tried to put on a show of good spirits. Even for a naturally cheerful man, his good humor was striking. The hospital he described was free of injuries and illness; no limbs were blown off or minds shattered. Quite the opposite. The other officers were "the cheeriest, jolliest bunch I have come across in a long time."

Superficially at least, his wounds seem to not have affected his spirit at all. Most of his letters home were about how badly he wanted to return to the front. His regiment was now in heavy fighting, and he was missing it all. His comrades were now heroes. Two privates from his regiment spent five days in a pile of charcoal in Bazoches that September 1918, without food and then without water, before killing two German machine gunners and leading a blinded and crazed infantryman to safety. Other engineers pulled the wounded out of rivers or ripped off their masks in a fog of mustard gas to save them. All around Bazoches, corpses were growing black in the hot sun.

While convalescing, Ralph heard reports that the Seventy-seventh was heading into something big. Finally the moment for the great advance had arrived. From the Vesle River the 302nd moved to the Argonne Forest, where the Seventy-seventh was to form the left flank of the American Expeditionary Force. During the day all was quiet; at night, details of engineers would creep out beyond the front lines, carrying bayonets, rifles, and fifty rounds of ammunition along with their tools, to cut through the thickets of barbed wire and create lanes through which the infantry could pass. Rumors flew that this was going to be the biggest assault the Allies had ever launched. Then the attack began, stretching from the North Sea to the Meuse, and the western front moved east.

Ralph reported the engineers' progress with glee, but he was clearly envious. "We got [to the Vesle] when the lines had become temporarily stationary, so I have missed the most exciting of all war events—an advance," he wrote to his mother. Ralph's wounds were all the more frustrating because they kept him from the fight. Having missed his chance for glory, he was anxious to return to the front. His commander wanted him there, too. "I am very anxious to retain his services within the regiment," Colonel C. O. Sherrill wrote to the commanding general of the Seventy-seventh Regiment a few days after Ralph was evacuated to the hospital.

He spent October in Bourré, recuperating in a loft above some goats and sheep at the home of Aunt Anna and Uncle Frank Welles—benefactors, as ever. His scars were still fresh, raw and red, and he would carry a piece of shrapnel in his lung for the rest of his life. Still, he hated to be stuck far from the fight. When he was well enough healed, he took a trip to Paris and saw it like a tourist, visiting Notre Dame and the Tuileries in the company of a friend whose right arm had been paralyzed by four machine gun bullets. His friend had been a pianist. Grim reminders of their strange situation were everywhere. At a party one night another friend casually mentioned that earlier that day he had learned that his brother had died, throwing off the comment like an insignificant aside. "The ONLY thing that will justify the losses is the complete defeat and elimination of Prussianism and militarism and *war*," Ralph wrote home.

At the end of October, while Ralph was still hoping to get back to the front for the last few weeks of fighting, letters from the United States arrived. The first batch had the news about Evan's hunger strike and time in the guardhouse. Ralph was stunned and a little guilty. The closer he had been to the fighting, the further his brothers' battles had been from his mind. Ralph could not help but admire and envy his brother. Reading about Evan's trials "hit me harder than anything I've heard," Ralph wrote to his mother. "I feel ashamed of myself to be having a good time in Paris and classed as a young tin hero because through no fault of mine a [German] shell dropped beside me." In France, Ralph had craved the authenticity of real battle—to put himself through strenuous effort and pain in the name of his convictions. To the soldier, Evan's suffering almost sanctified his principles, however wrong they were. "Much as I may disagree with him, I must say Evan has what in college we called guts."

After nearly three months, Ralph was cleared to return to his regiment. He left Bourré on November 11. It was not a normal day. That morning, the members of the engineer band gathered at division headquarters at Raucourt and pulled out the instruments, unused for months. At the eleventh hour of the eleventh day of the eleventh month of the year, peace was declared, and the band began to play. The crowd sang the "Marseillaise" and "The Star-Spangled Banner." The soldiers celebrated their victory with full enthusiasm. But when they looked at the French civilians who had gathered to celebrate with them, the soldiers could see that the end of the war meant something more extraordinary than they could ever

know, something they could imagine but not entirely understand. Only a
short time before, the town had been under the occupation of the German
military. Now the war was over, and the town was free.

·✛·

In New York, confetti floated through the air. After an early cold snap, the
air was springlike, and men and women filled the streets and sang. Norman
could hear the happy tumult outside and felt a surge of joy that he would
remember for the rest of his life. The next day the papers declared in two-
inch capitals: "ARMISTICE SIGNED: THE GREATEST DAY IN THE HISTORY OF
NATIONS HAS DAWNED."

It had been a trying week for Norman. Violet was ill, and, far more
worrying, four of their children had come down with influenza. This was
not just any flu. The first documented case of the Great Influenza had
occurred in Kansas in early 1918, but despite the strange symptoms and
significant death rate, no one thought too much of it, or considered how to
contain it, until it was too late.

Epidemiologists now estimate that the Great Influenza caused between
fifty million and one hundred million deaths worldwide. It killed more
men and women in one year that the bubonic plague in the Middle Ages
had killed in a century; it killed more people in six months than AIDS
killed in twenty-four years. The virus attacked people of all ages, but it
ravaged those who should have been the strongest: healthy young men and
women. They would appear in the infirmary or hospital with a bad case of
the flu. Quickly, within hours sometimes, cyanosis would sometimes set
in, and victims would turn blue after their lungs stopped transferring oxy-
gen to the blood, their faces turning the cool hue of veins seen through the
thin skin of the wrist. Blood poured out of nostrils and mouths and ears.
Hospitals could not keep up with the number of admittances, especially
on army bases, where men slept and lived in overcrowded quarters. The
sick lay on row after row of temporary cots, and the air was filled with
the stench of blood and vomit. When American soldiers left for Europe,
they took the virus with them. The most deadly weapon yet known would
kill them as well as their enemies indiscriminately. Back in the States, the
virus moved into the cities. In Philadelphia, after the city turned out for

a Liberty Loan parade, the virus exploded across the population. First a
few hundred were sick. Within ten days hundreds of thousands were sick
and hundreds died each day. Philadelphia ran out of caskets. The virus
appeared in San Francisco, Los Angeles, Boston, Baltimore, New York.
The dead were left in piles on porches.

A comparable figure to the number of deaths today, as a percentage of
population in the United States, is around 1.75 million, but a number does
not capture the fear the nation felt. There were common reports of men
and women who were walking down the sidewalk, feeling fine, when suddenly they would collapse to the sidewalk. They would show symptoms
and die within twelve hours. People stopped going outside. In one town, a
law was passed against shaking hands.

Though the government had facilitated the disease's spread through
troop movements and civilian rallies, Wilson stayed quiet. Only when
the flu had so debilitated the camps that drafts were canceled and training was curtailed did the president confront Army Chief of Staff General
Peyton March. By this point, writes the historian John Barry, "the transports became floating caskets." Wilson called General March to the White
House late at night on October 7. It was true, March admitted, that some
men were dying even before reaching France, but their lives were sacrificed
for the war effort: "Every soldier who has died just as surely played his
part as his comrade who died in France." He insisted, "The shipment of
troops should not be stopped for any cause." Wilson turned his gaze out
the window, into the darkness, and then he sighed. The shipping of troops
continued, and so did the spread of the disease. When the war stopped, the
ships would reverse directions, ferrying the sick back to the United States.

It was a strange time for all, and perhaps especially for Norman. He
was grateful that his children had recovered quickly but remained always
fearful for their health. While the armistice celebrations raged outside, he
knew that his friend Roger Baldwin was being led to a prison in Newark
that very day. Evan, too, was in a jail cell at that moment—in solitary confinement, with his hands manacled at chest height, standing chained to the
bars for nine hours a day.

Still, though, Norman could hardly constrain his joy. There was peace
at last.

·⼀·

Norman was relieved to hear from a contact in Junction City a few days
later that Evan had been transferred from Funston to Fort Leavenworth
on October 22. Norman had been anxious to get Evan out of the guardhouse at Funston, where the accounts of brutality—objectors called it the
"reign of terror"—were so sensational that even the reluctant War Department was investigating and taking action. Five army officers, including two
majors, were eventually fired. Evan unfailingly stressed the kind treatment
he had received while in the guardhouse, but Norman had heard too much
about guards at Funston beating and starving objectors—and knew Evan's
stoicism all too well—not to worry. Leavenworth was different. The commandant there, Colonel Sedgwick Rice, had a good reputation. But even
at Leavenworth, Norman cautioned his mother (with an "of course" that
signaled either resignation or wishful thinking), there would be trouble if
Evan refused to work.

    And before long, Evan did. Evan's impulse for martyrdom and protest
had not disappeared or been satisfied when he was sent to prison. He still
had an insatiable need to test the government and himself, to be absolutely
consistent and never give up. For a few days, Evan did work. Then he
heard that three of the Molokans, a small fringe sect that had emigrated
from Russia to avoid conscription and that felt compelled by the Holy
Spirit not to obey any military orders, were being held in solitary. The
Molokans had fascinated him since he had first spotted them at Fort Riley,
standing out with their long beards even in the crowd of misfit objectors.
After encountering them, Evan had burst into his tent and said to his tent-
mate Arthur Dunham, "By George! I thought I was a CO, but I've just
seen the *real thing*. . . . They've been mistreated in every sort of way, at
various times, but they have never done a stroke of work for the military,
and they have *never obeyed one military command*!" The *real thing*—what
Evan needed so badly to be.

    The news now spread through Leavenworth that for refusing to work,
the Molokans were being placed in solitary with their hands manacled
to the bars for the working hours of the day. They did not even eat the
prison food because it was not cooked according to their strict religious

requirements. Evan went to his boss and told him that he would no longer work, not because he conscientiously objected to working in prison, but in solidarity with the Molokans. "America surely is big enough and the American people liberal enough to allow these men liberty to conduct their lives in accordance with their own conscience as long as they do not injure others," Evan wrote in his first letter to his mother after finishing his first fourteen days in solitary.

Norman had known what the punishment for refusal to work would be. Months ago the NCLB had studied prison regulations and taken note of the military's policy of placing disobedient prisoners in solitary on a diet of bread and water and manacling their wrists to the bars, forcing them to stand for nine hours a day. Baldwin and other NCLB committee members had warned the objectors about that punishment, called the practice to the War Department's attention, and tried to publicize the treatment, but to no effect. It was some comfort for Norman, at least, that his brother had a strange ability to provoke admiration instead of rough treatment, even as he put himself in extreme and confrontational positions. "There is something about Evan that renders him immune from the brutalities of the guard," Norman wrote to Ralph.

Emma felt "absolutely hopeless" after reading Evan's letter, but she was not one to weep and worry and do nothing. What the NCLB could not do, she did. She went to Washington and met with Keppel and then Baker, who was accompanied by the general inspector of prisons. The War Department officials were polite but curt and dismissive, as they were to Jane Addams when she saw them that same day. When Emma told the men about the manacling, the general inspector cut in: "I don't believe that." When she asked if the treatment was a prison regulation, they said no. When she pleaded that the men were sincere conscientious objectors, not criminals, they told her that once in prison, they were prisoners, and their principles did not make them special.

But a letter from Colonel Sedgwick Rice told her, somewhat apologetically, that her son's hands were in fact manacled for nine hours a day. "You may rest assured that if he breaks down in any way—and it is not anticipated that he will—he will be given proper medical care," the commandant added. She did not rest assured.

Instead she took the overnight train back to Kansas to see her son for herself. He stood with his hands fastened to his cell bars, staring out into the electric light of the hallway. When he spotted his mother coming down the hallway, his expression turned to amazement. His happiness at her arrival was obvious when he reprimanded her for coming. She was just as stubborn as he, he said, which was, in some ways, true. Emma peered into the dark cell behind her son. There wasn't much to see: a six-by-eight-foot space with a toilet seat against the back wall and three boards fastened together to make a plank leaning against the wall, which Evan said he put down to sleep. He insisted he had done the right thing. Already he'd seen a change: The Molokans were now being served vegetables instead of food they couldn't eat. The mistreatment wasn't Colonel Rice's fault, Evan said, but Rice had to have the injustice called to his attention. Someone had to do it.

Out of both compulsion and determination, Evan had to keep fighting and keep escalating the stakes. In his "final statement" as he was sent into solitary, he declared that he was "protesting against the entire prison system as well as the fact that conscientious objectors are not distinguished from ordinary criminals and against the mistreatment of individual conscientious objectors."

Evan reassured his mother that he was fine, and Emma was soothed to find him in good health and spirits. He was not really fine, though. The pressure he had placed upon himself, torqued by the intense asocial and physical experience of being in solitary, did affect his spirit, body, and mind. Evan typed the first letter that he wrote after his first fourteen days of solitary confinement, as he had many of his letters before. But this time, his lines wavered up and down across the page, and his words were spiked with errors.

```
    Dear Mother-

         I have just completed my first 14 days of solitary con-
finement & am well & strong. You have no cause to worry. I have been on bread
and water  but will be on full diet now for the next two weeks. I promise
you faithfully to take the best possible care of myself. I know that you
suffer more  than I do in this whole wretched business  but you imagine this
worse than they are. Again I assure you I am in excellent health and in far
less danger of harm probably than either Ralph or Arthur. I hope that Arthur
may soon get home That is sad news of his friend's death. It must have
taken real nerve  to go up immediately after that accident.
```

✛

Before she left for Kansas, Emma forwarded the letter describing Evan's treatment to Norman. On Sunday evening, December 1, Norman called John Nevin Sayre. They now had proof contradicting Baker's insistence that no one was being manacled. Sayre left for Washington immediately, taking the overnight train, and called the White House as soon as he arrived.

He had only a tiny window in which to see the president; Wilson was leaving Washington the following night for Hoboken, where a ship was waiting to ferry him to Europe to begin peace treaty negotiations. Anxiously, Sayre waited at his hotel until an invitation for lunch at the White House arrived. Had Wilson known the reason for Sayre's visit, he might not have been so welcoming. It was the second time in a matter of weeks that Sayre had come to discuss the plight of a Thomas brother, and it must have been a little exasperating. Aside from that moment in September, the president had never shown much compassion for dissenters. To the contrary, he had declared that opposition must be crushed, and he had asked Congress to empower him to follow through. His desire for a unanimity of support was so great that he had asked the American people to vote for Democrats in the elections that November, so that he might be "unembarrassed" entering the peace negotiations. When the Republicans swept to a huge majority in the House and a slim but substantial majority in the Senate that November, he had suffered a severe blow.

On that day of all days, as he prepared to leave to negotiate the treaty he hoped would be his legacy, he would have been distracted. He was convinced that the course of world history was staked on the upcoming negotiations. It was an awkward moment to raise the question of amnesty for conscientious objectors or for the political prisoners, including Eugene Debs, whose release Sayre also requested.

But over lunch, Sayre found Wilson as gracious as he had always found him. Wilson listened to Sayre's plea with concern, interest, and even, Sayre was convinced, surprise. The news of Evan's imprisonment and rough treatment seemed to trouble Wilson particularly. His own former student—a Presbyterian seminarian—who was one of Sayre's closest friends was chained to the cell bars in solitary confinement? This was not what Wilson had imagined when he had warned dissenters not to oppose him. The manacling sounded barbaric, he agreed. "No such treatment ought to be meted out to conscientious objectors or any other prisoners in America," Wilson said.

"Can't you pardon now?" Sayre asked him. "Give proof to the world that with regard to democracy you mean what you say." Then he took another tack—one that he knew would appeal to Wilson in particular. "Evan Thomas is to me like Jesus Christ," Sayre said to Wilson, "being bruised for iniquities of other men."

Wilson was not about to pardon anyone, even a man that Sayre had repeatedly described as Christlike. But the brutal prison treatment did bother him. He took the testimonies that Sayre had collected from Evan, Emma Thomas, and others and promised to address Secretary of War Baker about the matter that afternoon.

Just before leaving Washington to board the SS *George Washington* bound for France, Wilson jotted a quick note to Sayre. With a note of reproach, he told Sayre that he had found Baker sympathetic. "Nothing barbarous or mediaeval will be permitted to continue in any form," Wilson wrote. Three days later, the War Department announced that prisons were no longer allowed to hang the hands of prisoners from cell bars, a modification that applied "not merely to political prisoners, but to those of every type." It was a small concession, but it was also real and rare. Perhaps Sayre's appeal had struck a chord, reminding Wilson why he was on his way to France. His description of the chaining as "mediaeval," perhaps, is telling: Wilson was looking forward, away from the dark past, to a better future.

The *George Washington*, carrying its illustrious load, left the next day. No sitting president had ever visited Europe, and many thought Wilson should have stayed behind and sent others. Those whom he did bring displeased his critics. Wilson had snubbed the Republicans when picking his fellow plenipotentiaries (or chief delegates), even though he would need their support to pass any treaty. The Republicans were simply waiting at home, plotting their opposition. Wilson had actually been reluctant to bring anyone except Colonel House. He had to bring his secretary of state, even though he told House, in House's recording, that Lansing had "no imagination, no constructive ability, and but little real ability of any kind." Wilson spoke to another delegate, General Tasker Bliss, the American military representative on the Supreme War Council, only five times during the whole peace conference (which was fine with Bliss, who preferred to lie in bed with a flask and a copy of Thucydides in ancient Greek). The token Republican, Henry White, turned out to be skilled mostly on matters of etiquette. Wilson wanted to do the work alone.

In France, Wilson was greeted as the "Champion of the Rights of Man." In Milan, he was the "Savior of Humanity." In Paris two million people welcomed him as "Wilson the Just." H. G. Wells would later marvel at that moment. "For a brief interval," he wrote, "Wilson alone stood for mankind."

·+·

Norman and Violet took their sons Billy and Tommy to Baltimore to celebrate Christmas with Emma, Norman's sisters—still living in Baltimore, where the younger Emma was in high school and Agnes had just begun college at Goucher—and Arthur, who was back from training camp in Texas, unhappy to have missed his chance to fight but no doubt relieved that he'd emerged unscathed.

They tried to be joyful, but the mood was somber. The absence of two of the four Thomas brothers weighed on everyone's minds. "Mother bears up better than I feared," Norman reported to Ralph, who was still in France, having returned to his regiment. Evan remained in solitary, after nearly seven weeks. On Christmas Eve morning, Emma, Violet, Norman, and Arthur traveled to Washington to join a delegation of families of conscientious objectors from across the country. They managed to meet with Baker, but the effort was a bust. Nothing was accomplished, no release forthcoming.

Ralph's own Christmas was not exactly cheerful. The 302nd Engineers were exhausted and discouraged. After the armistice, the regiment had marched 161 miles south to Chaumont, where they submitted to endless drills of their infantry skills and wondered why. It rained and rained. Rumors had spread in the beginning of December that the troops would be home by the new year, but by Christmas, there was still no promise of return. The soldiers were discontented and restless, seeking outlets where they could. The incidence of venereal disease in the Seventy-seventh Division rose sharply. Soldiers griped about their harsh treatment, passing along stories of unjust court-martial sentences. The war was over; they wanted to be home. The rain was washing away the roads. The engineers watched the pools of water form in the ruts and craters and despaired. There would be more work to do.

Ralph, too, was distracted, and his mind wandered sometimes to Evan. Wondering if there was something he could do, he wrote to a Princeton friend, John Buchanan, who had climbed the ranks in the JAG's office and asked him if he could look into Evan's case. But by the time Buchanan could report back, Evan had been freed. On December 2, the acting JAG had reviewed Evan's court-martial and found it to be in error. The charge that Evan had disobeyed an order had not been adequately proved, because the order had been to perform an action at some time in the future, and no evidence was presented that that action had not actually been performed. Also, no evidence had been submitted that Evan in fact had become too weak to become a soldier. The court-martial had found Evan guilty of his *intentions*, not his actions. The JAG's office recommended that the charges be dropped, but it took six more weeks for the bureaucracy to act. On January 14, Evan was called into the barracks office and told to sign his discharge. There had been a technical error in his court-martial, he was told. Above his signature, his enlistment record ran down the page. Most of the lines were simply crossed through. Next to "character," the discharging officer had written, "Bad (not honest and faithful)."

Bewildered and upset, not sure why he was being released, Evan was given his suitcase and led outside the gates. It wasn't fair, he told a friend, for him to be let out while other objectors remained in prison. He went straight to New York, where Norman and Violet welcomed him with relief. Evan, though, felt confused and ashamed. He spent the next week writing letters to the families of the objectors to whom he had grown close, telling them to be proud of their sons and apologizing for the fact that he was free and their sons were not.

On January 26, in the Green Room at the Hotel McAlpin, Evan addressed a crowd of a few hundred to describe his experience at Fort Leavenworth. The National Civil Liberties Bureau had advertised the event as the chance to hear about "actual conditions," implying that some kind of revelation was at hand. Norman was there to support his brother. He had given speeches on civil liberties hundreds of times, and he knew how to pique an audience's interest while telling an honest story. But for Evan, this kind of thing was very new, and he had never been one to give people the sensational tales that they wanted anyway. The *New York Herald* noted sneeringly that the audience was disappointed not to find a scarred man in tatters, but instead a self-composed, cleaned-up twenty-eight-year-old in a new blue serge suit, looking "like a prosperous young broker." The *Herald* was probably more perceptive than even the audience members would have liked to admit. Instead of regaling them with tales of torture racks, Evan described plainly what it was like to stand in solitary confinement, with bedbugs scuttling through the cracks of the walls, but not too much else to provoke disgust. The most forceful note he struck in his speech was a plaintive one: It was unfair and unjust that he had been released before the others. Instead of stirring the passion of the crowd with stories of abuse and deprivation, he told the audience that the worst effect of prison was the "moral selfishness" that it encouraged within the inmates. Coercion bred violence and contempt. "The best way to make for a violent and insane revolution in this country is to repress those who do not agree with the majority," he said.

A violent and insane revolution was precisely what the majority feared, but they saw the cause the other way around. The forces of repression that Wilson's administration had marshaled to rally a reluctant nation's support behind the war had not disappeared. They were intensifying.

Twenty

THE SANDIEST OF FOUNDATIONS

*In solitary confinement, Evan was manacled
to the bars in a standing position
for nine hours a day.*

The week before Evan spoke at the Hotel McAlpin, the relentless antiradical lawyer Archibald Stevenson addressed a Senate committee headed by Lee Overman, a North Carolina Democrat. Overman had worked as a particularly zealous Bureau of Investigation informant during the war; in one report, he had suggested that Germans were behind all Jewish businesses in the United States. His committee was supposed to investigate an alleged link between the Germans and the liquor industry, but it took a broad view of its mandate. Any subversive pro-German or anti-American network—perceived or real—was suspect. Bolshevism—more of a catch-all slur than a specific ideology—was the new enemy. On January 23, Stevenson reassured Overman's committee that Bolshevism, Germany, radicals, and pacifists were indeed in cahoots.

"Have you discovered that in many universities there were professors who subscribed to these dangerous and anarchist sentiments?" William Henry King, a Democrat from Utah, asked Stevenson.

"A very large number," replied Stevenson. In fact he had a list—a "Who's Who" that included nearly two hundred names. Over the next day, the Overman committee members removed all but sixty-two names, and then gave the list to the press. The *New York Times* printed it on the front page. Atop the roll call was Jane Addams. Roger Baldwin was on it, as were Oswald Garrison Villard, the historian Charles Beard (who had resigned from Columbia to protest the firings of two pacifist professors), Lillian Wald, Rufus Jones (a well-known Quaker)—and Norman Thomas.

Norman was all too familiar with Stevenson's method, but several on the list were furious at their inclusion. Charles Beard protested that he was not a pacifist, never had been, and had not even been part of "Mr. Wilson's sweet neutrality band" before the war. One professor from Brown University on the list had actually taken a leave to work at the War Department. He asked for a public apology; it was not offered. In fact, as one lawyer associated with the NCLB realized, the men and women on the list held a diverse set of opinions about the war. Several were not even opposed to the war. What they shared was their opposition to the tactics of repression.

Secretary Baker was mortified by the news reports of Stevenson's list and fired off a public letter stating that Jane Addams's name alone ennobled any crowd and denying any connection between Stevenson and Military Intelligence, which was part of the War Department. The first statement was true; the second wasn't quite, whether Baker was aware of it or not. In fact, Military Intelligence had employed Stevenson as a kind of freelancer throughout the war. He even carried a card identifying him as "Special Agent 650," which was embossed with the War Department's seal and signed by Marlborough Churchill, the head of Military Intelligence.

Baker's attempt to distance himself from the Overman committee's work was one more example of what infuriated and radicalized Norman. Liberals had put too much faith in their own good intentions. "One is building on the sandiest of foundations," wrote a chastened John Dewey after the war, "who expects much help in dealing with post-war problems, domestic or foreign, from the community of emotional consciousness generated by the war." The liberals had not harnessed these forces for the betterment of society; they had not been able to master the war and now could not master the peace. Those who hoped for an ambitious "reconstruction" plan on the socialistic scale of what the British Labour Party was proposing were quickly disappointed. Wilson, who had never given much thought to a wholesale program of domestic reform, was too distracted by his dream of a postwar international order.

⁘

During the summer of 1919, Wilson returned to the United States bearing a putative peace that would not last. Those who had looked forward to the new international order were quickly disillusioned. Some had already given up hope. Norman's magazine, the *World Tomorrow*, immediately condemned the treaty's "naked imperialism." Europe had simply redrawn the map again, Norman thought, bartering land for land and crippling the loser with indemnities. So much for a peace based on common brotherhood and common cause.

Wilson's cherished League of Nations was still in there, in etiolated form. Wilson himself had resisted shading in the details, preferring not to put it in a "straight-jacket." He wanted to let it evolve according to "changing circumstances of the time." In place of the clear and enforceable legal mechanisms that other internationalists (including, not least, Taft and Roosevelt) had hoped for, Wilson gave them the court of public opinion: "the moral force of the public opinion of the world—the cleansing and clarifying and compelling influences of publicity." To those who dismissed this as sentimentalism, Wilson had a stern reply. "Now a moral obligation is of course superior to a legal obligation, and, if I may say so, has a greater binding force." Wilson never adequately addressed the questions his conviction raised: What could public opinion do when faced with armies?

What kind of limits could the United States set upon its sovereignty? If collective security meant a specific commitment of force, how would that affect Congress's power to declare war? Who decided what was a "moral obligation," anyway?

In an attempt to sell the treaty directly to the people and to override hostility from the Senate, Wilson traveled around the country, giving speeches. On a warm day in Pueblo, Colorado, he sounded his most utopian note. The American people, he told the audience, understood "the truth of justice and of liberty and of peace. . . . We are going to be led by [that truth], and it is going to lead us, and, through us, the world out into the pastures of quietness and peace such as the world has never dreamed of before." It was Wilson's final speech. Debilitated by headaches and insomnia, he could not continue on his tour. Soon after returning to the White House he suffered a massive stroke that left him an invalid.

⁃⁑⁃

With Norman's encouragement and sometimes his help, Evan spent some time traveling around the country speaking out for the release of conscientious objectors, staying with the families of friends who were still imprisoned. These speeches did not go very well; Evan was never comfortable wearing a suit and standing on a stage. The government released the other conscientious objectors haphazardly. At the end of January, 113 men who had mistakenly not been tried or offered farm furloughs were set free, and others were released in small clusters, not always with explanations. The last men were released in November 1920, two years after the armistice, Howard Moore among them. Meanwhile, angry congressmen and nationalist organizations were criticizing Baker and the War Department for treating the objectors too kindly.

Real facts were hard to come by. So were cool heads. Radicals matched reactionaries for outrage. The Overman committee produced a 1,200-page report predicting a "reign of terror" by communists, while labor unrest across the country turned violent. Wilson's new attorney general, A. Mitchell Palmer, rivaled Postmaster General Burleson in taking the broadest possible interpretation (and then some) of the powers granted to him to punish subversive actions or speech. Palmer could make a convincing argument that security called for extraordinary measures. In Seattle, sixty thousand workers walked off the job in a general strike. The mayor asked for federal troops to occupy the city and punish the Reds who wanted to "duplicate the anarchy of Russia." On May 1, police fought soldiers who tried to disrupt a May Day concert at Madison Square Garden. At the Socialist newspaper the *New York Call*, four hundred soldiers beat families gathered to celebrate the opening of new facilities. "Blood flowed freely, and the crying and shrieking was horrible," an observer said. In Boston, the police and soldiers were on the same side in a melee with radicals. In Cleveland, soldiers tried to pull red flags out of marchers' hands; a nine-hour street battle broke out, finally dispersed by army tanks. A package of explosives sent by radicals arrived at the Seattle mayor's office, and another detonated in the hands of a Georgia senator's maid. Mail inspectors found thirty-four other packaged bombs intended for government officials. On June 2, bombs went off in eight cities simultaneously, killing two. One bomb damaged Attorney General Palmer's house in Washington, D.C. Congress refused to seat the duly elected (and relatively conservative) Socialist Victor Berger. A radical was shot for refusing to stand for the national anthem at the theater.

People were afraid, and they had reason for dread. From September 1918 to June 1919, approximately 675,000 Americans died from flu and pneumonia. Others struggled to not starve. Since 1914, when the war began in Europe, food prices had risen more than 80 percent and clothing prices more than 100 percent in parts of the country. For the average American family, the cost of living nearly doubled in five years, while wages stagnated. *Life* ran a cartoon depicting Uncle Sam asking a soldier what he wanted in return for his service. The reply: "A job." Who could blame Americans from across the political spectrum for feeling foreshocks and imagining that an earthquake was imminent? In becoming a Socialist, Norman had avowedly placed himself on the side of the workers, but he deplored violence and feared the conflict would only get worse unless political changes countered the upheaval and gave workers better basic economic security and more of a say in the governance of their lives.

Norman tried to address it all at once—and to expand the Socialists' concerns. Norman knew the Socialists—however inclusive in theory—did not have a great record on race, and he worked to call attention in speeches and in the pages of the *World Tomorrow* to the injustices perpetrated against blacks. Few things seemed more pressing. Race riots broke out in Chicago and spread across the country. Lynching increased, and so did the extralegal and vigilante suppression of blacks—despite the fact that many African Americans had supported, fought in, and died in the war. Violence against blacks, of course, was hardly new, but the government fostered a climate of racial distrust. Military Intelligence created a division of spies called "Negro Subversion," and Wilson wondered aloud aboard the *George Washington* whether blacks might be the "greatest medium in conveying Bolshevism to America."

Foreigners were also suspect. Attorney General Palmer deported hundreds of aliens suspected of radicalism. For some, Palmer did not go far enough. A Pacific Northwest businessman placed an ad in two papers saying, "We must put to death the leaders of this gigantic conspiracy of murder, pillage and revolution. We must imprison for life all its aiders and abettors of native birth. We must deport all aliens." The *Philadelphia Press* protested that the new laws were inadequate, for they did not reach the "intelligentsia" supported by the "so called intelligent Socialists . . . [who were] more dangerous than those who carry the red flag" because they preyed on the "weak-minded" and knew how to phrase a speech to dodge prosecution.

Palmer kept his eye on the intellectuals, too, empowering a young man named J. Edgar Hoover to run a new domestic intelligence service within the Justice Department. Hoover, who had spent time working at the Library of Congress, began an index card system for tracking information about radicals in America—the more moderate as well as the anarchist and Bolshevist. By the end of 1919, he had 150,000 cards. By the end of two years, he had 450,000. In New York, Archibald Stevenson volunteered to take the lead in investigating radicalism. At his prodding, in March the New York state assembly spent thirty thousand dollars to create the Committee to Investigate Seditious Activities. Known as the Lusk Committee after its chairman, Senator Clayton Lusk, it employed its own network of agents who conducted raids. Guns, ID cards, and press credentials came from the New York police department.

Spies sat in the audience when Norman urged sailors and soldiers returning from Europe to resist the push for universal peacetime military training. What had the soldiers won, he asked, if they had simply brought autocratic means and divisive attitudes home? Stenographers took notes at a meeting called by the Committee of Justice to the Negro in November 1919, when Norman condemned the sham trials and lynching of blacks. It was a shame and an outrage, he said, that a nation that would fight for freedom for the world would keep millions in conditions of near slavery. Norman knew he was being watched, and he slyly gave greetings to the undercover operatives in his speeches. The flagrancy with which the local and federal governments were abusing civil liberties stunned him, he wrote to Ralph, who was now home from France and back at his engineering job. Not only was it wrong, it was stupid, giving Norman plenty of material to publicize. The problem was that only the spies seemed to be listening.

The public was deaf to reports of abuse and repression. So also, much to Norman's bitterness and dismay, were liberals. The denial of freedom of speech, the hostility against foreigners and nonwhites, and the mob violence blooming across the country should have provoked outrage. Instead there was mostly silence and "shameful apathy." Few seemed to question the extraordinary powers the state had given itself to order the lives of its people and crush dissent.

But some things were changing. In his dissent to *Abrams v. United States*, Supreme Court justice Oliver Wendell Holmes—who had, only a short time before, written the opinion upholding Debs's conviction—argued that political speech should be checked only in those moments of imminent and absolute danger. Over the next decade, the Court would begin to craft a jurisprudence that took a broader view of the First Amendment, recognizing it as a cornerstone of democracy.

In July of 1919 Baldwin was released from prison. Norman and Violet hosted his welcome party, and two weeks later Norman officiated at Baldwin's wedding. They were happy events during times that could be dark. In January 1920 Norman joined Baldwin, John Haynes Holmes, John Nevin Sayre, and a group of civil rights lawyers in founding the American Civil Liberties Union. And liberals did respond to the call: John Dewey, Lillian Wald, Oswald Garrison Villard, and dozens of others gave their names and support.

Baldwin served as the ACLU's director for three decades. Norman was on the board and active in the organization, but he went in another direction. He was no philosophical anarchist, as Baldwin called himself. His ideals were fellowship and brotherhood. Those words seem quaint and vague now, but to him they meant something very real.

·+·

Socialism, too, now seems quaint—or, conversely, downright dangerous—despite the fact that many western European countries have successfully settled into some form of social democracy. In the United States, the party turned out to be a failure in national politics. Norman became a Socialist just at the moment the party ceased to be a real force, splintering into weak factions. The legacy of the Russian Revolution was part of the problem. It had given Socialists—and Norman—so much hope. Like so many during World War I, including, initially, the president himself, Norman saw the Russian Revolution as evidence and inspiration for the idea that people really do want to be free of tyranny and to control their own labor. His hope and optimism led him to make excuses and doubt at first the evidence coming out of Russia that tyranny and dispossession had followed in the revolution's wake. He could not see then that the revolution would become a bloody civil war, or that the civil war would lead to a regime where the maxim that the end justifies the means would become the doctrine of the monstrous state. He suspected that censorship and a culture of fear and intimidation against "Reds" in the United States kept Americans misinformed about what was really happening inside Russia. He had been heartened by the idea that the Russian people, the bulk of whom had for so many centuries suffered like slaves, now had control over their own lives. Norman, who had denounced the liberal pragmatists for their willingness to subordinate means to ends, did not yet know that Soviet Communist leaders would kill millions in the name of their cause. He was wrong about the Soviets, and he was wrong at first about what the Communists meant for American Socialists. He would soon learn that Communists, who looked to Moscow for orders, worshipped the state, and that the Soviet state would become tyrannical.

It would not take long for the Communists and the Socialists to split

the party. The Left Wing of the Socialist Party, sure that the revolution
was at hand, turned on the Socialists for their failure to "agitate exclusively
for the overthrow of capitalism, and establishment of Socialism through
a proletarian dictatorship" under the leadership of the Bolshevists, as one
Left Wing manifesto demanded. New York party meetings turned nasty.
The Left Wing advocated violence. They opposed efforts to gain amnesty
for political prisoners, calling it cooperation with the bourgeoisie. By the
end of the summer, the party had ruptured. The Socialists had suspended
or expelled most of the Left Wing. Two Communist Parties emerged,
dedicated to overthrowing not only capitalism but also the Socialist Party
as well. Norman had an early glimpse of Lenin's ruthlessness when the
Russian demanded the allegiance of American Socialists to Moscow, and
he was not sorry to see the Left Wing—the "pathological cases"—go. He
objected seriously to the Communists' emphasis on uniformity, arguing
that "there is room in this crusade for men of different gifts, temperaments,
and points of view so long as they seek to make real a fellowship of free
men here on earth." Still, it was several years before Norman discovered
just how ruthless the Russian dictators were. Once he finally learned, he
became one of their fiercest opponents.

Twenty-One

TO CARRY YOUR WATCH

Norman Thomas with his grandchildren Wendy,
Evan (the author's father), and Louisa

When World War I was over, Norman was left with a religious creed he could not quite believe in, a political creed he could not endorse without reservation, and a longing for something more profound than mere man could offer. He knew better than to trust that salvation could be found in abstract principles and was wary of those who believed it could. Still, he was optimistic. He had not yet given up on Christianity altogether, still remembering the sense of God's blessing. He still considered religion to be the basis for his pacifism, and he still talked about socialism as a kind of ethical Christianity. But that was changing, and he could only hope to find what once he took for granted: some "supreme loyalty which makes life worth while." The hope would fade; the longing wouldn't. The quest Norman would not abandon.

It was harder for Evan. After several unhappy occasions speaking on behalf of conscientious objectors, he more or less disappeared. His friends did not know where he was; at times his family did not know either. He worked odd jobs as a field hand, a lumberyard worker, a Fuller brush man, an ordinary seaman. For a little while he became a labor organizer working for a radical group, an experience that left him low. He was frustrated by the "ignorance and indifference of the masses . . . the selfishness of designing individuals . . . the irresponsibility and easy utopianism of others." He resigned from the Crusaders Club, telling Nevin Sayre that his "faith is pretty much shot to pieces."

In 1922, Evan went to Dublin, Ireland, where he hoped to get a scholarship to study medicine. Instead, he spent Sunday nights at salons discussing Irish revolutionary politics, and when the scholarship for his medical studies didn't come though, he fell into depression. For months, in letters to his mother and Norman, Evan lacerated himself. He wondered if the will to power was the only true force in the world, in which case he was a failure. He contemplated suicide. Instead, he ended up in London and underwent psychoanalysis, then came back to New York, where he landed at the home of Norman and Violet and where he finally began to pull himself together.

Evan became a lab technician at Roosevelt Hospital and then finally, at the age of thirty-nine, entered NYU Medical School. His specialty was venereal disease—an unpopular field in those days. He ran the syphilis unit at Bellevue Hospital and was a consultant to the World Health Organization and the United States Public Health Service. Being a doctor for those whom others would not touch gave him a way to live in society and yet care for its outcasts. He would hold clinics every afternoon, treating patients who gathered early on the street outside. He was strong tempered and blunt, but he radiated a calm good nature. The psychological scars from his wartime experience faded, but they did not disappear.

He was always a pacifist. During World War II, he served as chairman of the War Resisters League and the Metropolitan Board for Conscientious Objectors. He refused to register and was prepared to return to jail, but he did not have to. His work helped ensure that treatment of conscientious objectors during World War II was more systematic and humane than it had been during World War I, and indeed there was far less prejudice shown to them, even though the Second World War was far more popular than the First. Evan continued to disagree with his brother Norman about politics. Evan thought socialism was a "pretty dream," and an irresponsible one. Norman's daughter Francie remembers that her father and Evan—"Unk" to his nieces and nephews, and then to practically everyone—would argue terrifically, stalking the room with their long strides. But they never let their disagreements get in the way of their relationship. Unk was practically part of Norman's immediate family. The children of all his brothers adored him. He took them to the racetrack; he made them laugh; he was, they thought, a hero. Evan remained a loner in many ways. His relationships with women, with the notable exceptions of his sisters, his mother, and Violet, were never easy, for reasons he was probably not willing or able to explain. When he was forty-four, he confessed to Violet that he had been in love with someone since he had gone on a canoeing trip with her family when she was a child and he was in college (and possibly loved her mother as well; those feelings, he said, were more complicated), but even his descriptions of her were strained and tortured. He did not pursue her, and he idealized her in every way. She was, he wrote to Violet, "a fairy princess." Not long after, he was briefly and unhappily married to another woman.

Evan died in 1974. Among his papers was a scrap on which he had written, "Heresy is nothing but the Greek word for choice."

✛

Ralph arrived back in the United States at the beginning of May 1919. The first months of the year had been tiresome, despite his promotion to adjutant general of the regiment. The drills, the rain, the tenacious lice. There were also fun and boisterous times—drunken dinners, a sense of camaraderie that sustained the men, and the knowledge that they would be welcomed home as heroes. And they were. On May 6, they paraded through New York; on the seventh, they demobilized, on the twelfth, the regiment dissolved.

Ralph returned to Baltimore and to his job at the Pennsylvania Water & Power Company, where he set to work improving the efficiency of hydro-electric systems. Soon after he returned home, he began to court a young woman named Rebekah, the sister of twin classmates of his at Princeton. They married and remained in Baltimore, where Ralph went on to become the executive engineer and vice president of the Consolidated Gas and Electric Light and Power Company of Baltimore. Ralph was a man in the image of his father. He never suffered the crisis of faith that two of his brothers did, and he became an elder at Brown Memorial Church. He was active after the war in the American Legion, a patriotic group that provoked some of Norman's strongest denunciations. But he also tried to help his brothers' campaign to free conscientious objectors from prison, once writing the ACLU a long and thoughtful letter on why one mailing would have only the effect of alienating those whose minds the ACLU was trying to change. He was "much interested in any efforts to free the remaining CO's and want to do my part," he wrote. He meant it. Six weeks later, to a friend from Princeton, he wrote, "I am strongly in favor of amnesty for all conscientious objectors. . . . I think I would favor including nearly all purely political prisoners." But he objected to the ACLU's confrontational posture, arguing that it should have focused on supplying information about the objectors' treatment. The American Legion acted the way it did, Ralph argued, because it was "in complete ignorance of the facts." He refused to sign a petition of protest—but he would do his part, as promised. He and four other officers wrote a public statement describing in detail the treatment of objectors. "As officers in the Army . . . we did not and do not share the convictions of men who believed that it was wrong for them to participate in the war," they wrote, "but in the interests of truth and justice we believe that all members of the American Legion as well as the general public should be fully and accurately informed." One of the other undersigned was Thomas Guthrie Speers, a chaplain in the 102nd Infantry and the man who had asked Evan Thomas to join the Crusaders in 1912. Speers would go on to become the minister at Brown Memorial—which made him the pastor of Ralph, Agnes, Emma, and their mother.

Despite his early enthusiasm for Wilson, Ralph was a Republican and remained a Republican. After a few loyal votes for his brother during

Norman's perpetual campaigns, he never cast his ballot for his brother again. He would sometimes buy Norman's books on socialism and read them with a pen in hand, writing objections in the margins.

Ralph spent countless hours canoeing, sometimes with his sisters or his three children. His daughter died young, of illness, around the same time as his wife. During World War II, his son, Ralph Jr., went to fight in France. He had worse luck than his father. Ralph Jr. was killed during the Metz offensive in 1944. Over the next twenty years, Ralph and Rebekah went to France several times to visit the Lorraine American Cemetery, where he was buried.

Ralph and Norman saw each other whenever Norman blew through town to give a speech or on his way to Washington, and Ralph would come up to New York for the big birthdays and celebrations. He occasionally asked Norman to come to speak to one of his groups or clubs. Norman would grumble about it, but he would come. They went to Princeton reunions together when they were old, their bodies failing, and leaned on each other for support. Ralph died in 1965.

·+·

Arthur's experience during World War I was like that of many young Americans. He went because he was asked, not because of his idealism; he wanted to prove himself, but he struggled against strictures of the military and with his disappointment. He lived with the knowledge that his brothers were demonstrating their convictions in some extreme and decisive way. It was hard enough to live up to examples, and it was harder still that their examples were so hard to reconcile. It's not surprising that he felt sometimes so adrift, or that it took him some more time to find his footing. In the 1920s, he worked for textile mills in New York and South Carolina—not happily—and during the Great Depression, he lost his job.

But then his life was transformed. He became a social worker. It was a job he loved and was good at. He ran the Family Service Bureau in York, Pennsylvania, and helped reorganize the County Juvenile Probation Center. He also helped establish a day care center for mentally handicapped children in York, the first Teen Age Center, and the Planned Parenthood

Clinic. He served on the Interracial Committee in York's mayor's office. He lived, in many ways, a typical middle class life—a membership in the local Rotary Club, a position as church elder—and he was no socialist. He sometimes clashed with colleagues, his children remember, and he went through some more hard times. But he cared about his community and worked to make it fair, open, and just.

"My respect continues to grow for Arthur Thomas as a man with an unusual depth of wisdom and understanding," said the head of the Red Cross when he retired. "He is devoted to the high purpose of service to the total community without fear or favor."

After the war, he chased a girl named Christine, a classmate and close friend of his sister Emma. Finally—after a great deal of persistence on Arthur's part—she was won over and they were married. They had three children. Arthur's family remained especially close to Ralph's family, which was not far away, and to Arthur's sisters. The children loved Evan, who was the only person allowed to swear in their home. Norman was a "larger than life figure," Arthur's daughter remembers.

At the end of every fall, Arthur would take his children to the local orchard to order apples to send his brothers for Christmas. He sent those bags of apples until he died in 1967. Norman wrote his widow, Christine, "I was extraordinarily fortunate to belong to a group of brothers and sisters who didn't agree on a lot of things, but who found it very easy to feel a continuing respect and affection for each other."

·+·

After the war, Emma Thomas lived quietly in Baltimore with her daughters. She died in 1931, following a long and painful bout with cancer. Norman and Evan both waited until she died to demit from the ministry. Norman once wrote that he had always wanted to write about the impact his mother had had on him, but he could not find a way.

The Thomas brothers' sisters, Agnes and Emma, are not a part of this story because they were still so young when World War I began. (They did, though, contribute to the war effort, working on farms for the war effort as "Farmerettes.") Yet the trajectories of their lives, too, reflect the impact of their family's past. Neither Emma nor Agnes married. Both were committed to causes of social justice and to education. Agnes became a math teacher at a Quaker school, an active member of the Women's International League for Peace and Freedom (which grew out of the Women's Peace Party, founded in 1915), and tutored inner-city children.

Emma, like Arthur, was a social worker. She earned a master's in social work from New York University and was a medical social worker. She had, by all accounts, an infectious sense of humor and a radiating kindness. She was also willing to make unpopular and unusual choices. During World War II, when Norman was one of the few public figures to speak out against the Japanese internment camps, she did even more to lodge her own protest: She became a social worker at a hospital for interned Japanese. Later, back in Baltimore, she became a deacon at Brown Memorial. She died in 2000 at the age of 101.

·+·

Immediately following the war, the country, eager to return to "normalcy," had little tolerance for troublemaking dissenters, but Norman persevered. His family bolstered and supported him. In the summer of 1920, his children spent a stretch in Baltimore, visiting their grandmother, aunts, Arthur, and Ralph. At one point, eight-year-old Tommy copied out a stanza—taking some liberty—from John Whittier's "Anniversary" poem, read at a Friends meeting during the Civil War.

> The leveled gun,
> The battle brand
> We may not take
> But firmly loyal
> We shall stand
> For conscience sake.

To his father, he reported that a straw poll at Goucher College, his aunts' school, had Debs winning the presidential election. That fall, the Thomas children fell sick with streptococcus infections, and Tommy died of it in January 1921, at the age of nine.

✛

Not long after, Norman resigned as editor of the *World Tomorrow*. During the war, he had vaguely assumed that he would probably return to the ministry after the armistice. But the offers for a position in the church did not come, and Norman realized that he did not want them to. The seeds of doubt that had been planted during World War I had rooted and grown. He could not, he later wrote, believe in a God who was at once all-loving and all-powerful, who would be so capricious as to leave humans so weak. What he had wanted, what he had always wanted, was the God of his father and of the miracles, the God who had blessed the garden of Grandfather Thomas Thomas so many years ago. But he could no longer believe in such a God, and he came to realize that it had been some time since he had. At a meeting of the Fellowship of Reconciliation at his house on New Year's Eve 1918, he raised the question of whether the *World Tomorrow* should stop calling itself "A Journal looking toward a Christian World." "I must confess that I am increasingly doubtful whether the religion which must sweep the hearts of men if our ideals are to triumph will be content merely to take over and reinterpret the vocabulary or the categories of Christianity," he wrote, the awkwardness of his prose reflecting his discomfort. Shortly after, the doubt overcame him.

✛

Norman never stopped using the minister's religious vocabulary, even after he stopped calling himself a Christian. He was an evangelist for socialism and justice, but it bothered him when people said that he replaced Christianity with socialism. Socialism could not offer comfort and consolation. Norman respected the writings of liberal theologians like Paul Tillich and Reinhold Niebuhr, his friend and sometime political ally, but their theologies gave him neither what he wanted nor what he needed. Occasionally he would take his children to church, where, his daughter Frances remembered, he "embarrassed us, because he sang the hymns so loudly."

After Tommy's death, Norman wrote for Oswald Garrison Villard at the *Nation*, served on dozens of boards, and protested the incarceration of Eugene Debs—twice visiting President Warren Harding, the man who had been his boss when he was briefly a delivery boy in Marion, Ohio. In 1922 he became codirector of the League for Industrial Democracy, founded by a group including the radical authors Jack London and Upton Sinclair as the Intercollegiate Socialist Society. His parlor was the site of meetings upon meetings—many of which he ran, some of which (like the Women's Peace Party) he sympathized with and some of which he didn't. His living room was a safe harbor for those who championed unpopular causes—even if he thought they were unpopular for a reason. He ran for New York governor on the Socialist ticket in 1924—though he encouraged Socialists to throw their weight behind the Progressive Party candidate, Robert La Follette, for president. After Eugene Debs died in 1926, the party, dominated by foreign-born members, needed an American-born standard bearer. For nearly the next fifty years, that man was Norman Thomas.

Norman was the Socialists' most visible politician, and he made himself as visible as he could be. He spoke from hundreds of stages—the Ladies' Garment Workers' Union hall, Madison Square Garden, Yale, almost anywhere that would have him—every year until his body was so broken that he could hardly stand. He wrote hundreds of articles and scores of books, and he led or belonged to dozens of organizations. He never counted among the intellectuals of the Left, though many of them were friends. Issues and the people surrounding them, not concepts, and not even the give-and-take of politics, seized him. He wanted to be there, where things were happening—opposing Boss Hague in Jersey City, excoriating the Klan in Tampa. He was arrested and chased; in one famous picture, an egg is splattering off his head. He visited Franklin Roosevelt at the White House to protest the president's reluctance to intervene against men who were terrorizing poor sharecroppers and organizers in the South. "Norman, I'm a damned sight better politician than you are," FDR told him, and counseled patience. FDR was right about being a better politician, no question—but patience was something hard for Norman to swallow when black union leaders were being shot and Norman himself had been chased to the county line by men with shotguns.

✛

He spoke against imperialism, worked for nuclear nonproliferation, and opposed Vietnam, though he told protestors to wash the flag, not burn it. He began advising A. Philip Randolph, the civil rights leader, in the 1920s and never stopped working for racial equality. In a tribute to Norman, titled "The Bravest Man I Ever Met," Martin Luther King Jr. told the story of a young African American at the 1963 March on Washington who "listened at the Washington Monument to an eloquent orator. Turning to his father, he asked 'Who is that man?' Came the inevitable answer: 'That's Norman Thomas. He was for us before any other white folks were.'"

As a politician, Norman failed. During the Great Depression, he was backed by a group of intellectual stars (including the philosopher John Dewey, who had once mocked the pacifists but repeatedly voted for Norman and assisted his campaign). It seemed, as it had in 1912, as if the Socialist Party might become a strong political force in American politics. But the moment passed quickly, and Norman oversaw the party's precipitous decline. In his last presidential campaign, in 1948, he received 140,000 votes. Harry Truman won with twenty-four million. Norman could not hold the party together, with various factions of Marxists and non-Marxists and its intraparty battles. He waffled this way and that on matters of orthodoxy, militancy, and inclusivity. He could be rigid and uncompromising, as when he refused to support the New Deal, believing at the same time that it did not extend far enough and that it might lead to fascism. On the other hand, he wasn't enough of a "true believer" in Marxism and the socialist utopia, he later admitted, to really capture the hearts of people and lead them to socialism. "The tyranny of true believers living together over one another can be a pretty terrific affair," he wrote. He was suspicious of what true believers could do to others and suspicious of dogmatism. Though most of his critics called him a utopian, more concerned with moral purity than with practical results, some said he never went far enough—that he was a liberal in a Brooks Brothers suit who called himself a socialist because he didn't understand what the term really meant.

Norman never got the welfare state he wanted, although when he died it was closer at hand than it had ever been. When he graduated from college, there was no income tax to speak of, little regulation over industry and the financial system, and almost no social safety net. Many people today regard some of the measures he fought for—taxation as a tool for social justice, more extensive public ownership of natural monopolies and essential industries— as counterproductive and morally suspect. Government programs have become associated with snarls of bureaucracy and stifled innovation. Norman always believed that planning should be flexible, local, and nimble, but he did believe that the economy should be structured to satisfy human needs before wants.

By the end of his life, Norman had lost much of his faith in the viability of a collectivist society, humbled by the history of such experiments and more suspicious than he once had been of the bureaucratic state. When the country celebrated the Wilson centenary, he spent some time looking over the *World Tomorrow* and reflecting on those years. He was struck, he wrote to his 1948 running mate, Tucker Smith, by the innocence of his hope during those years. "I suppose the difference with me between now and then could mostly be summed up by saying that then I expected more of both God and man than today," he wrote. He had become more skeptical, less hopeful. "For instance, I hate war as much as I ever did but do not find an uncompromising belief in non-violence . . . as effective an alternative as once I did." He had to rethink socialism, too, "in the light of what we all are learning about bureaucracy and the difficulty of preserving individual freedom and initiative." He did not abandon socialism—he still believed that socializing natural monopolies was necessary for the human and fair treatment of workers and consumers—but his faith in what was possible was tempered.

He did change. After he decided that he could not call himself a Christian, he could not accept a Christian basis for pacifism. He supported intervention in the Spanish Civil War, only to readopt a pacifist stance at the wrong moment—during the run-up to World War II—and then drop it again after Pearl Harbor. He was not simply inconsistent—circumstances had altered, and he was committed to reevaluating his beliefs—but he could certainly be distracted. He moved from one speech to the next, one issue to another. Hard-liners thought he never went far enough. Conservatives (and most liberals) thought he was a utopian dreamer. He believed in the necessity of socialism, but he had a harder time making other people see why. Eventually he was absorbed into the mainstream, enshrined as a national gadfly. *Time* put him on the cover, *Life* ran a long feature on him, and he even appeared in the pages of *Playboy*. As something of a lifelong prude, he had misgivings about the last and appealed to his friend William Sloane Coffin Jr.—Yale's chaplain and the son of the man who had first noticed Norman as an assistant at Spring Street Presbyterian—for advice. "Had they asked you to write about sex," Coffin replied, "I might have suggested you were a mite old. But to speak on the peace movements you are without doubt the man most qualified."

Some Socialists (and non-Socialists) criticized Norman for not living like a proletarian. Violet's income took care of his family and left him free to pursue his political campaigns. The Thomases lived sometimes with servants, and Norman liked to end hot summer days with a swim at the segregated beach club in Long Island. They sent their children to private schools, and during the Depression, Violet insisted that her daughters each have a fur coat. She made sacrifices, but she drew lines. Norman had been sensitive to his wife's wealth from the early days of their marriage. He did not think it fair to ask her to give up her own money for his cause, even though she had also joined the Socialist Party. Whether he liked to admit it or not, he enjoyed the privileges that came with Violet's wealth. Later in life, he often pointed out that Violet made money by running a tea room and raising cocker spaniels, sometimes overemphasizing her earning power as if to distract from or diminish—to himself as much as anyone else—her inheritance. But it's also true that he never thought people should be ascetics. He loved beautiful things and thought more people should have them, not fewer.

When Violet, who traveled around the country with Norman as he campaigned, sitting in the front seat with a typewriter in her lap, died of a heart attack in 1947, Norman was bereft. Sid Lovett, then the chaplain of Yale, performed the small funeral in the Thomases' living room in Long Island, as Norman once had for Lovett's wife. In times like these, especially, he longed for faith, but it was elusive. "One of the facts about a doctrinal religion that has increasingly troubled me is this: earnest believers in any religion of salvation, eternal or temporal, feel constrained to enforce it on unbelievers for their own good," he wrote in middle age. "That is a truth illustrated almost equally by the history of organized Christianity, Islam, and Marxism." Religion may be a matter of personal conscience, but so-called men of conscience are usually more bent on bending others to their own convictions. Norman was never able to solve that contradiction, though in connecting democratic socialism to freedom of conscience, he spent his life trying. He was not afraid to fight like hell for what he believed in. He was not afraid to be angry. He was also not afraid to listen to those who disagreed.

·+·

Conscience can be a problematic notion. It's hard to say just what it is, and it's easy to see where it can become dangerous. It can make a person too rigid or self-righteous. It can be used to justify any action, even heinous ones (a group of right-wing Germans that prefigured the Nazi party titled its newsletter *Gewissen*—conscience). It can encourage egotism and self-absorption, the moaning of Hamlet; or it can seem a fool's speech, the prattle of Polonius, who said, "To thine own self be true." It can encourage intolerance, or it can conflict with responsibility, which sometimes means doing what's possible, even if it's not perfectly right.

Unlike his brother Evan, Norman was not inclined to think that dissent was a virtue in itself. "Belonging, is, of course, a part of life," Norman wrote late in his life. "For different purposes we belong to different groups and we live by our loyalties. . . . The secret of a good life is to have the right loyalties and to hold them in the right scale of values. The value of dissent and dissenters is to make us reappraise those values with supreme concern for the truth."

Norman suffered a stroke at the end of 1967 and was confined to a nursing home afterward. A few days after dictating his last book, *The Choices*, Norman turned eighty-four, and a few of his children and friends (including Roger Baldwin) came to toast him. The *New York Times*'s obituary man was there, too, taking notes. Norman died a month later.

The critic Irving Howe wrote:

> Even after he died Thomas remained, so to say, in my head,
> setting a standard of right action, pointing to the elusive path
> where the "ethic of ultimate ends" and the "ethic of responsibil-
> ity" join. When I did something unworthy in politics, it was to
> his memory I had to answer; when I acquitted myself well, it
> was his approval I would most have wanted.

The journalist Murray Kempton put it simply. "What Thomas conveyed was no sense of critical place in history (when I knew him any such
hope was fading) but rather a feeling that there is something glorious about
being forever engaged."

Norman was not a moral philosopher. He did not think in terms of
the "ethic of responsibility" or the "ethic of ultimate ends"; he did not
dwell on the tensions between responsibility and conscience. He tried to
be right and knew he might be wrong. All of the Thomases worked true
to carry out the dictates of their convictions, but confronted with differences between them, they had to respect the dignity and capacity of
others who disagreed, without endorsing the disagreement. Freedom of
conscience both secured and limited the right to the personal search for
truth. Norman believed this freedom could make a moral society out of
moral men. It would not be a utopia, but it would be a place where people
might be more thoughtful and honest, and more responsive to one another.
World War I undermined his faith in the inevitability of progress, but he
never lost faith that even if progress was not assured, it was possible. What
was true in his own family was true in the world at large. "The only thing
that he requires of his family is that as individuals we think," Violet once
said. "He doesn't demand that we think his thoughts." Then she smiled.
"Of course, I'm convinced he believes that if we think rightly, we'll agree
with him."

Right or wrong, he loved his family. In 1941, while Norman was still
publicly speaking out against the United States' entry into World War II,
his son, Evan Welling Thomas II, volunteered to drive ambulances for the
British. Just before he shipped out in November 1941, Norman sent him

a letter. "In a cruel and ugly world you never made you've chosen what is for you, I'm sure, the best possible course," he wrote.

> More than I can tell we shall be missing you and loving you and wishing for you the external good fortune and still more the inner courage and hope which may sustain you. Despite our follies and madness men are made for better things than constant exploitation and ever recurring wars.—It will be a great happiness always to carry your watch till you return to claim it.

Evan Welling Thomas II was my grandfather, and I have that watch now. It is a reminder of more than a father's love for his family; it is more, too, than a young man's desire to fight for freedom. It is a reminder that Norman's conscience was not the nation's; it was his own. That lesson he had learned long before.

ACKNOWLEDGMENTS

It states the obvious to say that a book involving one's family involves one's family, but in this case it really means something. I am indebted to several descendants of the Thomas brothers. Frances Gates, Norman's daughter, was a source and an inspiration throughout the research and writing of *Conscience*. Her memories and descriptions of her father and uncles helped me see and understand them, and her remarkable character gave me some insight into those who raised her. Her family papers, too, were invaluable. Francie's daughter, Nancy Gerber, was an unbelievable helpmate. She helped me track down letters and photographs (and descendants), spent hours discussing the Thomases with me, and read the manuscript with care. One of the greatest pleasures of working on this project was spending time with her. Christine Dunbar, Arthur's daughter, and her husband, Dave, welcomed me into their home, gave me access to scores of letters and photographs, and, along with Arthur Jr., told me about the branch of Thomases that settled around Baltimore and Pennsylvania. Christine also read the manuscript with sharp eyes. Norman's granddaughter Patricia Libbey (who is at work on a project about Violet) read the manuscript—twice—and generously shared her own research into the Thomas and Stewart families. I'm grateful and lucky, because there is not a more resourceful researcher around.

Many others provided crucial help with the book along the way. I'm especially grateful to Vanessa Mobley, Edward Orloff, Laura Griffin, David Plunkett, Louisa Hall, Jon-Jon Goulian, Shea O'Rourke, Jonathan Darman, Jack Sanders, Mike Hill, Marc Peyser and others at *Newsweek,* and Casey Blake. Much of this book was written at the MacDowell Colony—a writer's heaven. Matthew Price, Justin Jackson, and especially Jamie Johnston—who kept me sane, more or less—were fantastic fact checkers at the end. Of course, any errors are my own.

Several people read and commented thoughtfully on parts of the manuscript as I wrote it. Thomas Meaney clarified my themes, Rachel Reilich helped me think in chapters, and Stephen Wertheim seemed to know more about Woodrow Wilson than is probably healthy. The historian Kip Kosek guided me and corrected me on several key points. (I also relied on his book, *Acts of Conscience.*) Christian Lorentzen and Meehan Crist smoothed my prose. Laura Weinrib read several sections with a scholar's care. So did Jeremy Kessler, and his enthusiasm reminded me why I began this project in the first place.

Alix Rule, Gideon Lewis-Kraus, Katherine Marino, and Jon Meacham were part of this project from the start. They not only edited the manuscript (some parts more than once), but they helped me see what it could be. Alix clarified problems and showed me what was at stake. Gideon pushed me to be sharper, clearer, and a better writer. Katherine brought her own scholarship to bear on the manuscript and made the book stronger. Jon Meacham made several brilliant suggestions, including, at one point, scrapping what I had and starting over. I'm thankful for that advice—though I wasn't at the time! I have learned so much from him.

Many archives, libraries, and generous individuals helped me track down unpublished letters and papers. My thanks to the staffs at the Landon Trust and the Wheaton College Archives and Special Collections; the repository at the Library of Claremont School of Theology; the Inez Moore Parker Archives and Research Center at Johnson C. Smith

University; the Department of Rare Books and Special Collections at Princeton University Library; the Swarthmore College Peace Collection; the Elmira College Archives; the Tamiment Library at New York University; Sidney Lovett Jr. and Manuscripts and Archives at Yale University; the Astor, Lenox, and Tilden foundations and the Manuscripts and Archives Division at the New York Public Library; the Houghton Library at Harvard University; the National Archives in College Park; the Burke Library Archives at Union Theological Seminary; the Bentley Historical Library at the University of Michigan; the Presbyterian Historical Society; John Buchanan; and the Rare Book and Manuscript Library at Columbia University.

It is my good fortune to have Sarah Chalfant at the Wylie Agency for an agent. She also found *Conscience* a terrific home with Penguin Press. Ann Godoff has been an inimitable editor. I'm also very grateful to Lindsay Whalen for her editorial suggestions and for shepherding the book through publication.

My mother, Osceola, was—and always has been—the best editor of all. My father, Evan, began teaching me how to tell a story decades ago, and he still is. My sister, Mary, is a role model for me, the kind of person I imagine Norman Thomas would want to live in his socialist society.

My husband, Justin, deserves the most thanks. His insights were deep, his editing excellent, his patience heroic, and his love sustaining.

NOTES

Preface

x **Norman dwelled on:** Norman Thomas to Violet Thomas, August 30, 1918, Nancy Gerber collection.

x **"The situation of Mother":** For the sake of clarity, I have occasionally fixed the syntax and spelling in quotes from letters.

x **"the privilege of men":** Woodrow Wilson, *Woodrow Wilson: The Essential Political Writings*, ed. Ronald J. Pestritto (Lanham, MA: Lexington Books, 2005), 256.

xi **"He spoke to the feelings":** Alden Whitman, "Norman Thomas: The Great Reformer, Unsatisfied to the End," *New York Times*, December 22, 1968.

xiii **an idealist or a utopian:** See, for instance, the title of the most comprehensive book about Norman Thomas, W. A. Swanberg, *Norman Thomas: The Last Idealist* (New York: Scribner, 1976). Swanberg's admiring biography focuses on Norman's career as a Socialist politician, treating his early years lightly and his turn toward socialism almost as an inevitability. See also Gary Dorrien, *The Democratic Socialist Vision* (New Jersey: Rowman and Littlefield, 1986), 48–77. Dorrien's eloquent chapter on Norman emphasizes the impact of World War II on the evolution of Norman's beliefs, whereas I think that World War I was the more formative period. Daniel Bell draws on Max Weber's distinction between the ethic of conscience and the ethic of responsibility to explain Norman's failures in politics. See Daniel Bell, *The End of Ideology: On the Exhaustion of Political Ideas in the Fifties* (Cambridge, MA: Harvard University Press, 2000).

xiii **"My accepting of the Socialist":** Norman Thomas to Norman Alexander Trachtenberg, October 18, 1918, Norman Thomas Papers, Manuscripts and Archives Division, New York Public Library (hereafter NTP).

xiii **"not because of the exceptions":** Alexander Trachtenberg to Norman Thomas, October 25, 1918, NTP.

xiv **"TO THE BRAVE":** Norman Thomas, *The Conscientious Objector in America* (New York: B. W. Huebsch, 1923), dedication.

Chapter One: Fervent Wrestling Prayers

1 **"the wrong side down":** Emma Thomas to Mary Mattoon, December 3, 1884, Margaret and Kenneth Landon Papers, Wheaton College Archives and Special Collection, Buswell Memorial Library. The detail of Norman's weight comes from Swanberg, *Norman Thomas*, 2.

2 **"the more outstanding personality":** Norman Thomas, unpublished autobiography, 20. Much of the detail about his early years comes from Norman's autobiography.

2 **"What a setup"**: Thomas, unpublished autobiography, 5. Though Norman inconsistently numbered the pages of the copy of the unpublished autobiography at the New York Public Library, I will follow Norman's pagination.

2 **a sickly child**: Ibid., 7 and 10. Norman Thomas to Harry L. Golden, January 20, 1958, Stephen Mattoon Papers, JCSU Johnson C. Smith University Archives, Inez Moore Parker Archives & Research Center, James B. Duke Memorial Library.

3 **"is somewhere in the bushes"**: Untitled photograph of the Mattoon family, 1864, Margaret and Kenneth Landon Papers.

3 **"I don't see why"**: Norman Thomas to Emma Thomas, November 17, 1907, Patricia Libbey collection.

3 **born in 1816**: Some sources suggest that Stephen Mattoon was born in 1815. See "Finding Aid to Record Group 275," Mattoon Family Collection, 1827–1945, Presbyterian Historical Society. For a description of Stephen's biography, see "A Sketch of the Life and Career of Reverend Stephen Mattoon, D.D." (unpublished typescript), Mattoon Family Collection, 1827–1945.

3 **"I am not afraid"**: Robert T. Handy, *A History of Union Theological Seminary in New York* (New York: Columbia University Press, 1987), 65.

4 **"Cleanse me"**: Mary Mattoon Diary, Mattoon Family Collection, 1827–1945. For Mary's activity aboard the ship, see Mary Mattoon to "dearest of friends," November 9, 1846, Margaret and Kenneth Landon Papers.

4 **"They are not destitute"**: Stephen Mattoon to Alfred L. Williams, June 4, 1847, Margaret and Kenneth Landon Papers.

4 **"We are surrounded"**: Stephen Mattoon to Alfred L. Williams, November 24, 1847, Margaret and Kenneth Landon Papers.

4 **In 1855, Mongkut asked**: Mary Backus, ed., *Siam and Laos, as Seen by Our American Missionaries* (Philadelphia: Presbyterian Board of Publication, 1884), 378–79; Stephen Mattoon to Alfred L. Williams, June 4, 1847, Margaret and Kenneth Landon Papers; "A Sketch of the Life," 40. After Mongkut discovered that the women missionaries were proselytizing during lessons, he turned to a British widow named Anna Leonowens, whose (fanciful) memoir became the basis for the book *Anna and the King of Siam* and the Rodgers and Hammerstein musical *The King and I*. "Followers of Buddha are mostly aware of the powerfulness of truth and virtue, as well as the followers of Christ," Mongkut wrote to Leonowens, "and are desirous to have facility of English language and literature, more than new religions." (Margaret Landon, *Anna and the King of Siam* [New York: HarperCollins, 1999], 23.)

5 **"We esteem you"**: "A Sketch of the Life," 36.

5 **"There are slaves"**: Mary Mattoon Diary.

6 **"If [the rebellion] is not"**: Mary Mattoon to Anna Mattoon, December 18, 1862, Margaret and Kenneth Landon Papers.

6 **"I have just"**: Mary Mattoon to Anna Mattoon, August 26, 1862, Margaret and Kenneth Landon Papers.

6 **"with sinking Peter"**: Mary Mattoon Diary.

6 **"It can scarcely"**: Stephen Mattoon to Harriet Williams, July 14, 1853, Margaret and Kenneth Landon Papers.

7 **Stephen expanded the curriculum**: Details about the Mattoons at Biddle University are drawn from Ida Briggs Henderson, "Norman Thomas's Grandparents," *Charlotte Observer*, October 2, 1932; Inez Moore Parker, *The Rise and Decline of the Program of Education for Black Presbyterians* (San Antonio: Trinity University Press, 1977), 111–13; J. E. Rattley, "The Early Days at Biddle as I Recall Them," *Johnson C. Smith University Alumni Journal*, October 1927; Thomas, unpublished autobiography, 20; Norman Thomas to Harry L. Golden, January 20, 1958, Stephen Mattoon Papers.

7 **"a doubtful boon"**: Stephen Mattoon to sister, November, 17, 1876, Margaret and Kenneth Landon Papers.

8 **"She was ever"**: Rattley, "The Early Days at Biddle."

8 **the scariest punishment**: Norman Thomas to Harry L. Golden, January 20, 1958, Stephen Mattoon Papers.

8 **"When I think"**: Mary Mattoon to Mrs. Lee, undated, Margaret and Kenneth Landon Papers.

8 **"We must not scrutinize"**: Emma Mattoon (Mrs. Welling Thomas) Class of 1878 file, Elmira College Archives. See also "Elmira College Believes Young Women Should Be Trained for Public Life . . . ," *New York Times*, June 1, 1913.

9   **the son of Welsh immigrants:** Swanberg, *Norman Thomas*, 4; "Thomas Thomas," unpublished essay written in the hand of Welling Thomas, NTP; "Rev. Thomas Thomas," *Wyalusing (PA) Rocket*, June 22, 1904; Emily C. Blackman, *History of Susquehanna County, Pennsylvania* (Philadelphia: Claxton, Remsen, & Haffelfinger, 1873), 351–53.

10   **His professors at Union:** Gary Dorrien, *The Making of American Liberal Theology: Imagining Progressive Religion, 1805–1900* (Louisville, KY: Westminster John Knox Press, 2001), 338–47. The first two volumes of Dorrien's study of liberal theology heavily influenced my understanding of the roots and development of the Thomases' beliefs.

11   **"What? Another one!":** Welling Thomas to Anna Welles, August 2, 1899, Christine Dunbar collection.

11   **We are living:** "Bookmark," January 1, 1901, Harry Fleischman Papers, Tamiment Library/ Wagner Archives, Elmer Holmes Bobst Library, New York University; quoted in Harry Fleischman, *Norman Thomas: A Biography* (New York: W. W. Norton, 1964), 32.

11   **"Says Professor William James":** Welling Thomas, "Immortal Life with Christ," sermon delivered at First Presbyterian Church, Lewisburg, Pennsylvania, March 31, 1907, NTP.

12   **the local Republicans were rumored:** Emma Thomas to Arthur Thomas, November 10, 1911, Christine Dunbar collection.

12   **She cited Mary Wollstonecraft's:** Emma Thomas, "Women's Suffrage" (unpublished essay), Christine Dunbar collection.

Chapter Two: Preacher of the Word

14   **One of them was Amos Kling:** Swanberg, *Norman Thomas*, 2 and 6–7.

15   **"There is immortality":** Welling Thomas, "Immortal Life with Christ," sermon delivered at First Presbyterian Church, Lewisburg, Pennsylvania, March 31, 1907, NTP.

15   **William Jennings Bryan was the one:** Thomas, unpublished autobiography 4; Michael Kazin, *A Godly Hero* (New York: Random House, 2007), 61–63 (*Times* quoted on 63). See also Jackson Lears, *Rebirth of a Nation: The Making of Modern America, 1877–1920* (New York: Harper, 2009), 188–89. Kazin's biography, while not entirely admiring of its subject, tries to account for the more positive legacy of Bryan's brand of populism. For a bracing and darker look at the era, Lears's *Rebirth of a Nation* is especially good.

17   **But he was more in debt:** See, for instance, Nick Salvatore, *Eugene V. Debs: Citizen and Socialist*, 2nd ed. (Urbana, IL: University of Illinois Press, 2007), 150. Salvatore's book places Debs within the American democratic and republican tradition.

17   **"Coxey's Army":** Thomas, unpublished autobiography, 3–4.

17   **Norman was hardly aware:** Ibid., [0]–5. The detail about the trains comes from Ibid., 2.

18   **"It has been a splendid":** Evan Thomas, *The War Lovers: Roosevelt, Lodge, Hearst, and the Rush to Empire* (New York: Little, Brown, 2010), 364.

18   **"the most wholesome":** Lears, *Rebirth of a Nation*, 211.

19   **"No triumph of peace":** Ibid., 210–11; Miranda Carter, *George, Nicholas and Wilhelm: Three Royal Cousins and the Road to World War I* (New York: Knopf, 2010), 216.

20   **"so perfect a knowledge":** "Rev. Thomas Thomas," *Wyalusing (PA) Rocket*, June 22, 1904.

20   **"Dimly at least we understood":** Thomas, unpublished autobiography, 16.

Chapter Three: The World's Honors

22   **"blessed miracle":** Thomas, unpublished autobiography, 25.

22   **"We are not put":** William Barksdale Maynard, *Woodrow Wilson: Princeton to the Presidency* (New Haven, CT: Yale University Press, 2008), 66.

23   **"the most agreeable":** Maynard, *Woodrow Wilson*, 68 and 109.

23   **a cartoon of a lonely Wilson:** Swanberg, *Norman Thomas*, 13.

23   **Wilson's biographer John Milton Cooper Jr.:** John Milton Cooper Jr., *Woodrow Wilson: A Biography* (New York: Knopf, 2009), 84.

23   **When Norman's three-person:** Princeton University, *Nassau Herald* (1905), 99; "Princeton Wins," *Daily Princetonian*, March 29, 1905; H. B. Fine to Norman Thomas, April 3, 1905, Evan

Thomas III collection; Welling Thomas to Norman Thomas, telegram, March 29, 1905, Evan Thomas III collection.

24 **Norman graduated as valedictorian:** Princeton University, *Nassau Herald* (1905), 99; Princeton University 158th Commencement program (June 14, 1905), Evan Thomas III collection.

24 **"You better keep":** Emma Thomas to Norman Thomas, April 27, 1905, Evan Thomas III collection.

24 **"pleased me most":** Thomas, unpublished autobiography, 28–29.

24 **The most exclusive:** Maynard, *Woodrow Wilson*, 119.

24 **"like a Hollywood set":** Ibid., 115.

24 **"if I espoused unpopular":** Thomas, unpublished autobiography, 29.

25 **When Wilson first hired:** Maynard, *Woodrow Wilson*, 102.

25 **"gap of racial hatred":** Woodrow Wilson, *Papers of Woodrow Wilson*, ed. Arthur Stanley Link (Princeton, NJ: Princeton University Press, 1966–1994), 17: 223. In the letter, the student singles out his class's "finest debater"—probably Norman—as one of only two men who were "able to gulf and cross the gap." (Ibid.)

25 **the average expenditure:** Princeton University, *Nassau Herald* (1905), 95. Welling's salary was one thousand five hundred dollars. See "Application for Remission," Ralph Thomas student file, Princeton University Undergraduate Alumni Files, 1748–1920, Seely G. Mudd Manuscript Library, Princeton University.

26 **"foul core":** Jacob A. Riis, *How the Other Half Lives: Studies Among the Tenements of New York* (New York: Penguin Books, 1997), 46.

26 **After reading Riis's book:** Raymond B. Fosdick, *Chronicle of a Generation: An Autobiography* (New York: Harper, 1958), 58–60.

26 **"dangled before my eyes":** Thomas, unpublished autobiography, 41.

27 **the Age of Reform:** Richard Hofstadter, *The Age of Reform: From Bryan to FDR* (New York: Vintage Books, 1955).

27 **"no mystical sense of call":** Thomas, unpublished autobiography, 41.

28 **"cannot be handled like learning":** P. C. Kemeny, "University Cultural Wars: Rival Protestant Pieties in Early Twentieth-Century Princeton," *Journal of Ecclesiastical History* 53, no. 4 (2002): 741. My understanding of the religious character of Princeton's culture during Norman's years there is especially indebted to Kemeny's essay.

28 **"While our brother"** William Adams Brown, *A Teacher and His Times: A Story of Two Worlds* (New York: C. Scribner's Sons, 1940), 73.

28 **"probably brought me":** Thomas, unpublished autobiography, 44.

29 **"the ministry and the working man":** "Conference for the Consideration of the Opportunities and Work of the Ministry" program, March 31–April 2, 1905, NTP.

Chapter Four: The Fate of the Universe

30 **At Spring Street Presbyterian:** Swanberg, *Norman Thomas*, 17.

31 **"an apostle of riot":** David Nasaw, *The Chief* (New York: Houghton Mifflin, 2001), 197 and 199.

31 **"Come quick; Papa's killing":** Thomas, unpublished autobiography, 45–46.

31 **liquor as an "escape":** Ibid., 45–49.

32 **"What new anesthetic":** Albert Rhys Williams to Norman Thomas, September 28, 1909, NTP.

32 **His economics courses:** Thomas, unpublished autobiography, 25, 48, 49, 54, and 57; Fleischman, *Norman Thomas*, 38.

32 **"going all to pieces":** Thomas Carter to Norman Thomas, October 12, 1906, NTP.

33 **"Papa would be willing":** Emma Thomas to Norman Thomas, November 21, 1904, Evan Thomas III collection.

33 **"that life beyond the grave":** Welling Thomas, "Immortal Life with Christ," sermon delivered at First Presbyterian Church, Lewisburg, Pennsylvania, March 31, 1907, NTP. Swanberg, *Norman Thomas*, 23.

33 **letters home questioning:** Swanberg, *Norman Thomas*, 23.

33 **a trip around the world:** Ibid., 19–22; Thomas, unpublished autobiography, 50–51.

34 **"I took little interest":** Quoted in Rick Nutt, "G. Sherwood Eddy and the Attitudes of Protestants in the United States toward Global Mission," *Church History* 66 (September 1997): 505.

34 **"remarkable woman":** Norman Thomas to Emma Thomas, November 17, 1907, Patricia Libbey collection.
35 **"Siam's progress is marvelous":** Ibid.
35 **"selfish":** Violet Stewart to Frances Stewart, undated 1909, Patricia Libbey collection.
36 **"will lead inevitably":** Carter, *George, Nicholas and Wilhelm*, 213–15.
38 **"my mind was full":** Norman Thomas to Emma Thomas, June 4, 1908, Evan Thomas III collection.
39 **"Every day I live":** Wilson, *Papers of Woodrow Wilson*, 18: 335.
39 **"scientific study of theology":** Handy, *History of Union Theological Seminary in New York*, 122. For my portrayal of Union Theological Seminary at the turn of the twentieth century, I am indebted to Handy's book and to Gary Dorrien's multivolume study, *The Making of American Liberal Theology*.
41 **"Christian idealists must not make":** Walter Rauschenbusch, *Christianity and the Social Crisis* (New York: Macmillan, 1913), 410–11.
41 **"We shall never have":** Ibid., 420; Dorrien, *The Making of American Liberal Theology*, 105.
41 **"Ethical conduct":** Rauschenbusch, *Christianity and the Social Crisis*, 7; Gary J. Dorrien, *Soul in Society* (Minneapolis, MN: Fortress Press, 1995), 40.
41 **"disciples" of Rauschenbusch:** Swanberg, *Norman Thomas*, 27.
42 **"conventionally and cautiously liberal":** Thomas, unpublished autobiography, 53–54.

Chapter Five: Sympathy for the Unmarried

44 **a "wonder":** Norman Thomas to Emma Thomas, June 4, 1908, NTP.
44 **he fell in love:** Thomas, unpublished autobiography, 53.
44 **charged with embezzling:** "Another Big Defalcation," *New York Times*, August 17, 1886; "Treasurer Gray's Career," *New York Times*, August 18, 1886; "Defaulter Gray Buried," *New York Times*, August 20, 1886. I am grateful to Patricia Libbey for calling my attention to the scandal surrounding Gray's career and death and for generously sharing her research into the Stewart and Gray families, including their backgrounds. For Frances Gray Stewart's ancestors, see Edward Gray, *William Gray, of Salem, Merchant: A Biographical Sketch* (Boston: Houghton Mifflin, 1914).
45 **"John A. Stewart XVII":** Princeton University, *Nassau Herald* (1905), 13.
46 **"I'd not be surprised":** Violet Stewart to Mary Sheldon, November 9, 1909, Patricia Libbey collection.
46 **"full of news":** Violet Stewart to Frances Stewart, November 9, 1909, Patricia Libbey collection.
46 **"I'd hate to be England":** Swanberg, *Norman Thomas*, 29.
47 **"Don't tell her":** Violet Stewart to Frances Stewart, November 21, 1909, Patricia Libbey collection.
47 **"Mr. Thomas" became:** Swanberg, *Norman Thomas*, 29–30.
48 **"real preaching":** Violet Stewart to Frances Stewart, November 2, 1909, Patricia Libbey collection.
50 **"Considering their wealth":** Ralph Thomas to Norman Thomas, July 10, 1910, NTP.
50 **"the angel of Hell's Kitchen":** "Rev. N. M. Thomas Weds Miss Stewart," *New York Times*, September 2, 1910; "Fellow-Workers to Wed," *New-York Observer*, August 4, 1910; Swanberg, *Norman Thomas*, 34.
51 **"With sincere sympathy":** Princeton University, "The Record of the Class of 1905," 1910, 148–49.
51 **"all this and Heaven too":** Thomas, unpublished autobiography, 55.
52 **"Hindu pantheist":** Dorrien, *The Making of American Liberal Theology*, 57–58.
52 **William Adams Brown delivered a sermon:** Norman Thomas to William Adams Brown, January 26, 1911, Norman Thomas Student Records, UTS Collection, Burke Library Archives, Union Theological Seminary.
52 **"We are all delighted":** Cleveland H. Dodge to Norman Thomas, January 11, 1911, NTP.
52 **"I was feeling pretty blue":** Welling Thomas to Ralph Thomas, January 19, 1911, Christine Dunbar collection.
53 **"These sensational rumors":** Welling Thomas to George Alexander, January 23, 1911, Harry Fleischman Papers; quoted in Swanberg, *Norman Thomas*, 36.
53 **"in the winter of 1910–1911":** Thomas, unpublished autobiography, 81.

53 **not without misgivings and sadness:** Welling Thomas to Ralph Thomas, January 19, 1911, Christine Dunbar collection.
53 **"deplorable notoriety"** Welling Thomas to George Alexander, January 23, 1911, Harry Fleischman Papers.

Chapter Six: A Land of Brotherhood and Justice

56 **"had literally cursed the world":** Norman Thomas, sermon delivered at Brick Church, New York, April 16, 1911, NTP.
56 **"He preached a good sermon":** Thomas, unpublished autobiography, 57–58. In his autobiography, Norman refers to a Palm Sunday sermon, but the text of the 1911 Easter Sunday sermon found among his papers appears to be the same sermon.
57 **"So we rejoice":** Thomas, sermon delivered at Brick Church, New York, April 16, 1911, NTP.
57 **"the proclamation of the gospel":** "Form of Government," Office of the General Assembly, Presbyterian Church, http://www.pcusa.org/oga/boo/fog_ch1.htm (accessed April 27, 2010).
57 **"I am overwhelmingly distressed":** Swanberg, *Norman Thomas*, 36.
57 **He had followed with interest:** Thomas, unpublished autobiography, 57.
58 **"a penetrating and original mind":** Brown, *A Teacher and His Times*, 113.
59 **explicitly stated in the contract:** Board of Home Missions of the Presbyterian Church, "Agreement," April 1, 1916, NTP.
59 **Only twelve people came:** Home Missions Committee and Church Extension Committee, *The Church and the City: An Account of Home Missions and Church Extension in New York Presbytery* (New York: New York Presbytery, 1917), 79.
60 **could have been transplanted villages:** David Traxel, *Crusader Nation* (New York: Knopf, 2006), 138–40; Robert A. Orsi, *The Madonna of 115th Street* (New Haven, CT: Yale University Press, 2002), 17–18; David Laskin, *The Long Way Home: An American Journey from Ellis Island to the Great War* (New York: Harper, 2010), 6–7. For my depiction of East Harlem in the years before World War I, Orsi's book was especially helpful.
60 **around 15 percent:** Joseph M. Hawes and Elizabeth F. Shores, eds., *The Family in America: An Encyclopedia* (Santa Barbara, CA: ABC-CLIO, 2001), 1: 178. While child labor probably declined after 1870, Hawes and Shores note that the statistics are difficult to ascertain exactly. The 1910 figure was initially reported at 18.4 percent and then reestimated. (Ibid.)
60 **One survey:** Robert Whaples, "Child Labor in the United States," EH.Net Encyclopedia, http://eh.net/encyclopedia/article/whaples.childlabor (accessed April 30, 2010).
61 **"We soon got the idea":** Orsi, *Madonna of 115th Street*, 161.
61 **Between 1901 and 1910:** Louis Menand, *The Metaphysical Club* (New York: Farrar, Straus and Giroux, 2001), 381–88; Orsi, *Madonna of 115th Street*, 160.
62 **"I have done reasonably well":** Norman Thomas to "Harold," December 6, 1915, NTP.
62 **"These people who are coming":** "The Women's Board of Home Missions," *New York Observer* 91 (March 21, 1912), 382.
62 **On June 8, 1912:** *Princeton Alumni Weekly*, June 12, 1912.
62 **Woodrow Wilson, dined:** Cooper, *Woodrow Wilson*, 154.
63 **the fellowship for Christian action:** John Nevin Sayre, "After Fifty Years," Crusaders Club, John Nevin Sayre Papers, Swarthmore College Peace Collection.
63 **Evan wondered why:** Evan Thomas to John Nevin Sayre, October 14, 1912, John Nevin Sayre Papers.
64 **"The Son of man must suffer":** "Constitution" and "Service of Consecration," Princeton Crusader Fellowship Records, 1912–1979, Seely G. Mudd Manuscript Library, Princeton University.
64 **"I have a confession to make"** Evan Thomas to John Nevin Sayre, October 14, 1912, John Nevin Sayre Papers.
65 **a long ovation:** "Princeton Confers Honors and Degrees," *New York Times*, June 12, 1912.
65 **"I am always glad":** John A. Stewart to Norman Thomas, June 15, 1912, NTP.

Chapter Seven: The Promise of American Life

67 **hundreds of Socialists had been voted:** James Chace, *1912: Wilson, Roosevelt, Taft & Debs: The Election That Changed the Country* (New York: Simon & Schuster, 2004), 182–83.

67 **"the muddy tide of commercialism":** Quoted in Henry F. May, *The End of American Innocence: A Study of the First Years of Our Own Time, 1912–1917*, ed. Columbia University Press Morningside (New York: Columbia University Press, 1992), 5.
67 **he had left the country:** Chace, *1912*, 11–12.
67 **"A National Government cannot":** Ibid., 221.
67 **"fearless of the future":** Ibid., 116–23 (quote on 118).
67 **the character of religious revival meetings:** Ibid., 117, 161, 166–67.
68 **"The trust reposed in individual self-interest":** Herbert David Croly, *The Promise of American Life* (Charleston, SC: BiblioBazaar, 2006), 31–32.
68 **"The Bull Moose has stolen":** Morris Hillquit, " 'Comrade' Bull Moose," Morris Hillquit Papers, Tamiment Library/Wagner Archives, Elmer Holmes Bobst Library, New York University.
68 **The Socialist leader Debs:** For more on Debs's run in the 1912 election, see Chace, *1912*, 90 and 238–89; and Salvatore, *Eugene V. Debs*, 248 and 263–64.
69 **the warrior and the priest:** John Milton Cooper Jr., *The Warrior and the Priest: Woodrow Wilson and Theodore Roosevelt* (Cambridge, MA: Belknap Press of Harvard University Press, 1983).
69 **"third party":** Cooper, *Woodrow Wilson*, 168.
70 **"Evan came home to vote":** Welling Thomas to Arthur Thomas, November 6, 1912, Christine Dunbar collection.
70 **"Well I guess Evan is sorry":** Emma Thomas to Arthur Thomas, undated November 1912, Christine Dunbar collection.
70 **Ralph had also helped form:** "Peck Is President of Tech Wilson Club," *Tech* (Massachusetts Institute of Technology), October 18, 1912.
70 **"glad" at the result:** Welling Thomas to Arthur Thomas, November 6, 1912, Christine Dunbar collection.
70 **On election day:** Maynard, *Woodrow Wilson*, 276.
70 **He had finished his freshman year:** Princeton University Report Card for Arthur Thomas, June 1912, Christine Dunbar collection.
71 **"I know just":** Emma Thomas to Arthur Thomas, undated, Christine Dunbar collection.
71 **"Just remember":** Emma Thomas to Arthur Thomas, November 11, 1913, Christine Dunbar collection.
71 **"What is the particular cause":** Emma Thomas to Arthur Thomas, November 25, 1912, Christine Dunbar collection.
71 **The school recessed:** Maynard, *Woodrow Wilson*, 288.
71 **"the human cost":** Woodrow Wilson, *President Wilson's State Papers and Addresses*, ed. Albert Shaw (New York: George H. Doran, 1918), 2.
71 **a "gloom":** Emma Thomas to Arthur Thomas, November 10, 1913, Christine Dunbar collection.
72 **"already hostile to the Roman Church":** Thomas, unpublished autobiography, 64.
72 **As he saw it:** This may have been a little retrospective whitewashing. "I had a talk this p.m. with ten of Evan's scouts," wrote Norman to Violet in 1914, "seven of whom say they'll come to S.S. in the afternoon but their fathers want them to go to mass in the morning." (Norman Thomas to Violet Thomas, August 23, 1914, Nancy Gerber collection.)
72 **"You have no right":** "Some residents in 116th St" to Norman Thomas, undated, NTP.
73 **once refereed a basketball game:** Swanberg, *Norman Thomas*, 42.
74 **"Norman's letter sounded tired":** Emma Thomas to Arthur Thomas, October 14, 1913, Christine Dunbar collection.
74 **"With all my love":** Swanberg, *Norman Thomas*, 40.

Chapter Eight: Long Wars Will Occur

76 **When a Serbian nationalist:** My overview of the events leading up to World War I is especially dependent upon Martin Gilbert, *The First World War* (New York: Macmillan, 2004), 1–34; James Joll, *The Origins of the First World War* (London: Longman, 1984); John Keegan, *The First World War* (New York: Vintage, 2000), 48–70; and Barbara Tuchman, *The Guns of August*, 4th ed. (Toronto: Bantam Books, 1980), 33–44, 68, 91–104.
77 **"no chance":** James W. Gerard, *My Four Years in Germany* (Middlesex, UK: Echo Library, 2008), 82.

77 **"Friends in past"**: Gilbert, *First World War*, 18.

77 **"as quiet as the grave"**: Edward Mandell House, *The Intimate Papers of Colonel House: Arranged as a Narrative by Charles Seymour*, Vol. 1 (Boston: Houghton Mifflin, 1928), 270; quoted (with variation) in Walter Lord, *The Good Years: From 1900 to the First World War* (New York: Harper, 1960), 334.

80 **"every reason for war"**: Gilbert, *First World War*, 24.

80 **"Who rules in Berlin"**: Ibid., 27.

80 **Moltke won out**: Keegan, *First World War*, 48–70; Tuchman, *Guns of August*, 38–44, 68, 91–104.

81 **"A general European"**: Quoted in Traxel, *Crusader Nation*, 112.

81 **"one of the supreme opportunities"**: Norman Thomas, *The Reminiscences of Norman Thomas*, part 1 (1949), 56, Oral History Collection, Columbia University.

81 **few took seriously the practicability**: Joll, *Origins of the First World War*, 180.

81 **"To Berlin! To Berlin!"**: Traxel, *Crusader Nation*, 116.

81 **"I wonder if this"**: Ibid., 112.

82 **called the war "holy"**: Jeffrey Verhey, *The Spirit of 1914: Militarism, Myth and Mobilization in Germany* (New York: Cambridge University Press, 2000), 2. In recent years, historians have questioned the unity of enthusiasm for the war, arguing that reports of popular jingoism were less a reflection of common sentiment than a mobilizing (and self-mobilizing) tactic. See, for instance, Niall Ferguson, *The Pity of War* (New York: Basic Books, 1999), 177, Verhey, *Spirit of 1914*, 119, and Audoin-Rouzeau and Becker, *14–18*, 94–95

82 **"Blow, bugles, blow!"**: Rupert Brooke, *The Collected Poems of Rupert Brooke* (New York: Dodd, Mead & Company, 1915), 113; fragment quoted in Tuchman, *Guns of August*, 348.

82 **"We arrived in Paris"**: Audoin-Rouzeau and Becker, *14–18*, 163. Brooke died in 1915, of an infected mosquito bite, on his way to the battle of Gallipoli (around half a million total casualties). Apollinaire suffered a shrapnel wound in the head in 1916 and died two years after that.

82 **Husbands told their wives**: Gilbert, *First World War*, 29.

83 **"Le pantalon rouge c'est la France!"**: Tuchman, *Guns of August*, 46.

83 **"the friendliest intentions"**: Keegan, *First World War*, 80–81.

83 **a cruelty previously reserved**: Isabel V. Hull, *Absolute Destruction: Military Culture and the Practices of War in Imperial Germany* (Ithaca: Cornell University Press, 2006), 197–262.

83 **called town mayors "ringleaders"**: Tuchman, *Guns of August*, 1999, 255–59; Keegan, *First World War*, 78–84.

84 **"Espion! Espion!"**: Traxel, *Crusader Nation*, 121.

84 **"The European war is a most"**: Welling Thomas to Norman Thomas, August 25, 1914, NTP.

84 **the medieval university town of Louvain**: Keegan, *First World War*, 82–83; Tuchman, *Guns of August*, 356–60.

84 **They progressed so fast**: Keegan, *First World War*, 107–8, 111–26, 183.

85 **"War unlooses men's"**: Norman Thomas to Emma Thomas, October 20, 1914, Nancy Gerber collection.

86 **he would have enlisted**: Sidney Lovett to Elizabeth Lovett, undated 1915, A. Sidney Lovett Papers, Manuscripts and Archives, Yale University Library.

86 **"typifies . . . that deification"**: Norman Thomas to Emma Thomas, October 20, 1914, Nancy Gerber collection.

86 **"this old earth paradise"**: Norman Thomas to Violet Thomas, September 1, 1915, Nancy Gerber collection.

86 **"It seems as if"**: Norman Thomas to Violet Thomas, undated, Nancy Gerber collection.

Chapter Nine: Which Way Shall It Be?

88 **"take a couple of courses"**: Evan Thomas to Welling and Emma Thomas, January 20, 1915, Christine Dunbar collection.

88 **"I have half regretted"**: Ibid.

88 **"a damnable mistake"**: Evan Thomas to Emma Thomas, February 21, 1916, Christine Dunbar collection.

88 **"I wish that I was"**: Evan Thomas to Violet Thomas, January 17, 1915, Evan Thomas III collection.

89 **"Yes, [the church] preaches"**: Evan Thomas to Welling and Emma Thomas, January 20, 1915, Christine Dunbar collection.

89 **"not such an awful heathen":** Ibid.

89 **William Ashley Sunday was a force:** My description of Sunday is indebted to Roger Bruns, *Preacher: Billy Sunday and Big-Time American Evangelism* (New York: W. W. Norton, 1992). For Sunday's reception at Princeton, see Kemeny, "University Culture Wars," 11–17.

89 **He looked like a fop:** Bruns, *Preacher*, 14–17, 36–58, 85.

90 **"Take your evolution theory":** Ibid., 122.

90 **When Sunday arrived at Princeton:** Ibid., 111–12.

90 **The professors at Princeton:** "Princeton's Thrust at *Billy Sunday*," *Literary Digest* 50 (April 24, 1915), 959–60.

91 **Arthur wasn't sure:** Arthur Thomas to Welling Thomas, March 12, 1915, Christine Dunbar collection.

92 **She had loved:** Violet Stewart to Frances Stewart, 1909, Patricia Libbey collection.

92 **Ten years later:** Cooper, *Woodrow Wilson*, 285.

93 **"miscreants":** Arthur Stanley Link, *Wilson: The Struggle for Neutrality, 1914–1915* (Princeton, NJ: Princeton University Press, 1947), 373; Traxel, *Crusader Nation*, 166.

93 **"strict accountability":** Kendrick A. Clements, "Woodrow Wilson and World War I," *Presidential Studies Quarterly* 34 (March 2004): 62–64, 81–82; Traxel, *Crusader Nation*, 165.

93 **"I wish with all my heart":** Cooper, *Woodrow Wilson*, 286. Cooper puts this ambivalence at the heart of Wilson's actions following the sinking of the *Lusitania*, while Clements faults the president for not fully understanding the consequences of his response.

93 **J. P. Morgan acted as:** "Key Moments in J. P. Morgan's History," http://www.jpmorgan.com /pages/jpmorgan/emea/local/fr/history (accessed May 10, 2010).

94 **The most forceful advocate:** Thomas J. Knock, *To End All Wars: Woodrow Wilson and the Quest for a New World Order* (Princeton, NJ: Princeton University Press, 1995), 49, 61; Traxel, *Crusader Nation*, 168.

94 **"terrible and evil":** Cooper, *Warrior and the Priest*, 284–85. For a study of Roosevelt's obsession with manhood and its implications for his political mission, see Gail Bederman, *Manliness & Civilization* (Chicago: University of Chicago Press, 1996), 170–215.

94 **"poured out their blood":** Gilbert, *First World War*, 159; Cooper, *Warrior and the Priest*, 284–85. The phrase "poured out their blood like water" is a reference to Psalm 79.

94 **"The truth is":** Knock, *To End All Wars*, 49.

94 **"preparedness for peace":** See, for instance, "College Heads for War Drills," *New York Times*, January 24, 1915.

95 **"In the Plattsburg camp":** Arthur Stanwood Pier, "Harvard at the Plattsburg [*sic*] Camps: Impressions of a Graduate," *Harvard Alumni Bulletin* (Harvard Alumni Association), 1915, 30. "Plattsburg" was an alternative spelling.

96 **One night the Italian:** Swanberg, *Norman Thomas*, 41–42.

96 **a peace "bought":** John Grier Hibben, *The Higher Patriotism* (New York: Scribner, 1915), 39.

97 **"There are some pretty grim things":** Maynard, *Woodrow Wilson*, 303.

97 **"the choice men":** John Grier Hibben, "Martial Valor in Times of Peace," *Princeton Alumni Weekly*, June 16, 1915.

98 **wrote "unsettled":** "Application for Remission," Arthur Thomas student file, Princeton University Undergraduate Alumni Files, 1748–1920.

98 **"A year ago":** "Crusaders Talk—June 13th—1915," John Nevin Sayre Papers.

99 **"makes your blood run":** Evan Thomas to Agnes Thomas, November 8, 1915, Nancy Gerber collection.

100 **"The enemy could be seen":** Keegan, *First World War*, 202.

100 **Even the Scots:** Gordan Urquhart, "Confrontation and Withdrawal: Loos, Readership and 'The First Hundred Thousand,'" in *Scotland and the Great War*, eds. Catriona M. M. MacDonald and E. W. McFarland (East Linton, Scotland: Tuckwell Press, 1999), 140; E. W. McFarland, "Introduction: 'A Coronach in Stone,'" in *Scotland and the Great War*, eds. Catriona M. M. MacDonald and E. W. McFarland, 6; Ferguson, *Pity of War*, xix.

100 **hardly more than twenty:** Evan Thomas to Emma Thomas, November 21, 1915, Evan Thomas III collection.

100 **"I am ready":** Evan Thomas to Norman Thomas, November 12, 1915, NTP.

100 *"the lifting of resistance":* John Haynes Holmes, *New Wars for Old* (New York: Dodd, Mead and Company, 1917), 139; the emphasis is Holmes's.

101 "Love is the ideal": Evan Thomas to Norman Thomas, November 12, 1915, NTP.
101 "nothing is his own": Ibid.
101 "There is no such thing": Evan Thomas to Emma Thomas, November 21, 1915, Evan Thomas
     III collection.
101 "Have thought much": Evan Thomas to John Nevin Sayre, November 16, 1915, John Nevin
     Sayre Papers.

Chapter Ten: Courage of the Highest Type

103 The United States was in a recession: Clements, "Woodrow Wilson and World War I," 67–68.
104 "Some of my friends": Swanberg, *Norman Thomas*, 44.
104 "Well, that's done": Thomas, unpublished autobiography, 64.
104 "alphabet societies": "Minister Attacks Organized Charity," *New York Times*, October 5, 1915.
104 Norman, embarrassed, responded: "Churches and Charity," *New York Times*, October 13,
     1915.
105 "is a war in which": Welling Thomas, "Realizing God's Presence," sermon delivered by Enoch
     Perrine at First Presbyterian Church, Lewisburg, Pennsylvania, November 21, 1915, NTP.
107 "Please answer at once": Ralph Thomas to Norman Thomas, undated 1915, NTP.
107 "He looks thin": Emma Thomas to Norman Thomas, undated 1916, Nancy Gerber collection.
107 "so absolutely needless": Evan Thomas to Norman Thomas, November 30, 1915, NTP.
108 "one of the family": Evan Thomas to Emma Thomas, May 16, 1916, Evan Thomas III collection.
109 "I believe he would": Evan Thomas to Emma Thomas, January 25, 1916, Evan Thomas III
     collection.
109 After one tirade: Evan Thomas to John Nevin Sayre, January 5, 1916, John Nevin Sayre Papers.
109 "groping in the dark": Evan Thomas to Norman Thomas, December 30, 1915, NTP.
110 "I question it": Evan Thomas to Norman Thomas, December 30, 1915, NTP.
110 a "new start": Evan Thomas to John Nevin Sayre, February 14, 1914, John Nevin Sayre
     Papers.
110 Great Britain had just implemented: Paul Fussell, *The Great War and Modern Memory* (New
     York: Oxford University Press, 1975), 177.
111 "Such people": Evan Thomas to Emma Thomas, March 26, 1916, Christine Dunbar collection.
111 "the work not": Evan Thomas to Emma Thomas, April 24, 1916, Evan Thomas III collection.
111 "In the words of Jesus": Evan Thomas, sermon delivered at St. George's Church, Edinburgh,
     Scotland, April 23, 1916, Evan Thomas III collection.
111 "chiefly for the way": Evan Thomas to Emma Thomas, April 24, 1916, Evan Thomas III
     collection.
111 "faith alone saves": Evan Thomas, sermon delivered at St. George's Church, April 23, 1916,
     Evan Thomas III collection.
112 "You might send sermon": Evan Thomas to Emma Thomas, April 24, 1916, Evan Thomas III
     collection.
112 "Sit down": Author interview with Sidney Lovett Jr., October 7, 2010.
112 "the audience was so enthusiastic": Swanberg, *Norman Thomas*, 46.
113 "practical denial of brotherhood": Bernard K. Johnpoll, *Pacifist's Progress: Norman Thomas
     and the Decline of American Socialism* (Chicago, IL: Quadrangle Books, 1970), 21.
114 "a 'moral' but vindictive": Norman Thomas to Ralph Thomas, March 22, 1916, NTP.
114 "It's a good thing": Bruns, 16.
114 "Are you sure": Norman Thomas to Ralph Thomas, April 3, 1916, NTP.
115 "By thinking men": Ibid.
115 "I do not suppose": Ibid.
115 "It's the old story": Norman Thomas to Ralph Thomas, April 19, 1916, Christine Dunbar
     collection.
115 "not at all well": Sidney Lovett to Elizabeth Lovett, April 17, 1916, A. Sidney Lovett Papers,
     Manuscripts and Archives, Yale University Library.
116 "government of butchers": Arthur Stanley Link, *Woodrow Wilson and the Progressive Era,
     1910–1917* (New York: Harper & Row, 1963), 109.
116 "The field of self-government": Cooper, *Woodrow Wilson*, 240.
116 "almost parchmenty": Ibid., 243.

116 **"I should like"**: Norman Thomas to Ralph Thomas, April 19, 1916, Christine Dunbar collection.
117 **Flags lined Broadway**: "New York Ready for Big Parade," *New York Times*, May 13, 1916; "Every Calling in the Line," *New York Times*, May 14, 1916.
117 **"ABSOLUTE AND UNQUALIFIED LOYALTY"**: David M. Kennedy, *Over Here: The First World War and American Society*, 25th anniversary ed. (Oxford: Oxford University Press, 2004), 67.
117 **"its celerity of movement"**: "The Parade and Its Marshall," *New York Times*, May 15, 1916.
118 **"There is disloyalty"**: Wilson, *Papers of Woodrow Wilson*, 37: 223.

Chapter Eleven: *Muddle Headed*

119 **"bleed France white"**: "Battles—The Battle of Verdun, 1916," http://www.firstworldwar.com/battles/verdun.htm (accessed May 10, 2010); Keegan, *First World War*, 278–86; Gilbert, *First World War*, 230–35.
120 **"as if guided"**: Keegan, *First World War*, 289.
120 **"the great fuckup"**: Ibid., 290–99.
120 **The *Punch* cartoons**: Vera Brittain, *Testament of Youth: An Autobiographical Study of the Years 1900–1925* (New York: Penguin, 2004), 259.
121 **"sick" of the war**: Evan Thomas to Emma Thomas, June 23, 1916, NTP.
121 **the term "conscientious objector"**: Susan Pedersen, "Anti-Condescensionism," *London Review of Books*, September 2005, 7–8.
121 **Objectors were shunned**: For several prison memoirs by conscientious objectors in the UK during World War I, see Peter Brock, ed., *"These Strange Criminals": An Anthology of Prison Memoirs by Conscientious Objectors from the Great War to the Cold War* (Toronto: University of Toronto Press, 2004), 14–88.
122 **"take the consequences"**: Evan Thomas to Emma Thomas, November 14, 1916, NTP.
122 **Norman's "political moves"**: Evan Thomas to Emma Thomas, January 20, 1917, NTP.
123 **"Well, by God!"**: Evan Thomas to Emma Thomas, April 23, 1917, NTP.
123 **"My admiration for Pres. Wilson"**: Evan Thomas to Emma Thomas, December 17, 1916, NTP.
123 **"to a certain extent justify"**: Norman Thomas to Evan Thomas [October 1916], NTP.
124 **"ALL ARMOR PLATE"**: John Fabian Witt, "Crystal Eastman and the Internationalist Beginnings of American Civil Liberties," *Duke Law Journal* 54 (December 2004): 731–36.
124 **"our position"**: Norman Thomas to Evan Thomas [October 1916], NTP.
125 **The AUAM had come to the White House**: Knock, *To End All Wars*, 66–67.
125 **"world league for peace of righteousness"**: Ibid., 75–78.
126 **"the most important step"**: Ibid., 98.
126 **The *Independent* effused**: Ibid., 77.
126 **"bearded iceberg"**: Cooper, *Woodrow Wilson*, 338.
126 **"heroic mood"**: Cooper, *Warrior and the Priest*, 305.
127 **"We didn't go to war!"**: Cooper, *Woodrow Wilson*, 341.
127 **"Any little German lieutenant"**: Traxel, *Crusader Nation*, 240.
127 **"liberals" instead of "progressives"**: Forcey, *Crossroads of Liberalism*, 255.
127 **"remaking his philosophy"**: Cooper, *Woodrow Wilson*, 355; Forcey, *Crossroads of Liberalism*, 250–63.
127 **"I am a Socialist"**: Knock, *To End All Wars*, 94.
127 **On election night**: Cooper, *Woodrow Wilson*, 357–58.
128 **"more delighted"**: Evan Thomas to Emma Thomas, November 14, 1916, NTP.
128 **"America has an opportunity"**: Evan Thomas to Emma Thomas, January 20, 1917, NTP.
128 **"very depressing commentary"**: Norman Thomas to Evan Thomas, October 1916, NTP.
128 **"There will be no war"**: Link, *Wilson the Diplomatist*, 81.
128 **"vast, gruesome contest"**: Knock, *To End All Wars*, 107.
128 **"German militarism"**: Cooper, *Woodrow Wilson*, 363.
128 **"frantic with rage"**: Ibid., 363; Knock, *To End All Wars*, 108.
129 **"attention to the fact"**: Cooper, *Woodrow Wilson*, 365.
129 **"We are drawing nearer"**: Ibid., 366. For the argument that Wilson was too tolerant of disagreement among his aides, see especially ibid., 366–67.
129 **Wilson kept him waiting**: Barbara Tuchman, *The Zimmermann Telegram* (New York: Ballantine Books, 1985), 121.

Chapter Twelve: What Then Shall America Do?

131 "I have at last": Norman Thomas to Howard A. Walter, January 31, 1917, NTP.

132 "I cannot fail": Ibid.

133 "Peace now or at any time": Knock, *To End All Wars*, 107.

133 "not-unsympathetic": Sterling Kernek, "The British Government's Reaction to President Wilson's 'Peace' Note of December 1916," *Historical Journal* 13 (December 1970): 723–24.

133 "turnip winter": Keegan, *First World War*, 318.

133 "The people don't want war": Evelyn Mary Stapleton-Bretherton Blücher von Wahlstatt, *An English Wife in Berlin* (New York: E. P. Dutton, 1920), 159.

133 "the French coast from Dunkirk to Boulogne": Tuchman, *Zimmermann Telegram*, 119–20.

133 "*Durchhalten*": Keegan, *First World War*, 321.

134 "I do not intend": Tuchman, *Zimmermann Telegram*, 126.

134 "peace without victory": Cooper, *Woodrow Wilson*, 370–71. Papers of Woodrow Wilson.

134 "destined to an immortality": Knock, *To End All Wars*, 114.

134 "campaign of hysteria": Blanche Wiesen Cook, "Woodrow Wilson and the Antimilitarists, 1914–1917" (PhD diss., Johns Hopkins University, 1970), 179.

135 "However impractical our ideals": W. H. Tinker to Norman Thomas, January 22, 1917, NTP.

135 "reverence for personality": Charles Chatfield, "World War I and the Liberal Pacifist in the United States," *American Historical Review* 75 (December 1970): 1926.

136 "When you come to the positive": William Adams Brown to Norman Thomas, February 19, 1917, NTP.

136 "If you are interested": Norman Thomas to Leroy Sheetz, January 25, 1917, NTP.

136 "I would avoid the expression": Ibid.

136 "I might do better service": Norman Thomas to Leroy Sheetz, February 3, 1917, NTP.

136 "I guarantee that the U-boat": Tuchman, *Zimmermann Telegram*, 137–41; Arthur Stanley Link, *Wilson: Campaigns for Progressivism and Peace, 1914–1917* (New York: Princeton University Press, 1947), 245.

137 it would be a "crime": Cooper, *Woodrow Wilson*, 374–75.

137 "For defense of American rights": Kennedy, *Over Here*, 21.

137 "everything here depends": Knock, *To End All Wars*, 124. For an insightful discussion of Lodge's position on the League, see Stephen Wertheim, "The League That Wasn't: American Designs for a Legalist-Sanctionist League of Nations and the Intellectual Origins of International Organization, 1914–1920," *Diplomatic History* (forthcoming article, 2011).

137 "in my view a matter": Knock, *To End All Wars*, 127.

137 "a war against the civilization": Ibid., 117.

137 "the handmaid of nationalism": Murray Benjamin Seidler, *Norman Thomas: Respectable Rebel* (Syracuse, NY: Syracuse University Press, 1967), 21.

138 "unite friends of democracy": "Copy of Letter from Mr. Norman Thomas," American Union Against Militarism (AUAM) Records, Swarthmore College Peace Collection.

138 Around lunchtime on Saturday: Minutes of the Meeting of February 10, 1917, AUAM Records; Minutes of the Meeting of February 14, 1917, AUAM Records.

138 causing "disaffection": Geoffrey R. Stone, "Mr. Wilson's First Amendment," in *Reconsidering Woodrow Wilson*, ed. John Milton Cooper Jr. (Washington D.C.: Woodrow Wilson Center Press, 2008), 192–93, 215n14; Ernest Freeberg, *Democracy's Prisoner: Eugene V. Debs, the Great War, and the Right to Dissent* (Cambridge, MA: Harvard University Press, 2008), 49–51.

139 The day before, the papers: Cooper, *Woodrow Wilson*, 377–78.

139 "call through a crack in the door": Knock, *To End All Wars*, 118 and 120.

139 "The Prussian Invasion Plot": Tuchman, *Zimmermann Telegram*, 184–85.

140 "I shall skin him": Link, *Wilson: Campaigns for Progressivism*, 392.

140 "The fact that that meeting": W. Seaver Jones to Norman Thomas, February 1, 1917, NTP.

140 "I live and work": Norman Thomas to John Grier Hibben, March 28, 1917, NTP.

140 "half jesting": John Grier Hibben to Norman Thomas, March 30, 1917, NTP.

140 David Starr Jordan could find: Kennedy, *Over Here*, 15; Freeberg, *Democracy's Prisoner*, 43.

141 grasp the "instrumentality": John Dewey, "What Are We Fighting For?" *Independent* 94 (1918): 480–83; reprinted as "The Social Possibilities of War," in Joseph Ratner, ed., *Characters and Events* (New York: Holt, 1929), 2: 552–57.

141 "a vague but genuine vision": John Dewey, "What America Will Fight For," *New Republic*, August 18, 1917. For the theoretical foundations of Dewey's thought during World War I, see Robert B. Westbrook, *John Dewey and American Democracy* (Ithaca, NY: Cornell University Press, 1991), 202–12. For two brilliant—and complementary, though very different—explorations of the relationship between the *New Republic* liberals and World War I, see Charles Forcey, *The Crossroads of Liberalism: Croly, Weyl, Lippmann, and the Progressive Era, 1900–1925* (New York: Oxford University Press, 1961), 221–315 passim, and Christopher Lasch, *The New Radicalism in America, 1889–1963: The Intellectual as a Social Type* (New York: W. W. Norton, 1986), 181–224.

142 "the present crisis": Norman Thomas, "The Present Crisis," February 19, 1917, NTP.

142 "the effect of a great revival": Norman Thomas to "Jack," March 30, 1917, NTP.

142 "Race passions and prejudice": Ibid.

143 Czarist Russia covered: Carter, *George, Nicholas and Wilhelm*, 50, 60–61, 70.

143 "Fat Rodzianko has sent": Ibid., 398. The dates given are according to the Western calendar.

144 "yearning desire": Wilson, *Woodrow Wilson*, 256.

144 "as certain as anything": Peter Beinart, *The Icarus Syndrome: A History of American Hubris* (New York: Harper, 2010), 33.

144 "Once lead this people": Cooper, *Woodrow Wilson*, 382. The authenticity and date of Cobb's meeting are the matter of some controversy; see ibid., 642n51.

145 "the duty of this": Lasch, *New Radicalism in America*, 200–201.

145 "I do not care": Cooper, *Woodrow Wilson*, 383.

Chapter Thirteen: Let Every Man Be Faithful

146 They withstood the rain: Kennedy, *Over Here*, 10–13; Cooper, *Woodrow Wilson*, 385–88.

147 "in all its arrogance": Knock, *To End All Wars*, 121.

147 "I have just finished reading": Evan Thomas to Emma Thomas, April 3, 1917, Evan Thomas III collection.

148 "If conscience is separated": Edward G. Andrew, *Conscience and Its Critics: Protestant Conscience, Enlightenment Reason, and Modern Subjectivity* (Toronto: University of Toronto Press, 2001), 16.

148 "There may be some": Evan Thomas to Emma Thomas, January 20, 1917, NTP.

148 "I still think": Evan Thomas to Emma Thomas, February 21, 1916, Evan Thomas III collection.

149 "Your lives for me": Evan Thomas to Emma Thomas, January 20, 1917, NTP.

149 "felt like a man": Evan Thomas to Emma Thomas, June 6, 1917, Christine Dunbar collection.

149 "using the name": Evan Thomas to Emma Thomas, May 4, 1917, NTP.

150 would be a "relief": Evan Thomas to Emma Thomas, April 3, 1917, Evan Thomas III collection.

150 "To my mind": Evan Thomas to Emma Thomas, April 23, 1917, NTP.

150 "The abandonment of the use": Evan Thomas to Norman Thomas, April 12, 1917, NTP.

150 "If I could be": Evan Thomas to Norman Thomas, 1917, NTP.

151 "ceased all opposition": Crystal Eastman to the Executive Committee, June 14, 1917, AUAM Records.

152 "Unless a people retains": Charles Chatfield, *For Peace and Justice: Pacifism in America, 1914–1941* (Knoxville: University of Tennessee Press, 1971), 56.

152 "Rights" themselves were suspect: For a broader discussion of rights and freedom during the progressive era and World War I years, see Eric Foner, *The Story of American Freedom* (New York: W. W. Norton, 1999), 139–79; for pragmatism and rights, see Menand, *The Metaphysical Club*, 409–33.

152 As John Dewey reasoned: Freeberg, *Democracy's Prisoner*, 158.

153 "I believe that mutual understanding": Mabel H. Williamson to Norman Thomas, April 24, 1917, NTP.

153 "The only kind": Norman Thomas to E. B. Chaffee, March 12, 1917, NTP.

154 "mass action to shorten": "Socialist Party Proclaims Unalterable Opposition to War . . . ," *American Socialist*, April 21, 1917.

154 "You are my enemy": David A. Shannon, *The Socialist Party of America: A History* (New York: Macmillan, 1955), 102.

154 "Having failed to prevent": "'Declaration of War Policy' By the Dissenting Fifty," *American Socialist*, April 21, 1917.
154 "going into war upon": Kennedy, *Over Here*, 20–23.
155 "something in the air": Ibid., 23.
155 the birth of his wife: See, for example, "Easter Sunday," Norman Thomas journal, NTP.
156 "fit his voice": "Billy Sunday Can Preach to 20,000," *New York Times*, December 21, 1916.
156 "In these days": "40,000 Cheer for War and Religion Mixed by Sunday," *New York Times*, April 9, 1917.
156 "arrogance, narrowness, lack": Norman Thomas to Wilton Merle-Smith, November 20, 1916, NTP.
156 "coward and a sneak": "Denounce Germany in City's Pulpits," *New York Times*, March 26, 1917.
156 "parable of the state of our minds": Norman Thomas, "The Christian Patriot," speech delivered May 12, 1917, Philadelphia, Pennsylvania, NTP.
156 "In the estimation of Missourians": Kennedy, *Over Here*, 18.
157 "clothing, cots, camps": Ibid., 144.
157 "substitutes for American soldiers": Traxel, *Crusader Nation*, 275.
157 As late as April 18: Kennedy, *Over Here*, 18 and 148.
157 "nervously defective": "The Morality of Conscription," *New Republic*, May 5, 1917.
157 "less than 8 percent": John Whiteclay Chambers, *To Raise an Army: The Draft Comes to Modern America* (New York: Free Press, 1987), 73.
157 "Where is it written": Akhil Reed Amar, *The Bill of Rights: Creation and Reconstruction* (New Haven: Yale University Press, 1998), 57–58.
158 "I assure you very explicitly": Martha C. Nussbaum, *Liberty of Conscience: In Defense of America's Tradition of Religious Equality* (New York: Basic Books, 2008), 14.
158 He needed the draft: How and why Wilson decided to implement the draft is still the matter of some speculation among scholars. The timing of his decision to call for the draft—after earlier repudiating it—after reading a particularly forceful telegram from Roosevelt suggests that it was, at least in part, a reaction to Roosevelt's plan. See Chambers, *To Raise an Army*, 134–38.
158 "Universal training will jumble": Kennedy, *Over Here*, 145–47 (quote is on 145).
158 "gives a long and sorely needed": Christopher Capozzola, *Uncle Sam Wants You: World War I and the Making of the Modern American Citizen* (New York: Oxford University Press, 2008), 26.
159 not to use the word "censorship": Cooper, *Woodrow Wilson*, 391.
159 substituted the phrase "selective": Capozzola, *Uncle Sam Wants You*, 27.
159 met with Secretary of War Newton Baker: "Memorandum of Negotiations," April 1917, NTP; Lillian Wald, Jane Addams, and Norman Thomas to Newton Baker, April 12, 1917, American Civil Liberties Union (ACLU) Records, Public Policy Papers, Department of Rare Books and Special Collections, Princeton University Library.
160 "it is contrary": Henry P. McCain to Norman Thomas, April 26, 1917, NTP.
160 "I can assure you that the point": Wilson, *Papers of Woodrow Wilson*, 42: 179.
161 "wage war 'for the privilege'": Norman Thomas and Roger Baldwin to the Conference Committee, May 1, 1917, ACLU Records.
161 "a festival": Wilson, *Papers of Woodrow Wilson*, 42: 180.
161 "What Are You Doing": Capozzola, *Uncle Sam Wants You*, 3–4.
161 "It is in no sense": Ibid., 27.
161 On May 14: Gilbert H. Crawford, Thomas H. Ellett, and John J. Hyland, eds., *The 302nd Engineers: A History* (n.p., n.d.), 15; Ralph Thomas to Emma Thomas, May 20, 1917, NTP; Ralph Thomas to Emma Thomas, May 26, 1917, NTP.
162 "the glory of self-sacrifice": Ralph Thomas to Emma Thomas, May 26, 1917, NTP.
162 "I do not believe": Ibid.

Chapter Fourteen: A Caged and Cautious Liberalism

163 "never done": Swanberg, *Norman Thomas*, 38.
164 an anticonscription rally: "Harlem Pacifists Moved by Police," *New York Times*, April 18, 1917.
164 "not only of fire-crackers": Norman Thomas to James Brady, June 30, 1917, NTP.

165   **"not because of unusual":** Thomas, "The Christian Patriot."

165   **the "industrial autocracy":** Norman Thomas to William Covert, April 6, 1917, NTP.

165   **he thought the "punch":** Henry Sloane Coffin to Norman Thomas, March 31, 1917, NTP.

165   **"There is a very considerable":** Norman Thomas to William Covert, April 6, 1917, NTP.

165   **a "worthy citizen":** Thomas, "The Christian Patriot."

166   **"I bless the day":** Norman Thomas, untitled and undated essay on religion, NTP, 17.

166   **"forgiveness of sin":** Ibid., 5.

167   **"mere anti-war society":** Norman Thomas to members of the Fellowship, April 6, 1917, NTP.

167   **a more haunting problem:** Norman reflected back on the loss of his faith, including his struggle during World War I, in his untitled reflections on religion, NTP.

167   **a special meeting:** "Minutes of Special Meeting, June 1, 1917," AUAM Records.

168   **"Jane Addams is losing":** Capozzola, *Uncle Sam Wants You*, 147–49.

168   **"the little group":** "Topics of the Times," *New York Times*, July 4, 1917 (quoted in Samuel Walker, *In Defense of American Liberties: A History of the ACLU*, 2nd ed. [Carbondale, IL: Southern Illinois University Press, 1999], 11).

168   **"We are not, by habit":** Kennedy, *Over Here*, 35–36.

169   **"I feel very sorry":** Norman Thomas to Oswald Garrison Villard, June 6, 1917, Oswald Garrison Villard Papers, Houghton Library, Harvard University.

170   **"splendid courage":** Norman Thomas to Lillian Wald, June 7, 1917, Lillian Wald Papers, Rare Book and Manuscript Library, Columbia University.

170   **Later that Friday:** Norman Thomas to Oswald Garrison Villard, June 16, 1917, Oswald Garrison Villard Papers. It would be impossible to overlook the references to the example of abolitionism in Evan's letters, but for helping me place it in the larger context of the era's pacifist movement, I am grateful to Joseph Kip Kosek, "Liberal Pacifists and the Memory of Abolitionism, 1914–1933," graduate colloquium, Vanderbilt University, Nashville, Tennessee, April 19–20, 2002.

171   **"We have no intention":** "Rough Draft of Possible Basis for Immediate Statement to the Press," AUAM Records.

172   **"so throw the organization":** Paul Kellogg to Lillian Wald, June 6, 1917, Lillian Wald Papers.

172   **The United Press had written:** Robert C. Cottrell, *Roger Nash Baldwin and the American Civil Liberties Union* (New York: Columbia University Press, 2000), 55.

173   **"guarantee of good faith":** Crystal Eastman to the Executive Committee, June 14, 1917, AUAM Records.

173   **"of course, chimed":** Woodrow Wilson to Lillian Wald, April 28, 1917, ACLU Records.

173   **"We don't want to make":** Cottrell, *Roger Nash Baldwin*, 54; Emily Zackin, "Popular Constitutionalism's Hard When You're Not Very Popular: Why the ACLU Turned to the Courts," *Law & Society Review* 42 (June 2009): 374.

173   **"Obedience to the law":** Walker, *In Defense of American Liberties*, 18. The NCLB reiterated this position six months later, when it produced another pamphlet aimed at potential conscientious objectors, urging each man to "[comply] with the law to the limit of his conscience." (Roger Baldwin to "Citizens registered with the Civil Liberties Bureau," November 1, 1917, ACLU Records.)

173   **"entirely at the service":** Cottrell, *Roger Nash Baldwin*, 54. For the same sentiment expressed privately to Norman, see Roger Baldwin to Norman Thomas, May 23, 1917, ACLU Records.

174   **"white-handed or sissy":** "Teddy Raps Pacifists in Speech," *Marion (OH) Tribune*, September 29, 1917.

174   **forces of "sinister intrigue":** Wilson, *President Wilson's State Papers and Addresses*, 417–18. Freeberg makes the point that Wilson's failure to distinguish between threats made his warnings more menacing. See Freeberg, *Democracy's Prisoner*, 36–37.

174   **"What I am opposed to":** Kennedy, *Over Here*, 72.

174   **"general tenor":** Capozzola, *Uncle Sam Wants You*, 154.

174   **"The worst thing":** Ibid., 154–55.

175   **"grow to a control":** Walker, *In Defense of American Liberties*, 12.

175   **"No publisher who is at heart":** "Laws Denying Use of United States Mails," "The Official Bulletin," undated, ACLU Records.

175   **Modeled along the lines:** Norman Thomas to Oswald Garrison Villard, July 6, 1917, Oswald Garrison Villard Papers.

175 **When Villard had met with Judge:** Oswald Garrison Villard, account of interview with Enoch Crowder, AUAM Records.
176 **When a squadron of German planes:** Kirby Page to friends, July 4, 1917, Kirby Page Papers, School of Theology, Claremont Archives.
176 **Evan and his friend Harold Gray:** Harold Studley Gray, *Character "Bad": The Story of a Conscientious Objector, as Told in the Letters of Harold Studley Gray* (New York: Garland, 1971), 93–94; Mrs. Henry Hobhouse, *"I Appeal unto Cæsar": The Case of the Conscientious Objector* (London: George Allen & Unwin, 1917), 28.
177 **"You can shut me up":** Gray, *Character "Bad,"* 95.
177 **"hot old arguments":** Kirby Page to Max Chaplin and Harold Gray, October 13, 1917, Kirby Page Papers.
177 **"Submarine!" "Torpedo astern!":** Kirby Page to friends, October 22, 1917, Kirby Page Papers.
178 **"what could pacifism":** Gray, *Character "Bad,"* 84–85.

Chapter Fifteen: A Democratic Right

180 **dreamed of a proper shower:** Ralph Thomas to Emma Thomas, September 9, 1917, NTP. The information about drafted men is from "Enlisted Personnel of 302nd Engineers by Civilian Occupation," World War I Organizational Records: 77th Division: Historical: 302nd Engineer Regiment and Train, Record Group 120, National Archives.
180 **"blasting character":** Princeton-Yenching Foundation, *The Princeton Work in Peking* (New York: Princeton-Yenching Foundation, 1906, 2 and 15, also available online at, http://www .archive.org/details/princetonworkinp03prin (accessed October 22, 2009).
181 **"gospel sharks":** Kemeny, "University Cultural Wars: Rival Protestant Pieties in Early Twentieth-Century Princeton," 163.
181 **"The Relation of the Study of Sociology":** William Joseph Haas, *China Voyager: Gist Gee's Life in Science* (London: M. E. Sharpe, 1996), 229–30.
181 **"very anxious indeed":** John McDowell et al. to Arthur Thomas, March 9, 1917, Christine Dunbar collection.
181 **"so disappointed":** Wilson, *Papers of Woodrow*, 27:263.
181 **"some sportsmanship in it":** Norman Thomas to Emma Thomas, October 9, 1917, NTP.
182 **"the *minds* of men":** Kennedy, *Over Here*, 59–66 (quotes are on 61–62).
182 **"one white-hot mass":** John M. Barry, *The Great Influenza: The Epic Story of the Deadliest Plague in History* (New York: Viking, 2004), 144.
182 **donating the land:** George E. Davis, "Address on the Fiftieth (1917) Anniversary of the Founding of Biddle University," Stephen Mattoon Papers.
183 **"an aggressive policy":** Crystal Eastman to the Executive Committee, June 14, 1917, AUAM Records.
183 **"no forcible annexations":** Thomas Wirth, "The Economics of Peace: World War I and Scott Nearing's Radical America," *Concept*, http://www.publications.villanova.edu/Concept/2004 /Scott%20Nearing.htm (accessed May 19, 2010).
183 **"honest and open discussion":** Norman Thomas to Lillian Wald, August 27, 1917, NTP.
183 **"for the good":** Meeting Minutes, September 13, 1917, AUAM Records.
184 **"is reasonable and has judgment":** Cottrell, *Roger Nash Baldwin*, 55.
184 **"empty legal right":** Ibid., 61.
184 **"great respect":** Joseph Kip Kosek, *Acts of Conscience: Christian Nonviolence and Modern American Democracy* (New York: Columbia University Press, 2009), 32.
185 **"You may justly be called":** A. T. Carton to Norman Thomas, August 29, 1917, NTP.
185 **"Just think—five little pacifists":** Norman Thomas to Violet Thomas, May 20, 1918, Nancy Gerber collection.
185 **"wild rumors":** Tom Carter to Norman Thomas, July 6, 1917, NTP.
185 **"I would rather go":** Ralph Harlow to Norman Thomas, September 6, 1917, NTP.
185 **"ethical optimism":** Norman Thomas to Ralph Harlow, September 7, 1917, NTP.
186 **"Do you think Americans":** Ibid..
186 **"intolerable":** Norman Thomas to Emma Thomas, October 9, 1917, NTP.
186 **"What had been wrongheadedness":** Kennedy, *Over Here*, 73–74.
186 **"done its duty":** Ibid.

187 **"negroes and Mexicans":** Kosek, *Acts of Conscience*, 35; Norman Thomas, *The Case of the Christian Pacifists* (New York: National Civil Liberties Bureau, 1918), 3–15.
187 **"what's coming to him":** "Herbert S. Bigelow," *Ohio History Central: An Online Encyclopedia of Ohio History*, http://www.ohiohistorycentral.org/entry.php?rec=34 (accessed June 11, 2010).
187 **Radicalism of any kind:** Traxel, *Crusader Nation*, 303–305; Kennedy, *Over Here*, 73.
188 **The California State Board of Education:** Traxel, *Crusader Nation*, 316.
188 **jettisoning "Saxe-Coburg-Gotha":** Carter, George, Nichos, and Wilhelm, xxiii.
188 **"childish," he allowed:** Traxel, *Crusader Nation*, 316.

Chapter Sixteen: Courage of Convictions

190 **"prophetic spirit":** Richard W. Fox, "The Paradox of 'Progressive' Socialism: The Case of Morris Hillquit, 1901–1914," *American Quarterly* 26 (May 1974): 127–29, 133, 138 (quote is on 127). I am especially indebted to Fox's discussion of Hillquit's conception of socialism and of the Socialist's position within the party and without.
190 **"sense of duty of man":** Ibid., 132.
190 **called him a "Hillquitter":** Kennedy, *Over Here*, 70.
190 **"high treason":** "Calls on President to Punish Hillquit," *New York Times*, October 30, 1917.
190 **"I'd hang everyone":** "The Alumni," *Princeton Alumni Weekly*, November 7, 1917.
191 **"exalts competition instead":** Norman Thomas to Morris Hillquit, October 2, 1917, NTP.
191 **He had actually proposed:** See Fox, "Paradox of 'Progressive' Socialism," 132n9.
191 **"to prove that Socialism":** Swanberg, *Norman Thomas*, 80.
191 **"treasonable," she reminded:** Norman Thomas to Emma Thomas, November 2, 1917, NTP.
191 **"If you lived here":** Ibid.
192 **"Peace! Peace!":** "Hillquit Urges Peace to the End," *New York Times*, November 5, 1917.
192 **"last straw to break":** Norman Thomas to Oswald Garrison Villard, October 22, 1917, NTP.
192 **"but to be also a Socialist!":** Swanberg, *Norman Thomas*, 59.
193 **"embarrass":** Norman Thomas to Lavinia Tallman, July 12, 1918, NTP; Lavinia Tallman to Norman Thomas, July 15, 1918, NTP.
193 **"It would be idle":** Norman Thomas to the Board of Directors, February 9, 1918, Princeton University Student Christian Association Records, University Archives, Department of Rare Books and Special Collections, Princeton University Library.
194 **"a few proclamations":** Norman Stone, *World War One: A Short History* (London: Allen Lane, 2007), 129.
194 **befuddled Austrian aristocrats:** Ibid., 129–30.
195 **"be made safe":** Wilson, *Woodrow Wilson*, 259–64.
195 **"Frankly my own feeling":** Norman Thomas to Lillian Wald, March 1, 1918, NTP.
196 **One week he was raising:** Norman Thomas to "Billy," March 26, 1918, NTP; NCLB to Woodrow Wilson, April 2, 1918, ACLU Records.
196 **"challenges the existence":** Capozzola, *Uncle Sam Wants You*, 28–30.
197 **"be treated with kindly consideration":** Thomas, *Conscientious Objector in America*, 90; "Regulations Affecting Conscientious Objectors, by Order of the President, March 20, 1918," ACLU Records.
197 **"policy of drift":** Thomas, *Conscientious Objector in America*, 95.
197 **"We who are struggling":** NCLB to Woodrow Wilson, April 2, 1918, ACLU Records.
198 **"There is a general feeling":** Ralph Thomas to Norman Thomas, March 28, 1918, NTP.
198 **The 302nd Engineers boasted:** Crawford, *302nd Engineers: A History*, 20–25.
198 **"exceptional work":** C. O. Sherrill to Chief of Engineers, Washington, D.C., January 9, 1918, Records of U.S. Regular Army Mobile Units.
198 **"I am sorry we don't agree":** Ralph Thomas to Norman Thomas, March 28, 1918, NTP.
199 **"The interest of the officers":** Evan Thomas to Emma Thomas, May 5, 1918, Nancy Gerber collection.
199 **"constitutional slackers":** Evan Thomas to Emma Thomas, May 21, 1918, Nancy Gerber collection.
199 **"socialists of a not very intelligent":** Evan Thomas to Emma Thomas, May 31, 1918, Nancy Gerber collection.

199   "Was talking with Major Weeks": Evan Thomas to Violet Thomas, June 3, 1918, Nancy Gerber collection.
200   "many of this class": Walter Guest Kellogg, *The Conscientious Objector* (New York: Da Capo Press, 1970), 94.
200   "I should like to see": Norman Thomas to Emma Thomas, May 14, 1918, NTP.
200   "open scorn": Arthur Thomas to Emma Thomas, June 19, 1918, Christine Dunbar collection.
201   "very much pleased": Emma Thomas to Norman Thomas, undated letter fragment, NTP.

Chapter Seventeen: Into the Fracas

202   Violet was a "brick": Norman Thomas to Emma Thomas, May 25, 1919, Patricia Libbey collection.
203   "the principle of free self-determination": Cooper, *Woodrow Wilson*, 431–32.
204   "no desire to march": Ibid.
204   "utter, print, write": G. Stone, "Mr. Wilson's First Amendment," 186.
204   In a private letter: Cooper, *Woodrow Wilson*, 432.
204   Roger Baldwin was more optimistic: Cottrell, *Roger Nash Baldwin*, 66–72. My account of Baldwin's deteriorating relationship with Keppel depends on Cottrell's work. See also Roger Baldwin to F. P. Keppel, August 3, 1918, ACLU Records; Roger Baldwin to F. P. Keppel, June 22, 1918, ACLU Records.
205   "embarrassing situation": Cottrell, *Roger Nash Baldwin*, 67.
205   "I am of the opinion": Ibid., 70.
205   "ought to appeal": Ibid., 72.
205   "We are not doing business": Laurence Todd to Roger Baldwin, August 2, 1916, ACLU Records.
206   "I would many times rather": Evan Thomas to Norman Thomas, June 20, 1918, ACLU Records.
206   "I can't help but feeling": Evan Thomas to Norman Thomas, June 29, 1918, John Nevin Sayre Papers.
206   *How often do you pray?*: "Examination of Conscientious Objectors," NTP.
206   "Prussian idea of the State": Evan Thomas to Emma Thomas, July 21, 1918, Evan Thomas III collection.
206   "philosophical anarchy": Evan Thomas to Norman Thomas, July 19, 1918, ACLU Records.
207   "I want to establish": Ibid.
207   "If so I certainly bear": Evan Thomas to Emma Thomas, July 21, 1918, Evan Thomas III collection.
207   "I left Upton happy": Evan Thomas to Emma Thomas, July 23, 1918, Evan Thomas III collection.
207   "I am not sure": Ibid.
207   Around twenty-four million men: Capozzola, *Uncle Sam Wants You*, 56.
207   An estimated three million: Chambers, *To Raise an Army*, 211–13.
208   "The great mass of our citizens": Ibid., 59.
208   Evan called a meeting: Arthur Dunham, "The Narrative of a Conscientious Objector," Arthur Dunham Papers, Bentley Historical Library, University of Michigan, 41; Evan Thomas to Norman Thomas, July 28, 1918, NTP.
209   "The absolutists were no one's": Capozzola, *Uncle Sam Wants You*, 78.
209   "It is not always easy": Norman Thomas, "Justice to the War's Heretics," *Nation*, November 9, 1918.
209   108 degrees in the shade: Evan Thomas to Norman Thomas, August 3, 1918, NTP.
209   a "red-hot argument": Dunham, "Narrative of a Conscientious Objector," 37–38.
209   "I'll help keep": Ibid., 43–46.
209   a man named Howard Moore: Howard W. Moore, *Plowing My Own Furrow* (New York: W. W. Norton, 1985), 53–54 and 61–62.
210   "Carry on": Crawford, *302nd Engineers*, 29.
210   "With our backs to the wall": Gilbert, *First World War*, 414.
210   "Look! Look!": Ibid.
210   "It is best": Ralph Thomas to Emma Thomas, May 12, 1918, NTP.

210 "Inferno continues": Gilbert, *First World War*, 414.
211 "I think half our time": Ralph Thomas to Emma Thomas, May 23, 1918, NTP.
211 "I remember as a boy": Ralph Thomas to Emma Thomas, May 12, 1918, NTP.
211 the "great show": Ralph Thomas to Emma Thomas, May 23, 1918, NTP.
211 "on the go day and night": Ibid.
211 "Oh the army, the army": Laskin, *The Long Way Home*, 134 and 222–23.
212 "like the circus": Ralph Thomas to Emma Thomas, June 12, 1918, NTP.
212 "I think all of us": Ralph Thomas to Emma Thomas, July 21, 1918, NTP.
212 "an experience of a lifetime": Princeton University, "War Record of the Class of 1909," 180.
212 "I am not an American": Dunham, "Narrative of a Conscientious Objector," 50.
213 situation was "ridiculous": Evan Thomas to Norman Thomas, July 28, 1918, NTP.
213 "the principle of conscription": Dunham, "Narrative of a Conscientious Objector Camp," 61; Gray, *Character "Bad,"* 137–38; Thomas, *The Radical "No,"* 171–72.
213 "Quit bargaining": Evan Thomas to Norman Thomas, August 4, 1918, NTP.
214 However clumsily, he grasped: Kosek makes this point about the hunger strike and the early nonviolence movement well. See Kosek, *Acts of Conscience*, 39–40.
214 "The policy of the War Department": Quoted in Dunham, "Narrative of a Conscientious Objector Camp," 59.
214 "You know how much": Norman Thomas to Evan Thomas, August 24, 1918, NTP.
214 "utter folly": Julian Mack to Norman Thomas, August 27, 1918, NTP.
214 "I am fully aware": Norman Thomas to John Nevin Sayre, August 27, 1918, John Nevin Sayre Papers.
215 "We are leaving": Norman Thomas to Violet Thomas, August 30, 1918, Nancy Gerber collection.
215 "I still by no means": Norman Thomas to Roger Baldwin, August 30, 1918 [misdated August 31], NTP.
216 "to make some scratches": Ibid.
216 "He's the same dear": Emma Thomas to Emma and Agnes Thomas, undated September 1918, Nancy Gerber collection.
216 "I just nodded": Norman Thomas to Roger Baldwin, August 30, 1918 [misdated August 31, 1918], NTP.
217 "only a short talk": Gray, *Character "Bad,"* 148.
217 "FEDERAL AGENTS HAVE TAKEN": Roger Baldwin to Norman Thomas, telegram, August 31, 1918, NTP.

Chapter Eighteen: Treason's Twilight Zone

218 "against Baldwin and the Conscientious": Cottrell, *Roger Nash Baldwin*, 77–78.
219 "Treason's Twilight Zone": Chatfield, *For Peace and Justice*, 4.
219 "lock him up": Cottrell, *Roger Nash Baldwin*, 78 and 80.
219 "written by some ass": Swanberg, *Norman Thomas*, 62.
219 "particularly the editor": Ibid.
219 "If I had my way": Ibid.
219 "I can't see what": Cottrell, *Roger Nash Baldwin*, 82–83.
220 "nothing that everybody needs": "Interview with the President in the White House," John Nevin Sayre Papers.
220 "I know the principal": Wilson, *Papers of Woodrow Wilson*, 51:12.
221 led a "slacker raid": Capozzola, *Uncle Sam Wants You*, 46–48.
221 "If war is right": Freeberg, *Democracy's Prisoner*, 74–79; Salvatore, *Eugene V. Debs*, 291–96.
222 the Socialist produced: Freeberg, *Democracy's Prisoner*, 101.
222 "their hopes blasted": Salvatore, *Eugene V. Debs*, 295–96.
222 "all broken up": Gray, *Character "Bad,"* 148–49.
222 "You better collect": Emma Thomas to Norman Thomas, September 1, 1918, NTP.
223 "wiggled [their] jaws": Gray, *Character "Bad,"* 150.
223 "Never let the event": Arthur Dunham to Esther Dunham, September 2, 1918, Arthur Dunham Papers; Dunham, "The Narrative of a Conscientious Objector," 63.
223 "getting all the blame": Emma Thomas to Norman Thomas, September 2, 1918, NTP.

223 "Always nowadays": Emma Thomas to Agnes and Emma Thomas, September 2, 1918, Nancy Gerber collection.

224 "That's fine": Emma Thomas to Norman Thomas, September 3, 1918, NTP.

224 "I've been having": Ibid.

224 convinced him that continuing: Evan Thomas to Norman and Violet Thomas, September 5, 1918, NTP.

224 "he told me": Emma Thomas to Norman Thomas, September 3, 1918, NTP.

225 "tickled me greatly": Evan Thomas to Norman and Violet Thomas, September 5, 1918, NTP.

225 "I promised [the major]": Emma Thomas to Norman Thomas, September 3, 1918, NTP.

226 "Your son tried a method": Emma Thomas to Norman Thomas, September 4, 1918, NTP.

227 called Evan "Christlike": John Nevin Sayre to Woodrow Wilson, October 15, 1918, John Nevin Sayre Papers.

227 more "horse sense": Evan Thomas to Emma Thomas, September 28, 1918, NTP.

227 "My place is in prison": Evan Thomas to Emma Thomas, October 13, 1918, John Nevin Sayre Papers.

227 "I admit the 1st week": Evan Thomas to Emma Thomas, September 28, 1918, NTP.

227 a court-martial at Camp Funstion: "Proceeding of a General Court-Martial" for Evan W. Thomas, Records of the Judge Advocate General (Army), Record Group 153, National Archives.

229 "I take my hat off": Evan Thomas to Emma Thomas, October 13, 1918, John Nevin Sayre Papers.

229 a group of rowdy agents: "Reminiscences" (draft manuscript, Roger Baldwin Papers, Seely G. Mudd Manuscript Library, Princeton University), 68–72; Cottrell *Roger Nash Baldwin*, 83–85.

230 a Bureau of Investigation agent: Fleischman, *Norman Thomas*, 70–71.

230 "These are the days": Norman Thomas to Alexander Trachtenberg, October 18, 1918, NTP.

230 reviewed the transcript: "Proceeding of a General Court-Martial" for Evan W. Thomas, Records of the Judge Advocate General (Army), Record Group 153, National Archives; Norman Thomas to Ralph Thomas, January 10, 1919, NTP.

231 "I think you hold": Norman Thomas to Evan Thomas, September 11, 1918, NTP.

232 "If we are to love": Ibid.

233 "Perhaps to certain members": Norman Thomas to Alexander Trachtenberg, October 18, 1918, NTP.

233 "I have a profound fear": Norman Thomas to Anne G. Brush, September 24, 1918, NTP.

Chapter Nineteen: Mean What You Say

235 showed it to only Norman: Cottrell, *Roger Nash Baldwin*, 86.

236 "a flat contradiction": Walker, *In Defense of American Liberties*, 40; Cottrell, *Roger Nash Baldwin*, 87; "Roger N. Baldwin to Spend Year in Jail," *New York Post*, October 30, 1918.

236 "so-called 'civil liberties' ": Cottrell, *Roger Nash Baldwin*, 90.

236 "one of the rare experiences": Ibid., 86–90; (quote is on 90).

236 "proud flesh": Ralph Thomas to Emma Thomas, September 6, 1918, NTP.

237 Two privates from his regiment: Crawford, *302nd Engineers*, 62–63 and 76–84.

237 "We got [to the Vesle]": Ralph Thomas to Emma Thomas, September 5, 1918, NTP.

237 "I am very anxious": C. O. Sherrill to Commanding General, telegram, August 24, 1918, Records of U.S. Regular Army Mobile Units: World War I Organization Records 302nd Engineers, Record Group 391, National Archives.

238 "The ONLY thing": Ralph Thomas to Emma Thomas, November 6, 1918, NTP.

238 "hit me harder": Ibid.

238 That morning, the members: Crawford, *302nd Engineers*, 114–15.

239 "ARMISTICE SIGNED": Ann Hagedorn, *Savage Peace: Hope and Fear in America, 1919* (New York: Simon & Schuster, 2007), 7.

239 Violet was ill: Swanberg, *Norman Thomas*, 70.

239 Epidemiologists now estimate: Barry, *The Great Influenza*, 4–5, 187–88, 223, 238, 242–43. Barry gives a masterful account of the outbreak of the influenza, as well as its social and cultural context, and my description relies on his.

240 "the transports became floating": Ibid., 306–8.

240 **Norman could hardly constrain:** One sign of his optimism came, in all places, in his resigning from Princeton's Colonial Club three days after the armistice. He was doing so, he wrote, because he believed that the club system was detrimental to the school and to "that new era of democracy which it is my profound hope will dawn upon the earth." (Norman Thomas to the Board of Managers, November 14, 1918, NTP.)

241 **guards at Funston:** Norman Thomas summarizes the conditions at Camp Funston and the War Department's response in *The Conscientious Objector in America*, 155–62.

241 **"By George! I thought":** Dunham, "The Narrative of a Conscientious Objector," 52.

242 **"America surely is big enough":** Evan Thomas to Emma Thomas, November 21, 1918, Evan Thomas III collection.

242 **the NCLB had studied:** "Found 'Objectors' Chained, *New York Times*, September 14, 1918; "League Objects to Solitary Cells for Army 'Objectors,'" *New York Tribune*, September 14, 1918.

242 **"There is something about":** Norman Thomas to Ralph Thomas, January 10, 1919, NTP.

242 **"absolutely hopeless":** Emma Thomas to Norman Thomas, undated 1918, NTP.

242 **"I don't believe that":** "Extracts from Letter from Mrs. W. E. Thomas," November 26, 1918, Nancy Gerber collection.

242 **"You may rest assured":** Unidentified author to Emma Thomas, November 22, 1918, Nancy Gerber collection. From John Nevin Sayre's notes on his meeting with the president, it seems clear that the signatory is Colonel Sedgwick Rice ("Interview with President Wilson," [December 2, 1918], John Nevin Sayre Papers.

243 **He stood with his hands fastened:** Emma Thomas to "dear ones all," undated 1918, Evan Thomas III collection.

243 **"final statement":** "Bulletin," November 1918, Fellowship of Reconciliation Papers.

243 **"I have just completed":** Evan Thomas to Emma Thomas, November 21, 1918, Nancy Gerber collection.

244 **Norman called John Nevin Sayre:** "Interview with President Woodrow Wilson" [December 2, 1918], John Nevin Sayre Papers.

245 **"No such treatment":** Ibid.; "Interview with President Wilson," John Nevin Sayre Papers.

245 **"Nothing barbarous or mediaeval":** Wilson, *Papers of Woodrow Wilson*, 53: 307.

245 **"not merely to political prisoners":** Thomas, *Conscientious Objector in America*, 196.

245 **The *George Washington*:** Margaret MacMillan, *Paris 1919: Six Months That Changed the World* (New York: Random House Trade Paperbacks, 2003), 3–6; Cooper, *Woodrow Wilson*, 455–57.

246 **"Champion of the Rights":** Hagedorn, *Savage Peace*, 23.

246 **"Mother bears up better":** Norman Thomas to Ralph Thomas, January 10, 1919, NTP.

246 **a delegation of families:** "Pleads with Baker to Free Objectors," *New York Times*, December 25, 1918.

247 **he wrote to a Princeton friend:** John Buchanan interview with Evan Thomas III, undated 1977, Evan Thomas III collection.

247 **the acting JAG had reviewed:** "United States v. Private Evan W. Thomas, Medical Corps," Records of the Judge Advocate General (Army), Record Group 153, National Archives.

247 **Next to "character":** "Enlistment Record" for Evan Thomas, January 14, 1919, NTP.

247 **letters to the families:** See, for instance, Evan Thomas to Philip Gray, January 24, 1919, Harold S. Gray Papers, Bentley Historical Library, University of Michigan.

248 **"actual conditions":** Albert DeSilver to "Friend," January 23, 1919, ACLU Records.

248 **"like a prosperous young broker":** "No Prison Horrors for Edification of Pacifist Meeting," *New York Herald*, January 27, 1919.

248 **"The best way to make"** "Free 'Objectors,' Is Thomas's Plea," *New York World*, January 27, 1919.

Chapter Twenty: The Sandiest of Foundations

249 **Archibald Stevenson addressed:** Hagedorn, *Savage Peace*, 53–55.

250 **"Have you discovered":** Ibid., 57–58.

250 **a "Who's Who":** Ibid., 55–57; "62 Are Named in 'Who's Who' of Pacifism," *New York Tribune*, January 25, 1919.

250 **"Wilson's sweet neutrality band":** Hagedorn, *Savage Peace*, 57–58.

250 Secretary Baker was mortified: Wilson, *Papers of Woodrow Wilson*, 54: 398.
250 Military Intelligence had employed: Hagedorn, *Savage Peace*, 54.
251 "One is building on": Kennedy, *Over Here*, 247.
251 "naked imperialism": "Peace and Honor Yet to Be Won," *World Tomorrow* 2 (June 1919), 146.
251 "straight-jacket": Stephen Wertheim, "The League That Wasn't: American Designs for a Legalist-Sanctionist League of Nations and the Intellectual Origins of International Organization, 1914–1920," *Diplomatic History* (forthcoming article, 2011), 48 and 50.
251 "the moral force of the public": Wilson, *Papers of Woodrow Wilson*, 55: 175.
251 "Now a moral obligation": Cooper, *Woodrow Wilson*, 516.
252 "the truth of justice and of liberty": Ibid., 529.
252 The government released: "Conscientious Objectors," *New York Times*, February 16, 1919; Moore, *Plowing My Own Furrow*, 129; Thomas, *Conscientious Objector in America*, 248–49.
252 predicting a "reign of terror": Hagedorn, *Savage Peace*, 180.
253 "duplicate the anarchy of Russia": Kennedy, *Over Here*, 288.
253 "Blood flowed freely": Freeberg, *Democracy's Prisoner*, 156–57.
253 From September 1918: Hagedorn, *Savage Peace*, 276–77.
254 Military Intelligence created: Ibid., 31.
254 "We must put to death": Shannon, *Socialist Party of America*, 122.
254 did not reach the "intelligentsia": "New Laws Needed to Enable U.S. to Deal with Reds," *Philadelphia Press*, May 3, 1919.
254 began an index card system: Hagedorn, *Savage Peace*, 329.
254 Archibald Stevenson volunteered: Ibid., 152.
255 Stenographers took notes: "Verbatim Report of Mass Meeting Called by Committee of Justice to the Negro" at the Harlem Casino, New York City, November 13, 1919, NTP.
255 "shameful apathy": Norman Thomas, "Justice to War's Heretics," *Nation*, November 9, 1918.
257 The Left Wing of the Socialist Party: Shannon, *Socialist Party of America*, 130–31.
257 "pathological cases": Gloria Garrett Samson, *American Fund for Public Service: Charles Garland and Radical Philanthropy, 1922–1941* (Santa Barbara, CA: Greenwood Publishing Group, 1996), 38–39.

Chapter Twenty-One: To Carry Your Watch

259 "supreme loyalty:" Norman Thomas to Evan Thomas, September 11, 1918, NTP.
259 "ignorance and indifference": Evan Thomas to "Friends," June 15, 1921, John Nevin Sayre Papers.
259 "faith is pretty much": Evan Thomas to John Nevin Sayre, June 16, 1921, John Nevin Sayre Papers.
260 "pretty dream": Swanberg, *Norman Thomas*, 107.
260 "a fairy princess": Evan Thomas to Violet Thomas, January 1935, Nancy Gerber collection.
260 "Heresy is nothing but": Evan Thomas III, "A Case Study of Conscientious Objection in the First World War" (unpublished essay written at the University of Virginia, April 1977), 26.
261 "much interested in any efforts": Ralph Thomas to Albert De Silver, February 2, 1920, ACLU Records.
261 "I am strongly in favor": Ralph Thomas to John Buchanan, March 21, 1920, John Buchanan collection.
261 "As officers in the Army": Richard C. Tolman et al., to Franklin D'Olier, January 27, 1920, ACLU Records.
263 "My respect continues": "Arthur Raymond Thomas," Class of 1915 Fifty-Year Record, Princeton University Undergraduate Alumni Files, 1748–1920. The details about Arthur's life and character come from his daughter, Christine Dunbar, and son, Arthur Jr.
263 "larger than life": Christine Dunbar, e-mail message to author, March 11, 2009.
263 "I was extraordinarily fortunate": Swanberg, *Norman Thomas*, 485.
264 "The leveled gun": Norman Thomas Jr. to Violet Thomas, June 14, 1920, Nancy Gerber collection; Norman Thomas Jr. to Norman Thomas, July 11, 1920, Nancy Gerber collection.
265 "I must confess": Norman Thomas, "The Distinctive Place of the *World Tomorrow*," undated report, Fellowship of Reconciliation Papers, SCPC Swarthmore College Peace Collection, Swarthmore, Pennsylvania.

265 "embarrassed us": Swanberg, *Norman Thomas*, 70.
266 "Norman, I'm a damned sight": Ibid., 184.
267 "listened at the Washington Monument": Martin Luther King Jr., "The Bravest Man I Ever Met," *Pageant* (June 1965): 24.
268 "I suppose the difference": Ibid., 379–80.
269 "Had they asked you": William Sloane Coffin Jr., February 10, 1967, Nancy Gerber collection.
270 "One of the facts": Norman Thomas, untitled reflections on religion, NTP.
270 a group of right-wing Germans: Fritz Stern, *The Politics of Cultural Despair: A Study in the Rise of the Germanic Ideology* (Berkeley: University of California Press, 1974), 228.
270 "To thine own self": William Shakespeare, *Hamlet* (New York: Signet Classic, 1998), 22.
270 "Belonging is, of course": Norman Thomas, *Great Dissenters* (New York: W. W. Norton, 1961), 13.
271 "Even after he died": Dorrien, *Democratic Socialist Vision*, 75.
271 "What Thomas conveyed": Murray Kempton, *Part of Our Time: Some Ruins and Monuments of the Thirties* (New York: New York Review of Books, 2004), 324.
271 "The only thing that he requires": Fleischman, *Norman Thomas*, 305.
272 "In a cruel and ugly world": Norman Thomas to Evan Thomas II, November 6, 1941, Evan Thomas III collection.

BIBLIOGRAPHY

Archives

American Civil Liberties Union Records, Public Policy Papers, Department of Rare Books and Special Collections, Princeton University Library, Princeton, New Jersey.

American Union Against Militarism Records, Swarthmore College Peace Collection, Swarthmore, Pennsylvania.

Arthur Dunham Papers, Bentley Historical Library, University of Michigan, Ann Arbor.

A. Sidney Lovett Papers, Manuscripts and Archives, Yale University Library, New Haven, Connecticut.

Fellowship of Reconciliation Papers, Swarthmore College Peace Collection, Swarthmore, Pennsylvania.

Harold S. Gray Papers, Bentley Historical Library, University of Michigan, Ann Arbor.

Harry Fleischman Papers, Tamiment Library/Robert F. Wagner Labor Archives, Elmer Holmes Bobst Library, New York University Libraries, New York.

John Nevin Sayre Papers, Swarthmore College Peace Collection, Swarthmore, Pennsylvania.

Kirby Page Papers, School of Theology, Claremont Archives, Claremont, California.

Lillian Wald Papers, Rare Book and Manuscript Library, Columbia University Library, New York.

Margaret and Kenneth Landon Papers, Wheaton College Archives and Special Collections, Buswell Memorial Library, Wheaton, Illinois.

Mattoon Family Collection, Presbyterian Historical Society, Philadelphia, Pennsylvania.

Morris Hillquit Papers, Tamiment Library/Robert F. Wagner Labor Archives, Elmer Holmes Bobst Library, New York University Libraries, New York.

Norman Thomas Papers, Manuscripts and Archives Division, The New York Public Library, Astor, Lenox and Tilden Foundations, New York.

Oral History Collection of Columbia University, New York.

Oswald Garrison Villard Papers, Houghton Library, Harvard University, Cambridge, Massachusetts.

Princeton University Crusader Fellowship Records, Department of Rare Books and Special Collections, Princeton University, Princeton, New Jersey.

Princeton University Undergraduate Alumni Files, 1748–1920, Department of Rare Books and Special Collections, Princeton University, Princeton, New Jersey.

Records of U.S. Regular Army Mobile Units: World War I Organization Records 302nd Engineers, Record Group 391, National Archives, College Park, Maryland.

Records of the Judge Advocate General (Army), Record Group 153, National Archives, College Park, Maryland.

Roger Baldwin Papers, Department of Rare Books and Special Collections, Princeton University, Princeton, New Jersey.

Stephen Mattoon Papers, Johnson C. Smith University Archives, Inez Moore Parker Archives & Research Center, James B. Duke Memorial Library, Charlotte, North Carolina.

Student Files, Elmira College Archives, Gannett-Tripp Library, Elmira, New York.
UTS Collection, Burke Library Archives, Union Theological Seminary, New York.
World War I Organizational Records: 77th Division: Historical: 302nd Engineer Regiment and
    Train, Record Group 120, National Archives, College Park, Maryland.

Private Collections
John Buchanan collection, Washington, D.C.
Christine Dunbar collection, Allentown, Pennsylvania.
Evan Thomas III, Mary Thomas Miller, and Frances Thomas Gates collection, Washington, D.C.
Nancy Gerber, Mary Thomas Miller, and Frances Thomas Gates collection, New York, New York.
Patricia Libbey, Mary Thomas Miller, and Frances Thomas Gates collection, Afton, Minnesota.

Books, Articles, and Dissertations
Adler, Julius Ochs. *History of the 77th Division, August 25th, 1917–November 11th, 1918*. New
    York: W. H. Crawford, 1919.
Amar, Akhil Reed. *The Bill of Rights: Creation and Reconstruction*. New Haven: Yale University
    Press, 1998.
Andrew, Edward. *Conscience and Its Critics: Protestant Conscience, Enlightenment Reason, and
    Modern Subjectivity*. Toronto: University of Toronto Press, 2001.
Angell, Norman. *The Great Illusion: A Study of the Relation of Military Power in Nations to Their
    Economic and Social Advantage*. New York: Putnam, 1910.
Backus, Mary, ed. *Siam and Laos, as Seen by Our American Missionaries*. Philadelphia: Presbyterian
    Board of Publication, 1884.
Barry, John M. *The Great Influenza: The Epic Story of the Deadliest Plague in History*. New York:
    Viking, 2004.
Bederman, Gail. *Manliness & Civilization: A Cultural History of Gender and Race in the United
    States, 1880–1917*. Chicago: University of Chicago Press, 1996.
Beinart, Peter. *The Icarus Syndrome: A History of American Hubris*. New York: Harper, 2010.
Bell, Daniel. *The End of Ideology: On the Exhaustion of Political Ideas in the Fifties*. Cambridge,
    MA: Harvard University Press, 2000.
Blackman, Emily C. *History of Susquehanna County, Pennsylvania*. Philadelphia: Claxton, Remsen,
    & Haffelfinger, 1873.
Blücher von Wahlstatt, Evelyn Mary Stapleton-Bretherton. *An English Wife in Berlin*. New York:
    E. P. Dutton & Co., 1920.
Brailsford, Henry Noel. *The War of Steel and Gold: A Study of the Armed Peace*. 8th ed. London:
    G. Bell and Sons, 1917.
Brittain, Vera. *Testament of Youth: An Autobiographical Study of the Years 1900–1925*. New York:
    Penguin Books, 2004.
Brock, Peter, ed. *"These Strange Criminals": An Anthology of Prison Memoirs by Conscientious
    Objectors from the Great War to the Cold War*. Toronto: University of Toronto Press, 2004.
Brooke, Rupert. *The Collected Poems of Rupert Brooke*. New York: Dodd, Mead & Company, 1915.
Brown, William Adams. *A Teacher and His Times: A Story of Two Worlds*. New York: C. Scribner's
    Sons, 1940.
Bruns, Roger. *Preacher: Billy Sunday and Big-Time American Evangelism*. New York: W. W. Norton, 1992.
Capozzola, Christopher. *Uncle Sam Wants You: World War I and the Making of the Modern American Citizen*. New York: Oxford University Press, 2008.
Carter, Miranda. *George, Nicholas and Wilhelm: Three Royal Cousins and the Road to World War I*.
    New York: Knopf, 2010.
Chace, James. *1912: Wilson, Roosevelt, Taft & Debs: The Election That Changed the Country*. New
    York: Simon & Schuster, 2004.
Chambers, John Whiteclay. *To Raise an Army: The Draft Comes to Modern America* (New York:
    Free Press, 1987).
Chatfield, Charles. *For Peace and Justice: Pacifism in America, 1914–1941*. Knoxville: University of
    Tennessee Press, 1971.

———. "Pacifists and Their Publics: The Politics of a Peace Movement." *Midwest Journal of Political Science* 13 (May 1969): 298–312.

———. "Peace as a Reform Movement." *Magazine of History* 8 (Spring 1994): 10–14.

———. "World War I and the Liberal Pacifist in the United States." *American Historical Review* 75 (December 1970): 1920–37.

Clements, Kendrick A. "Woodrow Wilson and World War I." *Presidential Studies Quarterly* 34 (March 2004): 62–82.

Cook, Blanche Wiesen. "Woodrow Wilson and the Antimilitarists, 1914–1917." PhD diss., Johns Hopkins University, 1970.

Cooper, John Milton Jr., ed. *Reconsidering Woodrow Wilson: Progressivism, Internationalism, War, and Peace.* Washington, D.C.: Woodrow Wilson Center Press, 2008.

———. *The Warrior and the Priest: Woodrow Wilson and Theodore Roosevelt.* Cambridge, MA: Belknap Press of Harvard University Press, 1983.

———. *Woodrow Wilson: A Biography.* New York: Knopf, 2009.

Cortright, David. *Peace: A History of Movements and Ideas.* New York: Cambridge University Press, 2009.

Cottrell, Robert C. *Roger Nash Baldwin and the American Civil Liberties Union.* New York: Columbia University Press, 2000.

Crawford, Gilbert H., Thomas H. Ellett, and John J. Hyland, eds. *The 302nd Engineers: A History.* N.p, n.d.

Croly, Herbert David. *The Promise of American Life.* Charleston, SC: BiblioBazaar, 2006.

Dorrien, Gary. *The Democratic Socialist Vision.* Lanham, MD: Rowman & Littlefield, 1986.

———. *The Making of American Liberal Theology: Idealism, Realism, and Modernity, 1900–1950.* Louisville, KY: Westminster John Knox Press, 2003.

———. *The Making of American Liberal Theology: Imagining Progressive Religion, 1805–1900.* Louisville, KY: Westminster John Knox Press, 2001.

———. *Soul in Society: The Making and Renewal of Social Christianity.* Minneapolis, MN: Fortress Press, 1995.

Fairbank, John K., ed. *The Missionary Enterprise in China and America.* Cambridge, MA: Harvard University Press, 1974.

Ferguson, Niall. *The Pity of War.* New York: Perseus, 1999.

Fleischman, Harry. *Norman Thomas: A Biography.* New York: W. W. Norton, 1964.

Foner, Eric. *The Story of American Freedom.* New York: W. W. Norton, 1999.

Forcey, Charles. *The Crossroads of Liberalism: Croly, Weyl, Lippmann, and the Progressive Era, 1900–1925.* New York: Oxford University Press, 1961.

Fosdick, Raymond B. *Chronicle of a Generation: An Autobiography.* New York: Harper, 1958.

Fox, Richard W. "The Paradox of 'Progressive' Socialism: The Case of Morris Hillquit, 1901–1914." *American Quarterly* 26 (May 1974): 127–40.

Freeberg, Ernest. *Democracy's Prisoner: Eugene V. Debs, the Great War, and the Right to Dissent.* Cambridge, MA: Harvard University Press, 2008.

Fussell, Paul. *The Great War and Modern Memory.* New York: Oxford University Press, 1975.

Gerard, James W. *My Four Years in Germany.* Middlesex, UK: Echo Library, 2008.

Gilbert, Martin. *The First World War.* New York: Henry Holt, 2004.

Gray, Edward. *William Gray, of Salem, Merchant: A Biographical Sketch.* Boston: Houghton Mifflin, 1914.

Gray, Harold Studley. *Character "Bad": The Story of a Conscientious Objector, as Told in the Letters of Harold Studley Gray.* New York: Garland, 1971.

Haas, William Joseph. *China Voyager: Gist Gee's Life in Science.* Armonk, NY: M. E. Sharpe, 1996.

Hagedorn, Ann. *Savage Peace: Hope and Fear in America, 1919.* New York: Simon & Schuster, 2007.

Handy, Robert T. *A History of Union Theological Seminary in New York.* New York: Columbia University Press, 1987.

Hawes, Joseph M., and Elizabeth F. Shores. *The Family in America: An Encyclopedia.* Santa Barbara, CA: ABC-CLIO, 2001.

Hibben, John Grier. *The Higher Patriotism.* New York: C. Scribner, 1915.

Hobhouse, Mrs. Henry. *"I Appeal Unto Caesar": The Case of the Conscientious Objector.* London: George Allen & Unwin, 1917.

Hofstadter, Richard. *The Age of Reform: From Bryan to F.D.R.* New York: Vintage Books, 1955.

Holmes, John Haynes. *New Wars for Old, Being a Statement of Radical Pacifism in Terms of Force Versus Non-Resistance, with Special Reference to the Facts and Problems of the Great War.* Charleston, SC: BiblioLife, 2009.

Home Missions Committee and Church Extension Committee. *The Church and the City: An Account of Home Missions and Church Extension in New York Presbytery.* New York: New York Presbytery, 1917.

House, Edward Mandell. *The Intimate Papers of Colonel House: Arranged as a Narrative by Charles Seymour.* Vol. 1. Boston: Houghton Mifflin, 1928.

Howe, Irving. *Socialism and America.* New York: Harcourt Brace Jovanovich, 1985.

Hull, Isabel V. *Absolute Destruction: Military Culture and the Practices of War in Imperial Germany.* Ithaca, NY: Cornell University Press, 2006.

Johnpoll, Bernard K. *Pacifist's Progress: Norman Thomas and the Decline of American Socialism.* Chicago, IL: Quadrangle Books, 1970.

Johnson, Donald. "Wilson, Burleson, and Censorship in the First World War," *Journal of Southern History* 28, no. 1 (1962): 46–58.

Joll, James. *The Origins of the First World War.* London: Longman, 1984.

Kazin, Michael. *A Godly Hero: The Life of William Jennings Bryan.* New York: Anchor Books, 2007.

Keegan, John. *The First World War.* New York: Vintage, 2000.

Kellogg, Walter Guest. *The Conscientious Objector.* New York: Da Capo Press, 1970.

Kemeny, P. C. "University Cultural Wars: Rival Protestant Pieties in Early Twentieth-Century Princeton." *Journal of Ecclesiastical History* 53, no. 4 (2002): 735–64.

Kempton, Murray. *Part of Our Time: Some Ruins and Monuments of the Thirties* (New York: New York Review of Books, 2004).

Kennedy, David M. *Over Here: The First World War and American Society.* 25th anniversary ed. New York: Oxford University Press, 2004.

Kernek, Sterling. "The British Government's Reaction to President Wilson's 'Peace' Note of December 1916." *Historical Journal* 13 (December 1970): 723–24.

Knock, Thomas J. *To End All Wars: Woodrow Wilson and the Quest for a New World Order.* Princeton, NJ: Princeton University Press, 1995.

Kosek, Joseph Kip. *Acts of Conscience: Christian Nonviolence and Modern American Democracy.* New York: Columbia University Press, 2009.

———. "Liberal Pacifists and the Memory of Abolitionism, 1914–1933." "Limits of the Past." Graduate colloquium, Vanderbilt University, Nashville, Tennessee, April 19–20, 2002.

Landon, Margaret. *Anna and the King of Siam.* New York: HarperCollins, 1999.

Lasch, Christopher. *The New Radicalism in America, 1889–1963: The Intellectual as a Social Type.* New York: W. W. Norton, 1986.

Laskin, David. *The Long Way Home: An American Journey from Ellis Island to the Great War.* New York: Harper, 2010.

Lears, Jackson. *Rebirth of a Nation: The Making of a Modern America, 1877–1920.* New York: Harper, 2009.

Link, Arthur Stanley. *Wilson: Campaigns for Progressivism and Peace, 1914–1917.* Princeton, NJ: Princeton University Press, 1947.

———. *Wilson the Diplomatist: A Look at His Major Foreign Policies.* Baltimore, MD: Johns Hopkins Press, 1957.

———. *Wilson: The Struggle for Neutrality, 1914–1915.* Princeton, NJ: Princeton University Press, 1947.

———. *Woodrow Wilson and the Progressive Era, 1910–1917.* New York: Harper, 1954.

Lord, Walter. *The Good Years: From 1900 to the First World War.* New York: Harper, 1960.

Macdonald, Catriona M. M., and E. W. McFarlands, eds. *Scotland and the Great War.* East Linton, Scotland: Tuckwell Press, 1999.

MacMillan, Margaret. *Paris 1919: Six Months That Changed the World.* New York: Random House, 2003.

Marsden, George M. *Understanding Fundamentalism and Evangelicalism.* Grand Rapids, MI: William B. Eerdmans, 1991.

May, Henry F. *The End of American Innocence: A Study of the First Years of Our Own Time, 1912–1917.* Edited by Columbia University Press Morningside. New York: Columbia University Press, 1992.

Maynard, William Barksdale. *Woodrow Wilson: Princeton to the Presidency.* New Haven: Yale University Press, 2008.

Menand, Louis. *The Metaphysical Club.* New York: Farrar, Straus and Giroux, 2001.

Moore, Howard W. *Plowing My Own Furrow.* New York: W. W. Norton, 1985.

Nasaw, David. *The Chief: The Life of William Randolph Hearst.* Boston: Houghton Mifflin Company, 2001.

Nussbaum, Martha. *Liberty of Conscience: In Defense of America's Tradition of Religious Equality.* New York: Basic Books, 2008.

Nutt, Rick. "G. Sherwood Eddy and the Attitudes of Protestants in the United States Toward Global Mission." *Church History* 66 (September 1997): 502–21.

Orsi, Robert A. *The Madonna of 115th Street: Faith and Community in Italian Harlem, 1880–1950.* 2nd ed. New Haven, CT: Yale University Press, 2002.

Parker, Inez Moore. *The Rise and Decline of the Program of Education for Black Presbyterians of the United Presbyterian Church, U.S.A., 1865–1970.* San Antonio, TX: Trinity University Press, 1977.

Pedersen, Susan. "Anti-Condescensionism." Review of *Bodily Matters: The Anti-Vaccination Movement in England, 1853–1907,* by Nadja Durbach. *London Review of Books,* September 2005, 7–8.

Ratner, Joseph, ed. *Characters and Events.* New York: Henry Holt, 1929.

Rauschenbusch, Walter. *Christianity and the Social Crisis.* New York: Macmillan, 1913.

Riis, Jacob A. *How the Other Half Lives: Studies Among the Tenements of New York.* New York: Penguin Books, 1997.

Salvatore, Nick. *Eugene V. Debs: Citizen and Socialist.* 2nd ed. Urbana, IL, University of Illinois Press, 2007.

Samson, Gloria Garrett. *American Fund for Public Service: Charles Garland and Radical Philanthropy, 1922–1941.* Santa Barbara, CA: Greenwood Publishing Group, 1996.

Sayer, John. "Art and Politics, Dissent and Repression: *The Masses* magazine versus the Government, 1917–1918," *American Journal of Legal History* 32, no. 1 (1988): 42–78.

Seidler, Murray Benjamin. *Norman Thomas: Respectable Rebel.* 2nd ed. Syracuse, NY: Syracuse University Press, 1967.

Shakespeare, William. *Hamlet.* New York: Signet Classic, 1998.

Shannon, David A. *The Socialist Party of America: A History.* New York: Macmillan, 1955.

Stern, Fritz Richard. *The Politics of Cultural Despair: A Study in the Rise of the Germanic Ideology.* Berkeley: University of California Press, 1974.

Steward, Dwight. *Mr. Socialism.* Secaucus, NJ: Lyle Stewart Inc., 1974.

Stone, Geoffrey R. "Mr. Wilson's First Amendment," in *Reconsidering Woodrow Wilson,* ed. John Milton Cooper Jr. Washington D.C.: Woodrow Wilson Center Press, 2008.

Stone, Norman. *World War One: A Short History.* London: Allen Lane, 2007.

Swanberg, W. A. *Norman Thomas: The Last Idealist.* New York: Scribner, 1976.

Swisher, Carl Brent. "Civil Liberties in War Time." *Political Science Quarterly* 55 (September 1940): 321–47.

Thomas, Evan. *The War Lovers: Roosevelt, Lodge, Hearst, and the Rush to Empire.* New York: Little, Brown, 2010.

———. *The Radical "No": The Writings and Correspondence of Evan Thomas on War.* Edited by Charles Chatfield. New York: Garland Publishing, 1975.

Thomas, Norman. *As I See It.* New York: Macmillan, 1932.

———. *The Case of the Christian Pacifists.* New York: National Civil Liberties Bureau, 1918.

———. *The Conscientious Objector in America.* New York: B.W. Huebsch, 1923.

———. *Great Dissenters.* New York: W. W. Norton, 1961.

———. *A Socialist's Faith.* New York: W. W. Norton, 1951.

Traxel, David. *Crusader Nation: The United States in Peace and the Great War.* New York: Knopf, 2006.

Tuchman, Barbara. *The Guns of August.* 4th ed. Toronto: Bantam Books, 1980.

———. *The Zimmermann Telegram.* New York: Ballantine Books, 1985.

Verhey, Jeffrey. *The Spirit of 1914: Militarism, Myth and Mobilization in Germany.* New York: Cambridge University Press, 2000.

Vischer, Robert K. *Conscience and the Common Good: Reclaiming the Space Between Person and State.* New York: Cambridge University Press, 2010.

Walker, Samuel. *In Defense of American Liberties: A History of the ACLU.* New York: Oxford University Press, 1990.

Walzer, Michael. *Obligations: Essays on Disobedience, War, and Citizenship* Cambridge, MA: Harvard University Press, 1982.

Wertheim, Stephen. "The League That Wasn't: American Designs for a Legalist-Sanctionist League of Nations and the Intellectual Origins of International Organization, 1914–1920," *Diplomatic History.* Forthcoming article (2011).

Westbrook, Robert B. *John Dewey and American Democracy.* Ithaca, NY: Cornell University Press, 1991.

Wiebe, Robert H. *The Search for Order 1877–1920.* New York: Hill and Wang, 1967.

Wilson, Woodrow. *Papers of Woodrow Wilson.* Edited by Arthur Stanley Link. Princeton, NJ: Princeton University Press, 1966–1994.

———. *President Wilson's State Papers and Addresses.* Edited by Albert Shaw. New York: George H. Doran, 1918.

———. *Woodrow Wilson: The Essential Political Writings.* Edited by Ronald J. Pestritto. Lanham, MD: Lexington Books, 2005.

Witt, John Fabian. "Crystal Eastman and the Internationalist Beginnings of American Civil Liberties." *Duke Law Journal* 54 (December 2004): 705–63.

Zackin, Emily. "Popular Constitutionalism's Hard When You're Not Very Popular: Why the ACLU Turned to Courts." *Law & Society Review* 42, no. 2 (2008): 367–96.

Electronic Sources

"Battles—The Battle of Verdun, 1916." First World War. http://www.firstworldwar.com/battles /verdun.htm (accessed May 10, 2010).

"Key Moments in J.P. Morgan's History." http://www.jpmorgan.com/pages/jpmorgan/emea/local /fr/history (accessed May 10, 2010).

Princeton-Yenching Foundation, *The Princeton Work in Peking,* http://www.archive.org/details /princetonworkinp03prin (accessed October 22, 2009).

Whaples, Robert. "Child Labor in the United States." Economic History Association. http://eh.net /encyclopedia/article/whaples.childlabor (accessed April 30, 2010).

Thomas Wirth, "The Economics of Peace: World War I and Scott Nearing's Radical America." *Concept.* http://www.publications.villanova.edu/Concept/2004/Scott%20Nearing.htm (accessed May 19, 2010).

"Herbert S. Bigelow," Ohio History Central: An Online Encyclopedia of Ohio History. http:// www.ohiohistorycentral.org/entry.php?rec=34 (accessed June 11, 2010).

INDEX

Page numbers in italics refer to illustrations.

IMAGE CREDITS

In Order of Appearance

Chapter Title Pages

Chapter One
left, Welling Thomas; *right,* Emma Thomas; courtesy of the Thomas family

Chapter Two
left, Ralph and Norman Thomas; *right*, Evan and Arthur Thomas; courtesy of the Thomas family

Chapter Three
The Thomas Family; courtesy of the Thomas family

Chapter Four
Norman Thomas and Ted Savage on camels; courtesy of the Tamiment Library, New York University

Chapter Five
Violet Thomas; courtesy of the Thomas family

Chapter Six
East Harlem, New York; *The New-York Observer*

Chapter Seven
Norman, Ralph, and Arthur, with two of Norman's children; courtesy of the Thomas family

Chapter Eight
Polish infantry moves through Prussia; *The New York Times*

Chapter Nine
The Crusader Fellowship; courtesy of the John Nevin Sayre Papers, Swarthmore College Peace Collection

Chapter Ten
Fifth Avenue preparedness parade; collection of the New-York Historical Society

Chapter Eleven
Norman with son Billy; courtesy of the Thomas family

Chapter Twelve
Telegram; National Archives

Chapter Thirteen
President Woodrow Wilson before Congress; Library of Congress

Chapter Fourteen
Recruitment poster; Library of Congress

Chapter Fifteen
American soldiers training; National Archives

Chapter Sixteen
Arthur Thomas; courtesy of the Thomas Family

Chapter Seventeen
The Extreme Left tent; courtesy of the Arthur Dunham papers, Bentley Historical Library, University of Michigan

Chapter Eighteen
Eugene Debs; courtesy of the Debs Foundation, Terre Haute, Indiana

Chapter Nineteen
Ralph Thomas, from *The 302nd Engineers: A History*

Chapter Twenty
Solitary confinement cell; courtesy of the William Kantor Collected Papers, Swarthmore College Peace Collection

Chapter Twenty-one
Norman Thomas with grandchildren; courtesy of the Tamiment Library, New York University

A FRESH LOOK AT WORLD WAR I—AS TOLD THROUGH THE STORY OF FOUR BROTHERS, AND THE CHOICES EACH MADE

Conscience reveals how the war challenged the Thomas brothers' convictions and threatened to tear their family apart. The narrative centers on the life of the eldest brother, Norman Thomas, who began the war as a Presbyterian minister and ended it as a pacifist, a defender of civil liberties, and a Socialist (he would later run for president six times). His brothers chose different paths: Evan was a conscientious objector, imprisoned for his stand. Ralph and Arthur Thomas both became soldiers. Beautifully written, *Conscience* tells the story of a tumultuous time through the experience of one family—and in doing so recovers a way of talking about being true to oneself and to one another.

"The thrust of this enthralling book lies with its title: Through the experience of her forebears, Thomas examines how conscience fares when society considers it subversive." —*New York Times Book Review*

"Every once in a while the story of one man or one family is so well told that it becomes a vehicle for exhibiting an entire age. So it is with this triumphant work. Through the prism of the four Thomas brothers, the dramatic years at the turn of the twentieth century are recreated with such vitality that they seem to have happened only yesterday." —**Doris Kearns Goodwin**, author of *Team of Rivals*

"A fascinating story."   —*The New Yorker* **Book Bench**

Cover design: David Pearson. Cover photograph 8643; Gas Warfare Envelope; Box 51; Entry NM-92 1780. Historical Report of the Chief of Engineers of the AEF, 1917–19; Records of the American Expeditionary Forces (World War I), Record Group 120.

A PENGUIN BOOK

History

www.penguin.com